Live &
—IN—
AUSTRALIA
—AND—
NEW ZEALAND

Fiona McGregor
Charlotte Denny

Published by Vacation Work, 9 Park End Street, Oxford

LIVE AND WORK IN AUSTRALIA
AND NEW ZEALAND
by Fiona McGregor
&
Charlotte Denny

Series Editor: Victoria Pybus

ISBN 185458 115 5 (softback)
ISBN 185458 116 3 (hardback)

Publicity: Roger Musker

Cover design by
Miller, Craig and Cocking Design Partnership

Imageset and Printed by **Unwin Brothers** Ltd., Old Woking, Surrey

Contents

Australia

SECTION I — LIVING IN AUSTRALIA

GENERAL INTRODUCTION

RESIDENCE AND ENTRY REGULATIONS

SETTING UP HOME

DAILY LIFE

RETIREMENT

SECTION II — WORKING IN AUSTRALIA

EMPLOYMENT

STARTING A BUSINESS

New Zealand

SECTION I — LIVING IN NEW ZEALAND

GENERAL INTRODUCTION

RESIDENCE & ENTRY REGULATIONS

SETTING UP HOME

DAILY LIFE

RETIREMENT

SECTION II — WORKING IN NEW ZEALAND

EMPLOYMENT

STARTING A BUSINESS

Foreword

While the proximity of European countries to each other facilitates the movement of people and goods between them, the lands of Australia and New Zealand are a huge distance away from one of their main sources of immigrants, Britain. It is approximately 12,000 miles and a 26-hour flight to Sydney from Europe; flights to New Zealand take a few hours longer. Despite the vast geographical separation, there must be strong reasons why so many Britons and other Europeans yearn to travel, work or live in Australia or New Zealand. One obvious reason is that, of the Australian population at least 75% are of direct British origin, and the majority of New Zealanders are also of British descent. This means that almost every British person seems to have a relative or family friends living in either or both of these countries. Another reason for these countries' popularity is that the climates of both are very appealing and an increasing percentage of the populations of both countries are derived from many other nations giving the large cities especially, a lively ethnic and cultural mix.

A drawback, (or advantage depending on your view) of both nations is that they are comparatively 'new' having been settled by Europeans only in the last 200 years. In the case of Australia, a large proportion of the original 'immigrants' were forced labourers in the penal colonies, and many original New Zealand settlers were farmers. This has led to inevitable accusations that Australia and New Zealand are cultural backwaters. This is somewhat unfair given the emergence of Australasian cinema to international acclaim; not to mention the worldwide exportability of stars Dame Kiri te Kanawa and Barry Humphries. However it is true that the Antipodes have no long classical traditions and heritage, as has Europe.

Both New Zealand and Australia are developing increasing affinity, through economic links, with their Pacific and Asian neighbours and as a result the ties with Britain have inevitably loosened. One obvious sign of this is Australia's strengthening republican movement which aims to end what is perceived as the anachronistic consitutional link with the British crown. New Zealand, on the other hand has its own distinct Polynesian, particularly Maori, culture which is a growing influence on both politics and economics.

Increasingly, both countries are streamlining immigration procedures to favour young, educated and/or skilled migrants, while still allowing family-linked and humanitarian immigration to take place. Business investors and successful entrepreneurs are welcomed with open arms, and more importantly, financial incentives. This book outlines the categories under which you can enter Australia and New Zealand and shows you how to maximise your potential for qualifying and where to get help with your application. Working holiday visas for up to a year give those who are aged 18-30 the opportunity combine a holiday with the chance to discover whether they would like to commit themselves to a longer stay in the future.

In summary, going to live and work in one of these countries is as great a leap as going to live and work somewhere else in Europe. Permanent emigration, with which this book also deals, is an even more momentous decision. Whether you are going on your own, taking the family or retiring to the ANZAC countries, the *Living* sections of this book aim to help you set about the task and prepare you for the differences once you get there. Those with established skills may be looking for a way to get a fixed working contract or to start a business in Australia or New Zealand. Those with young families may want to have the best of both worlds: a good job and and a healthy environment in which to raise their children during their formative years. The *Employment* sections of this book give full details of all the possibilities.

Despite the popular misconceptions, there are great advantages to living and working in the Antipodean countries, as many successful immigrants and workers will testify. There are still sufficient ties with Britain in both countries to make new arrivals feel more comfortable than they would in many European countries. The main language is English (more or less) and the systems of government and health care in New Zealand reassuringly follow the British models, while the vast land of Australia is a organised on a federal system of states and territories which would not seem strange to North Americans.

Whatever those who have lived and worked in Australia or New Zealand say about these countries, they all agree that they are great places to live, work and/ or raise a family because of the space, the great outdoors and the quality of life. Additionally business and the economy are picking up again after the recession making these countries once more lands of opportunity. The key to making a success of the time you spend there is preparation which this book will help you make.

Fiona McGregor &
Charlotte Denny
February 1995

Acknowledgements

The authors and publishers would like to thank the following for their invaluable help in compiling this book. For Australia: Alastair and Kathleen McGregor for extensive research in Australia; also heartfelt thanks to Jonathan Crossen of Oxford University for his untiring technical and research assistance, patience and moral support. For New Zealand: Gillian and Andrew Denny for on the spot research along with Susan Lamb and Justine Munro. Many thanks also to Adrian Koppens for information he provided on taxation, Leah Fitzgerald for the introduction to Maori protocol, the staff of the information office of the New Zealand High Commission for their inexhaustible patience; Peter Brown and Jane Harris for their time and the use of their library facilities; Ernst Young and Co. for their help with the business section; Chris Jones for his role as all-round advisor to the author; Nigel Atkinson and Ann Oakthorpe for allowing their own experiences to be used for the case histories.

N.B. Every effort has been made to check the accuracy of the information given in this book and the authenticity and correct practices of all organisations, companies, agencies etc. mentioned. However, situations may change and telephone numbers etc can alter and readers are therefore strongly advised to check facts and credentials for themselves.

Australia

SECTION I

Living in Australia

General Introduction
Residence and Entry Regulations
Setting Up Home
Daily Life
Retirement

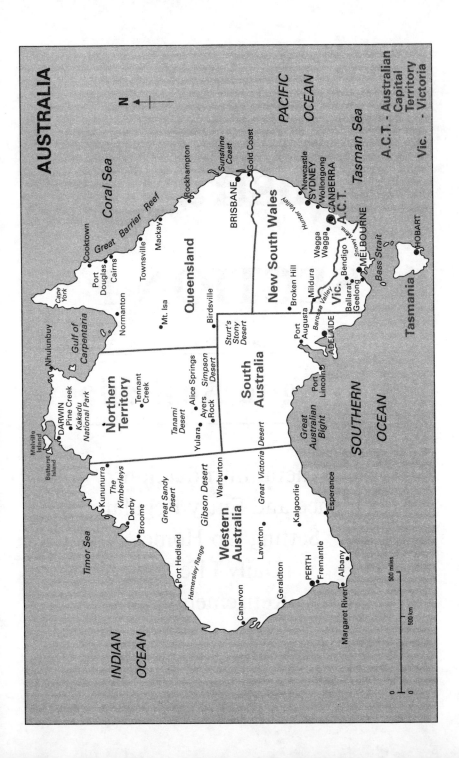

Introduction

Destination Australia

Until fairly recently, Australian immigration policies openly encouraged British applications for permanent residency and citizenship and as a consequence almost everyone in the UK seems to have at least one relative living in Australia. In the early days of colonial rule, the British Government actually gave away free land in order to entice those who would not otherwise be able to own land away from Britain's overcrowded shores into the apparently empty land of Australia. Times have, however, changed quite significantly, and Australia's current republican government is not so willing to accept British immigrant applications. This should not be seen as a deliberate rejection of British applications, but is merely a reflection of Australia's much more stringent and self-insulating immigration policies. Quite simply, Australia is now seen as a highly desirable place to live, and therefore the government feels it can pick and choose a bit more as to who it lets into the country. This is certainly a far cry from the compulsory immigration in the days of transportation.

As a consequence of the tightened immigration policies, immigration procedures for Australia are relatively complicated, time-consuming and expensive in comparison with immigration procedures within the EU and are, perhaps, more similar to the immigration procedures of North America. Having said this, an enormous number of British citizens emigrate to Australia every year, drawn by the weather, employment prospects, cheaper housing and the image of a more leisurely lifestyle. In general, these benefits are indeed characteristic of Australian life. Australia's relatively small population and vast natural resources have certainly meant in the past that Australians enjoyed better wages, a lower cost of living and a generally more affluent lifestyle than many of their counterparts in other developed countries. Recently, however, Australia has had its own recession from which it is, arguably, beginning to recover, and the situation does not appear to be as rosy as it was as few as three or four years ago. Having said that, there are certainly benefits which remain untouched by the economic or political climate of the country and which can be enjoyed by those under 25 who are backpacking around the country, by those emigrating with young families, or by those who wish to retire.

Pros and Cons of Moving to Australia

One of the most obvious benefits of life in Australia is the weather. The British Medical Association now recognises the detrimental psychological effects of tne lack of sunshine which gives medical authority to the claim that one simply feels better when the sun shines. Associated with the sunny climate is a totally different lifestyle which is much more outdoor-based, and this also has a certain appeal to many British people, particularly those with young families. Also associated with a better climate is the first-rate range of natural produce, such as fruit and vegetables, available at a significantly lower price than their British counterparts. In particular, meat is much cheaper than in Britain. Recently new season's lamb was selling in Western Australia at the equivalent of 54 pence per pound. One is generally able to buy a much wider variety of produce at a lower price than one can in Britain.

Although the image of the tough, macho, heroic man of the bush as projected by the *Crocodile Dundee* movies or the documentary series *Bush Tucker Man* recently shown on British television is still popular with advertisers, most of the Australian population lives in big, modern cities which compete successfully in an international market. Australian scientific and medical research leads the world in many areas, and technology, engineering, commerce and banking are just as important to the national and international economy as the wheat and wool produce.

Generally, Australian wages tend to be higher than those in the UK and British citizens working in Australia will find that they will be paid more for similar work. Importantly, manual labour is well respected in Australia and thus a job such as bricklaying/building or plumbing pays very well indeed.

The cost of living varies from city to city across Australia, but in general, it is significantly lower than in most UK cities. Due to the huge amount of land available, it is also, generally, considerably cheaper to buy/build a house in most Australian cities. Sydney and Melbourne are the most expensive cities in which to purchase property, however the price of real estate is still lower overall than the price of comparable properties in similar sized British cities.

There are important disadvantages which must be considered before deciding to move to Australia for any length of time. Perhaps the most obvious disadvantage is the feeling of isolation one experiences, not just from other cities within Australia, but, above all immigrants often experience a sense of being cut off from the rest of the world. This sense of exile is heightened by the cost of flights to Australia which prevents British relatives and friends of the immigrant from visiting each other as frequently as they would like. The isolation can by overpowering and has resulted in many emigrants returning to Britain within two years of their emigration.

While the cost of food and fuel may be cheaper than in Britain, imported goods tend to have a substantial luxury tax, as well as the standard duty (Australia's version of VAT), added to the cost price, and so items such as some electrical goods, books and cars are often more expensive. It is important to note that British electrical goods operate on a different voltage (110V as opposed to Australia's 240V) and so it is not really worth taking electrical goods such as stereos or televisions to Australia.

Australia is notorious for its flies, spiders, sharks and other creatures which are not particularly people-friendly. Flies are indeed everywhere, particularly in summer, and even though most doors and windows are fitted with fly-screens, they do, annoyingly, find their way into the home. Outside, especially at barbecues, flies can often be unbearable, and you will soon notice that you automatically fall into the way of the 'Aussie salute': your hand waving in front of your face to keep the flies out of your eyes, nose and mouth. Crickets, cockroaches and spiders are also prevalent and you need to be careful as spiders are often very dangerous. It is not that one's home is overrun with creepy-crawlies, but caution needs to be exercised, particularly when in the garden, regarding spiders. Most people have professional exterminators spray their homes with insecticide every five to seven years. Snakes are not so common in inner-city suburbs, but in the outer suburbs and the bush care should also be taken. Similarly, sharks are not as much of a problem as they have been made out to be. Most popular beaches have lifesaver towers where a lifesaver surveys the swimming area for sharks as well as swimmers' general safety and these towers are fitted with an alarm in order to warn and evacuate swimmers should anything suspicious be spotted. In the seventeen years I have spent in Australia,

mostly on beaches along the coast of Western Australia, I have only once been called out of the water by a shark alarm.

Given the disadvantages, one aspect of Australian life which contributes to Australia's sense of cultural vitality and zest is the fact that the population is completely cosmopolitan. This is reflected in all of the major cities in Australia in the choice of restaurants, and the range of entertainment and the arts constantly on offer.

In brief, the main pros and cons of living in Australia from the British point of view are:

Pros: Climate generally much warmer and sunnier than the UK.
Rates of pay tend to be as high or higher than in the UK.
Conditions of work better.
Land and property prices lower than in the UK.
World-leading scientific, particularly medical, & technological industries.
Multicultural diversity.
Better range of fruit and vegetables at a significantly lower price.

Cons: Isolated.
Expensive travel, both domestic and international.
Imported goods much more expensive than in the UK.
Annoying/dangerous insects and other animals.

Political and Economic Structure

Government and Politics

In 1901, the six Australian colonies federated to form the Commonwealth of Australia, which created the three levels of government in Australia; federal, state and local. The State government had actually existed first, as each colony had been self-governing, and the Local government was established under State legislation after federation. In 1991 Australia had 842 elected members of Parliament, of whom 224 were Commonwealth and 618 were State and Territory members.

Both State and Commonwealth systems of government derive from the British Westminster system, although the Constitution, including the Federal structure, is based on the US Constitution. The Legislative power of the Commonwealth of Australia is vested in the Parliament of the Commonwealth, which consists of the Queen, the Senate and the House of Representatives. The Queen is represented in the Commonwealth by the Governor-General. The powers and functions of the Governor-General include; powers to appoint times for holding the sessions of Parliament, to prorogue Parliament and to dissolve the House of Representatives: to cause writs to be issued for general elections of members to the House of Representatives; to assent in the Queen's name to a proposed law passed by both the Houses of the Parliament; to choose and summon Executive Councillors; to appoint Ministers of State for the Commonwealth of Australia; to be Commander-in-Chief of the Defence Forces. The Governor-General may also make regulations which give effect to Acts of the Commonwealth Parliament, and issue proclamations, e.g., to declare an Act to be in force. Australia's real political power is held by the Prime Minister, currently Paul Keating, and cabinet ministers who are elected by a democratic process every four years. The Prime Minister and cabinet ministers are answerable to the Senate and the House of Representatives.

In each Australian State there is a State Governor, who is the representative of the Queen for the State. The powers and functions of the State Governor include: exercising prerogative powers conferred by Letters Patent issued under the Great Seal of the United Kingdom and also various statutory functions stated by State Constitutions and the Commonwealth *Australia Act 1986*. A Governor of a State assents in the Queen's name to bills passed by the Parliament of the State. Since the 1986 *Australia Act*, an Act of Parliament of a State that has been assented to by the governor of the State is no longer subject to disallowance by the Queen, nor suspension pending signification of the Queen's pleasure. The State Governor acts on the advice of Ministers of State and can administer the prerogative of mercy by the reprieve or pardon of criminal offenders within his/her jurisdiction, and may remit fines and penalties due to the Crown in right of the State.

In the Commonwealth Parliament, the Upper House is known as the Senate, and in the bi-level State Parliaments as the Legislative Council. The legislature in all States was bi-level until 1992 when the Queensland Parliament abolished the Upper House. In the Commonwealth Parliament the Lower House is known as the House of Representatives, in the State Parliaments of New South Wales, Victoria and Western Australia as the Legislative Assembly, and in the State Parliaments of South Australia and Tasmania as the House of Assembly. The single House of Parliament in Queensland, the Northern Territory and the Australian Capital Territory is known as the Legislative Assembly.

The members of the Parliaments of each State are elected by the people, the franchise is extended to Australian citizens who are at least 18 years old and are qualified to become electors of the Commonwealth Parliament. In order to qualify, one needs to be any Australian citizen (or a British subject who was on the Commonwealth Roll as at 25 January 1984), over 18 years of age, and resident in Australia. Enrolment and voting are compulsory for all eligible persons. Those persons deemed ineligible to vote are those convicted of treason and not pardoned, those convicted and under sentence for any offence punishable by imprisonment for five years or longer, those of unsound mind, or those who hold temporary entry permits under the *Migration Act 1958* or are prohibited non-citizens under that Act.

The Queen's role as Head of State is essentially passive, reflected in her change of title through the years. On 7 February 1952, the Governor-General proclaimed 'Princess Elizabeth as Queen Elizabeth the Second, Queen of this Realm and of all Her other Realms and Territories, Head of the Commonwealth, Defender of the Faith, Supreme Liege Lady in and over the Commonwealth of Australia'. In 1973, the new *Royal Styles and Titles Act* proclaimed in Canberra on 19 October, amended the Queen's title to be in relation to Australia and its Territories, 'Elizabeth the Second, by the Grace of God, Queen of Australia and Her Other Realms and Territories, Head of the Commonwealth'. Australia's National Anthem was changed from 'God Save the Queen' (now known as the Royal Anthem and played on Royal visits) on 19 April 1984 to *Advance Australia Fair*. This was not the popular people's choice, which was *Waltzing Matilda*. The powers that be, however, deemed that *Waltzing Matilda* was unsuitable because it was about a thief who commits suicide.

Australia's national colours are green and gold, and the flag is a blue background with six stars of varying sizes (representing the Southern Cross) and a small Union Jack in the top left hand corner. This is subject to change if Australia becomes a republic.

Political Parties

There are six main political parties in Australia whose policies are continually changing. They are the Australian Labour Party (ALP), the Liberal Party (LP), the Country Liberal Party (CLP), the National Party of Australia (NPA), the

Independent Party (IND), and the Australian Democrats (AD). Each party has varying success from region to region across Australia, and their policies are also increasingly variable. In general, the LP is conservative, the INP is concerned with enviromental and social issues. The ALP is traditionally socialist, and the AD was originally formed 'to keep the bastards honest'.

The Economy

Australia has a predominantly free-market economy but this is subject to fairly extensive and rigorous regulation. The governmental regulation is three-tiered, parallelling the governmental structure, and regulation occurs at federal, state/ territory and local levels. The current government policy, however, favours privatisation and thus the government will reduce its participation in the national economy over the long term. The government is currently examining deregulating many of Australia's industries to make them more efficient and able to compete in the international market. It has ended government monopolies on domestic airlines, banking (there are now 34 non-Australian banks operating in Australia) and telecommunications (Telecom no longer has the monopoly).

In the early 1980s Australia experienced rapid economic growth which eventually stabilised and then slowed down by 1990. Australia's Gross Domestic Product for the 1989-90 tax year was $A247.6 billion, an increase of 3.22% from the previous year. Inflation ranged from 7%-10% after 1984, but fell to approximately 6% at the beginning of the 1990s. This relatively high rate of inflation and a significant balance of payments deficit have been exacerbated by a high level of National Debt which continues to rise.

Traditionally, Australia's exports have largely consisted of raw materials and primary products such as wheat, wool and metal ores, but these have been devalued during the last seven years due to the trade practices of the United States and the European Union. Australia's most essential industries are primary production (both agricultural and mineral), forestry, fishing, manufacturing and tourism. Although in the past the largest economic sectors were primary production, more recently manufacturing has taken over as the most influential sector of Australia's economy. This is largely due to the fact that the Australian manufacturing industry had been fiercely protected by heavy tariffs and quotas on imports which, in the 1980s, were reduced in order to encourage Australian manufacturers to become willing and able to compete in the international arena. This trend is likely to continue for the forseeable future. There are also stringent new anti-dumping laws. The Australian government is extremely conscious and protective about the environment, and thus there are very strict laws affecting the disposal of industrial waste which carry severe fines and legal implications (such as closure). Green industries are definitely favoured by the government, and even major mining companies such as ALCOA have for many years practiced re-planting and landscaping bauxite mining sites they have excavated.

The last twenty years have seen the increasing mechanisation of blue-collar industries and, as a consequence, the relative power of trade unions has been reduced. Although Australian trade unions have been extremely powerful bodies in the past, particularly when the ex-Prime Minister, Bob Hawke, was president of the Australian Council of Trade Unions (ACTU), now less than 50% of the Australian workforce belongs to a union.

Geographical Information

Area and Main Physical Features

Australia has often been referred to as the largest island in the world (or the smallest continent) with an area of 7,686,848 square kilometres. In order to be able to understand what this area represents, compare it with the area of the entire UK, 244,046 sq. kms. In other words, the UK fits into Australia just over 31 times. Australia's vastness enables it to span a variety of geographical and climatic regions. Rain forest meets the reef in Queensland, most of Australia's interior is desert, much of the coastal south-west of Western Australia and South Australia have a mediterranean appearance and climate, and yet the Australian Alps in the eastern states offer skiers more snow than the Swiss Alps.

Much of central Australia is a plateau, and it is bounded by the Indian Ocean to the West, the Pacific Ocean to the East, the Southern Ocean to the South, and the Timor, Arafura, and Coral Seas to the North. Most of Australia is literally empty, particularly the central region which consists mainly of desert, viz. the Great Sandy Desert, the Gibson Desert and the Great Victoria Desert. These areas contain red dust, low scrub and spinifex grass (extremely hardy, spiny grass which grows in tufts), and are extremely hot and dry. The harshness of this land is sometimes reflected in the names given to geographical features, e.g. Lake Disappointment in Western Australia.

There are mountainous regions throughout Australia. The Hamersley Rand, the Kimberleys and the Stirling Ranges in Western Australia, the Macdonnell Ranges in Central Australia, and the Great Dividing Range which runs down the entire length of Eastern Australia. The Great Barrier Reef, the largest natural reef in the world, runs almost parallel to the Great Dividing Range' from the northernmost tip of Queensland at Cape York down to Fraser Island (approx. 200 kms north of Brisbane).

Besides the Great Barrier Reef, perhaps Australia is best known for its beaches, the majority of which remain unspoilt. Australia's coastline is immense, and while this may pose a huge problem for the defence forces, it is hard to find beaches elsewhere in the world which match the endless stretches of fine white sand, such as the appropriately named Eighty Mile Beach near Broome.

The major rivers in Australia are the Swan, Ord, Darling and Murray, although there are many other long and large rivers throughout the country.

Neighbouring Countries

Australia's nearest neighbour is Papua New Guinea, less than 200 km to the north of Cape York in the east, and Indonesian islands also lie close to the coast of north-west Australia. Further away in the north-east lies the French Island of New Caledonia, beyond which lie the Solomon Islands, Fiji, Western Samoa and Tonga. To the South East, approximately 1,700 kms east of Sydney, lies New Zealand. To the south, beyond Tasmania, there is nothing before Antarctica, and to the west beyond Perth are the Seychelles, Mauritius and Madagascar, just before one reaches the African coast.

Internal Organisation

Although anthropologists and historians estimate that human settlement of Australia occurred around 40,000 years ago, Australia celebrates Australia Day on 26 January to commemorate the foundation of the first colony at Botany Bay in 1788. Australia is a federal monarchy, but it is divided into six states: Western Australia, South Australia, Tasmania, Victoria, New South Wales and Queensland, and two territories: the Northern Territory and the Australian Capital Territory. A large part of Antarctica is also Australian territory.

Tasmania was discovered by Abel Tasman in 1642 and, as he was commissioned by the Dutch East India Company, he named it Van Diemen's Land in honour of the Governor of the Dutch East Indies. It was granted political independence from New South Wales in 1852, and Hobart was declared its capital. It only became known by its present name in 1856. Queensland was settled in 1824, but did not gain independence until 1859. Captain Fremantle declared the entire west coast of Australia to be British Crown Territory in 1829. South Australia was founded in 1836, and Victoria was established in 1851. In 1900 the colonies united in order to encourage economic expansion, regulate the postal system, and build a military defence force. The constitution was presented to the House of Commons in 1900 and signed by Queen Victoria. Australia became the Commonwealth of Australia on 1 January 1901, known as Federation Day.

Although Australia is a united country, each state/territory has its own government which is separate, yet subordinate to the federal government. There are interstate discrepancies in areas such as the minimum driving age and education. Each state is also divided into separate local shires (municipal councils) which control rates and community facilities.

Population

Currently, the population of Australia is approximately 18 million. Most of this population is concentrated in the cities situated around Australia's coast, so although the average population density reads as two people per sq. km, the fact that almost all of central Australia is relatively empty means that this figure is not representative of life in the cities and suburbs. If immigration is stabilised at its current low rate, it is estimated that Australia's population in the year 2041 will be 26.7 million.

The specialist British tabloid *Overseas Jobs Express*, October 15 1994, states that immigrants from Britain and New Zealand compose approximately 50% of the permanent residents in Australia. The majority of the rest of the permanent residents are likely to have been born in the south-east Asian region or in Europe. There are relatively few American permanent residents in Australia, although Americans contribute substantially to the tourism industry. Permanent residents must not be confused with Australian citizens, who make up the rest of the country's population. Most Australian citizens are Australian-born, but there is also a large number of those who have been born overseas and have applied for citizenship. Applicants for citizenship tend also to reflect the trend in permanent residency and be from European or south-east Asian countries.

The country is literally a melting pot of hundreds of different nationalities, a consequence of Australia's 'Population or Perish' immigration policy during the 1940s and 1950s. If you walk down any city street, you are likely to encounter Italians, Scots, Irish, Greeks, Thais, Japanese, Lebanese etc., just as frequently as Australians.

The Aboriginals. Tragically, the one ethnic group you would perhaps expect to see tends to be poorly represented statistically. The Australian Aboriginal has suffered affliction and persecution ever since the arrival of Captain Cook at Botany Bay and their population, never very numerous, has steadily and dramatically declined over the last two hundred years. In those early years the British government actually sanctioned and instigated attitudes and measures which essentially decimated the Aboriginal population. The army was ordered at various times to undertake what amounts to systematic extermination campaigns in the form of 'hunting parties', where the 'game' was any and every Aboriginal. For example, within three years of the arrival of the First Fleet in Sydney, the Aboriginal population was reduced by two-thirds through smallpox and influenza (previously unknown in Australia), accidents and violent death. The barbarism revealed a predominant British attitude of the time that the Aboriginals were sub-human, and, sadly, this attitude has been particularly potent, infecting every succeeding generation of Australians. Until the law was abolished in the late 1970s, Aboriginals were prohibited from being in any city or town after dark, and were not even considered to be citizens of their own country. The refusal to grant Aboriginal people citzenship again demonstrated the fundamental belief that Aboriginals were not in fact human and so they did not have any basic rights. Over the last twenty years, the Australian government has tried to make amends to the Aboriginal population, but the problem lies in the fact that nothing can atone for the horrors of the last two hundred years. The Aboriginal people now suffer from high national and even international rates of alcohol dependency, infant mortality, deaths in custody, and involvement in crime. In addition, their average life span is shorter than other Australians. It is very difficult to find many, if any, pure-blood Aboriginal people in Australia today. Aboriginal people are considered to be Aboriginal if they have any Aboriginal ancestry, and so many Aboriginals have blonde hair and blue eyes. Although they do have distinctive physical characteristics, it is often not possible to tell simply by appearance whether someone is Aboriginal or not. Currently, the Aboriginal population stands at approximately 10,000. Two hundred years have seen a harsh reduction from 100,000 and left a people divorced from their cultural and historical roots. It is little wonder that many feel a sense of fragmentation, isolation, displacement and a certain bitterness towards, and lack of faith in, governments.

Many anthropologists and tourists are fascinated by the Australian Aboriginal. Anthropologists have found that the Aboriginal people, rather than being primitive, had distinctive sophisticated societies. They were not perhaps sophisticated in the way the western world defines the term, but developed a culture which worked in harmony with their environment. Their knowledge about Australian flora and fauna is extensive and astounding, and their ability to survive in harsh climates and terrain relied on such knowledge. The Aboriginal *dreamtime* is a system of beliefs, representing man, animals, nature and the land as being bound inseparably together, that forms the basis of Aboriginal life, culture and the heritage. To the Aborigine, the land is sacred and there has been an inevitable conflict of interests between the Aboriginal people and the Australian government which relies on mining as a crucial part of the country's economy. The Aboriginal people often see such mining operations as the literal rape of mother earth and/ or desecration of traditional burial sites, and the government is continually trying, usually unsuccessfully, to find a compromise. The power of the dollar generally prevails.

Climatic Zones
Weather Chart

Average Temp °F °C	Jan	Feb	Mar	Apr	May	Jun	Jul	Aug	Sep	Oct	Nov	Dec
Sydney	72	70	71	65	60	58	54	58	60	65	70	71
	22	21	21.6	18	15	14	12	14	15	18	21	21.6
Canberra	72	72	67	57	52	42	41	43	50	57	63	69
	22	22	19	13.8	11	5.5	5	6	10	13.8	17	20.5
Melbourne	70	70	67	62	56	52	48	52	55	60	62	66
	21	21	49	16.6	13	11	9	11	12.7	15	16.6	18.8
Hobart	64	64	61	52	50	48	45	48	52	54	58	60
	17.7	17.7	16	11	10	9	7	9	11	12	14	15
Adelaide	76	76	72	68	60	54	52	54	58	64	68	72
	24	24	22	20	15	12	11	12	14	17.7	20	22
Perth	73	73	71	68	62	58	56	58	60	62	70	72
	22.7	22.7	21.6	20	16.6	14	13	14	15	16.6	21	22
Cairns	82	80	77	76	73	72	72	74	74	75	77	80
	27	26.6	25	24	22.7	22	22	23	23	23.8	25	26.6
Brisbane	75	75	73	72	68	61	58	61	68	71	73	74
	23.8	23.8	22.7	22	20	16	14	16	20	21.6	22.7	23
Alice Springs	83	82	74	70	60	55	54	58	68	72	76	82
	28	27	23	21	15	12.7	12	14	20	22	24	27
Darwin	82	82	82	82	78	76	75	77	81	84	84	83
	27	27	27	27	25.5	24	23.8	25	27	28.2	28.8	28

This table shows the average monthly temperatures in the major cities of Australia throughout the year. Note that winter and summer are at different times of the year to the northern hemisphere. The winter months in Australia are June to August and the summer months are December to February. Tropical cities such as Cairns, Darwin and Brisbane, however, experience a wet season during the summer months rather than the winter months. This is demonstrated below in the table of average rainfall.

Average Rainfall in Main Australian Cities

Av. rainfall in inches cm	Jan	Feb	Mar	Apr	May	Jun	Jul	Aug	Sep	Oct	Nov	Dec
Sydney	4	4.5	5	5	5	5	4	3	3	3	3	3
	10.2	11.4	12.7	12.7	12.7	12.7	10.2	7.6	7.6	7.6	7.6	7.6
Canberra	2.5	2	2.5	2	2	1.5	2	2	3	2.5	2	1.5
	6.3	5	6.3	5	5	3.8	5	5	7.6	6.3	5	3.8
Melbourne	2	2	2	2.5	2	2	2	2	2	2.5	2.5	2
	5	5	5	6.3	5	5	5	5	5	6.3	6.3	5
Hobart	2	2	2	2	2	2	2	2	2	2.5	2.5	2
	5	5	5	5	5	5	5	5	5	6.3	6.3	5
Adelaide	1	1	1	2	3	3	3	2.5	2	2	1	1
	2.5	2.5	2.5	5	7.6	7.6	7.5	6.3	5	5	2.5	2.5
Perth	0.5	0.5	1	1.5	5	7	7	5	3	2	1	0.5
	1.3	1.3	2.5	3.8	12.7	17.8	17.8	12.7	7.6	5	2.5	1.3
Cairns	16	18	19	7	4	2	1	1	1.5	1.5	3	7
	40.6	45.7	48.3	17.8	10.2	5	2.5	2.5	3.8	3.8	7.6	17.8
Brisbane	6.5	6	5.5	3.5	3	3	2	2	2	3	4	5
	16.5	15.2	14	8.9	7.5	7.5	5	5	5	7.5	10.2	12.7
Alice Springs	1.5	2	1	0.5	0.5	0.5	0.5	0.5	0.5	1	1	1.5
	3.8	5	2.5	1.3	1.3	1.3	1.3	1.3	1.3	2.5	2.5	3.8
Darwin	16	13	10	4	0.5	0	0	0	0.5	2	5	10
	40.6	33	25.4	10.2	1.3	0	0	0	1.3	5	12.7	25.4

A Guide to the States and Territories

Most people who visit Australia for a holiday try to cram as much as possible into a short time. A survey released by the Federal Minister for Tourism for the Australian Tourist Commission found that British tourists spent an average of 37 nights in Australia, of which 17 were likely to be spent at the homes of friends and/or relatives. The sheer size of Australia and the time and expense involved in covering all the states and territories is, of course, prohibitive, so most tourists and residents of Australia never visit all of them. It is quite common for Australian families and young people to pack up for six to twelve months and travel around Australia, but even within a state or territory the terrain and climate can vary so much that if you visit one part of the state, you have by no means seen all there is to see. Every Australian state/territory has an enormous diversity of attractions to tempt the potential immigrant/traveller/retirer, and this section aims to give a short synopsis of the different regions in Australia and contact names and numbers in order to help the interested reader find out more information.

Welcome and Information Facilities

Australia's tourist industry is huge and enjoying an increasingly high profile in Australia's economy. Every capital city has a large and informative Tourist Bureau, and the larger towns usually have a smaller Tourist Information Office. Even in the tiny country towns and in the middle of isolated national parks, there are often tourist information points which comprise maps, general information and points of interest displayed on a board. In addition, at most railway or bus stations, there are information points which can give you information not just on how to get to your destination, but also detailed information on the area you are visiting.

The Australian Tourist Commission has an office in London which is open from 9am-5.30pm and they are happy to answer any queries and forward any relevant information. They have many free booklets which are available on request, and of course maps and guides. Most states also have their own tourist office in London, and offer free publications on request on both general and specific matters particular to that state.

Further information about the states/territories, cities, towns and national parks of Australia can be found at major bookshops in the form of tourist and independent traveller guides, or specialist travel and map shops.

Useful Addresses

Australian Tourist Commission, 1st Floor, Gemini House, 10-18 Putney Hill, London SW15 6AA, tel: 0181-780 2227/1424 or fax: 0181-780 1496. This is the number of the general switchboard which will transfer you to the person most able to deal with your specific query.

Western Australia House, 115 The Strand, London, WC2R OAJ, tel: 0171-240 2881 or fax: 0171-379 9826.

South Australia House, South Australia House, 50 The Strand, London WC2N 5LW, UK, tel: 0171-930 7471 or fax: 0171-930 1660.

Victoria House, Melbourne Place, The Strand, London WC2B 4LG, tel: 0171-836 2656 or fax: 0171-240 6025.

Queensland House, 392 The Strand, London WC2R OLZ, tel:- 0171-836 1333 or fax: 0171-240 7667.

New South Wales Tourist Commission, does not have an office open to the public in London. Any enquiries should be referred through Australia House in London or the Australian Tourist Commission. Their telephone number for enquiries at Australia House is 0171-283 2166.

Northern Territory Tourist Commission, 612 Kingston Road, London, SW20 8DN, tel: 0181-544 9845 or fax: 0181-544 9843.

Australian Capital Territory, no UK office so contact the Australian Tourist Commission, or fax: +61 6 205 0629.

Tasmania, Gemini House, 10-18 Putney Hill, London SW15 6AA, tel: 0181-789 7088 or fax: 0181-780 1496.

WESTERN AUSTRALIA
Capital: Perth.
Area: 1,515,300 sq. miles (2,525,500 sq. kms) = over 10 times the size of the UK.
% of total area of Australia: 32.87
Coastline: 7,500 miles (12,500 kms).
Climate: Average Perth daily maximum temperature in January (Summer) 27°C, in July (Winter) 15°C. Note that there is significant variation in temperatures throughout the state from the temperate South to the tropical North.

Western Australia's huge size (the whole of Western Europe can easily fit into Western Australia with a bit left over) enables it to encompass many different climatic and geographical regions and in this respect it is like a scaled-down version of Australia. From the tropical north around Broome and beyond, through the arid zones of the Nullarbor Plain to the fertile south-west corner where wheat, wool and vineyards abound, Western Australia also boasts its own lesser-known but equally spectacular Ningaloo Reef, majestic Karri forests, spectacular gorges and other geological formations such as the aptly named Wave Rock and the Pinnacles (an ancient fossilised forest now standing in a desert landscape) as well as the Stirling Ranges which occasionally see snow in winter.

The State is rich in a wide variety of natural resources, and is a leading producer of iron ore, gold, industrial diamonds, alumina, mineral sands products, wool, wheat, salt and forest products. Besides the common rural products of wheat and wool, which account for about 30% and 37% respectively of the total value of produce, Western Australia is also developing more unusual industries such as cashmere and angora goat farms, commercial rabbit farms, emu and deer farms. In addition, the Western Australian fishing industry's major products are rock lobster, prawns, shrimp and scampi, which are mainly exported to the USA and Japan. Mineral and petroleum production added $8 billion to the State's economy in 1990/91, which makes up 60% of the value of the State's overseas exports and one third of Australia's total mineral exports.

Since the 1960s, the Western Australian economy has grown faster than that of any other State, with an average real Gross State Product growth of 5.1%. The State's economy is export-based and it recorded a $7 billion overseas trade surplus with exports valued at $11 billion in 1990/91, twice as much per capita as the rest of Australia. Given Western Australia's strategic position within the Asian region, its major customers for exported products are Japan and the South-East Asian nations, as well as the US and the EU. Part of the reason for Western Australia's economic success is that the West Australian Government is one of the few governments in the world to have a Minister for Productivity, whose policy is threefold; to establish co-operative labour relations, to maintain an optimal, safe working environment, and to create a highly skilled workforce.

Western Australia is experiencing a growth rate of approximately 3% per year. This is largely spurred on by overseas immigrants, particularly business immigrants. Western Australia attracts almost a 20% share of Australia's total business immigrants from all over the world. More than a quarter of Western Australia's population was born overseas, and it consequently enjoys a broad and harmonious ethnic mix, creating a truly cosmopolitan lifestyle. It also has a young population, second only to the Northern Territory, with an average age of 30.4 years. In addition, Western Australian medical and health services are among the best in the world. At a doctor-patient ratio of 1:500, the State ranks with Norway, Sweden, Finland, Denmark, France and the Netherlands, and is considerably ahead of the USA, UK and Japan. The average life expectancy in Western Australia is high at 74 years for men and 80 for women.

Western Australian education is of a very high standard, both in the public and private schools. With four universities in Perth, five advanced education campuses, a network of technical and further education colleges and private colleges throughout the State, Western Australia has world class education facilities.

Real estate costs are among the cheapest in the country, and Western Australians enjoy a high rate of home ownership with more than two-thirds of all residences being privately owned.

Perth: Western Australia has a population of 1,600,000 and of this number, just over one million live in Perth, truly the most isolated capital city in the world. Its isolation has helped Perth avoid becoming impersonal as it has developed, and has encouraged the city to retain its relaxed and friendly atmosphere, characteristic of its easy-going lifestyle. Perth is a stunning city, situated along the banks of the Swan River, extending to the coastal beachside suburbs of Cottesloe and Scarborough, and inland to the suburbs built on the side of the escarpment which marks the edge of the coastal plateau. In summer, although the average temperature is only 27°C, the thermometer can certainly soar up to 38°C for a few days at a time. This is a dry, not humid, heat and so it does not seem to sap your energy as tropical heat can. The hottest day I have ever experienced in Perth was 46°C (in the shade!) and, spent at the beach, it was quite bearable. It is, however, never this hot for a sustained period of time. In fact, Perth's saving grace is the sea-breeze which almost invariably comes in off the Indian Ocean every summer afternoon and cools the place down, affectionately known as 'The Fremantle Doctor'. Interestingly, Perth is Australia's windiest city, and the third windiest city in the world, which not only cools the city down in intense summer heat, but also clears the city of any air pollution. Perth enjoys more sunshine and more clear days than any other Australian capital and while it also has one of the wettest winters, rains are usually short and sharp, with beautiful crisp sunny days interspersed. The amount of sunshine, together with Perth's beaches which, like those all along Western Australia's immense coastline, are beautiful, indicates why Western Australia is sometimes called 'The Golden State'.

In the centre of Perth is a large park which is the pride of the city; King's Park, which consists of approximately 1,000 acres of natural bushland and landscaped gardens only a ten minute walk from the city centre. The park displays a dazzling array of wildflowers every year, demonstrating why Western Australia is also known as the 'Wildflower State'. The city of Perth, viewed from the hill on which King's Park is situated, looks quite breathtaking at any time of the day, or at night, when one can easily understand why Neil Armstrong named it 'The City of Lights' as he travelled high over Perth on his way to the moon.

Besides sheer beauty and magical weather, Perth also has a very active ethnic community and cultural scene. Western Australia has its own Symphony Orchestra, Ballet Company and Opera Company, which are all based in Perth at the city's two main arts venues: the modern Perth Concert Hall and His Majesty's Theatre. The Entertainment Centre is where many of the big international artists play, such as Paul Simon, Whitney Houston, Dire Straits and Simply Red. Massive outdoor venues, football grounds converted especially for the occasion, have also been played by Pink Floyd amongst others.

Perth has an efficient public transport system consisting of buses and trains. A new rail line was opened in late 1992 to service the city's northern suburbs, and so the city centre is now within 30 minutes travel for the majority of city workers, although most of these would spend less than 20 minutes getting to work.

The beaches and the Swan River provide perfect water-playgrounds for Perth's population, and swimming, water-skiing, windsurfing, surfing and sailing are just part and parcel of Perth leisure. Not suprisingly, there are more boats owned per capita in Perth than in any other Australian state. The other major sports played in Perth include cricket (the Western Australian Cricket Association, affectionately known as the WACA, often hosts One-Day International and Test matches), various codes of football (Aussie rules, soccer, rugby), horse-racing, tennis, hockey, lawn bowls and golf. Basketball and baseball are also becoming increasingly popular, due to the recent successes of the State's teams.

Western Australia's healthy economy, its growing population, developing industries and technology, its glorious outdoor lifestyle, cheap real estate, and prime facilities contribute to a general feeling of well-being, and a sense that one is privileged to live there.

Useful Addresses

Real Estate Institute of Western Australia, 215 Hay Street West, Perth, Western Australia 6005, tel: 00-61 9 381 8866. REIWA produce an illustrated weekly guide to houses for sale. Copies should be obtained directly from REIWA.

Ministry of Education, 151 Royal Street, East Perth, Western Australia 6004, tel: 00-61 9 420 4111.

Department of Commerce and Trade, PO Box 7234, Cloisters Square, Perth, Western Australia 6850, tel: 00-61 9 327 5666 or fax: 00-61 9 327 5699. Contact the DCT or Western Australia House for a quarterly economic briefing on Western Australian Economic Conditions.

Investment Attraction Branch, Department of Commerce and Trade, tel: 00-61 9 327 5993 or fax: 00-61 9 327 5526. The IAB offer a free 'Locate Western Australia' booklet available on request.

NORTHERN TERRITORY

Capital: Darwin.
Area: 807,720 sq. miles (1,346,200 sq. kms) = 5.5 times the size of the UK.
% of total area of Australia: 17.52
Coastline: 3720 miles (6,200 kms).
Climate: Average daily maximum temperature in January 31°C, in July 31°C. In Alice Springs there is much more variation of temperature as the town lies in the semi-arid region rather than the tropical region of Darwin. The average daily maximum summer and winter temperatures respectively for Alice Springs are 35.2°C and 20.5°C.

The Northern Territory (also known as 'The Top End') is situated in central northern Australia, to the east of Western Australia. It is also bordered by South Australia in the south and Queensland to the east. The Northern Territory's history of development is closely linked with that of South Australia as in 1863 the British Government handed over control of the Northern Territory to the Colony of South Australia. Within a year, the first sale of land in the Territory was held in Adelaide. In 1869 an expedition led by the Surveyor-General George

Goyder resulted in the final establishment of a permanent settlement, now known as Darwin, the capital. South Australia's control had to be relinquished in 1901 due to the constitutional unification necessary for Federation, and control over the Northern Territory was held by the Commonwealth Government until 1 July 1978, when the Territory was granted self-government and the powers of government were transferred to the Northern Territory Government. The powers of the Northern Territory Government differ from those of other states in title only. For example, there is an Administrator instead of a Governor, and a Chief Minister instead of a Premier.

The Northern Territory lies within the torrid zone of the Tropic of Capricorn and much of its area is semi-arid. It contains part of Australia's great 'dead heart' in a large area 805 km long and 322 km wide, which is sand dune and claypan desert, yet in the tropical northern part of the Territory, some coastal areas are luxuriantly verdant. These two climatic regions result in a diversity of vegetation to be found within the Territory, including mangrove and freshwater swamps and billabongs (pool or backwater), rainforest, eucalypt and mulga woodlands, spinifex grasslands, gibber and sandy deserts (the former stony and full of boulders), and rocky gorges. There are no major rivers in the Northern Territory's interior; rivers and creeks here only flow after rains in the wet season (October-April), e.g. the Todd River across which Alice Springs is located. The wet season is a period of high humidity and rain, and torrential rain and thunderstorms occur in the transition from dry (May-September) to wet, and wet to dry seasons. The torrential rains often cause flooding, and transport and communications in the Northern Territory may be difficult or even disrupted at times. All of the Territory's major rivers are on the coastal fringe. The Roper River, which flows into the Gulf of Carpentaria, is the Territory's largest river, and other larger rivers include the Daly, Victoria, Adelaide, Mary, South and North Alligator rivers, as well as the Cox and the McArthur rivers. The torrential rains caused by deep tropical depressions result in what Australians term cyclones (hurricanes). The most infamous cyclone in the history of the Northern Territory, Cyclone Tracy, hit Darwin on 24 December 1974, devastating the city. There were few Christmas celebrations that year for the city's inhabitants as a massive evacuation reduced Darwin's population from 47,000 to 11,000 in a matter of days. Ironically, the Darwin cinemas were showing *Gone With the Wind* at the time, and billboards advertising the film stood besides areas which had been literally blown away.

The remoteness and harshness of the Northern Territory have made it unique in many ways, not the least of which is its relatively tiny population and lowest population density of only one person per nine square kilometres. In August 1991, the populations of the major NT centres were:

Darwin	Alice Springs	Katherine	Nhulunbuy
78,401	25,585	9,372	3,934

Despite the fact that the Territory appears to be virtually empty, it has in the recent past experienced the fastest population expansion in Australia. Over the census intervals from 1961-1991, the population grew at an average rate of 4.7% per annum, nearly three times the national growth rate. This rate has slowed recently due to changing patterns of interstate migration, but the Northern Territory continues to have the youngest population in Australia, with an average age of 28 years (as at June 1991), compared with the Australian average of 34.7 years. 28% of the NT population is aged 14 or less, compared with the national percentage of 22.7%. In terms of the ethnic composition of the NT population, it is interesting to note that almost one quarter is identified as Aboriginal, although Aboriginal and Torres Straits Islanders account for only 1.5% of the Australian population. Within the Aboriginal population, a massive 39% are aged 14 or less. More than 50 different ethnic groups are represented in Darwin, and 24% of the people speak a language other than English. 18% of the people resident in the NT were born overseas.

Although the Territory is hampered by distances from major Australian economic and political centres, and the restricted transport and communications links, its economy has experienced a growth rate in Gross Domestic Product (GDP) which has generally exceeded that of Australia as a whole. Its rapid growth can be attributed mainly to developments in mining, especially oil, and the tourist industries. The tourist industry is in fact the Northern Territory's fastest growing industry and the source of approximately $490 million in direct revenue in 1991/2. The abundance of natural resources such as alumina, manganese, gold, bauxite and uranium as well as oil and gas, have enabled the Northern Territory to participate substantially in the international market. In 1991/2, the value of exports from the Northern Territory was valued at $1,466 million. The value of exports for the Northern Territory per capita for the same period was calculated to be $8,695, almost three times the national figure.

There are three main interstate highway links in the Northern Territory, the Stuart Highway from Darwin to the South Australian border, the Barkly Highway from Tennant Creek to the Queensland border, and the Victoria Highway from Katherine to the Western Australian border. Although there are road houses along these highways, there are stretches of road as long as 265km which are not serviced. It is always advisable to notify the Automobile Association of the Northern Territory before embarking on an unfamiliar road (especially in the wet season), and/or long journeys over unsealed and/or unserviced roads. It is also advisable to install a CB radio in your vehicle which can be used both for general interest's sake to relieve the monotony, or in the case of an emergency.

The cost of housing varies dramatically within the Northern Territory from city or town, to homestead on a settlement or station. The cost of rented accommodation is, surprisingly, among the highest of all capital cities in Australia, due to the lack of availability of private rental accommodation, particularly in Darwin and Alice Springs. In 1991 the Northern Territory government introduced a portfolio designed to promote home ownership in the Northern Territory. This portfolio includes a deposit assistance grant scheme, a first mortgage loan scheme and a vendor-finance sheme, with favourable interest rates for the home buyer. Contact the relevant department listed above for further details.

Education in the Northern Territory has been its own responsibility since 1979 and it has modified its own schools' curriculum to reflect the multicultural nature of its classrooms, promoting intercultural understanding as well as proficiency in English. There are also correspondence schools which involve the use of electronic media such as a two-way radio, video and audio cassettes, and computers, for isolated students. The Northern Territory Secondary Correspondence School offers an excellent range of secondary courses up to university entrance level for those who do not have access to normal school facilities. Tertiary education in the Northern Territory is usually undertaken through either the Northern Territory University or the University's Insititute of Technical and Further Education which specialises in trade and technical courses. In 1983, the postgraduate research institution, the Menzies School of Health Research, was established at the Royal Darwin Hospital and it is currently enjoying a reputation as a centre of scientific excellence in its field. One of its primary objectives is to assist in improving the health of people in tropical and central Australia. The School has an academic link with the University of Sydney and its students may qualify for the higher degrees of that university.

The Northern Territory Health Services are remarkable, considering the distance and difficult terrain that must be covered. There are modern, well-equipped hospitals in Darwin, Alice Springs, Katherine, Tennant Creek and Nhulunbuy. All hospitals provide general in- and outpatient, accident and emergency services. The Royal Darwin and Alice Springs Hospitals offer a wide range of specialist services and are both special teaching hospitals affiliated with the University of Sydney. A private hospital is also available in Darwin. Mobile services are also provided in remote areas, or the Northern Territory government subsidises missions, pastoralists or Aboriginal organisations to provide health services. While there are health centres in all major towns and settlements, in extremely remote regions the Royal Flying Doctor Service (RFDS) and the Aerial Medical Service operate in cases of serious injury or illness. There is a Patients' Assistance Travel Scheme (PATS) which provides financial assistance to people from isolated areas who have had to travel for specialist consultations and treatment. The Northern Territory government also provides mental health services, blood banks, services for the aged, family, youth and children's services, services for the disabled and women's information services as well as women's refuges and shelters, a Sexual Assault Reference Centre, and the Ruby Gaea Darwin Centre Against Rape which provides counselling, support services and emergency accommodation.

Most non-Australians and even a significant number of Australians think of the Northern Territory only in terms of Ayers Rock (situated in the Uluru National Park) or the Kakadu National Park, which is partly a tribute to the success of the marketing strategy employed by the Northern Territory Tourist Commission. It must be stated, however, that the Northern Territory is a place of development and growth, both of the general population and industry, at a rate almost invariably higher than those elsewhere in the country. The capital, Darwin, is a modern city on a par with other Australian capitals in terms of the quality of community services it provides. Like any other Australian state, the Northern Territory offers a huge range of outdoor activities, including a wide variety of sports, as well as diverse arts, including theatre and festivals. In general, although the towns are small, they are less crowded and have a more relaxed atmosphere and a strong sense of familiar community.

Useful Addresses

Department of Immigration, Local Government and Ethnic Affairs, PO Box 864, Darwin, Northern Territory 0801, tel: 010-61 89 46 3100 or fax: 010-61 89 81 6245/ 010-61 89 41 2297.

Department of Mines and Energy, GPO Box 2901, Darwin, Northern Territory 0801, tel: 00-61 89 89 5286 or fax: 00 61 89 89 5289.

Department of Primary Industry and Fisheries, GPO Box 990, Darwin, Northern Territory 0801, tel: 00-61 89 89 4365 or fax: 010-61 89 41 0825.

Department of Transport and Works, GPO Box 2520, Darwin, Northern Territory 0801, tel: 00-61 89 89 7693.

Department of Education, GPO Box 4821, Darwin, Northern Territory 0801, tel: 00-61 89 89 5605/6.

Department of Health and Community Services, GPO Box 1701, Darwin, Northern Territory 0801, tel: 00-61 89 89 2709.

Northern Territory Department of Lands, Housing and Local Government, PO Box 40246, Casuarina, Northern Territory 0810, tel: 00-61 89 51 5344.

SOUTH AUSTRALIA

Capital: Adelaide.
Area: 380,070 sq. miles (984,377 sq. kms) = four times the size of the UK.
% of total area of Australia: 12.81

Coastline: 2,300 miles (3,700 kms).

Climate: Average daily maximum temperature in January 29°C, in July 15°C.

South Australia is situated in the middle of the southern coast of Australia along the Great Australian Bight. It is bordered by Western Australia to the west, the Northern Territory to the north, both New South Wales and Victoria almost due east, and Queensland to the north-east. It has a Mediterranean climate and as a consequence, vineyards are prolific throughout the Barossa Valley, established by German settlers. South Australia produces more wines that any other state or territory in the country, and South Australian wines are readily available in the UK at highly competitive prices and have cornered a large section of the international market. South Australia has a population of 1,407,984 which is approximately 8.5% of the total population of Australia. Most of South Australia's population lives in Adelaide, the capital, which has a population of 1,023,517. Adelaide is situated between peaceful gulf waters and a range of low hills on a coastal plateau, by the River Torrens. Although the river was formerly the lifeline for early settlers, it is now a major recreation area, supporting diverse aquatic wildlife less than 500 metres from the central business district. Adelaide covers an area of 984 sq.kms, and stretches 63 kms from its southernmost to northernmost suburbs. The rest of the population is scattered throughout the state in the major regional centres of Whyalla, Mount Gambier, Port Augusta, Murray Bridge, Port Pirie and Port Lincoln.

Adelaide: Adelaide's transport system is a well-oiled machine that is rarely experiences breakdown or congestion. This is largely due to the city's first planner, Colonel William Light, who planned Adelaide with such geometric symmetry that all major city roads are straight and wide. Adelaide also boasts a unique bus service called *O-Bahn* which is a right-of-way guided transport system on which commuters are shuttled to and from the city at speeds of up to 100km/h.

Most of the housing follows the pattern of a single-storey bungalow on spacious blocks ensuring off-street parking and a private back garden. The standard of homes in South Australia is among the highest in the country, and rented accommodation can be up to 18% cheaper than elsewhere.

Unlike Victoria and New South Wales, South Australia was not developed by convict labour, but by free settlers. The result of this is that South Australia has an industrial tradition and so electrical appliances bought in South Australia are most likely to have been built by South Australians at a South Australian factory. Science and technology are also developing and expanding in South Australia, particularly the electronics industries. South Australian technicians are leading the way in laser research, and the Advanced Engineering, Electronic Research and Electronic Surveillance laboratories at the Defence Science Technology Centre are experiencing considerable, if secret, success. The academic centres of the Adelaide and Flinders Universities support these developments, as well as enjoying a fine reputation in many other disciplines. The University of Adelaide ranks ahead of universities in Victoria, Queensland, Western Australia and Tasmania in its ability to attract funds through the Australian Research Grant Scheme. Australia's first planned centre for high-technology development and manufacture, Technology Park Adelaide, is integrated with the campus of the University of South Australia. In addition, there are vast mineral resources in the form of oil, gas and other hydrocarbons which are being tapped in the Cooper Basin area, brown coal at Leigh Creek, one of Australia's biggest opal fields at Andamooka, and copper, uranium and gold at Roxby Downs.

South Australia has a warm, friendly ambience, and Adelaide is a rapidly developing city. It also hosts the Australian Formula One Grand Prix, has excellent sporting and entertainment facilities, and a fine system of education.

With a relatively low cost of living and real estate, South Australia is an appealing and easy place in which to live.

Useful Addresses

Immigration Promotion and Settlement Unit, Office of Multicultural and Ethnic Affairs, 24 Flinders Street, Adelaide, South Australia, 5000, tel: 00 61 8 226 1943 or fax: 00 61 8 226 1955.

The Department of Industry, Trade and Technology, GPO Box 1264 Adelaide, South Australia, 5001, tel: 00 61 8 210 8333 or fax: 00 61 8 231 0440.

TASMANIA
Capital: Hobart.
Area: 26,375 sq. miles (68,331 sq. kms) = 0.22 times the size of the UK.
% total area of Australia: 0.88.
Coastline: 1,920 miles (3,200 km).
Climate: January 22°C, July 11°C.

Tasmania is Australia's smallest state and is an island separated from the south-east corner of the mainland by the Bass Strait, a shallow body of water with an average width of 240kms. Tasmania's remaining coastline is bounded by the Southern Ocean on the south and west, and the Tasman Sea on the east. Tasmania spans 296 km from north to south and 315 km from east to west at its greatest width. Despite the fact that it is Australia's smallest state, it must be pointed out that it is still twice the size of Wales. Tasmania is the only Australian state which does not have a desert region and so irrigation is virtually unnecessary. It is also the most mountainous state and one of the most completely mountainous islands in the world. At the same time, it has the largest rural population in relation to its size of all the Australian states, and is one of the most richly mineralised areas world-wide. Tasmania is the leading Australian state in terms of the production of minerals in point of value of output per capita and almost all of Australia's tungsten is extracted from King Island.

Orchard and berry fruits are grown in the south of the state. Due to its high production of apples and its almost love-heart shape, Tasmania is often referred to as the Apple Isle. Industries in the southern region include the Cadbury Schweppes cocoa and confectionary factory, the Electrolytic Zinc Company, the Australian Newsprint Mills, Stanley Works (manufacturers of hand tools such as the Stanley knife), Sheridan Textiles, International Catamarans and the Cascade Brewery, which was established in 1824 and is the oldest brewery still in operation in Australia.

The east coast of Tasmania is a popular holiday destination as there are miles of beautiful beaches and plenty of surfable waves. Fishing is the major industry in this region, based in the ports of St Helens and Bicheno, and catches include crayfish and abalone.

In the north-east of the state, the fertile soil provides ideal farming land. Beef and dairy cattle, wool sheep and prime lambs, all important to the State's economy, are all run here. Vegetables are also a significant component of the region's agriculture. This is also true of the north-west region of the state, where vegetable and dairy farming are predominant. United Milk Products and Lactos cheesemakers have been established on the coast to process the large quantities of milk and vegetables produced. Other types of farming in the north-west include pig, sheep and also poppy farming (to provide oil for pharmaceutical preparations). Manufacturing here is dominated by forest-based industries whereas in the central northern region of the state industries include the knitting yarn producers Coats Patons, the automotive parts manufacturer ACL Bearing Company, and the aluminium smelter and refinery Comalco. In addition, in central northern Tasmania, there are vineyards and also the Ben Lomond Ski Fields. The use of the Scottish name is significant as many people find that many parts of Tasmania are reminiscent of the green and rolling, yet sometimes wild and windswept, landscapes of some parts of Scotland and England, and for this reason perhaps, a large number of British and other European immigrants settled in Tasmania. According to the latest (1991) census, the population of Tasmania is 452,841 and of this number, 396,313 were born in Australia. A large proportion of the remaining people who had identified their country of origin were born in European countries. For example, 19,449 were born in England, 3,051 in Scotland, 2,959 in the Netherlands, 2,039 in Germany, 1,334 in Italy and 1,174 in Poland. In addition, Tasmania's climate and farming are the most easily comparable with those of the UK, which also helps new British settlers feel more at home than they would perhaps do in the harsh dry regions of the Northern Territory or the tropical areas of Queensland.

The west of the state is a region of dense forests and mountain ranges, raging rivers and rugged hills, and has a treacherous coastline of untamed beaches. Mining is the predominant industry in the west, and metal ores such as copper, zinc, tin and iron are extracted. Much of the south-west region is inaccessible and uninhabited, containing some of the most spectacular scenery in the world. The South-West Wilderness Area has been listed by the World Heritage Commission and it consists of dense rainforest, scrub, wild rivers, rapids and ravines, unpredictable weather and harsh mountains which can only be tackled by experienced bushwalkers. Approximately 20% of Tasmania is World Heritage area, and there are extensive cave systems many of which are Ice Age Aboriginal cave-art sites.

The central lakes area is dominated by hydro-electric schemes which produce the State's electricity. Trout-fishing is also popular. In the flatter midland area, sheep farming, particularly for wool, and beef cattle grazing are also popular.

Hobart is Tasmania's capital city, situated in the south-west of the state, 20 km from the mouth of the Derwent River. It is Australia's second oldest city, being founded in 1804, and it extends over both sides of the river, being bordered in the west by Mount Wellington (1,269 metres). The city essentially originated as a penal colony, and many old colonial songs, both in Britain and Australia, voice the anguish felt by prisoners punished by transportation to Van Diemen's Land. Despite its harsh and cruel beginnings, the city flourished in the mid-nineteenth century due to its ship-building, whaling and port facilities, and now it is a popular port of call for luxury cruising liners and is also distinguished in terms of being home to Australia's first casino. Nowadays, Hobart is much more likely to hit the international headlines during the famous Sydney-Hobart or the Westcoaster yacht races, which it hosts.

Tasmania has been more progressive than other states in educating its population. In 1869 Tasmania became the first colony in the British Empire to make education compulsory and in 1898 school attendance was made obligatory between the ages of seven and thirteen, expanding to between six and fourteen years in 1912. In 1946 Tasmania became the only Australian state to make attendance up to the age of sixteen compulsory. It now has its own universitv, the University of Tasmania, and the total number of enrolments in 1992 was 11,313.

Tasmania's main employment sectors are retailing and manufacturing, and it is perhaps easiest to find employment in either of these areas. The employment situation is perhaps not as rosy as in other Australian states and territories. Employment peaked in Tasmania in April 1990 with 198,700 people employed which was a remarkable increase from the figure of 185,100 recorded in February 1989, but after this peak there was a steady decrease until mid-1992. During

1992 employment reached a low of 188,800 in May before rising in September and dropping again in December to 190,000. For the year ending December 1992, employment fell 0.9%, compared with the national average of 0.1%. Female employment, however, showed an annual increase of 0.3% while male employment showed a fall of 1.7%.

Since September 1989 there has been a marked increase in unemployment in Tasmania. In December 1992, there were 26,400 unemployed Tasmanians, and at 12.5% it had the highest unemployment rate for all the states. During the year to December 1992, significant changes in employment rates were experienced throughout the nation; however only Western Australia experienced a drop in the unemployment rate, so Tasmania is certainly not alone in seeing a rise in unemployment.

Tasmania is often considered a bit too far off the beaten track to initially interest migrants to settle, however, the statistics show that it is becoming increasingly popular. The high standard of education, modern health facilities and cheap housing are all strong attractions, but it must be noted that the cost of living can be slightly higher than in other states due to freight costs. In addition, although some love the small-community feel to the state, others feel that the sense of isolation which almost inevitably affects new settlers to Australia, particularly from European countries, can seem even worse due to the fact that Tasmania is separate even from mainland Australia. Tasmania's geographical isolation has, however, enabled the state to retain certain distinctive character-istics in terms of fauna. Tasmania has ten species of mammal not found elsewhere, including the Tasmanian Devil and the Tasmanian Tiger, fourteen indigenous species of birds and two of reptiles. The duck-billed platypus is more common in Tasmania than elsewhere and the Tasmanian mountain shrimp which is only known outside Tasmania as a fossil has remained almost unaltered and very much alive.

In the final analysis, there is simply no disputing the fact that in terms of weather and landscape, Tasmania is breathtaking, and perhaps feels a little more like home to the European settler than the harsh, sandy, sunburnt land of mainland Australia.

VICTORIA
Capital: Melbourne.
Area: 136,560 sq. miles (227 600 sq. kms) = 0.93 times the size of the UK.
% of total area of Australia: 2.96.
Coastline: 1,080 miles (1,800 km).
Climate: January 25.1°C, July 14°C, but Victoria's, particularly Melbourne, weather is notoriously unpredictable. Victoria's exposure to frequent cold fronts and southerly winds results in changeable weather patterns, and a phrase 'Four Seasons in One Day' which the antipodean band *Crowded House* immortalised in their hit titled with the same phrase.

Victoria is situated in the south-eastern corner of Australia, bordered by South Australia to the west and New South Wales to the north. Even though Victoria is the smallest of all Australian States, it still can offer such geographical diversity as the Victorian Alps, which lie on the shared border with New South Wales, fertile wine-growing regions such as the Murray and Yarra River Valleys, rainforest in the Gippsland region (in the south-east corner of Victoria) in the Errinundra Plateau, and desert beauty in the north-west inland Mallee region. Victoria also boasts the world's third largest volcanic plain in the Western District. The Great Dividing Range, which forms a spine down the inland back of Victoria and New South Wales, is known as the 'High Country', and the breathtaking scenery was captured by the excellent cinematography of the Australian film, *Man From Snowy River*, based on the nineteenth-century poem of the same name by the famous Australian poet 'Banjo' Patterson.

The land on which Melbourne was built was purchased in 1835 from Aborigines of the local Dutigalla clan. The Aborigines had no concept of land as a commodity at that time, but in exchange for their land, they were paid in terms of articles of clothing, 50 pounds of flour, handkerchiefs, knives, tomahawks, looking-glasses and blankets. The driving force behind the founding of Melbourne was John Pascoe Fawkner, the son of a convict. He was a self-educated bush lawyer and he established several newspapers. He also sat on the Legislative Council of Victoria for 15 years, where he was an energetic campaigner for the rights of small settlers and convicts, and for the ending of transportation. His energy was drawn from his own personal experience of the harsh penal code — he received 500 lashes when he was 22 for assisting seven convicts to escape, and he bore the scars for the rest of his life.

The population of Victoria is currently estimated as 4.4 million, and consists of immigrants from the UK and EU as well as the Middle East and South-East Asia. There are also more than 12,000 Aborigines in Victoria. All of these different ethnic groups give the state real cultural diversity and have an influence on Victorian culture. Of Victoria's 4.4 million residents, over three million live in Melbourne. The other major regional centres are Geelong, Bendigo, Ballarat, Horsham, Mildura, Warrnambool, Castlemaine and Shepparton.

Victoria's economy has suffered in the past from strikes in education and industry, and questionable governmental industrial and economic decisions. It was hit the hardest by the Australian recession in 1991, which perhaps accounts for the high numbers of Victorians who have moved interstate mid-1990, but there are already signs of recovery within the Victorian economy. The signs of recovery and more optimistic outlook can be attributed to the change of government which occurred in October 1992, when Jeff Kennett was elected Victoria's Premier, and, as the leader of the Liberal-National coalition, Labour's ten-year reign was ended. In an attempt to boost the State's economy, the Victorian Government can sponsor successful overseas entrepeneurs and senior executives intending to live permanently in Victoria through the Australian Government's Independent Business Skills Migration Category. Victoria is the site of research and development in the areas of food, paper, chemicals and petroleum, transport equipment, electrical equipment and biotechnology.

The standard of tertiary education in Victoria is particularly high. There are eight universities in the State, as well as numerous technical and further education institutions. The Commonwealth Scientific and Industrial Research Organisation is based in Victoria.

On the whole, Victoria can still be seen as a lucky and affluent State.

Melbourne: The Population Crisis Committee, based in Washington DC, recently rated Melbourne the world's most livable city in an analysis of one hundred of the world's largest cities in respect to aspects such as safety, health, noise and atmospheric cleanliness. Melbourne's location on the coastal plain between the Pacific Ocean and the beautiful Dandenong hills (where one can take a scenic trip on 'Puffing Billy', a quaint old steam train) must have made a significant contribution to this result. In addition, Melbourne offers cultural and sporting facilities unequalled elsewhere in Australia, if not the world.

Melbourne was built out of the great gold rush of the 1850s, and as a consequence it became the Australia's centre of business and commerce. Even today, 15 of Australia's top 25 companies have their headquarters in Melbourne. In the 1880s, Melbourne was known as 'The Paris of the Antipodes', and it was the capital of Australia from 1901 (Federation) until 1927, when the capital was moved to Canberra.

Melbourne is one of Australia's leading exporters of computers, engines and pharmaceuticals, and it is the location of eight major medical research institutes, including the Walter and Eliza Hall Institute which is the home of modern immunology and one of the world's best known medical research centres. Telecom Australia's main research and development facilities are based in Melbourne, and the city is the site of 70% of Australia's telecommunications output. Melbourne is the second most popular destination in the Asian region, behind Singapore, for conventions, meetings and exhibitions.

The population of Melbourne is truly cosmopolitan and, with nearly 160 different nationalities represented, it is one of the most multicultural cities in the world. It has the world's third largest Greek community, behind Athens and Thessalonia.

Culturally, Melbourne has been called Australia's cultural capital. The Australian Ballet Company is based in Melbourne, which also boasts a huge Arts Centre. Some famous Melbournians include Barry Humphries (alias Dame Edna), Kylie and Danni Minogue, Sir Sydney Nolan, Olivia Newton-John, Nick Cave, Rupert Murdoch, Dame Nellie Melba, Peter Carey and Germaine Greer. Melbourne is also home of the Australian film industry, and famous movies such as *Picnic at Hanging Rock*, the *Mad Max* series, *The Big Steal, Death in Brunswick, Malcolm, Spotswood, Proof* and *Sirens* have been made there. The famous soaps *Neighbours* and *The Flying Doctors* are also made in Melbourne.

Melbourne is also the retail capital of Australia, offering an outstanding range and standard of shops at highly competitive prices. For other Australians, a trip to Melbourne necessitates a raid of the 'seconds' warehouses, where big-name brand names and designers sell clothes directly to the public.

In terms of sport, Melbourne's facilities are almost unparalleled elsewhere in the country. Melbourne is host to the nation's biggest horse-race, The Melbourne Cup, the Australian Rules Football's Grand Final, and the Australian Open at the impressive Koorong Tennis Centre.

Melbourne is a lush, green city with plenty of parks and botanical gardens. Its diversity in terms of restaurants, shopping, theatre and entertainment, and business, as well as the high standard of research and development in the commercial and medical fields will continue to make Melbourne one of the world's most habitable big cities well into the future.

Useful Addresses

Department of Business and Employment, 228 Victoria Parade, East Melbourne 3002, tel: 00-61 3 412 800 or fax: 00-61 3 419 7872.

Investment Centre Victoria, 29th Floor, 120 Collins Street, Melbourne, tel: 00-61 3 655 899 or fax: 00-61 3 650 2248.

AUSTRALIAN CAPITAL TERRITORY

Capital: Canberra.
Area: 1,440 sq. miles (2,400 sq. kms) = 0.01 times the size of the UK.
% of total area: 0.0003.
Coastline: 0 (except for 35km of the Jervis Bay Territory).
Climate: January 28°C, July 11°C.
All other capital cities in Australia developed because they were built on the banks of rivers and so were accessible to trade. Canberra is the exception, established in 1901 at Federation, precisely because it was not the centre of anything. Sydney had threatened to refuse to join the federation unless the capital was in New South Wales, which Melbourne hotly contested, with the result that Canberra was chosen as a compromise which, it has been said, was acceptable to everyone, but satisfactory to nobody.

The American architect, Walter Burley Griffin, won the international competition to design the capital city. Canberra is a completely planned city, with such attention to detail that even the sites of trees have been carefully selected. The effect is eerie to other Australians, and can even appear sterile in its neatness and obvious planning. This eeriness is reinforced by the fact that 60% of Canberra's residents are employed by government departments. The weekends see an evacuation of the politicians back to their state of origin, giving Canberra the reputation for being dead.

During the week, however, Capital Hill, through which the artificial Lake Burley Griffin cuts, is the hub of the nation's political activity. Canberra is a derivative of an Aboriginal word *kamberra* which means 'meeting place', and it is here that the country's top leaders and international leaders meet. Interestingly, the British High Commission was the first diplomatic office to establish its headquarters in Canberra.

My own experience of Canberra was as a teenager on a high school music tour of Canberra and Sydney. I was billetted on the second largest battery chicken farm in the southern hemisphere. I remember feeling that I should have been a lot more excited about this fact than I actually was. The Territory was incredibly cold at night (it can go below 0°C in winter, which for Australians is bitter!). At the risk of seeming negative, I also remember feeling that the city was dull, which many other Australians seem to feel, but my boredom could have been caused by my frustration about being placed on a chicken farm while all my schoolfriends who had scored more central billets were busy socialising. For many Australians, one day in the Australian Capital Territory is enough.

On the positive side, Canberra is home to the Australian National University, the Australian Insititute of Sport, the Australian National Gallery, the Australian War Memorial and Museum. The new Parliament House, opened in 1988 by the Queen, is certainly impressive. My memory of the old one is slightly absurd. Our school band had set up outside Parliament House in order to play to an assortment of political figures who were due to saunter outside and enjoy the free entertainment. They never came. Instead, we played to four punks on hunger strike in a tent, and a man and his camels who had just crossed the Nullarbor. We thought it was funny at the time, but were a bit miffed that the camels received more media attention than we did!

The Canberra Centre is a shopper's haven, with 150 shops under one roof. Canberra's residents feel a kind of pride that their city does not have a commercial centre. Instead, the city has multiple parks and recreational areas, and traffic congestion is virtually unknown.

The city is certainly beautiful; it is just that other Australians, perhaps more used to the rugged and harsh beauty of their respective states and territories, find the planned and highly ordered beauty of Canberra somewhat difficult to appreciate. Canberra's atmosphere is certainly friendly and it is not inferior to the rest of Australia, just different.

NEW SOUTH WALES

Capital: Sydney.
Area: 309,572. sq. miles (802,000 sq. kms) = 3.25 times the size of the UK.
% of total area of Australia: 10
Climate: The mean January termperatures along the coast are usually between 8°C and 21°C, but 22°C at Sydney. The plateaux are about 4°C cooler and the temperatures in the plains increase in direct relation to the distance from the sea. Temperatures at the Queensland border are about 27°C to 31°C. The maximum temperature in July is 17°C and the minumum is 8°C.
New South Wales is probably the Australian state most visited by tourists and

business people, and is also the state which receives most international publicity. Most of this is largely due to its spectacular capital city, Sydney, which lends itself so well to any Australian Tourist Commission marketing campaign. There is, however, so much more to New South Wales than Sydney, and it is well worth venturing beyond the city limits to explore its diverse regions.

New South Wales is bordered to the north by Queensland, to the east by South Australia and to the south by Victoria. The Australian Capital Territory lies wholly contained within the south-east corner of New South Wales. From Sydney it is 1,157 km west to Broken Hill, almost on the South Australian border, 908 km north to Tweed Heads which borders Queensland, and 498 km south to Eden, the last sizable town before Victoria. Within these borders lie mountain ranges, beaches, fertile farming land, rainforests and arid desert.

It is possible to catch a bus or train to spend a day at Katoomba in the Blue Mountains, Australia's version of the Grand Canyon, 100 km west of Sydney. The area is a national park and it contains some of the most breathtaking scenery in the world. Standing at one of the numerous lookouts it is easy to feel as though you are on the top edge of the world as you survey hundreds of miles of unbroken, uninhabited bush, or at the immense unusual rock formations at Echo Point called 'The Three Sisters'. Many people are bowled over by the sheer scale of the beauty of the appropriately named Blue Mountains and can find that the Grand Canyon is a little disappointing in comparison. Perhaps this is due to the fact that the Blue Mountains are not as well publicised as the Grand Canyon which may have been somewhat overexposed. The area now known as the Blue Mountains National Park was once home to Aboriginal people at least 14,000 years ago, who have left their mark in the form of rock carvings and cave paintings. The rugged 250,000 hectare park is composed mainly of sandstone which has been eroded over the ages by rivers and creeks, to form dramatic valleys and sheer escarpments.

Approximately 150 km north of Sydney is the wine region of New South Wales, the Hunter Valley. The Valley is divided 'into two distinct areas, the Lower Hunter region and the Upper Hunter region. Cessnock, 183 km from Sydney, is the centre of the Lower Hunter region and was originally founded on the coal-mining industry. The area produces some of the state's best wines and famous wineries include McWilliams, Mount Pleasant, Lindemans, Hungerford Hill, Tyrells and Brokenwood. Wineries are generally open between 9am and 5pm daily for tasting, tours and buying. 100 km further to the north-west is the smaller, newer and less popular Lower Hunter, but the famous Rosemount Estate winery and the lesser known but equally excellent Arrowfield winery are both established in this area. Muswellbrook is the centre of this region and is also known for its coal and agriculture.

In the south-east of the state lie the Snowy Mountains, less than a three-hour drive from Canberra in the ACT. Thredbo is a popular ski resort which has hosted various World Cup Ski events, and it is possible to take a chair lift to the top of Crackenback and then hike up Australia's highest mountain, Mount Kosciusko which, at 7,328 feet (2241 metres), is less than half the height of Mont Blanc. On the northern side of Mt Kosciusko are two very popular ski resorts in Perisher Valley, Perisher and Smiggins Holes. This is Australia's alpine country which, surprisingly, contains more snow covered area than Switzerland, but instead of the pine trees one associates with alpine scenes, the area is peppered with gum trees, looking somewhat incongruous against the vast snow fields. The ski season runs from June to October and the snow is usually best between late July and mid-September. Mt Kosciusko is located at the heart of the Kosckiusko National Park, which contains 629,000 hectares of rugged moorland, glacial lakes, caves, the source of the Murray River, Australia's largest waterway, more than 200 species of birds, and an abundance of wildlife including kangaroos, possums and wombats. The Snowy Mountains are really more a series of plateau blocks than the soaring peaks of the Alps, and they house seven hydroelectric stations which supply a large proportion of the state's power grid.

The Murray River rises in the Great Dividing Range and flows for over 2,500 km, creating most of the border between Victoria and New South Wales. From Wentworth in the far west of New South Wales, the Murray continues through South Australia and veers south, entering Lake Alexandrina and the ocean. It is used extensively for irrigation and is therefore, crucial to the agricultural industries. One of the state's most important agricultural districts is the Riverina which lies along the northern borderlands of the Murray River. Crops as diverse as rice, vegetables and citrus fruits are grown here, and cattle and merino sheep are also important. Albury is at the heart of this fertile region and its population is approximately 37,000. It is a National Growth Centre, the aim of which has been to encourage the decentralisation of industry from major state capitals. Wentworth is important as the heart of the region's irrigation scheme and both the citrus and avocado growing areas.

Broken Hill is one of the state's most eastern settlements, lying almost on the border with South Australia. It is isolated and remote, but nearly 26,000 people live here as it is famous for its silver mines and Royal Flying Doctor Services. The mining industry has survived and silver, lead and zinc are still mined in significant quantities. In addition, Broken Hill is the birthplace of Broken Hill Proprietary Limited (BHP), which is Australia's biggest company. The nearby ghost town of Silverton was made famous as the rugged, inhospitable and eerie setting for the *Mad Max* films which starred Australia's own Mel Gibson. In the northern desert region of the state along the border with Queensland lies the town of Lightning Ridge, famous for its opal mines. Over 1,000 people representing over 30 different nations are based at Lightning Ridge, and manage to survive the extreme weather conditions and limited water supply (artesian bore water is the only kind available here) to mine the fields, particularly for the highly prized black varieties of opal. Visitors are allowed to tour various mines and to *fossick* (prospect) for the gems.

New South Wales' north coastal region is one of the state's favourite holiday destinations as the region contains beautiful surf beaches, lakes, rivers, small coastal towns and gorgeous inland scenery. Byron Bay is considered to be the unspoilt gem of the entire New South Wales coast. It is Australia's most easterly point and, so far, is one of the world's last remaining touches of paradise. The beauty of this region is natural and the beaches are seemingly endless, and Cape Byron is home to many people who prefer an alternative lifestyle away from the rat-race of the busy cities. Coffs Harbour, closer to Sydney, is a popular harbour and port town, with many top-class tourist resorts. There is plenty of good surf to be enjoyed, and it is also a famous yachting centre. Bananas are grown in this semi-tropical area, and the nearby Dorrigo National Park contains rainforest, waterfalls and lush vegetation. Inland from Coffs is the Nymboida River, a popular spot for white-water rafting. Grafton is situated in this area, some 65 km inland, and is at the centre of a region which specialises in the unlikely combination of dairy and sugar-cane industries.

New South Wales also controls Lord Howe Island and originally owned Norfolk Island, although it is now a Territory of Australia which has no income or sales taxes. Lord Howe Island is a tiny island 11 km long and 2.8 km at its widest point, some 700 km northeast of Sydney. It has a population of 300 and was listed as a World Heritage area in 1982 because of its soaring volcanic peaks, the world's most southerly coral reef, exceptional birdlife and general scenic beauty. Lord Howe Island was first sighted in 1788 and was named after the first Lord of the Admiralty. The numbers of visitors to the island is strictly controlled to prevent it from becoming crowded, and the island's 37 km coastline provides plenty of opportunity for fishing, coral reef viewing and plain relaxation. Norfolk Island is a much larger and more isolated island 1,600 km to the east of Sydney. It was first discovered by Captain Cook in 1774 during his second round-the-world voyage. Its history is that of a brutal and much feared penal settlement for the colony of New South Wales between 1788 and 1855, and it later became the home of the Pitcairn Islanders who included descendants of the *Bounty* mutineers moved to the island in 1856. There are still many Pitcairn descendants on the island who speak 'Norfolk', a curious mixture of Tahitian and English. The island has a population of about 2,000, most of whom are involved in either tourism or agriculture.

Sydney;

Sydney contains 60% of New South Wales' population of 5,500,000. At 3,400,000, Sydney's population is easily the biggest in the state and more than the total population of most of Australia's other states and territories. The second largest city in New South Wales is Newcastle, on the northern coast 170 km from Sydney, with a population of 423,000, and Wollongong is the third largest city in the state, some 82 km south of Sydney, with a population of 230,000.

The city itself is open and spacious, surrounded on three sides by many national parks and on the fourth by 60 km of beautiful and quite spectacular coastline. Sydney Harbour, on which the city is built, has 240 km of foreshore, much of which has remained as it was when the First Fleet made its initial investigative journey up the waterway in 1788. Joseph Conrad wrote of Sydney in 1906, that the view from Circular Quay was that of 'no walled prison-house of a dock...but the integral part of the finest, most beautiful, vast, and safe bays the sun ever shone upon' (*The Mirror of the Sea*) and Antony Trollope had written earlier that 'Sydney is one of those places which, when a man leaves it knowing that he will never return, he cannot leave without a pang and a tear. Such is its loveliness' (*Australia and New Zealand*, 1873). Other sayings have also remained true through the years, despite the original speakers having been forgotten. Sydney has been described as 'the best address on earth', and it has been said that Sydneysiders 'by the standards of the world at large...live magnificently'. Although Sydney has its fair share of problems usually associated with big cities, such as pollution, ugly industrial areas, traffic congestion, homelessness, unemployment, drugs and crime, one still cannot help but feel that Sydney is perhaps even more beautiful now than it was over 100 years ago. The Sydney Harbour Bridge and the Opera House, which are certainly dramatic features of the Harbour, were not opened until 1932 and 1973 respectively. I will never forget sitting at South Head in 1988, watching a re-enactment of the First Fleet entering Sydney Harbour as part of the bicentennial celebrations. The day was perfect and the view included the craggy cliffs of the North Head opposite, an almost solid bank-to-bank flotilla of small pleasure boats vying for a closer look, the old 'Coathanger' and Centrepoint Tower in the background, in front of which stood the Sydney Opera House, the sun gleaming off the millions of highly polished white tiles that make up its shell. As we made our way down to Circular Quay to watch the firework extravaganza later in the evening, the excitement and beauty were nothing less than intoxicating. There is no doubt that Sydney Harbour is simply stunning and the city is an exciting and privileged place in which to live. Some Australians do, however, tire of the bright lights and relatively fast pace and prefer to move to quieter, calmer and perhaps safer cities, each with their own distinctive beauty.

As well as being a modern city, Sydney is one of Australia's most historical cities, as it was into Botany Bay, just south of Sydney, that Captain Cook sailed in the *Endeavour* in 1710. In May 1787 the First Fleet of 1,044 people, including 759 convicts (191 of whom were women) set sail from Portsmouth and arrived eight months later. Unimpressed with Botany Bay's windswept barrenness, the Fleet moved north in search of a more suitable site and six days later the ships arrived at what became Port Jackson, described by Captain Phillip as 'the finest harbour in the world'. Even though Port Jackson was superior to Botany Bay, the first days of the colony were harsh as crops failed and the anticipated supply ships failed to arrive. Somehow, however, the colony managed to survive and slowly began to grow. Captain Phillip was replaced by Governor Macquarie, known as the 'Father of Australia', in 1810 and over the next 11 years streets and fine new buildings were built. Convict transportation to New South Wales continued until 1840, but free settlers began to arrive from 1819. From 1831 to 1850 more than 200,000 government-assisted migrants streamed into the colony to begin a new life as far away as possible from what they perceived as the urban nightmare of Victorian Britain. During the 1850s, a goldrush brought a new influx of settlers which continued until the end of the nineteenth century, and by 1925 the area around Sydney had a population in excess of one million.

Sydney today boasts Australia's most influential Central Business District (CBD) and most national and international businesses choose to have their major Australian offices in Sydney. Darling Harbour houses the Sydney Aquarium, Chinese Gardens, Powerhouse Museum and the National Maritime Museum, and is linked to the CBD by monorail. The Rocks is Sydney's most historical area, and much of it has been restored to its former glory. Doyle's Restaurant at the foot of the Rocks is a haven for the seafood connoisseur, with fresh fish a house speciality. There are many beaches around the Sydney area, the most famous of which are, perhaps, Bondi (grossly overrated) and Manly (slightly overrated). The most beautiful, unspoilt and uncrowded beaches lie further north or south of the city. The northern coastal suburbs are particularly beautiful as the coastline is made up of rugged headlands broken with long sandy beaches. Each beach tends to have a sea-water swimming pool carved out of the rocky headland to provide safe, sheltered swimming areas. The beaches of Dee Why, Long Reef, Collaroy, Narrabeen, Newport, Avalon, Whale Beach and Palm Beach, from which you can catch a ferry to the shores of the Ku-ring-gai Chase National Park. Palm Beach has been famous as the setting for *Home and Away*, shown in the opening credits. Coogee, Mroubra and Cronulla are the nicer southern beaches.

In terms of culture, Sydney boasts the Australian Opera based at the lovely Opera House. Standing tickets for the opera can be bought for as little as $14.00, and many agents sell last-minute tickets at half price. Even if one is not an opera buff, it is certainly worth investing an evening at perhaps the world's most famous opera house, for where else on earth would you see men and women immaculately dressed in evening attire, climbing on each other's shoulders to grab one of the enormous helium balloons (used to decorate Dame Nellie Melba's farewell performance in *The Merry Widow* before retirement), and clutching them all the way home on the train? The acoustics are wonderful, the setting incomparable, and the atmosphere is unique.

Sydney is also home to the Museum of Contemporary Art and the Sydney Observatory. For the less refined culture, the Sydney Showclub offers more of a cabaret-style entertainment, but the Aboriginal Culture Show is also performed here. The city's Mardi Gras is also an eye-opener and entertaining as the country's gay, bisexual and transvestite population take to the streets in bizarre and outlandish costumes, once again challenging the stereotypical image of the Australian male. Animal watching can be had at the famous Taronga Zoo, but beware of the entry price which seems a little high in comparison with zoos in other Australian capital cities.

The Queen Victoria Building houses many chic boutiques and plenty of bargain shops, but better bargains tend to be found at Paddy's Markets in Paddington. On the whole, however, the shopping in Sydney is excellent.

New South Wales has many special events during the calendar year. The Festival of Sydney usually takes place in January, as does the New South Wales Tennis Open and the Country Music Festival in Sydney. The Sydney Royal Easter Show usually occurs in March to April, and the Sydney Film Festival tends to take place in June as does the Darling Harbour Jazz Festival. The Rugby League Grand Final is held in Sydney in September, and the other major state sporting events are the Tooheys 1000 Bathurst Touring Car Race at Bathurst in October, and the Sydney to Hobart yacht race which usually commences on Boxing Day every year.

In terms of the housing prices, Sydney is one of the most expensive areas in Australia, but many of the outer suburbs and regional areas are less expensive. Rent in Sydney is extortionate by Australian standards, but is still markedly lower than current rental rates in London for comparable properties. The state's unemployment rate is average, with a higher rate of unemployment in the city than in country areas. Major employment sectors in the city are commerce (banking, insurance and finance), retail, manufacturing, hospitality and tourism. Agriculture and tourism are the biggest employment sectors in regional areas.

Education and health services are exceptionally good in New South Wales, which is home to many large and excellent tertiary educational institutions, and there are many hospitals throughout the state which are listed in Chapter Four,*Health Insurance and Hospitals*. New South Wales currently attracts more new settlers than any other state/territory.

QUEENSLAND

Capital: Brisbane.
Area: 1,035,000 sq. miles (1,725,000 sq. kms) = seven times the size of the UK.
% of total area of Australia: 22.48.
Coastline: 4,440 miles (7,400 km).
Climate: In Brisbane, the average daily maximum in January is 29°C and in June is 21°C. In Cairns, the average daily maximums for the same months are 31°C and 26°C.

Queensland is the second largest state, but if one defines habitable area as that which receives at least 200mm of rain per annum, at 90%, it has the largest habitable area. Queensland's habitable area is a staggering 1,554,000 sq. kms, whereas only 57% of Western Australia is habitable (1,440,000 sq. kms). Queensland is situated in the north-eastern corner of Australia and it is bounded by the Northern Territory to the west, South Australia to the south-west and New South Wales to the south. It stretches from the temperate and densely populated south-east to the tropical sparsely populated Cape York Peninsula in the north.

Many tourists' preconceptions of Australia often match up with what they find in Queensland, particularly because many of the images used to market Australia by the Tourist Commission are of Queensland. With the Great Barrier Reef, the Whitsunday Islands, World Heritage areas such as the Daintree Rainforest and Fraser Island, and a beautiful climate, it is not suprising that Queensland is one of the most popular tourist destinations in Australia. Queensland is known as 'The Sunshine State', and Queenslanders are affectionately called 'banana benders' by other Australians, due to the high production of bananas and pineapples, and also because native Queenslanders have the reputation (completely unfounded) of lacking intellectual powers (i.e., being a few shrimps short of a barbie)!

Like most of Australia, Queensland is also rich in natural resources. Its four major products are sugar, meat, grains and wool, and the growing areas are spread all over the state. Australia is the world's second largest exporter of raw cane sugar, and 95% of Australia's production comes from Queensland. The State also contains vast mineral deposits, including coal, bauxite, gold, copper lead, zinc, silver and magnesite. Besides agricultural and mining industries, Queensland's other big industries are manufacturing and tourism. Although there are claims that, like anywhere in the world, tourists are ripped off, it was recently reported that accommodation was about 10% cheaper, eating out 20% cheaper, and car hire 50% cheaper, than the UK. Queensland's economic growth has recently been significantly higher than the national average.

For more than 20 years, Queensland has experienced a consistently higher rate of population growth than the national average. This trend continued during 1991-2 when the State's population increased at a rate 1% higher than the national rate of 1.4%. In the year to 1992, Queensland's population growth can be accounted for by overseas immigration (18.0%), natural increase (35.7%), but perhaps most importantly, interstate migration (46.2%). To state it quite simply, Queensland is the place where most Australians want to live. In the year ending June 1992, the net migration to Queensland from other States and Territories totalled 32,971. Compare this with the net migration to the Australian Capital Territory (2,566) and Tasmania (719) or to the net losses experienced by Victoria (18,203), New South Wales (16,373), the Northern Territory (1,123), Western Australia (480) and South Australia (243). 1992/3 saw a record number of 51,600 interstate migrations, which accounted for 62.8% of the State's growth. In comparison, New South Wales and Victoria lost 19,500 and 17,300 respectively. In the year ended June 1993, Queensland accounted for 45.9% of Australia's total population growth for that year. These statistics plainly show that more Australians are moving to Queensland than any other State/Territory.

An increasingly popular myth is that Australians are moving to Queensland to retire, in a similar way to the myth that the population of Florida is composed almost entirely of retired people. The Australian Bureau of Statistics 1986 census shows that in fact this is far from being the case. Not only did interstate migration account for a mere 12% of the total State population, but the largest age group, making up 31% of Queensland's population, was the 25-44 year olds.

Queensland's population is much more decentralised than any other state. Its population of just over 3,000,000, is scattered over major regional centres such as the Gold Coast, Bundaberg, Toowoomba, Rockhampton, Longreach, Townsville, Cairns and Mount Isa, as well as Brisbane, which is home to 1,327,006 Queensland residents.

Until recently, the Queensland Government had a reputation (going back more than 35 years) of being ultra-conservative. For most of those years it was under the leadership of the Premier, Sir Joh Bjelke-Peterson, and it became notorious for its repressive and racist attitudes which, some suggest, are inherited from the Protestant/Catholic intolerance originally imported from Ireland. Unfortunately, there are still vestiges of this xenophobia, especially against the Japanese, mainly because many Australian soldiers died in Japanese POW camps in WWII. There is a certain antipathy towards the Japanese even today, particularly because they are investing in large amounts of Queensland property, but it is a love/hate relationship as Japanese investments and tourists play a significant part in promoting Queensland's healthy economy.

The Queensland Government has suffered from allegations of being extremist right-wing and that the police force is corrupt at both low and high levels (illegal gambling, shady escort agencies, etc.). The Labour Party was re-elected in September 1992, and the Premier, the Hon. W K Goss, is the first Labour Premier in Queensland since 1957. This new government signifies the attitude of Queensland's residents that they had simply had enough of the corruption and hypocritical moralising of the old government, and wanted the old regime completely swept away.

Queensland health and education services are comparable with the outstanding national standard. Queensland is home to the University of Queensland and Bond University established by Alan Bond. Ironically, the one-time entrepreneur and multi-millionare Western Australian after whom it is named, is now serving a prison sentence for illegal business ventures; however, the university that bears his name is none the less regarded as a centre of excellence.

Most Queensland residents own their own home. This, together with the idyllic islands, beautiful coast, rainforest and reef, indicates that Queensland is indeed a kind of paradise. Significantly, the number of Australians moving to Queensland indicates that this assertion is more fact than fiction.

Useful Address

Trade and Investment Development Division, PO Box 185, Albert Street, Brisbane, Queensland 4002, tel: 00-61 7 224 8573 or fax: 00-61 7 835 1002, or contact the Director, Queensland Government Office at Queensland House as listed above.

Getting There

QANTAS is Australia's international airline which, as Dustin Hoffman's character pointed out in the film *Rainman*, has the best safety record in the world. Many international carriers fly directly to Australia — mostly to Perth and/or Sydney. British Airways, Singapore Airlines, Malaysian Airlines System, Garuda (Indonesian), Royal Brunei, Cathay Pacific and Thai Airways are just a few of the carriers which service Australia.

The cheapest time to fly to Australia is from 16 April-15 June as this is considered to be the low season. It is much more expensive to travel during high season which runs from mid-September until the end of December. Peak season is the most expensive time to travel which is from 9-22 December. It is certainly worth travelling at low season if possible as the prices of flights can vary dramatically. For example, Qantas quoted London-Sydney return fares of £755 in low season and £1185 in peak season. A family of four can save up to £1,000 if travelling in low season.

Scheduled fares may not however be the cheapest available as existing laws prevent the airlines from selling tickets at reduced rates to the general public and that substantially cheaper fares can be found through High Street travel agents.

Travel agents are now legally obliged to request proof of residency (visa or emigration papers) in order to sell a one-way ticket to Australia. If a traveller without proof of residency arrives with a one-way ticket at Gatwick airport, they will not be allowed to check in. If a traveller manages to leave Britain on a one-way ticket and cannot provide proof of residency upon arrival in Australia, they will be returned to Britain on the first available flight and be subject to the cost of their detainment in Australia and the return flight. It is possible, however, to cash in the second half of a return flight to Australia when you arrive in Australia, but this is not advisable unless you have been granted residency or an extension of your visa.

For the younger travellers seeking to live and work in Australia for up to a year, both STA and Campus Travel (also known as USIT) usually offer competitive fares which are, on occasion, markedly lower than those to be found elsewhere. You must be under 35 to be eligible for these fares. Both STA and Campus Travel can be found in almost all cities and major towns nationwide, so check your phone book for your local office. The London offices are:

Campus Travel: 52 Grosvenor Gardens, London SW1W OAG, tel: 0171-730 8111. Their opening hours are Mon-Fri 8.30am-6.30pm, Thurs 8.30am-8pm, Sat-Sun 10.00am-5pm.

STA Travel: 86 Old Brompton Road, London, tel: 0171-938 4711 or Oxford 01865-240 547.

Students and anyone else are also advised to check fare prices with the many agencies which specialise in Australia and New Zealand flights as they are likely to have some of the most attractive deals. :

Discount Fare Specialists for Australia & New Zealand

Ausflights, 102 New Street, Birmingham B2 4HQ; tel 0121-633 3232; fax 0121-633 4081.

Auspac Travel, 87 Regent Street, London W1R 7HF; tel 0171-437 2328; fax 0171-437 2339.

Austravel 50-51 Conduit Street, London, W1R 9FB, tel: 0171-734 7755 or fax: 0171-494 1302, Manchester: 0161-832 2445, Bristol: 0117-9277425, Bournemouth: 0202-311 488. Austravel's fares guide compares fares between different carriers throughout the year.

Connections, 93 Wimpole Street, London W1M 7DA; tel 0171-495 5545; fax 0171-408 4450. Connections' brochure gives fares and tours pricing for different seasons and offers ideas as how best to build itineraries.

Cresta World Travel; 44-6 George Street, Altrincham, Cheshire WA14 1RH; tel 0161-927 7177; fax 0161 929 0433.

Golden Wings Worldwide, 29 Kent House, First Floor, 87 Regent Street, London W1R 7HF; tel 0171-734 3070; fax 0171-494 3936.

Modern Air Travel. 61 Reform Street, Dundee DD1 1SP; tel 01382-322713; fax 01382 201079.

Jetabout Sovereign House, 361 King Street, Hammersmith, London W6 9NJ, tel: 0181-741 3111.

Travelbag 12 High Street, Alton, Hampshire, GU34 1BN, tel: 01420-88724 or 373/375 The Strand, London WC2R OJF, tel: 0171-497 0515.

Most of these agencies will be able to arrange international accommodation and accommodation, air, bus and rail travel within Australia (and New Zealand). Some can also organise tours in Australia. Some will also provide migrants' one-way flights on chartered carriers such as Britannia Airways. The Australian Youth Hostels Association (Level 3, 10 Mallett St, Camperdown, NSW 2050; tel +61 02-612 565 1699; fax +61 02-565 1325), also offers complete travel packages including accommodation and 12 months coach travel.

YHA AUSTRALIA OFFERS

HOSTELLING INTERNATIONAL

YHA Australia have complete travel packages which include accommodation, 12 month valid coach travel, entrance tickets to Australia's favourite tourist places & more.

Packages are from as little as AUD$25 a day - e.g. Aussie Explorer 'Best of East' bus pass with Australian Coachlines with 60 nights' accommodation for AUD$1,415.

Stay in over 140 Australian YHA Hostels. There are also over 5,500 Hostels world wide, all with friendly, helpful hostel staff.

No age limits in any Australian YHA Hostels. Self-catering facilities to help you save money.

A centralised booking system where YHA Hostels can be booked for your next destination.

Access to over 600 discounts throughout Australia - a saving of thousands of dollars to YHA members only. The discounts are listed in the 1995 YHA Accommodation Guide.

YHA Hostels that feature clean and comfortable accommodation at all of Australia's favourite tourist destinations.

Travel Agencies in every State capital city as well as Alice Springs, Cairns, Airlie Beach and Canberra. Each Travel Office offers special discounts to YHA members on a wide range of travel products from international airline tickets, coach passes, travel insurance and local tours.

Please send further information on the excellent travel packages available from YHA Australia

Name _____

Address _____

_____ Postcode _____

VW-95

Country _____

Send to: Australian YHA, Level 3, 10 Mallett Street, Camperdown, NSW 2050 Australia

A.T.I. SERVICES
• ATLAS • TRAVEL • INSURANCE •

These are just a few of the many low prices and comprehensive quality covers the A.T.I. Group offers together with a seven day approval.
Long stays, special family rates, sports premiums, annual plans, specified article insurance, also one way insurance.

EUROPE
£7.00
for 5 days

For the BEST HOLIDAY INSURANCE deals

COMPREHENSIVE COVER

MEDICAL/AIR ASSURANCE	CANCELLATION/CURTAILMENT
£4,000,000	£3,000
PERSONAL LIABILITY	PERSONAL BAGGAGE
£1,000,000	£2,000
PERSONAL ACCIDENT	MONEY
£100,000	£500
LEGAL EXPENSES	TRAVEL DELAY
£25,000	£250

WORLDWIDE
£18.00
for 5 days

CALL NOW
0171 609 5000

37 Kings Exchange, Tileyard Road, London N7 9AH
NEAREST UNDERGROUND STATION KINGS CROSS

Insurance
Working travellers and those on speculative job finding trips to Australia are strongly advised to take out comprehensive travel insurance. Among the companies specialising in Australasia are ATI Services and Downunder Insurance Services. Golden Wings Worldwide (address above) also have some low-priced, comprehensive insurance designed for long stay students and independent travellers.

Atlas Travel Insurance Service Ltd.(ATI), 37 Kings Exchange, Tileyard Road, London N7 9AH; tel 0181-579 3700; fax 0171-609 5011.

Downunder Insurance, 24a Bristol Gardens, London W9, (Warwick Ave tube); tel 0171-286-2425; fax 0171-289 6562.

Residence and Entry Regulations

The Current Position

According to the Australian High Commission and the newspaper *Australian Outlook* (both of which are useful sources of information for prospective emigrants) the current Australian position on immigration and working visas appears to be good. The Federal Government has made it easier for people with good English to gain extra points towards their acceptance for emigration to Australia. Up to an extra 20 points may now be awarded if the applicant holds a degree, higher degree, diploma or trade certificate which required at least three years full time study and all the instruction was carried out in English. A new report on Australian immigration released by the Bureau of Immigration and Population Research suggests that migrants were more likely to own successful small businesses or be self-employed, and the Australian government is actively trying to recruit more of this kind of entrepreneurial migrant. Migrants with skills in demand (the categories are always changing), are also viewed as likely to benefit the Australian economy. Australia does try to attract the cream, particularly in the fields of business, industry, science and technology from all over the world and for the years 1993/4, the immigrant targets were 76,000 and 86,000 respectively. The most recent estimate for 1994/95 at the time of printing, puts the target number of new emigrants at about 73,000.

Talk to people who have been trying to emigrate, however, and it is a different story. Many people claim it is much harder now than ever before to enter Australia either on a year's working holiday visa or as an immigrant. A recent article in *The European* newspaper even claimed that there is discrimination against French applicants. Although the number of French citizens applying to go to Australia is increasing, the number of successful applicants is decreasing, suggesting that to be successful, a French applicant would have to speak English perfectly, be 25 years of age, and a chef. Indeed, the process one has to go through in order to apply for any particular kind of visa is time-consuming, difficult, confusing and expensive, to such an extent that there is an increasing number of 'Migration Consultancies' which claim to help you prepare a much better application for migration or temporary residence than you could do yourself. If you try to phone the 0891 number given by the Australian Tourist Commission for visa applications, you can run up a huge phone bill as you listen to the incredibly lengthy phone message and try to get the information you actually need. As an article in the *The Independent* complained in February 1994, the system is inadequate.

At present, the procedure is to get application forms from the Australian High Commission, complete and forward them, together with the your passport, to the Australian Government, which then issues the visa. Currently, the visa process is estimated to take anything between three and six weeks, but the

Australian Government is looking at ways of streamlining this process into a 24 hour service. However, it will be some time before the current system is changed.

Useful Addresses

Emigration Consultancy Services, De Salis Court, Hampton Lovett, Droitwich, Worcestershire WR9 ONX; tel 01905-795949; fax 01905-795557.

AUSTRALIA/NEW ZEALAND

* ASSESSMENT
* VISA APPLICATION ASSISTANCE
* DISCOUNTED AIRFARES & REMOVALS
* FULL RESETTLEMENT ADVICE
* EFFECTIVE JOBSEARCH SERVICE

Network Migration Services are Europe's largest migration consultancy. For further information call us now on: **(01793) 612222 or write to: Network Migration Services, Oxford House, College Court, Commercial Road, Swindon, Wiltshire. SN1 1PZ**

Network Migration Services, Oxford House, College Court, Commercial Road, Swindon SN1 1PZ; tel 01793-612222; fax 01793-542554.

Oz-Link-UK, Higher Elstone Cottage, Elstone, Chulmleigh, Devon EX18 7AQ; tel & fax 01769-58013. Also office in Australia.

OZ LINK UK

Migration & Visa Entrant Agents for all Australian & New Zealand entry classes.
Temporary, permanent, independent, concessional, working etc.
Also office in Australia to assist in other areas, 'Most competitive fees in United Kingdom' - 'If you're going to do it- do it right!'
OZ LINK UK: Higher Elstone Cottage, Chulmleigh, Devon, UK EX18 7AQ.
P/F: 01769 580318.

Relocations International, P.O. Box 6112 Wellesley Street, Auckland, New Zealand; tel 64 9 378 9888; fax +64-9 378 8072; Wellington Office: tel +64-4 473 9461; +64-9 473 9404. Operates throughout Australasia.

Entry for Australian Citizens

Anyone with an Australian passport, or British passport with a visa of permanent residence, does not require a visa to enter Australia. This is also true for Australian or New Zealand citizens travelling on a New Zealand passport. Unless you are on an Australian or New Zealand passport, or you have a visa for permanent residence, you will have to obtain some sort of visa in order to enter Australia. If you arrive in Australia without a visa, you will simply be deported immediately. If you are in doubt over whether you are an Australian/New Zealand citizen, or whether you have permanent residency, contact the Australian High Commission, who handle all visa and migration queries. In general, if you are travelling purely as a tourist, you will need a Visitor's Visa. If you are planning to go on a working holiday or to retire, you will need a Temporary Residence Visa, and if you are planning on living in Australia for the rest of your life, you will need to be accepted as an immigrant and be granted permanent residence.

Visitor's Visa

If you just want a holiday in Australia, then you are most likely to need a Visitor Visa (Tourist Class), for which you will need Form 48 from the High Commission. Visitors' visas are valid for three months and six months from the date of entry into Australia. You must enter within 12 months from the date of issue for the three month visa and four years, or the life of the passport (whichever occurs first) for the six month visa. If you are retired parents of Australian citizens, you can get a Visitor Visa valid for a period of 12 months in Australia. In order to be eligible for such a visa, you need to have a valid passport and proof of funds if you are applying for a six-month visa. You will need to provide photocopies of recent bank statements which show that your account is £2,000-£3,000 in credit. If you will be staying for friends or family for any or all of that time, you will not be expected to have as much money in your account as you would if you are simply touring for six months.

There are rumours at the time of printing that the Australian government intends to scrap the tourist visa requirement for tourists from 'low risk' countries defined as the USA, Canada and Japan. Britain however is likely to be excluded from this proposed liberalisation of the visa rules.

The three-month Visitor Visa is the only visa which is FREE, and the processing time by post is approximately two weeks. Applications can be made in person at the High Commission in London, Manchester or Dublin, and three-month visas can also be issued at the Qantas Travel Centre (a travel agent, related to but not to be confused with the airline) in Birmingham. This is a free service if your tickets are purchased from Qantas Travel Centres, add a charge of £15 per passport applies for tickets purchased through another travel agent or with another airline. You can contact the Qantas Travel Centre at 36 Union Street, Birmingham B2 4SR, tel: 0121-643 8703 or fax: 0121-633 4096. Opening hours are Monday to Friday, 9am-5.15pm. Please note that it is not possible to obtain a visa by fax or telephone, you must go in to the centre personally.

It is possible to obtain a multiple entry visa for both the three and six-month Visitor Visas, but this costs an extra £15. It is also possible to extend your three-month visa to a six-month visa, but to do this in Australia costs around $200 whereas to buy a six-month visa in the UK will only cost you £15, so it makes good financial sense to extend your visa *before* you leave. It is very important that you extend your visa before it has expired as Australian Immigration will immediately deport you if you try to extend a visa that has already expired. You must leave the country on a valid visa, and then renew it from overseas before returning. You must be careful here as some travellers have been refused re-entry into Australia despite leaving Australia on a valid visa and renewing their visas in New Zealand or Singapore.

Temporary Residence

These are issued to people who intend to enter Australia temporarily for short or long-term periods to engage in employment or other activities such as sportspeople and support personnel, religious personnel, staff exchanges and special programmes, extended temporary stay in retirement, occupational trainees, working holidaymakers, executive, technical and professional staff for organisations in Australia, and staff for Australian educational and research institutions. There are 22 different categories of visa according to what you will actually be doing in Australia. Below is a list of the categories and a brief description of the kind of traveller they apply to.

Retirement (410) This allows entry on the basis of an extended temporary stay for people wishing to retire in Australia. For more information on this category, please see below.

Exchange (411) This promotes opportunities for people to experience other cultures and enhance international relations by entering Australia under staff exchange schemes or an agreement between the Australian Government and that of another country.

Independent Executive (412) Allows entry of individuals to establish new or existing businesses in Australia where permanent residence is not intended.

Executive (overseas) (413) Senior management personnel are allowed to join established businesses in Australia or to establish branches of overseas companies in Australia.

Specialist (overseas) (414) Allows employers to temporarily recruit skilled workers from overseas when they cannot readily find of train suitable people in Australia for the position.

Foreign Government Agency Staff (415) Allows entry of people as employees, including language and culture teachers, of foreign government agencies which have no official status in Australia, and of foreign goverment oficials who have no diplomatic or official status in Australia indending to conduct official business in Australia.

Special Program (416) Allows entry of people under a Churchill Fellowship, to take part in an approved yoth exchange programme, or to take part in an approved community-based programme of cultural enrichment or community benefit.

Working Holiday (417) Promotes international understanding by providing opportunities for young people to experience other cultures by holidaying and travelling in Australia with the opportunity to work to supplement their funds. For further information on this category, please see below.

Educational (418) Allows entry of staff for Australian educational and research institutions.

Visiting Academic (419) Allows entry of people as Visiting Academics at Australian educational and research institutions.

Entertainer (420) Allows entry of actors, entertainers, models and their associated personnel for specific engagements or events in Australia.

Sport (421) Allows entry of sportspeople, including officials and their support staff, to take part in specific events in Australia, and of sportspeople joining Australian sports clubs or organisations.

Medical Practitioner (422) Allows entry of medical practitioners where the relevant State or Territory Medical Board recognises the applicant's medical qualifications as suitable to practise in that State or Territory.

Media and Film Staff (423) Allows entry of foreign correspondents to represent overseas news media organisations in Australia and television or film crew members or photographers, including actors and support staff, involved in the production of films, documentaries or advertising commercials in Australia which are not being produced for the Australian market.

Public Lecturer (424) Allows entry of people to deliver public lectures in Australia.

Family Relationship — young single person (425) Allows young people, usually of secondary school age and under 18 years, the opportunity to learn about Australia while staying with relatives or close family friends in Australia.

Domestic (Diplomatic/Consular) (426) Allows entry of domestic workers for diplomatic and official personnel in Australia where Australian Department of Foreign Affiars and Trade supports the entry.

Domestic (427) Allows entry of domestic workers for senior executives of overseas companies temporarily in Australia.

Religious Worker (428) Allows entry of religious and evangelical workers to serve the religous objectives of religious organisations in Australia.

Supported Dependant of Australian or New Zealand Citizen (430) Allows for dependants, who are not exempt from Australian visa requirements, to accompany Australian or New Zealand citizens who are exempt from visa requirements for temporary residence in Australia.

Expatriate Dependants (432) Allows for the dependants of expatriate employees stationed in remote locations in South-east Asia, the South Pacific or Papua New Guinea, to reside temporarily in Australia for the duration of the employee's assignment in that remote location.

Occupational Trainees (442) Allows entry of persons for occupational training which is compatible with their background and/or employment history, to acquire or upgrade skills which they will be able to utilise readily on their return home.

People who wish to enter Australia must meet the normal health and public interest requirements for entry. Some applicants may be asked to have a medical examination before a visa will be granted. In most cases, if you have your application for temporary residence approved, you will then be granted a multiple entry visa for the period of the approved stay. If you need a further re-entry visa, you will need to apply to an office of the Department of Immigration, Local Goverment and Ethnic Affairs (DILGEA).

The two most popular temporary resident visa categories are the Working Holidaymaker and Retirement, and there is further information pertinent to both that is worth including here.

Working Holiday: If you wish to go to Australia and combine working with travelling, this is the visa you need. You must ask for Form 147, Class 417 at the High Commission. The main purpose of this visa is to encourage young people aged 18-30 to explore Australia while working in order to be able to support themselves. You are not allowed to work full-time for any one employer for more than three months at a time, and so you are, by necessity, on the move for the entire year. The visa is valid for 13 months from the day your passport is stamped, but you are only allowed to spend a maximum of 12 months of those in Australia. Having said this, if you did not arrive in Australia until some time after your visa was issued, you are able to go to the local immigration office and have your visa 'topped up' to the maximum 12 months. This must be done approximately two months before the expiry of your visa. It does cost about $200 for this service, which is not guaranteed, but is does save the trouble of bothering with overseas consulates on your way there.

You are eligible for this visa if you hold a valid UK, Irish, Dutch, Canadian or Japanese Passport, you are aged between 18 and 30 on the date of your application, you have no children (even if the children are not in your custody) and you have not entered Australia on a Working Holiday Visa before. If you are aged between 18 and 26 you will be far more likely to be granted the visa than those between 26 and 30. It is rumoured that it is impossible to get a visa if you are over 26, but if you can give a good reason as to why you did not choose to travel to Australia earlier, such as 'studying' or 'establishing a career', this is considered acceptable. You will also need to think of reasons as to why spending a year in Australia will benefit you, and to what kind of benefits you can hope to give to Australia. You should return your completed visa application form no more than four weeks before you are due to leave as this will enable you to enjoy the full 12 months of your visa. In order to be granted a Working

Holiday Visa, you will also need to provide proof that you have enough money to pay for your return airfare and have sufficient money to support yourself initially. Currently, this amount is about $2,000 (including the airfare) and recent bank statements which show the account is yours considered to be valid proof. As noted in the General Introduction, you will not be allowed to enter Australia unless you have a return ticket, and purchasing your ticket prior to your visa application form can actually help your case in terms of being granted a visa.

A Working Holiday visa is usually multiple entry, which means that you may leave and re-enter the country as many times as you like (within the time restriction of your visa) once you have arrived. When your passport has been returned and your visa has been granted, make sure to check that it has been stamped 'multiple entry'. You **cannot** get an extension on a Working Holiday Visa, you must leave the country before or on the expiry date of your visa.

Retirement Visa: If you wish to retire to Australia, there is a section further on in this book specifically dealing with Retirement in Australia. It is possible to retire to Australia permanently, but you will only be issued with a Temporary Residence Retirement Visa (Form 147, category 410). This visa functions in a slightly complicated manner, not allowing you permanent residence per se, but really allowing you to stay indefinitely. Your first visa allows you to make multiple entries into Australia during the first six months, and only applies for the first six months of the visa being issued. Whenever you arrive in Australia during this first six-month period, you will receive an entry permit allowing you to stay in Australia for four years. Because the multiple entry facility expires after six months, should you leave Australia again temporarily after this time, you **must** get another visa (before you leave Australia) allowing you to return. You should contact your local Department of Immigration and Ethnic Affairs for details of this. Once your first four-year visa is due to expire, you can apply for an extension of your stay. If you still meet the criteria necessary for the Retirement Visa, you may be granted a further stay of four years.

In order to be eligible for a Retirement Visa, you may be single, or couples in a married or de facto relationship. You must be at least 55 years of age, have no intention of entering the workforce, have no dependants other than your spouse, and meet health and character requirements. You must also be able to meet 'Funds transfer requirements' on the day you lodge your application. This means that you should have sufficient funds to maintain yourself (and your spouse/partner, if applicable) in Australia. You need to prove that you have capital for transfer of at least $500,000, or that you have a combination of both capital for transfer of at least $150,000 and a pension or income, or further capital providing an income of at least $35,000 yearly. If you need to sell a house to meet the funds transfer requirements, the Immigration Department requires that the sale must be completed within 12 months of the date of your application.

Permanent Residence:

As with the temporary resident visas, there is also a variety of categories for application for permanent migration. Most migrants enter Australia under one of three main categories, the Family Migration (you must have a relative in Australia who is able to sponsor you), Skill Migration (you must have skills or outstanding abilities that will contribute to Australia's economy), or Refugee, Humanitarian and Special Assistance Migration. Generally, in order to migrate to Australia the application forms state that you must meet the personal and occupational requirements of the category for which you are applying; be able to settle in Australia without undue cost or difficulty to the Australian community; and be of good health and character. In addition, if your application is successful, you should have enough money to travel to and settle in Australia.

According to Allen Young of Emigration Consultancy Services, getting a permanent visa can take up to 12 months and for most people it takes at least ten months.

Family Migration: This visa category allows for family members overseas to be reunited with Australian citizens and permanent residents. You can either be a 'preferential' or a 'concessional' family migrant. Both classes must be sponsored by a relative who is an Australian citizen or permanent resident and is at least 18 years of age. Your relative (sponsor) must agree to help you with accommodation and financially during your first year in Australia. There are different visa classes of Preferential Family Migration:

Class 100 — Spouse which is a husband, wife or de facto partner (who you must have been living with for at least the previous six months); *Class 300-Prospective Marriage* which is as the prospective spouse of your sponsor in Australia (Although you will be initially issued with a six-month provisional visa/entry permit, permanent residence will be granted if you marry your sponsor and remain resident in Australia for the first six months after your arrival in Australia); *Class 101-Child* which means that as the child or adopted child of your sponsor and you are dependent on your sponsor, you will be granted permanent residency (you are ineligible if you are married or engaged to be married); *Class 102-Adoption* there are two slightly different classes within this class, for adoptions within and without Australia, but it caters for adopted children under the age of 18 years of age; *Class 103-Parent* which means that as a parent of your sponsor, you are entitled to permanent residency providing your sponsor has lived in Australia for at least two years before lodging the sponsorship; *Class 104-Orphan Relative* which caters for orphans (as defined in the Migration Regulations), under 18 years old, unmarried and a relative of the sponsor; *Class 104-Special Need Relative* is for a relative capable of providing 'substantial and continuing help' to an Australian citizen or permanent resident in need of permanent or long-term help; *Class 104- Aged Dependent Relative* if you are unmarried, old enough to be granted an age pension under the *Social Security Act 1991* and dependent on the sponsor, you are eligible under this category and class, providing your sponsor has lived in Australia for at least two years before lodging the sponsorship; *Class 104-Last Remaining Relative* which caters for the last remaining brother, sister or non-dependent child outside Australia. You or your spouse must not have a parent, sibling or non-dependent child or step-relative (within the same degree of relationship) living outside Australia, and again your sponsor should have lived in Australia for at least two years prior to the sponsorship being lodged.

If you are a non-dependent child, a parent of working age, a brother or sister, niece or nephew, you are eligible to apply for the category of *Concessional Family Migration* (Class 105). This means that you must be sponsored by your actual relative in Australia. As well as meeting health and character requirements, you must also be of working age and have passed the points test, details of which are outlined below.

Skill Migration: This is designed to make a direct contribution to Australia's economic growth, and so if you possess special skills or a business background which is easily transferred to the Australian business world, and for which opportunities exist, you may be able to enter Australia on one of the following visa classes: *Class 120-Labour Agreement* which allows the entry of skilled people with specified skills, qualifications and experience under a labour agreement. You must have been nominated by an employer within the framework of a labour agreement, and almost invariably, be aged under 55 years (if you have exceptional qualifications and skills, and are over 55, you may still be allowed to enter the country on this visa); *Class 121-Employer Nomination Scheme* which allow the migration of highly skilled people for a job vacancy which cannot be filled by the Australian workforce, and again, unless you are exceptional, you must be under 55; *Class 124 and 125 — Distinguished Talent* I just wish I were eligible for such a visa! Imagine all the pre-migration parties you could swan around, casually mentioning that you were entering Australia as a person of Distinguished Talent. This really allows for exceptional artists or sportspeople to enter the country 'who have outstanding abilities that would be a clear gain for Australia'. Unfortunately, for those of us with average talents you need to have a record of exceptional achievement in your particular field; *Class 126 — Independent Entrant* this visa covers the entry of highly skilled people whose education and skills will contribute to the Australian economy and they are readily employable. Like the Concessional Family Migration Category outlined above, visa approval for the independent entrant is determined by the points test; *Classes 127, 128, 129 and 130 — Business Skills Migration* These visa classes allows business people who have had recent experience running a successful business as an owner or part owner, or as a senior executive in a large comapny, and have passed the Business Skills points test, to enter Australia. Points are awarded for the size and sector of business as well as age, ability in English and assets, with additional points for State/Territory sponsorship.

Others: you may also be considered for migration if you lost your Australian citizenship (for a number of approved reasons) and have maintained ties with Australia (*Class 150 — Former Australian Citizens*); you have spent most of your life before the age of 18 in Australia, you left Australia without acquiring citizenship, and you have maintained ties with Australia (*Class 151 — Former Residents of Australia*); or you are the dependant of a New Zealand citizen where the New Zealand citizen has settled or intends to settle permanently in Australia (*Class 152 — Dependants of New Zealand Citizens).*

The Points Test:
The Australian Immigration Department operates a 'points system' for international immigration applications only in the 'Concessional' category of the Family Migration and 'Independent' category of the Skilled Migration component. This means that an applicant is allocated a certain number of points for different qualifications, age, skills, relatives resident in Australia, etc. It is quite a complicated system, and there are a number of consultancies which advertise in *Overseas Job Express* or *Australian Outlook* offering assistance with preparing your case in order to help you accrue as many points as possible. Australia used to produce a list of wanted skills and/or jobs specificallly designed for potential immigrants, called the Priority Occupations List. The situation was that if you were able to offer skills that were needed in Australia, you would almost automatically be granted permanent residency. This has now changed. There is no list of jobs available as there are no specific skills or occupations that Australia lacks. The High Commission basically decides whether you will be employable on your immediate arrival in Australia, and grants residency on that basis. You should, however, assess your own employment opportunities in Australia, ard further details are given in the *Employment* section. The success of applications seems to be much less predictable than it was. However, if you are able to see exactly what you need to do to be given permanent residency (whether that be to get a degree, learn English, acquire more trade skills etc.) and apply again when you feel you are able to earn enough points.

Generally, to pass the points test you must be a male under 65 years old or a female under 60 years of age at the time your application is lodged, you must reach either the pool or pass mark in force at the time of assessment of your application (note that these may not necessarily be the same as the marks at the time your application was lodged), and you must be proficient in English if your occupation is listed as an Occupations Requiring English (which means you must be fluent in both spoken and written English).

Points for skill are based on your usual occupation and the qualifications required to work in that occupation in Australia. Your usual occupation is one which you have worked continously for at least six months in the two years prior to lodging your application to migrate. If you have held more than one job which fits this description, you will be assessed against both of your usual occupations. The skill level of your occupation will determine how many points you can score. For example, if your usual occupation requires a degree or trade certificate in Australia, you will earn 60-70 points, but if it requires a diploma, you will only earn 50-55 points. Your points score will also depend on the amount of post-qualification work experience gained immediately before lodging your application.

It is possible to obtain a self-assessment table from the High Commission in order to estimate your points score, but this is only a guide. As of December 1993, the Pass and Pool marks were:

Concessional Family visa class

Pass mark	95 points
Pool mark	90 points

Independent Entrant visa class

Pass mark	100 points
Pool mark	95 points

Note that the timing of your application can be extremely important. Your circumstances may be about to change and improve your points score, in which case it would be better to wait. For example, it may be better to wait until your sponsor has Australian citizenship before you apply as this entitles you to five points on the citizenship factor.

In order to apply to migrate in the Concessional Family visa class, you need to make sure that you score at least the Concessional Family pool mark and then you should ask your relative to get a sponsorship form from the local Department of Immigration and Ethnic Affairs in Australia. They should complete the sponsorship form and sent it to you with the required supporting documents for you to lodge with your application. Your sponsor will have to complete an Assurance of Support which is a legal commitment by the assurer (who is not necessarily the sponsor) to repay the Australian Government certain welfare benefits if they are paid to the migrant during his/her first two years in the country. Assurance of Support is mandatory for the class 103 and all types of class 104. In these cases, a refundable bond and a Migration (Health Services) Charge are payable. The refundable bond is currently $3,500 for the principal applicant and a further $1,500 per person above 18 years included in the application. The Health Services Charge is to cover the cost to the health budget added by migrants in their first two years of residence in Australia, and the current charge is $846. Other costs you will be liable for are Immigration Fees. These fees are listed below:

Application for Migration to Australia Forms Package	£5.00
Sponsorship for Entry to Australia for Temporary Residents	£95.00
Application for Migration to Australia	£194.00
Application for Temporary Residence	£65.00
Application for Holiday Maker	£65.00
Application for Occupation Trainee	£65.00
Application for Student	£65.00
Application for Visitor Visa (more than 3 months)	£15.00
Business Migration Programme Application Fee I	£499.00
II	£299.00

You should also note that the average processing times (in months) by visa class are:

Spouse (including de facto)	5	Prospective marriage	4
Dependant Child	3	Concessional family	12+
Parent	10	Employer nomination	4
Other preferential family	15	Independant	12+

There is no doubt that moving to Australia, whether it is as a working-holiday backpacker, to start up a business or to retire, is a complicated and expensive process. This process can be made easier with plenty of time, patience and some expert advice.

Useful Addresses

Passport Offices, Clive House, 70 Petty France, London SW1H 9HD, tel: 0171-279 3434. There are also offices in Belfast, Glasgow, Liverpool, Newport and Peterborough.

High Commission, Australia House, Strand, London WC2B 4LA, tel: 0171-379 4334. Open: Mon-Fri 10am-4pm. The Visa Section is separate, and the recorded message number is 0891 600 333. It is virtually impossible to get to speak to anyone at the Commission, there seems to be an endless series of interminable recorded messages. If at all possible, it is well worth your while to go into the High Commission or one of the offices listed below, where you will be met with friendly and efficient service. A useful hint is to avoid going to the London office between October and early February, where you can expect to find long queues. In addition, make sure you are in the right queue to start with as the queue for migration details is much shorter than the queue for temporary residence and you may find yourself waiting unnecessarily in the wrong queue.

Consulate, Chatsworth House, Lever Street, Manchester M1 2DL, tel: 0161-228 1344. Open: Mon-Fri 9.30am-3.30pm.

Embassy, Fitzwilton House, Wilton Terrace, Dublin 2, tel: +3531 676 1517. Open: Mon-Thur 9am-3pm, Friday 9am-12noon.

Other Australian embassies and consular offices within the EU and Europe are:

Denmark: Kristianagade 21, 2100 Copenhagen, tel: 3126 2244.

France: 4 Rue Jean Rey, Paris 15ème, tel: 1-40 59 33 00.

Germany: Godesberger Alee 105-107, 5300 Bonn 1, tel: 0288- 8 10 30/8 10 31.

Greece: 37 Dimitriou Soutsou Street, Ambelokpi, Athens 115 12, tel: 01-644 7303.

Italy: Via Alessandria 215, Rome 00198, tel: 06-83 27 21. (There is also a consulate in Milan.)

Netherlands: Carnegielaan 12, 2517 KH The Hague, tel: 070-310 8200.

Sweden: Block 5, Sergels Torg 12, Stockholm C, tel: 08-613 2900.

Switzerland: Alpenstrasse 29, Bern, tel: 031-43 01 43. (There is also a consulate in Geneva.)

Setting Up Home

How do the Australians live?

The traditional family unit still rules in Australia with 49% of its residents being married with children and 30% being married without children. Young people also seem to live at home longer than in most European countries, perhaps due to the fact that urban students attending university usually stay in their own home city rather than go elsewhere in the country. Eighty percent of children under 24 live with their natural parents, and 96% of these live with their natural mother. 13% of Australian homes consist of single parent families and 84% of these parents are women.

Most adults in Australia own, or are in the process of buying, their own home. The Commonwealth Bank of Australia's *The Cost of Living and Housing Survey Book* shows that nearly 75% of Australian homes are occupied by their owners or by people buying them on a mortgage basis. Flats and multiple unit residences are common in more central city suburbs, but most Australians tend to live in detached bungalows with a spacious garden at both the front and the back of the house. The average home has three bedrooms, a combined lounge/dining room, kitchen, bathroom, toilet and laundry (with a large sink for washing and fitted plumbing for a washing machine). Two and four-bedroom houses are also easy to find, and houses with two bathrooms and a family room (also known as a rumpus room) are becoming increasingly popular. If you are buying a home in Australia, you will find the kitchen fitted with a cooker and cupboards, and carpets, curtains and light fittings throughout the home are generally included in the price. Gas and electricity are also both usually available, but this can vary in more remote areas. Australians really enjoy outdoor living, indeed 1994 was Australia's 'Year of the Great Outdoors', and many homes have a balcony, terrace or patio and a barbecue, often found beside the swimming pool in the back garden. Even though most Australians live at or near the coast, nearly 50% of home owners have a swimming pool, which must by law be completely fenced off and childproof as they have all too often been the site of a domestic tragedy.

Australian homes are generally made of brick, but there are also brick veneer, weatherboard or fibre cement houses available. A brick veneer home looks exactly like a brick home from the outside, but its internal structure is wooden and it is lined with plasterboard. Brick veneer is cheaper than a full brick home and is just as suited to the Australian climate, but full brick homes are far more popular in Western Australia. Roofs are generally tiled with terracotta or cement tiles, but colourbond steel decking or corrugated fibre cement sheeting are currently fashionable. Most Australian homes are fitted with insulation in the roof and, less commonly, the walls. Insulation helps to keep the house cool in summer and warm in winter. All homes are fitted with fly-screens over the doors and windows, which enable you to keep your doors and windows open to let the cooling summer breezes in without admitting any unwanted insects. The real trick to keeping cool is to keep the air circulating within the home. On really hot days when there does not seem to be the slightest breeze to lift the oppressive heat, the best place to head is the beach, where there is almost invariably a refreshing sea breeze, accompanied by a beach umbrella to provide shelter from the fierce sun.

If you intend to reside in Australia long-term or permanently, it does make good financial sense to purchase property as there are no legal or financial restrictions on new settlers owning their own houses and land. Just as in Britain or the EU, you would be well advised to consult a solicitor if you wish to purchase a home or land in Australia, as a solicitor will look after your interests as the buyer. It is wise to have your solicitor approve any documents requiring your signature before you sign them.

Many people buy established homes, but it is also very popular both for Australians and for immigrants to build their own home. There are basically two ways to build a house in Australia. One way is to buy land, prepare plans and contract a builder to construct your house for you. The average building time can range from four to 12 months, but it usually takes an average of six months to build a house. Local governments have strict building regulations and any plans for any new structure or additions must be submitted for approval to the local council and the Metropolitan Water and Sewerage Board before work begins. Usually, the contract builder arranges this. It is important to note that certain sections of the construction, specifically plumbing and electrical work, must be undertaken by qualified and authorised tradesmen only. For this reason, plumbers and electricians who are authorised and highly qualified are often very expensive.

The second method of building a house is to buy a new home as part of a package deal from a land and/or building company. These deals are offered in capital cities and involve the sale of new homes on sub-divisions developed by a particular company.

Prices

Between cities and even within a given city, the price of land can vary dramatically, depending on the distance from the city, availability of services, proximity to the coast, desirability of the area, etc. The best way of knowing which suburbs might suit your price range is through the various real estate magazines produced for the different cities. The magazines consist entirely of advertisements and photos of the house or unit (flat) for sale, so you have an idea of what realistic prices are as well as getting an impression of the wide variety of housing styles available. It is possible to order these magazines through *Australian Outlook* using their special order form, but allow a few weeks for delivery as the magazines come from Australia.

To give a rough idea of the current situation, the following table shows the availability and cost of vacant land in each capital city. Immigrants would probably be interested in the last two groupings in each city as these are the areas in which most of the modest and comfortable new homes are being built. All prices are approximate and are given in Australian dollars. Ha stands for hectare.

Availability and Vacant Land Prices in and around Main cities

City	8km from city	8-16km city	16-24km city	24km from city
Sydney	Very little available.	Limited avail. $150,000	Limited $120,000	Available $55,000 for residential, $130,000 for 2 hectare (ha) semi-rural lots.
Melbourne	Very little available. Usually old houses which are demolished and rebuilt.	Limited. $80,000-$140,000 in eastern & S.E. suburbs. $40,000-$70,000 in northern & western suburbs.	Greatest avail. western, northern & some eastern suburbs. $50,000-$80,000 in eastern suburbs, $40,000-$55,000 in northern & western suburbs.	Regional centres: Werribee, Melton, Sunbury, Cranbourne & Frankston; $35,000-$60,000.
Brisbane	Very little available. Refurbishing or redeveloping of old houses, or demolition and rebuilding.	Limited. $55,000-$110,000.	Adequate. Numerous staged developments $70,000-$130,000 in northern & southern corridors.	Adequate. Surburban sized & larger blocks $55,000-$120,000. Canal development in north & south sides of Moreton Bay $250,000 for canal frontage.
Adelaide	Very little available. $70,000-$180,000.	Limited. $35,000-$135,000. Very expensive in eastern foothills.	Adequate in northern & southern suburbs, $25,000-	Ample, particularly in southern areas, $20,000-$45,000. 'Hobby farms' of 3-4 ha $55,000-$120,000.
Perth	Virtually no vacant land available, but considerable redevelopment of sites $120,000.	Reasonable. $35,000, but $50,000-$100,000 in better suburbs.	Readily avail. $25,000-$95,000. Larger hill & coastal blocks more expensive.	Ample in the lower south and eastern areas, $20,000. Special rural 2ha bush blocks $65,000 which may not be fully serviced.

City	8km from city	8-16km city	16-24km city	24km from city
Hobart	Limited, $35,000-$50,000. Prime land with harbour views, $40,000-70,000.	Adequate, $25,000-$45,000. Semi-rural 1-2ha blocks, $40,000-70,000.		Readily available, $12,000-$20,000. Semi-rural 1-20ha $30,000-$50,000.

Canberra.There is no freehold land system in the ACT. Ninety-nine year leases only are available on residential blocks, which are released by the Australian Government as the city's growth demands. All residential blocks are sold at public auction and unsold sites are available for sale at the Land Sales Office. Reserve prices are set at 80% of the assessed market value and although recent reserve prices have ranged from $35,000-$85,000 per block, an average reserve price is $60,000. Lessees are obliged to commence construction within twelve months and to complete construction in 24 months. All leases are within 30km of the city centre, and all sites are fully serviced with water, power, sewerage, sealed roads, etc. Suburban development occurs as the population warrants, and schools, shops, playing fields etc., are all provided to meet the demand.

The approximate cost of constructing a home is given in the table below. Prices are based on individual house construction with a tiled roof and a medium standard finish for a house of approximately 150-350 sq. metres. Figures apply per sq. metre, but the standard of fittings and finish can make a dramatic difference. Builders' project homes are often cheaper and house and land packages are also cost effective, but you are limited by the locational availability.

Table of Approximate House Construction costs in Main Cities (per sq. metre)

City	Brick	Brick veneer	Weatherboard	Fibre Cement
Sydney	$625-$700	$585-$660	$535-$670	$535-610

Brick veneer houses are the most popular in Sydney.

| Melbourne | $500-$650 | $490-$650 | $500-$550 | |

Brick veneer houses are the most popular in Melbourne.

| Brisbane | $500-$600 | $480-$600 | $400-480 | $390-420 |

Brick veneer and timber cladding houses are the most popular in Brisbane.

| Adelaide | $595-$665 | $560-620 | $510-570 | |

Brick veneer constructions are less reactive to Adelaide's volatile soil types.

| Perth | $400-$500 | $350-$450 | $350-$500 | $600-$700 Usually for upper floor extensions. |

Perth homes are almost exclusively full brick.

| Hobart | $600-$750 | $550-$750 | | |

Brick veneer houses are the most popular in Hobart.

City	Brick	Brick veneer	Weatherboard	Fibre Cement
Canberra	$650-$900	$620-$770		

Brick veneer houses are the most popular in Canberra.

Finding Property/Land for Sale

One can find lists of builders, including sample plans and special building deals on a particular style of house, and also vacant land for sale in most state/territory newspapers, in the real estate section, including the auction section of the newspaper. Local (shire) newspapers also occasionally have notices of land for sale, particularly Crown (or Government) land. It is a very good idea to go and visit show (display) homes by different building companies, and indeed this is a popular Sunday afternoon occupation of Australians who are not particularly interested in buying or building a new home, but are simply searching for good design ideas for their existing house. Often a few companies will build show homes adjacent to each other, and it can take a whole afternoon to stroll around the beautiful houses and gardens on display while getting an excellent idea of what the actual end product of the plans looks like.

If you wish to buy an established home, these are also advertised in real estate magazines, in real estate windows, and in newspapers in the real estate section. You may often see a 'Home Open' sign on the kerb outside a house for sale which means that the owners have gone out for the day and the agent is inside the house waiting to show interested customers around. In this case, it is not necessary to make an appointment to view the house, but in all other cases it is essential you book an appointment through the agent before you go.   Below is a table of examples of established houses for sale throughout Australia. It includes examples from different suburbs within a given city and a short description of that suburb. Again the purchase price is given in Australian dollars.

Table of Approximate Property Prices countrywide

Suburb	Type	Age (yrs)	Size (sq. metres)	Contains	Purch. price (incl. land)	Description of area.
Sydney						
Blackett	W/brd	30	140	5 bedrooms, living, double carport, single garage.	$95,000	Well established residential area 45km west of city. handy for school & shops.
Punchbowl	Brick veneer	40	10	3 bedrooms, kitchen, dining/lounge, garage.	$180,000	Residential area 16km south of city. Train to city.
Mt. Colah	Brick veneer	5	130	3 bedrooms, 2 bathrooms, lounge, dining.	$205,000	30km north-west of city.
Ambervale	Brick veneer	5	125	3 bedrooms, family, living, dining, lounge, garage.	$120,000	New residential area 56 km south-west of city.
Melbourne						
Cheltenham	Brick veneer	10	150	3 bedrooms, lounge/ diner, kitchen, bathroom, laundry, double garage, tennis court, swimming pool.	$280,000	16km south of city. Train to city, close to shops.
Glen Waverley	Brick veneer	8	140	3 bedrooms, spacious open plan lounge/ dining room, kitchen, bathroom, laundry, double garage.	$145,000	20km east of city. Train to city. Close to school & shops.

Suburb	Type	Age (yrs)	Size (sq. metres)	Contains	Purch. price (incl. land)	Description of area.
Blackburn	Brick veneer	25	98	2 bedrooms with built-in wardrobes, lounge, dining, kitchen/diner, laundry, bathroom, garage.	$115,000	18km east of city. Train to city, close to schools & shops.
Epping	Brick veneer	3	108	3 bedrooms, lounge/diner, kitchen, bathroom. laundry, carport	$105,000	20km north of city. Train to city, close to local shopping centre.
Brisbane						
Aspley	Lowset brick	3	235	4 bedrooms, 2 living rooms rumpus room.	$192,500	14km north-west of GPO. Medium-good quality housing, large shopping centre, public transport to city.
Capalaba	Lowset brick	2	180	3 bedrooms, 2 living rooms, lock-up garage.	$135,000	19km east of GPO. Developing residential area, good local shopping, bus/train to city.
Kenmore Heights	Brick	4	220	4 bedrooms, 3 living rooms, double garage, in-ground pool.	$378,000	15km west of GPO. Well established area of high quality housing, good local amenities, train/bus to city.
Taringa	Highset brick veneer	10	130	3 bedrooms, 2 living rooms, carport under house.	$180,000	4km west of GPO, inner city suburb, older style housing, train/bus to city.
Adelaide						
Parkside	Stone	93	135	5 main rooms, garage	$200,000	Popular inner suburban area, 4km south of GPO.
Mitchell Park	Brick	25	13	26 main rooms, carport, garage.	$115,000	10km south of GPO, Medium standard residential area.
Belair	Brick	15	242	7 main rooms, double garage	$250,000	12km south of GPO, in Adelaide Hills, residential area in rural setting, good local amenities.
Reynella	Brick	17	12	45 main rooms, carport.	$91,000	25km south of GPO, average-good quality homes, close to all facilities.
Perth						
Ballajura	Brick & New Tile			4 bedrooms, lounge, laundry, bathroom, kitchen, WC, carport, ensuite	$102,000	Medium locality, 15km north of city, all amenities.

Suburb	Type	Age (yrs)	Size (sq. metres)	Contains	Purch. price (incl. land)	Description of area.
Bassendean	B & T	30		4 bedrooms, 2 living rooms, kitchen, laundry, bathroom, garage, WC.	$149,000	Medium locality, 10km north-east of city, all amenities.
Leeming	B & T	8		4 bedrooms, 3 living rooms, 2 bathrooms, laundry, WC, double carport.	$165,000	Medium locality, 14km south of city, all amenities.
Willagee	B & T	30		3 bedrooms, living room, kitchen, laundry, WC, bathroom, garage, ensuite.	$92,000	Modest locality, 11km south of the city, all amenities.
Hobart						
Howrah	Brick	15		3 bedrooms, lounge, dining, family room off kitchen, bathroom, laundry, garage.	$130,000	Popular residential area on east shore of the Derwent River.
Bellerive	Brick veneer	4		4 bedrooms, main with ensuite, shower room, lounge, dining room, sundeck, family room, kitchen, double garage, water views.	$245,000	Established residential area on east shore of Derwent River, 5 mins to city.
New Norfolk	W/bd	14		3 large bedrooms, lounge, laundry, double garage.	$52,990	20 km north-west of area.
Dromedary	Brick	4	1.49ha	semi-rural, large lounge, spacious kitchen/family room, with formal dining room, 3 bedrooms, main with ensuite.	$123,950	Country area, 28km north-west of Hobart, rural and water views.
Canberra						
Macgregor	Brick veneer	11	180	4 bedrooms, lounge, dining, bathroom, ensuite, laundry, double garage.	$175,000	Average residential area, 12km north-west of city, 2kms to shops & schools, bus transport.
Griffith	Brick	55	130	3 bedrooms, kitchen, lounge/dining, bathroom, laundry, attached garage.	$385,000	Older southern suburb, 7 kms from city, 2kms from shops & schools, convenient to all local amenities.
Garran	Brick veneer	27	183	5 bedrooms, lounge/ dining rooms, kitchen/family area. bathroom, ensuite, laundry, single garage.	-$225,000	11km south of city centre, average-good standard area, 1km to shops & schools, bus to city.
Rivet	Brick veneer	20	123	4 bedrooms, lounge, dining/kitchen, bathroom, laundry, single garage.	$138,000	14km south-west of city, average standard housing, close to local amenities, 4km to town centre.

Apartments: Due to the large amount of land available in Australia for building and residential purposes, there are relatively few high-rise apartment blocks compared with most European cities. You will find terraced housing in older inner city suburbs, and you will also find apartment blocks in some suburbs, but these blocks are usually no higher than three or five floors, and they tend to be rented rather than bought. If you do not wish to buy a large fully-detached house on its own block of land, then the alternative is a semi-detached house (known in Australia as a 'duplex') or purpose-built low-level residential schemes (known as 'units') which consist of an area the size of an average flat situated in communal gardens, sometimes with a pool for the residents. The closest example of such housing in Britain would be a large house subdivided into flats, although in Australia units are always purpose-built and never conversions of larger residences into smaller ones. Units can be in a single or double storey block, and if you own a unit in a double storey block, this means that your unit is split level (i.e., with an upstairs and downstairs). You never have people living above or below you in a unit, although you may share outer walls with your immediate neighbours. Most people who cannot afford a large detached house in the area of their choice, or have no need of a large amount of living space, prefer to buy a unit rather than a flat as there is outdoor living space attached to a unit which flats cannot offer. Many single people and first home buyers choose to invest in a unit rather than pay rent on a flat, and retired people also tend to prefer units as they require considerably lower maintenance than most suburban houses

Finance

Mortgages with Australian Financial Institutions

The major sources of housing finance in Australia are banks, building societies and government housing authorities. As a home buyer, you must provide a proportion of the cost of the house (usually 20%) from your own sources.

Banks: Lending terms and conditions can vary considerably between banks, but at the time of writing each bank sets its own maximum loan limit and the interest rates range from 8.75%-8.95% per annum for standard variable home loans. The maximum term for a standard home loan is 25-30 years, and all banks charge establishment fees at the time of setting up the mortgage arrangements. Some institutions also charge an additional valuation fee and ongoing administration fees to cover the cost of documentation and other administration duties required by your loan.

Australia has two national banks, the Commonwealth Bank of Australia and the National Bank. The Commonwealth Bank of Australia is Australia's largest lender for housing. It grants loans for building new houses, buying new or established homes and units, for vacant land, for holiday homes and for home improvements. The Commonwealth Bank has no fixed maximum loan limit and although loans don't normally exceed 80% of the market price of the property, loans of up to 95% are available if mortgage insurance (which requires a once only premium) is in effect. Total repayments are usually limited to 30% of the borrowers' combined gross income.

Interest rates are variable from time to time at the Commonwealth Bank's discretion (as with any other Australian bank). Currently, the interest rate of 8.75% per annum applies to new home loans irrespective of the amount of the loan, valuation ratio or the term of the loan. Interest is calculated on the daily loan balance and is charged monthly. Fixed interest rate loans are also available -

five years fixed at 9.50%. A special 6.95% Capped Rate offer is also available to new borrowers where repayments are capped for six months from the date the loan is first drawn upon, returning to the standard variable repayment rate after that.

The Commonwealth Bank has introduced a Home Loan Protection Plan (HLPP) which enables the borrower to repay their debt in cases of death or permanent disability. The HLPP means that the borrower's home can be secured for the immediate family and/or relatives in the event of a tragedy. The Bank also provides a special account for its home loan borrowers, the Mortgage Interest Saver Account (MISA), which enables the borrower to save thousands of dollars in interest and take years off the term of the loan by making a larger part of each repayment go towards reducing the principal. In the long term, there is a significant saving in interest on the home loan, which leads to the mortgage being paid off more quickly.

Housing Loan enquiries may be made, or applications may be lodged at any Australian branch of the Commonwealth Bank of Australia. If you require further detailed information about financial arrangements, housing and the general cost of living in Australia, contact the Commonwealth Bank of Australia's Financial & Migrant Information Service Office in London (address given below). This service is extremely helpful in terms of answering any questions you have relating to any sort of financial business; in addition to providing information over the phone, they also have various useful publications available on request and conduct open days throughout the year specifically aimed at potential migrants.

Useful Addresses

Australian and New Zealand Banking Group, 55 Gracechurch Street, London, EC3, tel: 0181-280 3100.

The Commonwealth Bank of Australia, Financial & Migrant Information Service, 3rd Floor, 1 Kingsway, London WC2B 6DU, tel: 0171-379 0955.

Westpac Banking Corporation, Walbrook House, Walbrook, London EC4, tel: 0181-525 4500.

Permanent Building Societies: Lending terms and conditions also vary between societies, but generally the interest rate is currently 8.75%-9.5% and the maximum term of the loan is 25-30 years. Similar to the banks, each building society sets its own guidelines, and many societies can charge borrowers for legal fees associated with the society's preparation of loan documentation.

Government Housing Authorities: The Commonwealth and State Governments provide funds for housing loans through the Commonwealth/State Housing Agreement. The governmental authority generally provides interest subsidies during the early years of the mortgage. The loan repayments are linked to the borrower's income and the subsidies given are repaid to the government when the borrower's income allows such additional repayments to be made. This kind of financial assistance is generally restricted to families with low/moderate income and the waiting period in some areas can be quite lengthy. In most states the borrower applies for the loan through building societies, and a central list of these societies is kept by the Registrar of Co-operative Societies in each state.

Registration & Mortgage Costs

You will not be charged by any of the above mentioned financial institutions for making general enquiries, but in general an establishment fee is charged upon the registration of your mortgage. This fee varies according to the amount and structure of the loan. Some finance agencies also charge a valuation fee and fees to cover administration and legal costs incurred over the course of the loan. It is worth shopping around for a mortgage as these extra fees can add a substantial amount in the long run to the total amount of your loan. It is important to check whether you have the flexibility to make extra repayments if you are in a position to do so, as some institutions do not offer the facility to make extra repayments and other agencies may even make a charge on extra repayments to cover additional administration costs.

In addition to the mortgage costs, you will be expected to pay Stamp Duty and Legal Fees which are not in any way connected with the mortgage, but are payable upon the purchase of the house/unit. See the section *Purchasing and Conveyancing Procedures* below for further information.

Repayment Conditions

Australian financial sources have variable repayment conditions, but they all generally stipulate that equal instalments, including interest, be repaid monthly. Some banks offer the option of fortnightly repayments. The Commonwealth Bank of Australia allows payments of A\$20 or more to be made at any time on variable rate loans. As already stated, other banks do not always offer this facility and may even charge for extra repayments to be made.

On page 71 is a table of Owner Occupied Housing interest rates across the different banks, including establishment fees (payable on application), valuation, maximum percentage of value lent, repayment percentage of income (both single and joint).

Purchasing & Conveyancing Procedures

There is no overall procedure to follow as far as purchasing property in Australia goes, as the rules and regulations vary between states and territories. For example the process is more complicated in the Australian Capital Territory than it is in Queensland. In addition, depending on which visa you enter Australia on, the rules and regulations may be different again. For example, if you enter the country on a Retirement Visa or some other temporary resident visas, you will have to ask permission to buy property in Australia from the Foreign Investment Review Office, (address below). Basically, regardless of which state or territory you choose to buy property in, you will need professional assistance at every stage of the purchasing and conveyancing procedure. The following section aims to outline the basic procedure in order to point you in the right direction.

Dealing with Estate Agents

If you wish to find a property, you can start the process before you even enter Australia in terms of getting an understanding of the kind of area you wish to live in and the kind of price range you are likely to be able to afford. This can be done by looking at various publications such as Consyl Publishing's *Owner's Own* and *Australian Outlook*, and the various Australian state and national papers. This is advisable in terms of giving you a basic idea about the kinds of features houses are likely to include and the prices of properties in different suburbs, regions or states.

This kind of preparation gives you some idea of what to ask for when you visit estate agents once you have arrived in Australia. Once arrived, you can browse round real estate agents' premises, where photographs of properties

Owner Occupied Housing	Advance	ANZ	Bank of Melbourne	Bank of New Zealand	Bank of Queensland	Challenge	Commonwealth Bank of Australia	Metway	National Bank of Australia	St George	State Bank of New South Wales	Westpac
6 month cap	6.75	n/a	n/a	n/a	6.00	5.00f	n/a	6.00f	6.95f	5.00	n/a	n/a
12 month cap	6.75	n/a	n/a	7.75	n/a	n/a	6.95	n/a	n/a	6.75	5.50	n/a
variable	8.75	8.75	8.75	8.75	8.75	8.75	8.75	8.75	8.75	8.75	8.75	8.75
1 year fixed	7.35	6.95	6.95	7.95	6.90	6.95	n/a	7.25	6.95	7.50	7.75	6.95
2 years fixed	8.45	8.25	8.75	8.95	n/a	8.50	8.75	8.50	8.25	9.00	8.95	8.25
3 years fixed	9.25	8.75	9.25	9.45	9.25	9.25	9.25	9.25	8.95	9.95	9.75	8.95
4 years fixed	n/a	9.00	9.50	n/a	n/a	n/a	9.50	n/a	9.25	10.25	10.25	9.25
5 years fixed	10.25	9.25	9.95	9.90	n/a	9.95	9.75	9.90	9.50	10.50	10.50	9.50
10 years fixed	n/a	n/a	n/a	n/a	n/a	n/a	n/a	n/a	n/a	n/a	11.45	n/a
home equity	8.75	9.50	9.95	8.90	11.75	10.25	9.75	8.75	8.75	8.75	9.50	9.75
application	$0-3%	$0*	$0	$500-$950	$500-$950	$350-$500	$0-$600	$500-$1000	$400-$600	$1-$500	$600-$750	$600
valuation	$0-$150	n	n	n	n	n	n	110	n	n	n	n
max % of value lent	95	80-95	95	95	95	80-95	80-95	95	80-95	95	95	80-95
repayment % of 30 income, single/joint	25	25	33	n/a	32.5/27.5	33	30	32.5/27.5	25/20	30	varies	n/a

* = Conditions apply

f = fixed, not capped   Source: Market Infofax Interest RateMonitor, *Australian Outlook.*

currently on the market are displayed, and you can also visit display home centres. It is a good idea at this stage to make a list of the kinds of things you are looking for in a property, in order of priority, trying to take as many factors into consideration as possible. For example, do you wish to live in a quiet family suburb or a more exciting and perhaps trendy inner city suburb? Do you wish to live near the beach or do you want to live in the more rural setting of the hills around the city? Do you wish to live somewhere near state primary and/or secondary schools that enjoy a fine academic reputation, so there will not be any difficulties getting your children enrolled because you live in the immediate area? Do you wish to have a property with a large garden and/or swimming pool, or would you prefer a smaller garden which required less maintenance. Would your needs be more suited to a unit rather than a larger house? Where are the best areas that you can afford? Where do you absolutely *not* want to live? How much decorating do you wish to do, if necessary? If none, what kind of basic decoration and fittings do you expect to find in the home? The list is almost endless, and will be different for each person as everyone will have quite unique needs. When you have compiled such a list, it really is time to approach real estate agents for their essential and often invaluable assistance .

It is important to keep in mind that real estate agents are usually paid some sort of commission on sales, and will be likely to try to convince you to purchase property in order to earn their commission. You should, therefore, make sure that you keep your prepared list of important required features firmly in mind so that you are not persuaded to settle for anything unsuitable. In addition, you should perhaps consult building companies with regard to any house and land packages they may currently be offering. Sometimes it can work out much cheaper for you to purchase a house and land package, which may be more suited to your needs, rather than an established home.

You can find real estate agents by consulting listings in the yellow pages telephone books throughout the country. Estate agents also tend to advertise on television, the radio and in the printed media. In addition, agents will often distribute leaflets within their local area. L.J. Hooker (1st Floor, 175 Pitt Street, Sydney, NSW 2000; tel + 61 2239 1111/1130; fax +61 2239 1181) a leading Australian real estate company with decades of experience helping new residents to find suitable properties.

Professional Assistance

You will need to have a solicitor in order to draw up contracts and conduct searches on prospective properties, and it can be very useful to ask your solicitor's advice about different properties and prices as he/she is more likely to give you honest, independent advice. In addition, you may choose to contract a surveyor and/or valuer for an independent assessment of the property.

When you have found the right property, your solicitor should draw up a contract to be signed by you and the owner of the property at the agreed price. This contract is subject to confirmation that you have available finance within a specified time, usually between seven and fourteen days. It is important to note that there is no such thing as a 'cooling off' period on this contract. Once it is signed, you are legally obliged to buy the property, so you must be absolutely certain that the property is really what you want. In order to ensure you are making the right decision, you should have at least two inspections before signing the contract. The contract is usually settled within 30 days of being signed by both parties. During this period your solicitor should carry out necessary searches on the property. Provided that everything is satisfactory after 30 days, you are then free to move into your new home.

Regardless of whether you choose to consult a real estate agent, a building company, or both, it is extremely important to get professional advice as to the procedures involved in purchasing property. There are complex legal processes involved and necessary documentation to complete, as well as different taxes to pay such as stamp duty (between 1% and 3% depending on whether the property has been purchased for residential or investment purposes) and your agent and solicitor should be able to guide you through the legal minefield unique to your state/territory safely. You must be careful to check precisely what charges you will be liable for when you are considering engaging an agent as some can hit you with hidden charges, such as a percentage of the price, after a sale. In terms of legal fees, you will be expected to pay between $450 and $1,000, depending on the cost of the property.

Useful Publications

Consyl Publishing are distributors of:

Melbourne houses for sale (£3.70), *Brisbane houses for sale* (£3.70), *Adelaide houses for sale* (£2.70), *Gold Coast houses for sale* (£2.55), *NSW houses for sale* (£4.20), *WA houses for sale* (£3.70), and *Owner's Own - houses and businesses for sale* (£6.95). Contact the Subscription Department, Australian Outlook, 3 Buckhurst Road, Bexhill-on-Sea, East Sussex, TN40 1QF, for further details.

Foreign Investment Review Board, c/o the Treasury, Parkes Place, Parkes ACT 2600.

Registration Tax

The table above outlines the registration (application) fees payable to the banks, but in addition, there are certain taxes payable to the State and Territory governments. All Australian State/Territory governments require Stamp Duty to be paid on property transfers and mortgages. For first home buyers purchasing a property priced at approximately $150,000, the following approximate duty would be payable on the transfer.

Sydney	$3,740
Melbourne	$5,200
Brisbane	$1,100
Adelaide	$4,830
Perth	$3,525
Hobart	$3,925
Canberra	$3,765

Higher rates can apply in some states for subsequent home purchases.

In 1992/3, the approximate average range of legal fees for the purchase of a house/property over $100,000 was as follows:

Sydney	$600 for $100,000
Melbourne	There are no set fees based on purchase price of property. Conveyancing charges depend upon the amount of work involved and are established by negotiation with the solicitor. An appropriate average is $750.
Brisbane	$1,400 + $100 per $10,000 over $100,000
Adelaide	The majority of settlements are handled by land brokers whose normal charge for preparing a transfer ranges from $400-$500. A solicitor may execute this if desired.
Perth	$400-$500, with the majority of settlements being handled by settlement agents.
Hobart	$900
Canberra	$650-850

Renting Property

In order to have time to shop around for a new home, many immigrants either stay with relatives or friends for a short time on arrival in Australia. Those for whom this is not a feasible option usually consider short-term renting for a period of between three and six months. This is a practical, though more expensive, alternative. Australians do, as a rule, buy rather than rent, so most tenants occupy a rented property for less than a year. Until recently rented housing in Australia was considerably less expensive than in Europe, as the landlords were able to gain a taxation incentive if they let houses/units for less than the mortgage repayments on the property. This taxation incentive is no longer available, and as a result rents have risen and the property market for domestic letting has diminished. In addition, a capital gains tax was introduced which taxed the sale of an investment property (i.e., a property you own other than the one in which you live). Currently, under Australian taxation law, an individual may only own one investment property in addition to their actual residence.

Rent control is not common in Australia, and has been abolished in both Tasmania and Western Australia. In other States a certain degree of control is established over residential rents; however this control does not extend to new premises or tenancies after a certain date. If you are intending to rent a home upon your arrival, or indeed at any time during your stay in Australia, you should specifically question the landlord/letting agency about rent control and the procedures involved in rent rises.

When looking for a home, it can be useful to keep in mind that there are Federal Discrimination Acts in effect which may be pertinent at the time. It is important to be aware of these in order to understand your rights as a prospective tenant. For example, it is illegal for property owners to discriminate against a potential tenant on the grounds of sex or marital status or because they are pregnant, under the Sexual Discrimination Act, or on the grounds of ethnic origin. If you suspect that the owner has made an illegal refusal of your application to rent his/her property, you should contact the nearest Consumer Affairs office who will be able to advise you further. In general, those of European ethnic origins will be less likely to encounter discrimination than those of Asian or Aboriginal origins. Accommodation officers at certain universities, for example, may be confronted with blatant prejudice when taking Indonesian, Chinese or Japanese students to view potential rented accommodation. In general, however, landlords are interested in having their property occupied by rent-paying tenants, and you are unlikely to have your application for tenancy turned down, particularly if you are of British or other European origin.

The best place to start looking for a home to rent is in the 'To Let' section of the daily local newspapers, or at local real estate agents who often specialise in property management. Finding your way through an Australian advertisement for a house to let can be a daunting experience, as there is a very specific jargon, usually abbreviated, used only to advertise property.

Tenancy Agreements

Very short term rented accommodation is quite difficult to find in Australia as most property owners will only accept tenants prepared to sign a tenancy agreement valid for six months. This can cause problems for people travelling on a Working Holiday Visa which restricts them to work in one place for no longer than three months. Occasionally, it is possible to find an owner prepared to make a short term lease available, and in turn this is sometimes extendable by private agreement with the landlord who allows the tenant to stay on a weekly or monthly basis after the expiry of the lease. Obviously, this is a fairly unstable arrangement, and not advisable unless you would be willing to move at very short notice should the owner decide to give the lease to another more permanent tenant. In general, a first lease is given for six months and is extendable provided that you and the owner can negotiate an agreement on rent rises. Properties are let either furnished or unfurnished, and the former is more expensive. Usually, the leases drawn up for domestic residential purposes are fairly self-explanatory and easily understandable. Unless you intend to rent commercial property, it is not necessary to pay for legal advice at this stage.

As a general rule, letting agents or property owners require tenants to pay a bond which is equal to four weeks rental, and they will also usually require a month's rent in advance. This bond can sometimes be as much as six weeks' rent, and owners may occasionally ask for up to two months' rent in advance. This can add up to hundreds, even thousands, of dollars, so you need to be prepared to be able to make these payments if required. The bond can be used in part or entirely forfeited if the tenant defaults on payment or conditions of the lease. If you leave the premises with the furniture and fittings in a reasonable condition (i.e., reasonable wear and tear), your landlord will refund your bond. It is extremely useful to ask for an inventory of items in the property, particularly if the property is furnished, to be drawn up with the lease in order to give yourself an idea of what should be left behind, and what kind of condition the house was in before you entered (e.g., scuff marks at bottom of front door). It is well worth studying this list of furniture and fittings carefully before you sign to make sure it is accurate, as you do not want to be left being charged for lots of little problems which existed before you moved in.

It is important to note that the owner is responsible for all property rates payable on rented property, but the tenant is responsible for all utility costs such as electricity, gas and the telephone.

Rental Costs

In most states, there is governmental housing available though often on a limited basis. The main criterion for eligibility is that the applicants must demonstrate an inability to secure decent accommodation in the private sector at a rent within their capacity to pay. The availability of houses and/or units to rent in the different states can vary, but in general units are easier to find than houses to rent. Below is an approximation of the costs of weekly rental rates for various sizes of houses and units in the different cities. The prices are based on an unfurnished property:

Sydney: Governmental housing is available from the Housing Commission of New South Wales and waiting times for rental accommodation vary considerably depending on the type of accommodation and the location required. Privately there are a reasonable number of houses available for rental and units are available for rental in most areas.

Type	No of rooms	modest	medium	good
Houses	two	$120-155	$185-250	$250+
	three	$150-200	$200-280	$280+
Units/Flats	one	$90-120	$120-150	$150+
	two	$120-160	$160-200	$200+
	three	$150-200	$200-250	$250+

Melbourne: Governmental housing is available from the Ministry of Housing. The waiting time varies according to the kind of housing and the location required, but there is a long waiting list for Ministry of Housing properties. Privately, the situation is quite good due to the fact that rent levels bottomed in the last quarter of 1991 and advertised rent levels remain below the peak levels reached in mid-1990. Presently there is a glut of properties, especially flats/units, on the market. Flats are becoming increasingly difficult to let as rent levels for houses have fallen in the last twelve months, making the rental of a house only marginally more expensive than that of a flat/unit.

Type	No of rooms	modest	medium	good
Houses	two	$110-120	$120-150	$150+
	three	$120-140	$140-250	$250+
Units/Flats	one	$75-85	$90-120	$120+
	two	$90-110	$110-140	$140+
	three	$120-140	$140-160	$160+

Brisbane: Govermental rental accommodation is available through the Department of Housing and Local Goverment and allocation is made by a waiting list with priority given to those with special needs and urgency. This type of housing is increasingly in demand. Privately, there is a marked increase in demand for rented property but there is a very limited selection of both houses and flats available.

Type	No of rooms	modest	medium	good
Houses	two	$100-130	$120-160	$200+
	three	$120-140	$140-200	$240+
Units/Flats	one	$80-100	$85-$100	$130+
	two	$90-120	$120-160	$160+
	three	$100-140	$140-200	$200+

Adelaide: Governmental accommodation is available from the South Australian Housing Trust (SAHT) to low income households that do not own residential property and are in need of housing assistance. There are waiting lists for up to five years due to the heavy demand on this type of housing, but the waiting period for flats is generally shorter than that for houses. In addition, family accommodation within the inner metropolitan area has a waiting list of up to five years whereas in the outer suburbs the waiting period is between 18 months and three years. There is a reasonable selection of houses and flats in the private sector as there has been little reported growth for residential properties and many owners have had to offer discounted rentals.

Type	No of rooms	modest	medium	good
Houses	two	$80-110	$110-140	$140+
	three	$110-130	$120-170	$170+
Units/Flats	one	$55-70	$70-90	$90+
	two	$75-90	$70-130	$130+

Perth: Governmental accommodation is provided through Homeswest and is subject to an income test. Waiting time for flats/units in the metropolitan area is between six and 18 months, and for houses it varies between two and three years. The waiting time can be significantly less for accommodation in some outer areas of the city. Privately there is a good range of accommodation available in most areas, particularly in the lower rental bracket, and in many instances rental incentives are being offered.

Type	No of rooms	modest	medium	good
Houses	two	$90-110	$110-135	$135+
	three	$110-135	$135-160	$160+
Units/Flats	one	$65-$75	$75-85	$85+
	two	470-80	$80-120	$120+

Hobart: Governmental accommodation can be obtained through the Tasmanian Government Department of Housing and Construction, but eligibility is restricted by an income/needs test and there is a very high demand. The Department will accept application upon arrival in the State, but waiting periods vary from eight to 18 months depending on the type of accommodation and the location required. Privately, there is a very limited selection of rental accommodation available; both flats and houses are scarce.

Type	No of rooms	modest	medium	good
Houses	two	$130-150	$150-180	$180+
	three	$140-170	$160-200	$230+
Flats	one	$90-100	$100-110	$110+
	two	$110-120	$120-140	$130+

Canberra: Governmental housing is available from the Australian Capital Territory Administration Community Services and elegibility is dependent upon both a means test and whether the applicant is employed or resident in the ACT. In order to be eligible for family accommodation, the total family income must be less than $579 gross per week plus $58 for each person in the family. Assets must not be valued at more than $20,000. For single accommodation, the income limit is $348 per week and assets must not exceed $20,000. There are currently long waiting lists for all forms of accommodation; for example you will wait an average of three years for a bedsitter, between two and three years for a two-bedroomed flat, three to four years for a three-bedroomed house, and four to five years for an Aged Person's Unit. Privately, the situation is much better for the prospective tenant as new construction in the outer suburbs of Canberra has reduced the demand for rental accommodation.

Type	No of rooms	modest	medium	good
Houses	two	$130-140	$140-180	$180+
	three/four	$150-180	$180-240	$240+
Town Houses/ Flats	one	$90-110	$110-130	$130+
	two	$130-150	$150-190	$190+

Please note that all rents are approximate at the time of writing and are subject to inflation and fluctuations in the building trade.

Relocation Companies

Although relocators are common in the EU for intra-European moves, and also perhaps trans-Atlantic moves, they do not appear to be in demand for moves between Europe and Australia. This is largely due to the distances and, consequently, costs involved. There are very few companies indeed offering relocating services to Australia which include finding you or your family a new home, schools for your children, employment for your spouse etc. Almost all of the companies that do offer relocation services in Australia tend not to cater for the domestic move of the migrant, but for corporate moves. This is also due to the fact that the costs involved are huge and therefore usually only affordable by larger corporations. Rather than look for a relocation firm to make arrangements for you in Australia if you are making a domestic rather than an executive or corporate move, it is better to enquire with removal companies, some of whom offer more than the usual packing and freight service. Your best option for domestic relocation services is, therefore, to scan your local yellow pages telephone directory, and enquire whether your local removal firm offers relocation assistance in Australia, or whether they are affiliated with any companies in Australia that may be of service to you.

Relocation Companies in Australia. It is better to contact relocation firms directly in Australia for assistance rather than in the UK as UK relocation firms tend to act on behalf of overseas clients moving to Britain. Alternatively you could try contacting one of the larger national relocators independently from your present country prior to departure, and ask if they are able to assist you before you actually arrive in Australia as many of them operate within an international network. Below is a list of relocators that, although specialising in corporate or executive relocations, also offer domestic services. Please also refer to either *Australian Outlook* or *Australian News* as both publications contain lists of removal companies that advertise specialist services for emigrants.

Useful Addresses

Carroll, Dardis & Associates, PO Box 468, Claremont WA 6010, tel: 09-383 2677 or fax: 09-383 2677 (same number). Meet and greet service at the airport upon your arrival/, introductions to reputable real estate agents, bank

Personal caring assistance in Settling;
Finding a Home; Orientation;
Education; local information
and social networking.

**RELOCATIONS
INTERNATIONAL**
——— NEW ZEALAND ———
The Relocation Group – Australasia Worldwide

PO Box 6112 Wellesley St
Auckland, New Zealand
Telephone (64 9) 378 9888

managers, accountants, solicitors, insurance brokers, motor car dealers etc.,
and information on education and health care in Western Australia.

Coyle & Hitchcock International, Relocation and Migration services, 502 South
Tower, Chatswood Plaza, Railway Street, Chatswood NSW 2067, tel: 02-412
1505 or fax: 02-411 2155.

Emigration Consultancy Services, De Salis Court, Hampton Lovett Droitwich,
Worcestershire WR9 ONX; tel 01905 795949; fax 01905 795949. Can arrange
introductions to specialists in the practical aspects of emigration, removals,
flights, banking transfers and accommodation.

Expat International offer expatriate consultancy to corporations worldwide, visa
documentation, international and interstate relocations, cultural awareness
and training, and they are affiliated with the Migration Institute of Australia
and the Employee Relocation Council (USA). They have offices worldwide,
so check the white pages telephone directory of your capital city, or contact
them at 207 George Street, East Melbourne VIC 3002, tel: 03-419 9351 or
fax: 03-416 0786.

Relocation Information Services, 160 London Road, Croydon, Surrey CR0 2TD,
tel: 0181-681 3692 or fax: 0181-686 4061.

Relocations International, P.O. Box 6112, Wellesley Street, Auckland, New
Zealand; tel +64-9 378 9888; fax +64-9 378 8072. Assistance in finding a
home/orientation/education/social networking in Australia and New Zealand.

Network Migration Services, Oxford House, College Court, Commercial Road,
Swindon, Wilts. SN1 1PZ; tel 01793 612222. Can help with discounted
airfares/removals/resettlement including jobsearch/accommodation/meet and
greet on arrival.

Church Assistance

The Anglican Church Overseas Settlement Department
Although strictly non-commercial, the Anglican Church has an *Overseas Settlement Secretary* whose job is to ensure that you are put in touch with your local
Anglican Church in Australia and given a warm welcome into the country. Many
people find that this is a great way to meet helpful locals as the common bond
of faith opens up friendships which would perhaps never otherwise occur. For
further details, write to the Overseas Settlement Secretary, Board for Social
Responsibility, Church House, Great Smith Street, Westminster, London
SW1P 3NZ.

Other Denominations. Alternatively, should you not be a member of the Anglican
Church but of another denomination or religion, you should contact the head
office of your denomination/religion (if there is one) in your present country in

order to obtain a list of the relevant churches/mosques in Australia. The Australian Council of Churches offers *Refugee and Migrant Services* and further information can be obtained from their office at 379 Kent Street, Sydney NSW 2001, tel: 02-229 2215.

Insurance and Wills

Home Insurance

There are many big insurance companies in Australia, all of which deal in home and contents, vehicle, business, boat and caravan, and life insurance. A list of these companies is given in *Daily Life, Buying a Car* . Naturally, there are many different housing insurance policies available from the different companies. Most Australians who own their own homes choose to insure their homes against fire, flood, earthquake and other natural disasters or accidents. It is important to read policies very carefully before you sign, as some policies may not cover flood or earthquake, and you do not want to discover that you are not covered for flood damage after torrential rains have caused a freak flood in your street, as does occasionally happen. The cost of the policy will be dependent upon factors such as the age of the house, the type of house (i.e., brick, brick veneer, etc.), the value of the house, its size and location. Home insurance is usually payable on a yearly or half-yearly basis, and will cost between $200- $400 per year for an average family brick home in a typical location. For example, a 30-year-old brick house with four bedrooms and two bathrooms, kitchen, study, lounge/dining and rumpus room, in an average suburb moderately close to the city centre, valued at $93,000 (please note that this house is considerably undervalued, a more realistic value would be $120,000), is covered by an insurance payment of $202.30 per annum, with an earthquake excess of $500. This means that in the event of an earthquake, the home owner is expected to cover the first $500 damage, and the insurance company will cover the rest of the damage.

Contents Insurance: Most Australians, regardless of whether they own their own homes or not, also choose to be covered by a Contents Insurance. This insurance is either Replacement, which means that, in the case of theft or damage, your contents will be replaced by the insurance company, or Indemnity, which means that you will be reimbursed for the stolen/damaged contents. To purchase a Contents policy, you need to make a clear itemised list of goods which you would expect to have replaced or be reimbursed for, should you be burgled or should the goods be damaged in any way, and the approximate value of the goods. You total the values to find the sum you wish to be insured for, and this value is noted on your policy. Obviously, the more you wish to be insured for, the higher your premiums will be. The cost of contents insurance may also depend on how secure your home is, and some insurance policies offer lower premiums if your home is fitted with an approved security alarm, or even with security lights. In addition, Replacement insurance is more expensive than Indemnity insurance, simply because it is the insurance company's responsability to go shopping for you to replace your contents (which may, in the meantime, have increased in value and/or cost), whereas with Indemnity, you must spend time yourself replacing what has been stolen/damaged, and you may find that items such as televisions or videos have increased in price since you purchased your originals. Replacement and Indemnity insurance policies are usually also payable on an annual or six-monthly basis, and an example of the relative cost of the policies is given below. This example of the Replacement/Indemnity policy for the insured value of $26,000 is based on the same house as in the example given above:

Sum Insured	Amount Payable	6 months	12 months
Replacement	$26,000	$96.70	$173.00
Indemnity	$26,000	$73.90	$136.10

Personal Insurance: Personal, or life, insurance, is also available through the big insurance companies. Depending on the company, if you take out home, content, vehicle and life insurance with the same company, you may be eligible for substantial discounts on your premiums, or even for a premium-free period. It is well worth questioning any potential insurer if it is to be to your financial advantage to take out a number of policies with the same company. You must then shop around and total the number of best and most economical individual policies with different companies, and see whether taking out a number of policies with a single company is in fact a good financial move. There are a number of different life insurance policies available. Combined savings/personal insurance policies are becoming increasingly popular. These entail making deposits, the amount of which is decided by you and the company representative/ financial advisor at the time of discussing the possibility of taking out a policy, which begin to earn interest after a substantial period of time, usually about five to seven years. It is possible to draw on or cash in this policy at any time, but it would not make good financial sense to do so until your premium payments (which really function as long-term savings deposits) have begun to earn significant interest. The longer you leave the money in the policy and continue to add premium payments, the more interest and bonuses you accumulate along the way. This kind of policy is very popular with young people who have newly entered the full-time workforce as by the time they wish to retire at 55 or 60, they will have a large nest-egg. At this point, or at any other they choose, the policy may be cashed in. It is not a case of having to die before anyone benefits by the return of their premium payments. Of course, there are the standard life insurance policies available, which tend to have lower premium payments, but it is well worth consulting a financial advisor or insurance company representative, who will often come to your home for a free consultation, in order to assess what kind of policy is best suited to you.

If you already have life/personal insurance before you enter Australia, consult your own insurance company and explain the move you are intending to make. Your own company should advise you as to what steps, if any, you should make concerning your present policy. Alternatively, take details of your present policy with you and show them to an advisor in Australia. It is possible that your policy may be transferred and that you receive benefits in terms of reduced premiums or bonuses.

Wills

If you have not made a will prior to your death, all your property will pass to certain people according to the provisions and statutory order of the various statutes in each state dealing with intestacy upon your death. For example, in New South Wales if you die leaving a spouse but no children, then your spouse would inherit the whole of the estate. If you leave a spouse and children, then the spouse may get most of the estate and children would perhaps only get part of it, depending on the size of the estate and the nature of its assets. If you die without any kin, your estate may pass to the State of New South Wales Treasury. Perhaps the most urgent reason for having a will is that it enables you to choose to whom you wish to pass control of the distribution and/or administration of your estate.

There are basically two ways to make a will: either you do it yourself or you do it with the assistance of a lawyer. Given that a will must fulfil certain formal and legal requirements in order to be valid, it is advisable to seek professional legal advice, even if only to obtain professional approval of your own attempt at making a will in order to gain peace of mind. A solicitor's professional assistance can often make an important contribution in the area of capital gains tax in relation to the administration of an estate, and therefore it would be financially prudent, particularly in the long term, to consult a solicitor. Australia has recently seen a certain relaxing of the rules concerning will-making formalities in most states in an attempt to protect the true intentions of the testators, but there are still some necessary guidelines which must be followed which should ensure that your last wishes are executed.

A will must be in writing and must be signed by the testator. This signature must in turn be witnessed by two other people who must attest to the fact that they were present with each other and saw the testator sign the will. If a witness is a beneficiary, or married to a beneficiary of that will, the gift to that beneficiary will fail (although the whole will may not necessarily fail). It is of the utmost importance that beneficiaries are not requested to witness the will. Wills may be revoked by the testator at any time after execution, by destruction, by a later will or by marriage, but it is important to note that divorce does not automatically revoke a will.

Both Commonwealth estate duty and State Death Duty have been abolished. Consequently, under the present law, no probate or estate duty is payable in respect of a deceased person's estate, regardless of its state.

Interestingly, if you have a will made overseas which is valid according to the law of the country where it was made, it will be accepted for probate in Australia (a probate is an order or grant by the Supreme Court in favour of the executor authorising him/her to collect the assets of the deceased and deal with those assets according to the terms of the will), even despite the fact that the will may not be valid according to the law of the particular state to which you have moved. It is possible to deal with Australian assets by means of a separate will.

Utilities

The rates for electricity, gas and water vary between cities, and can be more expensive if you live in a remote area. Furthermore, within any city the charges can vary from suburb to suburb due to a number of differing determining factors.

Electricity and Gas

Each State/Territory has its own Energy Commission, owned and administered by the government, in charge of electricity and gas. Most new homes are fitted with both gas and electricity outlets. Many older homes do not contain gas fittings, but it is a simple process to contact the relevant energy authority in order to have gas fittings installed. In general, gas is used in Australian homes for cooking, and is less popular for both water and home heating. Solar power heaters fitted to roofs are very popular as the average hours of sunshine per day usually provide sufficient energy to heat a family's water supply. Solar power heaters are environmentally friendly and economical, and are usually connected to an electric booster system which can be operated on overcast winter days, or when there is an unusually high demand for hot water. Most Australians have portable electric radiators in the main living areas of their homes, brought out of their summer storage during the winter months. Central heating is not generally a feature of the average Australian home, simply because the climate does not warrant it. Pot-belly stoves or other solid fuel enclosed fires are becoming increasingly popular as a means of heating the main living areas of the home and may even be installed to heat the water supply as well. Rather than focusing on the heating, most Australians find that keeping cool is the major issue, and almost every home seems to have electric pedestal/ceiling fans, and/or an air-conditioner. Air-conditioning is essential in the northern regions of Australia, both in the home and the car, and the vast majority of professional businesses throughout Australia are air-conditioned. The more modern homes may have ducted air-conditioning, powered by electricity, with a climate-control to reverse the cycle in winter and provide ducted heating. Generally, this is considered an indulgence of the wealthy, and for most people in the more temperate regions of Australia, a small portable electric fan heater will be sufficient to heat the lounge room. It is extremely unusual to have a heater in the bathroom, and heated towel rails are almost unheard of, delighting any Australian visitor to the UK.

An example of a gas and electricity bill covering the winter months from the end of May till the end of July, based on the State Energy Commission of Western Australia's charges is:

Domestic Electric Tariff (12.29 cents per unit)	$100.35
Domestic Gas Tariff (2.64-6.70 cents per unit)	$129.68
Total charge	$230.68

The voltage in Australia is 240/250V and the current is alternating at 50 Hz. The power points take three-pin plugs which have two diagonally slanting pins above one straight pin.

Water

As stated above, water rates may differ from area to area, but in general, they are charged annually. Each city and major region has its own water board, a department of the State/Territory government, and payments should be made to these boards.

An example of a bill from 1 July 1993 to 30 June 1994, based on a 4 bedroom, 2 bathroom house with laundry, front and back lawns irrigated using the main metropolitan water supply, is $118.45. On top of this, there are sewerage charges of approximately 6.00 cents per unit, totalling $373.70 for the year. The total of the annual water bill for this family of four is $492.15 for 1993/4.

The good news for those who have retired is that, as registered Senior Citizens, a rebate of up to $117.65 can be offered on the above total. Seniors are entitled to a 25% rebate of the water and sewerage bills if payment of the bill is made using one of the water board's preferred payment options outlined below:

Option	Instalments	Due dates	Total	1st instalment due
One instalment(prompt) (additional discount $7.75)	$357.25	31/7	$357.25	$357.25
Two instalments (normal) (no discount, no cost)	$117.75 $187.25	31/7 31/12	$365.00	$177.75
Four instalments (extended) (cost of option $6.70)	$85.80 $95.30 $95.30 $95.30	31/7 31/10 31/12 31/3	$371.70	$85.50

Due to the long, dry summers in most regions, many Australian homes have irrigation/sprinkler systems (known as reticulation) to keep their gardens green. If there is no reticulation system, lawns are usually hand-watered using a garden hose and/or sprinkler system attached to the garden tap. The region's main water supply can be used as the source of water to be used in the garden, but it is also very popular to sink a bore and tap the artesian water at depths of up to 150 metres below the suburban surface. Bores can be expensive, particularly if you live on a hill or in a high-lying area, as the cost of the bore is determined by its depth and the geographical structure of the land. Although huge savings are eventually made on water bills, bore water tends to stain fences, houses and even roads a rusty-brown colour due to its rich mineral content. They are particularly handy in summer, when water restrictions apply on the main water supply because of a drought. At these times, bore owners are free to use as much water as they like on their gardens, while mains users must water their gardens sparingly every third day either before dawn or after dusk. In fact, this makes practical sense, as most of the water used on gardens during the day in the height of summer immediately evaporates and can result in scorching, rather than soaking, your lawn. It is becoming increasingly popular to steer away from the traditional British style of cottage garden towards gardens of native Australian plants which need little or no additional water apart from seasonal rains and require little maintenance. Wood chips and gravel are also popular alternatives to lawns, which are expensive and time-consuming to maintain in Australia.

In an effort to save on water bills, many families, particularly in rural areas, have rain-water tanks which collect precipitation that can be used for gardening or baths/showers.

The water that comes through the kitchen and even garden taps in Australia is safe, and the taste is generally good. In some areas, the quality of taste may not be as good because of mineral deposits etc., (e.g., bore water tastes awful), but it is possible to have a water-purifier fitted to the kitchen tap for about $60.00 which tends to improve the taste. Unlike the water supply in many British areas, Australian water supplies do not tend to contain 'limescale', so tap fittings, sinks and other surfaces tend to require less maintenance. During the summer months, however, garden hoses and domestic swimming pools can be the site of amoebic meningitis, and it is extremely important to clean pools thoroughly and frequently, and to let the water run for a while before allowing children to play with or drink from garden hoses. Amoebic meningitis is caught from contaminated water being forced up the nose, as can easily happen when jumping into a pool or playing with a hose, and care should be taken during extremely hot summers.

Other Rates and Charges

In addition to the electricity, gas and water charges, there are also council rates which are payable on an annual basis. These rates include a Refuse Charge for the collection of domestic rubbish, and charges for amenities provided by the council. This rate is determined by the location of the property. Rates will be higher if you buy a house in a high demand area which boasts excellent services and amenities. An example of rates and charges payable on the same house used in the example of water rates given above, in a suburb of a medium to good standard of housing and good/high demand is:

Refuse charge	$110.00
General charge	$478.57
Instalment surcharge	$15.00
Total charge	$603.57

Rates and charges are payable to the local (shire) council and it is possible to pay in two instalments. For example, on the above rates and charges for the financial period 1 July 1994 - 30 June 1995 issued on 12 August 1994, $364.28 is payable on 16 September 1994 and $239.29 is due on 15 January 1995. If the amount is paid promptly in a single instalment, you can get a substantial discount and are only liable to pay $568.57.

Telephones

Until relatively recently, Australia's telecommunications have been monopolised by the government owned Telecom Australia. In the last two years, the federal government has allowed a competitor, Optus, to enter the telecommunications market. The market has tended to divide between Telecom, specialising in local and national calls, and in charge of installing and leasing phone, fax and telex lines, and Optus, offering cheaper services, yet of an exceptionally high standard, on overseas calls. International telephone, telex and facsimile links are also provided by the Overseas Telecommunication Commission (OTC). OTC also offer MIDAS, providing users with access to international databases and computer resources; INTERPLEX, which provides clients with their own private international telephone line exchange; MINERVA, an international electronic mail service (used mainly by businesses and universities); and ITCNET, which provides customers with exclusive use of facilities in the international telephone exchange for voice/data transmissions. Almost without exception, Australian homes are fitted with a telephone line, and if you are building a new home, or wish to have another telephone line installed (perhaps for business purposes), you should contact Telecom Australia for further details. The installation of a phone line costs approximately $A216, but you pay an advance of $300 from which the fee is deducted. If there are existing telephone lines in the premises, then you will only have to pay $50, which is deducted from an advance payment of $150.

At the time of writing, telephone bills are issued quarterly by Telecom Australia, even if you have an established Flexi-Plan facility with Optus. This bill includes metered calls (local), STD (interstate/long distance national calls), mobile calls, international calls (Optus or Telecom), and service, equipment and any other charges.

It almost seems too good to be true, but local calls (i.e., calls within a given distance of any region), cost 25 cents from a domestic phone (payphones are more expensive) *regardless* of the length of the call. That is, it does not matter whether you are on the phone for three seconds or three hours, the cost of the call is the same. Long distance national and international calls are, however, charged according to the distance and the length of the call. The time at which you call also affects how much you will be charged. Day rate (9am-6pm) is most expensive, Economy rate is (7am-9am, 6pm-9pm) is slightly cheaper, and Night rate (9pm-7am and all weekend) is the cheapest rate for national calls.

Optus offers a significant reduction in the cost of international calls if you use the Optus Flexi-Plan, dialling direct at the cheap rate. If you dial direct through Telecom, the same call would cost up to 28% more, depending on the time at which you call. The call charges from Australia to the UK are approximately $1.36 per minute at the normal rate and $1.03 per minute at off-peak times which are 6pm-9pm Monday to Friday and 6pm Friday to 9am Monday. If you have arranged to participate in some sort of flexiplan, then there are various deductions which are made on these rates. The local white pages telephone directory used to contain information on rates and codes for local, STD and international calls, but since the telecommunications industry has been deregulated, there are now so many different rates and charges that you must now call the company direct for information about the cost of telephone calls. These numbers are given at the front of the white pages telephone directories.

The quarterly services and equipment charge can also vary, but an average charge is between $40-$50.

The codes for dialling Australia directly from the UK are:

Sydney 00-61 2	Brisbane 00-61 7
Perth 00-61 9	Darwin 00-61 89
Melbourne 00-61 3	Adelaide 00-61 8
Hobart 00-61 02	Canberra 00-61 6

This code should prefix the local number, which will be 7 digits long in most capital cities, and 5-6 digits long in more rural areas.

In addition, both AAP-Reuter and AP-Dow Jones offer services targeted at the business world, specifically for helping businesses keep up with international trade, commodity and money markets via computers. These services operate 24-hours per day.

Removals

The easiest way to gain information about removal companies is to obtain a copy of *Australian Outlook*, the newspaper produced specifically for potential Australian migrants and travellers, published by Consyl Publishing. Besides advertisements for all sorts of different specialist comapanies on almost every page, there is always a list of all the advertisers in the newspaper. You could cut out the list, tick the advertisers you wanted to get in touch with you, add your name and address, post it off to the publishers, who would then forward your name and address to the relevant companies or services. These companies would then forward you free information, often in booklet form, giving you help and advice about such varied fields as banks, employment, car exports, animal removals, migrant services etc. For current and back issues of the newspaper, contact *Australian Outlook*, Consyl Publishing, 3 Buckhurst Road, Bexhill-on-Sea, East Sussex, TN40 1QF, tel: 01242-223 111.

Household Goods: There are a huge number of shipping services available for household removals. The bigger ones offer free estimates, which involves a company estimator visiting your house in order to answer your questions, offer advice, explain the service offered and the packing methods, as well as giving a quote. It is certainly worth shopping around for competitive rates, but it is also worth questioning the company closely to make sure the service you are getting is highly professional and completely suited to your needs. You can often be charged extra for services you may not really need.

It is also worth thinking very carefully about exactly what household items you are going to take with you. Some people feel it is helpful to make lists of essential, and non-essential items which can make the decision of what to take more easy. The British Association of Removers has compiled a checklist for their overseas specialist removers which is worth consulting early in order to make sure you have everything covered. Eleanor Greet, in her book *Coping With Australia* recommends that wardrobes, televisions, refrigerators and cookers (gas or electric) will be redundant, as most homes come with built-in wardrobes, a refrigerator and a gas or electric cooker, and British televisions do not work in Australia. In addition, Australian refrigerators have extra fan-assisted power to cope with the heat. PVC-covered furniture will be inappropriate in Australia because the heat makes many plastic surfaces, vinyl in particular, uncomfortable to sit on.

Avalon Overseas International Movers have twice won the the Queen's Award for Export Achievement twice (1993 & 1994). They provide a door-to-door service. They have offices in London (0181-451 6336), Manchester (0161-237 1120) and Denny, Scotland (01324-634 170).

Importing a Car

Most removal companies offer a car shipping service as well. Details of customs charges and procedures are given under 'Buying a Car'. In brief, there are specialist motor vehicle shipping specialists who will supply all the necessary information including lists of customs and port charges, and also give a quote for shipping a private motor car from the UK through to an Australian location. The services provided should include full preparation for shipment including placing car floor mats, seat covers and Silica Dessicant bags/pillows to help avoid the possibility of condensation damage in the car. The car is packed into a 'sole use' twenty foot ISO Reefer Container and is secured in accordance with manufacturers' recommendations at their private warehouse. The quote should include return haulage of the container to the UK export loading berth, all UK port and handling charges, all export and customs documentation, provision of Bills of Loading to your nominated address once shipment has been effected and freight through to arrival at the port of Melbourne. This type of first-class service costs in excess of £1,000. If you are very thorough you will ask the company for recent letters from satisfied customers who have used the UK to Australia service. Additional charges may include insurance (calculated at 1.5% of the car's value), Australian port/unpacking and quarantine inspection charges which are payable on arrival and are approximately $A600/700. Shipping to Australia takes between 4.5 and 7.5 weeks, depending on the final destination. The additional charges sometimes mean that when all the costs are worked out, it is only worth shipping your motor vehicle if it is a particular type and year. Please see the 'Buying a Car' section for more detailed information and advice on which kinds of cars are worth exporting to Australia for private use.

For furtherinformation about shipping private motor vehicles to Australia, contact: Karman Shipping Services Ltd., Motor Vehicle Shipping Specialists(44 Chestnut Hill, Leighton Buzzard, Bedfordshire LU7 7TR, tel: 01525 851 545 or fax: 01525 850 996).

Importing Pets

Moving your pets to Australia is a complicated and expensive process, on a par with moving yourself. Rules and regulations for pets entering Australia are liable to change but currently state that they must have blood tests, vaccinations and be wormed before they enter the country, and on arrival be quarantined for 30, 60 or 120 days in Australian Customs kennels. The length of the quarantine depends on the country of origin. Dogs and cats from countries recognised as rabies-free (Cyprus, Malta, Norway, Sweden and the United Kingdom) need only have a 30-day quarantine period. Pets from Austria, Belgium, Canada, Denmark, France, Germany, Greece, Italy, Luxembourg, Holland, Spain, Switzerland or the USA must have the maximum quarantine of 120 days. If your pet is from a rabies-free country, it must have been resident in that country for the previous six months before exportation or from birth, and if the pet is from another country, it must have been resident in that country for six months and must also be vaccinated six to twelve months prior to exportation.

Costs for importing pets are high but have not increased for the last 12 years. The approximate cost of shipping a cat to Australia can range from £300 to

£350, and the cost of a dog the size of a labrador, can range from £750 to over £1,000. The cost of the veterinary treatment needed to certify your pet has had regulation blood tests etc. before entering Australia also needs to be taken into account, as do the quarantine costs, payable in Australia, (currently about A$20 per day). If your pet requires the full 120 days in quarantine, you will be liable to pay approximately $A2,400 in quarantine fees alone. Be prepared for a large part of your moving costs being absorbed by that otherindispensable family member, your pet.

As for the household removers, there is also a wide selection of pet movers available, and details are found in *Australian Outlook*.

Useful Addresses
Ladyhaye, Livestock Shipping, Hare Lane, Blindley Heath, Lingfield, Surrey RH7 6JB; tel 01342-832161; fax 01342-834778.
Par Air Livestock Shipping Services (Stanway, Colchester, Essex CO3 5LN, or tel: Amsterdam 020-653 2000).
Worldwide Animal Travel, 43 London Road, Brentwood, Essex CM14 4NN; tel & fax 01277-231611; 0181-522 5592.

Customs
Australian Customs are incredibly strict and this is because to date, Australia has managed to remain free of many of the diseases affecting plants, animals and people such as rabies and foot-and-mouth disease. You are prohibited from bringing any wood or wooden artifacts including furniture, which will either be burned or quarantined and fumigated. Even straw hats and wooden spoons need

to be shown to officials for inspection. You are asked to declare all goods of animal and plant origin, including all fresh, frozen or tinned food, fruit, vegetables and flowers. You are prohibited from even taking fruit and vegetables interstate. If you are travelling interstate by coach, your bus will stop at the border and a customs official bearing a bin will ask you to deposit any fruit or vegetables in order to maintain Australia's clean bill of ecological health. When you arrive in Australia from an international flight, the cabin will be fumigated before you disembark. This is to make sure that no diseases carried on you, your clothing or luggage, can get a free ride into the country. Although it does add an annoying extra ten minutes onto your journey time, and can be slightly irritating (it is a good idea to cover your nose and mouth even though the chemicals have been declared perfectly safe), it is an important part of the process of making sure Australia stays relatively disease-free. Other restricted goods are products made from protected wildlife species, non-approved cordless phones, live animals and weapons and firearms (which are either prohibited or require a permit and safety testing).

You are also prohibited from taking an illicit drugs, including marijuana, into the country. Due to its proximity to South-East Asia, a number of drug rings exist, and Australian Customs have been forced to become very efficient in stopping drugs from entering the country. If you are travelling from Asia, be especially careful - under *no* circumstances bring any illicit drugs with you and *never* agree to carry a package for anyone else. You will be held responsible for whatever you are found with.

In terms of the duty-free allowance, you can bring almost any duty-free article into Australia as long as you can satisfy Customs that they are for your own use and that you will be taking the goods with you when you leave. The duty-free allowance includes one litre of alcohol, 250 cigarettes and up to $400 of duty-free goods. It is your responsibility to declare anything else that may be liable for sales tax or duty.

Buying a Car

Australian cars are right-hand-drive and, since 1989, the importation of left-hand-drive vehicles into Australia has been prohibited. There is a tiny number of LHD vehicles imported before 1989, but in general these cars are not particularly suited to Australian driving conditions, and they are expensive for parts and servicing. Australians seem to drive larger cars than those generally driven in Europe. The old Australian-made Ford Fairlane and Holden Kingswood cars are big, run on six cylinders, and are virtually indestructible, but, as afficionados will testify, the absence of power steering on the older models means that they have the manoeuverability of a large tank. More recently Japanese cars have become very popular for city driving. Hyundais, Subarus, Toyotas, Mitsubishis, Hondas, Daihatsus, Mazdas and Nissans easily outnumber the European cars such as BMWs, Saabs, Audis etc. The costs of importing these cars are much higher than importing cars from South-east Asia. This is largely due to the trading deals which operate between South-east Asian and Australian car manufacturers. The result is a cheaper car which is partially built in the South-east Asian region and then finished in Australia.

Unlike Britain, there is no MOT system in Australia, and so you are much more likely to see older cars, including absolute 'bombs' which are basically holes tied together with bits of rust, clattering through the streets. Many people drive their cars until they or their cars die because there is no compulsory vehicle standards check unless you are importing a car or if you let your car's registration lapse. If you let a car's registration expire, renewal of that car's registration cannot be given until the car has been over the 'pits', which means the police do a thorough safety and standards test on the car. Usually, if a car is put over the pits, the police will issue a list of repairs and/or modifications which must be carried out on the car in order for registration to be renewed. This step can be avoided, however, if registration payments are not allowed to fall into arrears. Having said this, the police are often on the lookout for vehicles in a bad state of disrepair and have the authority to pull over any car and carry out a safety and standards check if they think there is something obviously amiss with a particular vehicle. Frequently, this kind of test results in a police Yellow Sticker being affixed to the car's windscreen which basically means the car is not roadworthy and cannot be driven until the car is passed, having gone through the pits. The lack of a strict MOT system, combined with the fact that most young people of driving age own their own cars, means that the used car business in Australia is booming.

The procedures of buying a new car and buying a used car are slightly different, and so it is helpful to deal with the procedures and issues involved with each separately.

Buying a new car: The first piece of advice is really just common sense — shop around. Look at the car section of the classified advertisements and visit sales rooms. Do not allow yourself to be pushed around, or more subtly manipulated, by the salespeople, particularly in terms of making a quick decision or of paying more than you intended for a lot of optional extras you did not really want. Consyl Publishing have a *New Car Buyers' Guide* which provides information on which cars are faster, more powerful, less expensive, roomier and more economical than others as well as mechanical specifications, opinions based on personal experience and a summary of vital statistics such as length, wheelbase, width, height, turning circle, fuel tank capacity and towing ability. It also outlines which cars are available with automatic transmission, which have fuel injection, and which have two or three year warranties, making it easier to work out which car would best suit your budget.

Besides buying a new car for personal use, two out of every five new cars bought in Australia are registered in company names. You may wish to buy a car for business purposes, and Ford, Holden, Toyota and Mitsubishi all provide special business versions of their popular models. Ford has introduced a one-stop-shop operating lease which enables fleet owners to select cars from Ford's range and run them on a virtual fixed-cost basis through a fully maintained operating lease. Under this scheme, the owner has the use of the car for a set term and distance, and is covered for fully scheduled servicing and also for unscheduled maintenance items such as wheel alignment and the replacement of windscreen wiper blades. Ford can tailor the lease to cover registration, new tyres, a petrol credit card and management reporting, including fringe benefits tax.

When buying a car, as when buying a house, the advertisements use abbreviated terms which are worth knowing, e.g., abs (anti-lock braking system), ac (air conditioning), at (automatic transmission), cc (cruise control), cl (central locking), ps (power steering), pw (power windows), srs (supplementary restraint system — airbag), mags (alloy wheels). In addition, although cars names may be the same as UK models, they are often used for totally different models in Australia, or the models themselves may be completely different.

Used Cars: Given that most new cars depreciate greatly in value as soon as they are driven out of the showroom, many people choose to buy used cars. Similar to Britain, it is possible to buy a used car from a dealer or through private sales usually delivered in state newspapers, often under the classified section *Auto Mart*. Many dealers in new cars also deal in used cars, and although they may

be more expensive, they are also usually the safest places to buy from as you will be more likely to buy a car that has been serviced at the dealer's workshop, and it is more likely to be accompanied by some sort of dealer's warranty. State and Territory governments in Australia have specific legislation regarding used cars bought from dealers. It is illegal for dealers to sell used cars of a certain price (which varies from state to state) without a warranty, the terms of which also differ between states. Some dealers may give, at no extra cost to the customer, an additional warranty on their used cars.

If on arrival in Australia you want to avoid hiring a car which would be expensive, but want time to look around for the perfect used car, or if you are travelling round Australia on a working visa there is another option. There are firms that specialise in selling cars with a guaranteed buy back agreement. They will supply the vehicle complete with the necessary roadworthiness certificate or 'pink slip'. One such company with over eleven years experience is Mach 1 Autos based in Sydney (495 New Canterbury Road, Dulwich Hill, Sydney NSW 2203; tel 02-569 3374; fax 02-569 2307). Mach 1 are the originators of the buy-back system.

Car theft is common in most capital cities in Australia, so if you choose to buy a car from a private sale, there may be a risk that the car is stolen. In order to ensure that your prospective new/used car is neither stolen nor otherwise financially encumbered, you can check the car against government registers of encumbered vehicles. The addresses and phone numbers of these registers are given below:

NT — contact NSW

VIC — Vehicles Security Register, Cnr Princess & Drummond Streets, Carlton VIC 3053, tel: (03) 348-1222.

QLD — QLD Motor Vehicles Security Register, 7th floor, 126 Margaret Street, Brisbane QLD 4000, or PO Box 38, Brisbane QLD 4001, tel: (07) 227-7111 or freephone 008-177 883.

SA — Vehicle Security Register, 60 Wakefield Street, Adelaide SA 5000, or PO Box 616, Adelaide SA 5001, tel: (08) 232-0800.

NSW — Register of Encumbered Vehicles, 47 Scott Street, Liverpool NSW.

WA — Register of Encumbered Vehicles, 6th floor, 251 Hay Street, East Perth WA 6004, or PO Box 6355, East Perth WA 6004, tel: (09) 222-0711 or freephone 008-198 333.

TAS — Road Transport Tasmania, Registration Section, Security Interests, 1 Collins Street, Hobart TAS 7000, or GPO Box 1002K, Hobart TAS 7001, tel: (002) 389-289.

It is also possible to have an authorised, qualified mechanic from one of the automobile associations check over a used car. It can pay to join one of the motoring organisations before buying a car so that one of their mechanics can go over it with a fine-tooth comb and give you honest, independent advice. There are federal safety regulations governing safety standards for cars such as seat belts, emission standards, tyres, engine noise etc., and states may also have individual extra legislation. If the vehicle doesn't conform with the safety standards, then it may not be registered until modifications have been made. Enquiries should be directed to the transport authority of the state concerned. It is advisable not to sign a deal offering a free vehicle check as this may only be done *after* you've bought the car and you can end up stuck with the vehicle no matter what problems come to light. Consyl Publishing also have a useful publication, *The Used Car Buyers' Guide* which covers all kinds of cars, advice on how to inspect cars, a guide to the codes of Australian models, a survey of the best value cars, and information about finance and insurance.

If you are trying to decide whether to take your existing car to Australia or sell it and buy one there, you must take into account the costs involved with importation. While European cars are prestigious, this is because they are subject to luxury tax, and the cost of parts and servicing reflects this attitude. It may be more simple to sell your car in your present country of residence and buy one on your arrival in Australia.

Motor Insurance

Once you have bought your car, it is a relief to know that Third Party Insurance is compulsory in Australia, and that the cost of this is included in the registration fees for the vehicle paid to the State/Territory government. This covers insurance for injury done to anyone else, but insurance for property damage is voluntary and is handled by private insurance companies. About 80% of Australian car owners are also privately insured. This section deals with insurance available in addition to the compulsory Third Party Injury Insurance obtained from private insurance companies.

Insurance premiums are higher in urban areas, where the risk of accident and/ or theft is calculated as being higher, but car insurance is generally cheaper than equivalent policies available in the UK. In Australia, the car is insured, not just the driver, and so anyone driving your car with your permission (providing they have a full Australian or equivalent licence and the car is privately owned) is covered by your insurance. At the time of writing, an average cost for private insurance and registration for a private car is approximately $650 per annum, but obviously this can vary greatly from company to company, state to state etc. Insurance can also be more expensive if you have to borrow money to buy the car rather than if you pay cash. You should check with the insurance companies what their policy is on this matter when you are shopping around for insurance and/or a car. There are basically two types of private insurance available, Third Party Property (as distinct from the compulsory Third Party Injury) which covers damage your car does to other cars and/or property (which does not belong to you), and Comprehensive insurance, which covers damage done to your own car as well as other people's property. On both kinds of policy you will be expected to pay an excess on any claim for damage for which you apply. This is the amount of money you must pay for any single insurance claim. It is usually for the first $200-$300 of a claim, but may be greater if the driver is under 25 or has had previous accidents. It is really to prevent people claiming for minor things, as the cost to the insurance company is not much different whether it is processing a $200 or a $2,000 claim. It is possible with some companies to pay extra when the insurance policy is initially taken out, or when it is renewed, to reduce the excess or to cut it out altogether.

Third Party Property Insurance: If you inadvertently stepped on the accelerator instead of the brake as you were approaching a red light at a busy intersection, smashed into the back of a brand spanking new BMW, careered off that into the middle of the intersection right into the path of a truck carefully packed with various treasures bound for Sotheby's Auctions, which in turn spun you out of the intersection through a garden wall and into the swimming pool of a prominent politician (stranger things have happened!), Third Party Property Insurance (TPPI) would cover the cost of all the damage done *by* your car, but not the damage done *to* your car. Given that TPPI can cost less than $100 and rarely exceeds $200, it is difficult and even frightening to comprehend why some drivers do not bother to take out even this most basic of private insurance policies.

Comprehensive Insurance: Comprehensive cover costs more than TTPI and the average can range between $275-$400, though it can also be either considerably more than $400 or less than $275 in certain circumstances. Insurance companies charge according to particular factors such as:
age: of both you and your car (if you are less than 25 years old, you will pay more).
residence: do you live in a high risk area? .
experience: how long have you been driving?
accident record: do you have one?
sex: in certain age groups in particular, females have fewer accident claims than males.
cost: of the car.
make and model: some have statistically more accidents or are more expensive to repair.
business or private: business cars are more likely to be involved in accidents than privately owned vehicles.
payment: statistics show that cars with money owed on them borrowed from certain types of loans tend to be involved in more accident claims (you will pay less for a car bought with cash).
trailer/caravan: you may need to get a separate policy for these as some policies do not cover damage caused by your trailer/caravan side-swiping another vehicle.
Comprehensive insurers offer a no claims bonus (NCB) which means that if you do not make a claim you get a bonus, usually a 20% discount, after the first year of insurance. The bonus rises by a further 10% each consecutive year, providing they are also claim free, until it reaches a maximum which is generally 60%. That is, if you are insured for five years without a claim, you only have to pay 40% of the insurance premium. If you do make a claim, your bonus will be reduced, usually by 20%, but this can be built up again by 10% for each claim-free year.
Companies differ in their approach to NCBs. Some reduce the NCB a certain

amount for every claim, others reduce the claim for a 12 month period by a set amount, which means you do not suffer further reduction of the NCB for any subsequent accidents in the same year. Most give preferential treatment to their long-time customers with a record of no claims, and allow them to have one claim without losing any NCB, or even allow more than one claim if these occur over a sufficiently long period of time. Some companies will not reduce the bonus if you can identify the other person that caused the accident. This does not cover the other kinds of accident such as the one in which a kangaroo decided to wrestle with a little old 1975 Toyota Corolla while it was zipping along a country road at 110km/h. The kangaroo did $1,800 damage to the front of the car, the owner lost his NCB, and the beast (i.e., the roo, not the owner) did not even have the decency to lie down and die, it just jumped off merrily into the bush, apparently unscathed. Many companies do not reduce the NCB if the claim is only for a damaged windscreen, but many limit the windscreen claims to one per year. Some companies may offer a no claim discount on a second car bought for the use of someone else in the family if your own NCB history is good.

Your insurance policy will either be for the agreed or market value which applies to how much you will be paid if your car is written off after an accident. Agreed-value policy means a definite value is decided upon at the time at which the policy is taken out and is then re-set every time the policy is renewed (usually every year). In the event that the car is written off, you are paid the agreed value minus the excess. A market-value policy means you are paid whatever the car is worth at the time of the accident. If the car has depreciated in value, you will get less than you paid for it, but if the car is now worth more, you will be paid accordingly. Some companies will pay for a brand new replacement car if your new car is written off less than a year after its purchase. In this case, your car will be replaced with one of the same make and model, even if these have gone up in price since you bought the original. The message is certainly to shop around. Go through the yellow pages telephone directory and phone insurance companies for quotes and deals. You should also take evidence of your present car insurance arrangements with you as any special benefits to which you are entitled in your present country of residence may be taken into account in Australia.

If you have an accident in which you suffer personal injury, it may be possible to make a Motor Vehicle Personal Injury Claim. It is important to contact your GP regularly so that he/she may keep detailed medical records (often used as evidence in such claims) and also a solicitor who specialises in such claims and will be able to assist you make a claim. You should check the yellow pages phone book to see which solicitors advertise as specialising in motor vehicle injury claims. An example of the cost of comprehensive insurance on a 1988 Mitsubishi Colt Sedan, valued at $5,100, as at 24 May 1994 for private usage, with a NCB of 60% and basic excess removed is $269.30 for 12 months. This is based on a comprehensive policy offered by RAC Insurance Pty. Ltd.

Useful Addresses

The biggest insurance companies offer both Car Insurance and Home & Content Insurance. The largest national insurance companies in Australia (which also cover boat, business and life insurance) are listed below:

FAI
Perth — 186 St George's Tce, Perth WA 6000.
Sydney — FAI Insurance Building, 185 Macquarie St, Sydney NSW 2000.
Melbourne — 422 Collins St, Melbourne VIC 3000.
Brisbane — FAI Insurance Building, 100 Eagle St, Brisbane QLD 4000.
Adelaide — 101 Flinders Street, Adelaide SA 5000.

National tel: 13-1000
GIO
Perth — 66 St George's Tce, Perth WA 6000.
Sydney — 50 Clarence St, Sydney NSW 2000.
Melbourne — 480 Collins St, Melbourne VIC 3000.
Brisbane — 200 Mary St, Brisbane QLD 4000.
Adelaide — 101 Pirie St, Adelaide SA 5000.
National tel: 13-1010
MMI
Perth — 15-17 William St, Perth WA 6000, tel: (09) 261-0221.
Sydney — MMI Centre, 2 Market St, Sydney NSW 2000, tel: (02) 390-6222.
Melbourne — 380 St Kilda Road, Melbourne VIC 3000, tel: (03) 685-0555.
Brisbane — 370 Queen St, Brisbane QLD 4000, tel: (07) 212-2222.
Adelaide — 136 Greenhill Rd, Hayley SA 5000, tel: (08) 372-6444.
National Mutual
Perth — 111 St George's Tce, Perth WA 6000, tel: (09) 327-7677.
Sydney — 44 Market St, Sydney NSW 2000, (02) 563-3333.
Melbourne — National Mutual Centre, 447 Collins St, Melbourne VIC 3000,
    tel: (03) 616-3911.
Brisbane — 144 Edward St, Brisbane QLD 4000, tel: (07) 227-3227.
Adelaide — 80 King William St, Adelaide SA 5000, tel: (08) 217-9666.
NZI
Perth — 218 St George's Tce, Perth WA 6000, tel: (09) 322-5888.
Sydney — 10 Spring St, Sydney NSW 2000, tel: (02) 212-7444.
Melbourne — 50 Queen St, Melbourne VIC 3000, tel: (03) 616-9509.
Brisbane — 215 Adelaide St, Brisbane QLD 4000, tel: (07) 221-8633.
Adelaide — 113 King William St, Adelaide SA 5000, tel: (08) 213-4222.
RAC
Perth — 228 Adelaide Tce, Perth WA 6000, tel: (09) 421-4444.
Sydney — 89 Macquarie St, Sydney NSW 2000, tel: (02) 233-2355.
Melbourne — RACV, 22 Little Collins St, Melbourne VIC 3000, tel: (03)
    790-2000.
Brisbane — RACQ, 30 St Paul's Tce, Fort Vy QLD 4000, (07) 361-2444.
Adelaide — RAA, 41 Hindmarsh Sq, Adelaide SA 5000, (08) 202-4500.

Useful Publications

Australian Outlook as mentioned above is an extremely useful monthly newspaper
    which gives invaluable infomation on the current situation in Australia in
    terms of migration, housing, employment and cost of living. In addition, the
    list of advertisers is handy for quick and easy access to information about
    related services you require. Subscription for 12 issues costs £3.50 and is
    available from Consyl Publishing & Publicity Ltd. (Buckhurst Road, Bexhill-
    on-Sea, East Sussex, TN40 1QF).
Budget Travel Australia (BTA) is an independent publication available every
    four months throughout the UK and Europe. It provides relevant information
    on travelling to and within Australia, visas, useful contacts and suggestions
    for employment and accommodation. It is aimed at the young backpacker
    and working traveller, but also contains useful regional information for the
    migrant. You pick up a free copy from the Australian High Commission or
    you can order it by post from Red Sky Distribution (70 Brunswick Street,
    Stockton-on-Tees, Cleveland, TS18 1DW) including a s.a.e.
Coping With Australia, by Eleanor Greet, published in 1990 by Basil Blackwell,
    contains useful information and hints.

Daily Life

Schools and Education

Australian education is roughly equivalent to education within the UK. There are both private and state school systems in Australia, as in Britain; however a wide range of private schools at the upper end of the market does not exist in Australia. There is generally no problem in enrolling children at their local state school, or even another of their choice. On the other hand private schools usually have long waiting lists which may extend years into the future.

Australian Outlook publishes a booklet called *Choosing a School for your Child* specifically aimed at emigrants to New South Wales, Victoria and Queensland, details of which are given below. These publications give extremely useful information regarding the kinds of schools available in these states, and answers the questions that tend to arise when one is faced with the need to select the most appropriate school.

In general, however, the system is relatively simple and the quality of education offered at the various levels is high.

Unlike many countries in the northern hemisphere, Australia's academic year follows the calendar year, so it runs from January to December, and as the period around Christmas is during Australia's summer this is when the long summer holidays (usually six or seven weeks) are taken.

The Structure of the Education System

In both the private and state systems, primary education in Australia takes six or seven years, depending on the state/territory legislation, and secondary education takes either five or six years. Wherever you are in Australia, the combined length of primary and secondary education is twelve years. Western Australia, Queensland, South Australia and the Northern Territory offer seven years of primary school and five years of secondary school. New South Wales, Victoria and the Australian Capital Territory offer six years of primary and secondary education, and Tasmania offers either six or seven years of primary and either six or five years of secondary, depending on the location of the school and the age of the student.

Primary & Secondary Education. State primary schools are almost invariably co-educational, while some private schools may offer single-sex education at the primary level. The starting age of primary school varies by state and there is a table below outlining this and other information about Australian education. Education is compulsory for Australian children until the end of their third/fourth year of secondary education at 15/16 years of age, after which the final two years of secondary education (known as 11 & 12/Upper School) are voluntary. In recent years, the upper school retention rate has dramatically increased as jobs are proving more difficult to find for unqualified young Australians, and now up to as many as 76% of a school's secondary students can be expected to stay on and complete years 11 and 12. The retention rate can, however, vary dramatically from state to state, as the table below shows:

Region	1992 %	1993 %
New South Wales	68.5	70.6
Victoria	81.1	79.1
Queensland	85.0	82.9
South Australia	92.7	86.3
Western Australia	72.8	75.6
Tasmania	60.2	60.6
Northern Territory	56.7	47.5
Canberra	97.2	94.2
Australia Overall	77.1	76.6

Although the national retention rate has decreased by 0.5% over the year 1992/3, the table clearly shows that this has not been the trend in all states. New South Wales, Western Australia and Tasmania all experienced retention rate growth, while the other states and territories saw their retention rates decrease. This can be attributed to a number of factors, two of which are the employment situation and the quality of education (both the teaching and facilities). If a state or territory is experiencing real economic growth which is reflected in the subsequent expansion of the employment market, more students will leave school as early as possible because they have a good chance of getting a job or apprenticeship. Alternatively, the employment market, while experiencing growth, may only see the creation of extra jobs in sectors requiring tertiary qualifications, such as teaching, law, physiotherapy etc. In this case, the retention rate of a state/territory may be very high as students realise that they need to complete the full five or six years of high school in order to enter further education.

Secondary Education. The most common type of secondary school, known in Australia as high school, is the comprehensive school which offers a wide range of subjects. Often in order to attract government funding, schools choose to establish specialist programmes in music, theatre studies, art or sport, and offer scholarships to talented students from all over the state/territory. High school students tend to enjoy modern surroundings and facilities, and are taught a variety of subjects from commercial to home economics, metalwork to technical drawing. In many high schools, students in the first year must take the whole range of subjects available despite personal preferences in order to try and help them develop wider interests or recognise previously undiscerned talents. This means that, regardless of gender, all students will have to study cooking, sewing, woodwork, metalwork, art, music, drama and sport, as well as the core subjects of maths, science, social studies (geography and history) and English. As students progress through the high school system, they are allowed to become gradually more specialised. In the final two years, students have complete autonomy over what subjects they would like to study, and the choices are usually much wider.

Special needs children. Special schools also exist for physically and/or mentally handicapped children, and within the state system, children with learning disabilities are often offered special tuition within the regular primary or high school situation.

The Academic Year. Most schools begin their academic year at either the end of January or the beginning of February, and the year ends before Christmas in December. The year is divided into four ten-week terms, and between the middle terms there are holidays of approximately two weeks. There are usually no mid-term breaks. The starting ages for both primary and secondary schools vary between states and territories, but in general, the fundamental structure is similar nationwide. You will also notice that the secondary education authorities of New South Wales, Queensland, Western Australia, Tasmania and the Australian Capital Territory all issue certificates to students who have completed their compulsory education. These certificates are especially important if the student wishes to leave school at that stage and enter the full-time workforce, as this is really the only authorised qualification he/she will have. In general, students leaving at this point will have managed to find themselves an apprenticeship with a particular industry or trade, whether that be hairdressing or spray-painting and panel-beating.

Fees & Uniforms. State school education is free, whereas tuition fees are payable at private schools. Parents do have to pay the costs of books and uniforms for both private and state schools, but on the whole the uniform expenses are far less at a state school than those at private schools. In addition, depending on the state school, uniform may or may not be compulsory. It is very likely that the state school uniform will seem very casual by British or European standards. Below is an approximate table of costs for both primary and secondary state school uniforms.

Item of Clothing	Boys (Primary)	Girls (Primary)	Boys (Secondary)	Girls (Secondary)
Hat	$10	$6	$20	$15
Dress	n/a	$30	n/a	n/a
Shirt	$20	$20	$25	$27
Shorts (boys)	$14.50	n/a	$27	n/a
Shorts (unisex)	$20	$20	n/a	$24
Skirt	n/a	$20	n/a	$32
Trousers	n/a	n/a	$30	n/a
Sports shorts	$8	n/a	$10	n/a
sports skirt	n/a	$12	n/a	$18
Socks & Shoes	$30	$30	$50	$50

Note that in primary schools, hats are provided free to all pre-school and first year students and are usually of a legionnaire-type design. Secondary schools tend to have the Australian Akubra-type hats (wide-brimmed and made of felt) or straw hats. Factor 15+ sunscreen is also provided free to all pre-school and year one students. Shirts tend to have short sleeves, although long-sleeved shirts are available for secondary school students, and are generally loose fitting to be comfortable and to keep the students cool. They tend to be made of tightly woven fabric which reduces the amount of UV penetration. Many schools also allow both male and female students to wear tracksuits (usually in approved school colours) or jeans during winter. Uniforms can be bought new, but most schools also have second-hand shops where one can pick up uniforms and text books in good condition at a reduced price.

Independent & Private Education. Independent or private schools account for 25% of Australia's 9,865 schools and are becoming an increasingly popular choice despite the often considerable expenses involved. Private school fees usually begin at around $2,000 per year per child, but may go up to as much as $7,000. The non-Government schools are usually church schools associated with the Catholic Church or the Church of England. In addition a number of independent non-government schools have been established which are associated with the Baptist Church, non-denominational churches, the Jewish Church, and other religions such as Islam and Buddhism. The latest figures from the Australian Bureau of Statistics 1993 Schools Survey indicate that during the year June 1992 to June 1993, an extra 5,436 students enrolled at private schools whereas 6,027 students left the state school sector. This reflects an enrolment increase of 0.6% at private schools and a decrease of 0.3% at state schools. The increase of enrolments in the private education sector can be attributed to the fact that there were 82 government school closures during that year, of which 79 were in Victoria. Victoria's education system has had turbulent times recently, and in 1992/3, the Victorian Government, as an attempt to implement a debt-reduction strategy, overhauled its education system with the result that a disproportionate number of state schools were closed. Many parents feel that their children are likely to get an enhanced education at a private school, as the teacher-student ratio is usually lower. Class sizes in Australian schools average 32-35, but may be significantly higher or lower than this, depending on the school's budget and resources. Upper-school classes also tend to be much smaller, and in private schools the upper school class sizes are often 15-20 students, while in state schools the size is more likely to be 18-25. There are, however, some outstanding state schools which consistently achieve standards of excellence in academic, sporting and/or arts fields. It is not difficult to find them out as their students will often attract media attention in suburban newpapers. To get a list of state schools with excellent reputations, you can also ask locals which schools they think are the best as they or their children will probably be speaking from experience. As a source of general information just contact the local Education Authority, via the Department of Education in your state/territory, who will be able to give you a list of private and state schools, and perhaps also tell you which state schools have reputations for consistently high academic standards.

Extra-Curricular Activities. Typically, Australian students are involved in a number of extra-curricular school activities such as camps, excursions and socials (discos). Many schools have a concert band or orchestra, a choir, a dance troupe and/or dramatic society which perform throughout the year.

Procedure for Grading New Arrivals. If you have children currently enrolled in the UK or European education system, you should provide recent school reports, including a reference from their teacher or Head Teacher, and samples of their work so that any school at which you wish to enrol your child can have a clear indication of what grade to start them at. Ordinarily, children are be placed in a grade according to their age. However, children who are significantly advanced or behind the level of work being done by other children of the same age will be placed according to their ability. If this situation occurs, it is extremely rare that the child will be placed with children more than a year older or younger.

Parents & Citizens Committees in Schools. Parents can expect to be more involved in their children's education than they are probably used to. Every Australian school has its own committee which consists of parents, teachers and student representatives, known as a Parents' & Citizens Committee (P&C). These committees raise funds for school excursions or tours, and school equipment, and assist in the administration of some aspects of the school, such as the canteen. The Australian school canteen is quite different to the British school canteen, as hot lunches cannot generally be bought. The canteen is usually just a small building from which students purchase their lunch (but don't generally enter), and food tends to consist of sandwiches (including toasted sandwiches), rolls, pies, pasties, drinks, ice-creams and light snacks. Recently, parents have become more concerned about their children's health, and many P&C committees have designed healthy, yet economical and tasty, lunch menus which have seen chips and crisps banned in favour of less fattening alternatives. P&C committees also decide on issues such as school uniform (including the design), homework policies and behaviour management policies.

Further Education

Universities

Like the schools, the university academic year follows the calendar year, and enrolments usually take place from September-November the year previous to commencement. Australian further education institutions offer a wide choice of subjects and qualifications. Currently, for a population of 17 million, there are about 51 universities, which, according to Mr Kim Beazley, the current Minister for Education, is as many as the country's economy can support. The vast majority of tertiary institutions are state-funded, at a cost to the government of approximately $40,000 per four year degree. This is second only to the USA's spending of approximately $US13,639 per annum as the Australian government spends an average of $US10,943 per annum on its tertiary students. However, unlike the USA, Australian education is relatively cheap.

Fees & other costs. Until 1989, tertiary education for university students was absolutely free in terms of tuition fees. In 1990, however, the system changed so that students are liable to pay fees called a Higher Education Contributions Scheme (HECS). This is really a nominal sum, approximately $1164 per semester of tertiary education, which is automatically paid on the student's behalf by the government during the course of their degree or diploma and is then paid back in the form of tax (at an additional rate of 2-4% above the normal tax rate) when that graduate earns more than $27,748 per annum. In effect, although you may pay back a HECS debt over a number of years, because it is deducted as tax, it is not really as painful as having to pay the amount up front. There is an option which allows you to pay back your HECS debt at any time, which enables you to avoid accruing interest on your debt. If you pay the amount at the beginning of each academic year, you are also eligible for a substantial discount of the amount payable. Students who opt to complete an additional honours year on top of pass degree can be eligible for HECS exemption for that year, which is known as a HECS scholarship. Students enrolled in higher degrees can also be exempt from HECS and may also be eligible for significant government and/or university funding. Below is a table of Higher Education Contributions correct at the time of writing:

Option 1	Payment up front	$873 per semester
Option 2	Taxable income below $27 748	HECS assessment of debt nil
	$27,748-$31,532	2% of taxable income
	$31,532-$44,146	3% of taxable income
	$44.146 or more	4% of taxable income

In addition to tuition fees, students can expect to pay between $500 and $1,000 per year on text books, depending on the course, but many institutions have excellent second hand bookshops where texts can be found at cheaper prices. Students are also charged fees to join their student organisations, known as unions, associations or guilds. These organisations provide, and are involved in, the administration of a large number of benefits and facilities, including sporting facilities, discounts, the issuing of student identification cards, insurance cover, photocopying, bookshops, catering, social functions such as balls, and student newspapers. Membership costs range from $65-$300 per annum, and are usually compulsory. However, if a student objects to joining the institution's student organisation on ethical or political grounds (e.g., they do not agree with some of the association's policies and practices), they may be allowed to state the name of a registered charity to which their association fees will be paid instead.

Choosing a University. Selecting a university can be very difficult as most capital cities house a number of different institutions. Most universities try to develop a reputation of excellence in particular fields of research. For example the University of Adelaide has a reputation for having a first class Department of English Literature while the University of Western Australia houses an excellent Physics Department. It is possible to contact each of the institutions and obtain a prospectus (though most good university libraries will hold a number of these from a range of universities throughout the country) in order to see what they have to offer, but there is also a *Good Universities Guide* published by *Australian Outlook*, which can help you make a more informed choice. The guide is published annually and is available from the Readers Department, (Australian Outlook, 3 Buckhurst Road, Bexhill-on-Sea, East Susses TN40 1QF). This book covers all 51 universities in Australia, giving a brief summary of each, including breadth of course offerings, depth, toughness to get in, admissions flexibility, opportunities for adults, student-staff ratios, gender balance, research track record, affluence, graduate salaries, employment prospects, library quality, popularity with fee-paying students and tuition fees. Details of various courses run by the different institutions, the entry marks required for each course, and entry procedures for the various courses are also given as well as a rating of Australia's top ten universities and details of comparative graduate employment rates and starting salaries. Although similar publications exist in Australia, this book has been specifically written for the British market, and as a consequence everything which needs explaining is detailed in familiar language.

The table given below shows the top twelve universities based on a survey of 150 major companies around Australia which rated the quality of graduates they had employed:

1   Monash University (Melbourne)
2   University of Melbourne
3   University of Sydney
4   University of New South Wales (Sydney)
5   Macquarie University (Sydney)
6   Australian National University (Canberra)
7   University of Queensland (Brisbane)
8   Sydney University of Technology
9   Royal Melbourne Institute of Technology
10 Swinburne University of Technology
11 University of Western Australia (Perth)

Readers should note that these ratings are particularly business-oriented, which may not give a true reflection of the overall rating of the university. A recent report by the Organisation for Economic Co-operation and Development (OECD) ranked Australia fourth behind the USA, Finland and Japan on entry into full-time tertiary education and also fourth, behind Canada, Norway and the USA, in the percentage of graduates produced. The report also found that, of all degrees awarded, engineering accounts for approximately 5.3% of degrees conferred by Australian institutions compared with 22.8% in Japan, 18.9% in Germany and 7.1% in the USA (the OECD average is 12.1%). In natural sciences, however, Australia is a world leader with 14.1% compared with 9.1% in Germany, 4.7% in the USA and 2.9% in Japan.

Austudy Grants
Australian university students usually survive financially on scholarships, part-

time jobs, Austudy, which is the name of the national student grant system in Australia, or their parents (about 50% of all university students still live with their parents throughout their academic careers). Only about 33% of students receive Austudy, which is designed as an income support scheme rather than a full living allowance. Many students are not eligible for any Austudy allowance whatsoever, and relatively few are eligible for the full Austudy allowance. The rules governing eligibility for Austudy are complicated and adjusted to suit each student's situation. The Department of Employment, Education and Training (DEET), which administers Austudy, has collaborated with the National Union of Students (NUS) to produce a guide to Austudy. The guide is free and available from any Commonwealth Employment Service (CES) office or student organisation office. If you receive an offer of a place at any tertiary insitution, you will automatically be sent a copy of the booklet. Basically your eligibility for Austudy and the amount you receive will depend on four factors. Firstly, you must be doing an approved full-time course (almost all university courses are approved). Secondly, your income and assets, including those of your parents, family and, if applicable, spouse, will be valued in order to determine your true financial situation. Thirdly, the period of time you have been enrolled in full-time study of approved courses to date: and lastly your age and living circumstances will affect the amount you get. You can apply for Austudy through centres around the country, and authorities recommend you should always apply as the rules are so complicated that it is not really possible to predict whether you will be eligible or not. The Austudy booklet tables the relevant payments.

If you are eligible for Austudy, you are also allowed to earn an income up to $6,000 per annum without affecting the allowance. If you earn above this amount, your Austudy payments will be reduced in proportion to the amount over $6,000 that you earn.

TAFEs. Besides the universities, further education is also available at Technical and Further Education Centres (TAFEs) which tend to offer more vocational and bridging qualifications than universities do. There are approximately 230 TAFE institutions in Australia, but many of these have additional campuses and training centres. For example, in South Australia there are 19 TAFE institutions, but 120 other teaching centres. Some universities also house TAFE divisions. Every state and territory has a large number of TAFE colleges and centres, which tend to be concentrated in the capital cities, though some are situated in the major regional areas. More than 1,000,000 students are enrolled in a TAFE course, though many of these are part-time students. Many school leavers who want to upgrade their skills, or adults who wish to retrain or re-enter the workforce, attend TAFE couses, which can be taken on a full-time or part-time basis. TAFEs specialise in trade training and pre-apprenticeships in a diverse range of trades, such as building, vehicle, metal, electrical and automotive trades, electronics, plumbing, printing, catering, gardening, dairy farming, hair-dressing, textiles, jewellery and watch-making, as well as secretarial and business studies. Both evening and day classes are usually held for most courses and School Certificate and Higher School Certificate subjects, for mature students. TAFEs also offer small group classes for people wishing to learn better reading, writing, spelling or mathematical skills, or to learn the English Language. There are also a number of short-term part-time courses available in subjects like Bar Service, Typing, Commercial Floristry and Woolclassing.

The standard of TAFE courses should not be considered to be inferior to university courses, but in reality university qualifications tend to be more prestigious than TAFE qualifications, simply because it is more difficult to get into university than TAFE colleges. The cost of fees, however, is significantly lower at TAFE colleges, and an average cost of tuition fees would be from $500-

$600 a year for a full-time course. Fee-exemptions may be given to students in receipt of Austudy or similar benefits, and there are concession rates for low-income earners. In 1992, the West Australian government waived all fees for 1992 school-leavers who enrolled directly in TAFE. Usually TAFE colleges will allow you to pay fees in instalments. If you attend a TAFE college, you are still liable to pay HECS (see above).

In a recent survey conducted by Mrs Susan Dawe of the National Centre for Vocational Education, nearly 87% of TAFE students rated their lecturer's knowledge of course content and teaching skills as either 'very good' or 'good'.Only 6.6% of the 25,000 students surveyed were dissatisfied with the time and day on which their classes were offered.

Foreigners at Australian Universities

Australian universities are now tending to serve countries beyond its own shores. In particular, students from the South-east Asian region make up a significant proportion of student populations, and tend to study business, commerce and economic subjects as well as medicine and law. At the time of writing, there are more than 70,000 overseas students in Australia. Half of these are studying at a secondary level, attending short intensive English language courses (ELICOS) in public or private institutions, enrolled on TAFE courses, or are preparing for university through special bridging courses. The other half are at university. Between 1990 and 1991, the number of overseas students attending Australian universities grew by 50%, and some universities now hold graduation ceremonies in Singapore and Kuala Lumpur, to cater for the increasing and significant number of southeast Asian alumni.

The Australian government requires all institutions which accept overseas students to register with state authorities in order to assure management and financial stability, and educational quality. If you wish to study in Australia, you will need to apply for a Student Visa, and this cannot be issued until you can provide evidence that you have been accepted for a course of study and have paid for at least one half of the first year's annual fee for your course. It is important to note that you cannot change from Visitor status to Student status while you are in Australia, but that application for a Student Visa can only be made in your own country of residence. In order to retain your visa, you must have a satisfactory record of attendance at your institution, and achieve satisfactory academic results. Upon completion of your course, you must leave Australia when your Student Visa expires, and the Australian Government is incredibly strict about this.

In terms of fees, obviously overseas students cannot enjoy the privilege of government-funded education offered to Australian citizens and permanent residents. Universities differ in how much they charge overseas students, and fees are dependent upon the demand for the course, the location of the institution and its level of prestige. The government sets a minimum fee structure for each course, but institutions are free to charge above this level, which they frequently do. Fees also vary greatly between disciplines. For example an Arts course may cost between $7,500-$10,000 per annum whereas a Science course may cost from $11,000-$14,500. Professional courses are the most expensive: Engineering costs between $11,000 and $15,000, Dentistry from $15,000-$23,000, and Medicine between $19,000 and $26,000 per annum.

Most universities do have some student accommodation associated with the campus, and overseas students are generally given priority for housing. Accommodation can cost between $60 and $150 per week, depending on whether it is self-catering and on the type of accommodation.

Overseas Students Societies. There are many societies specifically for overseas students at universities, and you will usually find a society or association consisting of other students from your neck of the woods. These associations often organise camps, social functions, speakers and orientation programmes, and can be worth contacting before you arrive at the institution. You should contact the student organisation at the relevant institution for information regarding student societies and clubs.

Useful Addresses

Choosing a School (NSW, QLD or VIC) magazines are available from the Subscription Department, Australian Outlook, 3 Buckhurst Road, Bexhill-on-Sea, East Sussex TN40 1QF and the prices are £5.95, £4.90 or £6.50 respectively.

International Education Branch, Department of Education, PO Box 826, Woden ACT 2606.

State Admissions Centres:

NSW & ACT — Universities Admissions Centre (UAC), Locked Bag 500, PO Lidcombe, NSW 2141, tel: (02)-330 7200.

QLD — Queensland Tertiary Admissions Centre, PO Box 1331, Milton QLD 4064, tel: (07)-368 1166.

SA — South Australian Tertiary Admissions Centre (SATAC), PO Box 2, Rundle Mall, Adelaide SA 5000, tel: (08)-223 5233.

VIC — Victorian Tertiary Admissions Centre (VTAC), Suite B, 40 Park Street, South Melbourne VIC 3205, tel: (03)-690 7977.

TAS & NT — Students must apply directly to the admissions offices of the relevant institutions. Contact the institutions for closing date for applications.

WA — Tertiary Institutions Service Centre (TISC), 39 Fairway, Nedlands WA 6009, tel: (09)-389 1466.

TAFE:

VIC — Vocational Orientation Centre, 131 Latrobe Street, Melbourne VIC 3000, tel: (03)-663 5800 or 008-13 3550.

NSW — TAFE Information Centre, 47 York Street, Sydney NSW 2000, tel: (02)-212 4400.

SA — TAFE Information Centre, 31 Flinders Street, Adelaide SA 5000, tel: (08)-226 3409 or 008-882 661.

QLD/WA — There are no central information centres, but information can be obtained directly from your nearest college and details of the colleges are found in the government section at the beginning of the telephone directory.

TAS — Training Division, Equity House, 110 Murray Street, Hobart TAS, tel: (002)-33 7132.

NT — Institute of TAFE, NT University, Darwin NT, tel: (089)-46 6465.

AUSTUDY

ACT — Student Assistance Centre, QBE Building, Auslie Avenue, Canberra ACT 2601 or Locked Bag 1010, Civic Square ACT 2068, tel: (06) 274 4099 or 008-04 1042 (country students). Personal enquiries should be made at the lodgement centres.

NSW — Student Assistance Centre, Parker Street, Haymarket NSW 2000 or PO Box K710, Haymarket NSW 2000, tel: (02)-911 0300 or 008-04 3401 (country students).

NT — Student Assistance Centre, TCG Centre, 3rd Floor, 80 Mitchell St, Darwin NT 0800, or PO Box 3071, Darwin NT 0801, tel: (089)-82 9218 or 008-11 2338 (country students).

VIC — Student Assistance Centre, 21st Floor, 222 Exhibition Street, Melbourne

VIC 3000, or PO Box 4314TT, Melbourne VIC 3001, tel: (03)-666 7777 or 008-11 2338 (country students).

WA — Student Assistance Centre, Durack Centre, 263 Adelaide Terrace, Perth WA 6000 or PO Box 6032, East Perth WA 6004, tel: (09)425-4694.

QLD — Student Assistance Centre, Level 2 Commonwealth Centre, Cnr Gympie Road & Banfield Street, Chermside QLD 4032, or PO Box 264, Chermside QLD 4032, tel: (07)360 0999 or 008-11 2338 (country students).

SA — Student Assistance Centre, 1st Floor, Wyatt House, 115 Grenfell Street, Adelaide SA 5001, or GPO Box 2568, Adelaide SA 5000, tel: (08)-224 6433 or 008 11 2338 (country students).

TAS — Student Assistance Centre, 85 Macquarie Street, Hobart TAS 7000, or GPO Box 9880, Hobart TAS, 7001, tel: (002)-35 7223 or 008 11 2338 (country students).

International Schools

International Baccalaureate Schools are not that popular in Australia, but each capital city with the exceptions of Canberra and Hobart have at least one such school. A useful organisation which can give further information is the Worldwide Education Service (Strode House, 44-50 Osnaburgh Street, London NW1 3NN, tel: 0181-387 9228).

Below is a regional list of the schools offering the International Baccalaureate (IB):

NSW

Australian International Independent School Ltd., 110 Talavera Road, North Ryde NSW 2113, tel: 02-888 7422.

New England Girls' School: Uralla Rad, Armidale, New South Wales 2350 Australia; tel 61 67 72 5922; fax 61 67 72 7057.

St. Pauls Grammar School: Locked Bag 16, Penrith, New South Wales 2751; tel 61 47 774 888; fax 61 47 774 841.

S.C.E.C.G.S Redlands: 272 Military Road, Cremorne, New South Wales 2090; tel 61 2 909 3133; fax 61 2 909 3228.

VIC

St Leonard's College

Lauriston Girls' School. 38 Huntingtower Road, Armadale, Victoria 3143; tel 61 3 822 9021; fax 61 3 822 7950.

Wesley College: Melbourne, 577 St. Kilda Road, Prahran, Victoria 3181; tel 61 3 510 8694; fax 61 3 510 9739.

Kilmore International School: POB 163, Kilmore 3764; tel 61 5 782 2211; fax 61 5 782 2525.

Presbyterian Ladies' College: Burwood Highway, Burwood, Victoria 3125; tel 61 3 808 5811; fax 61 3 808 5998.

Mount Waverley Secondary College: PO Box 346, Mount Waverley, Victoria 3149; tel 61 3 603 6811; fax 61 3 887 9308.

St. Leonard's College: POB 62, Brighton East, Victoria 3187; tel 61 3 592 2266; fax 61 3 592 3439.

Tintern Anglican Girls' Grammar School: 90 Alexandra Road, Ringwood East, Victoria 3135; tel 61 3 879 4466; fax 61 3 870 6002.

SA

Glenunga International High School: L'Estrange Street, Gelnunga, South Australia 5064; tel 61 8 379 5629; fax 61 8 338 2518.

Mercedes College: 540 Fullarton Road, Springfield, South Australia 5062; tel 61 8 379 6844; fax 61 8 379 9540.

Narrabundah College: Jerrabomberra Avenue, Kingston, South Australia 2604; tel 61 6 205 6999; fax 61 6 205 6969.

Pembroke School: 18 Holden Street, Kensington Park, South Australia 5063; tel 61 332 6111; fax 61 8 364 1525.

WA

Kingsley Montessori School: 18 Monstessori Place, Kingsley, Western Australia 6026; tel 61 9 409 9151; fax 61 409 9158

Wesley College: Perth, POB 149, South Perth, Western Australia 6151; tel 61 9 367 5777; fax 61 9 474 1051.

QLD

Brisbane Boys' College: Kensington Terrace, Toowong, Queensland 4066; tel 61 7 371 9977; fax 61 7 371 2679.

NT

Kormilda College Ltd: POB 241, Berrimah, Northern Territory 0828; tel 61 89 22 16 11; fax 61 89 470792.

Media and Communications

Australian film, television and radio productions are rated highly in the international arena, and the national newspapers are also of a high standard. Australian media is owned and controlled by a few corporations, who have blatant political interests, and the newspapers have often been criticised for containing obviously biased reporting. In addition, the size of the newspapers is often dictated by the amount of advertising available. That is, even on a big world news day the daily newspaper may be relatively thin because there was only a small amount of advertising available to fill the pages. One newspaper executive admitted that the newspaper he worked for could only function profitably if the news-advertising ratio was 35%-65%. Having said this, there is a high amount of international news coverage, and each paper contains a section outlining the major international world events.

Newspapers

At the time of writing, Sydney has six major daily newspapers, Melbourne and Brisbane have three each, and the other capitals and major regional centres have at least two. There are also local newspapers produced by regional shires and suburbs, which are usually privately owned.

There are also two national daily newspapers, *The Australian* and *The Australian Financial Review*, and the national weekend paper is *The Weekend Australian.*

Expatriates from the UK can keep up with the news from there by subscribing to the *International Express* sold throughout Australia and New Zealand. It is based on articles drawn from the London daily and Sunday Expresses satellited to Australia and printed in Sydney, Melbourne and Perth. Available in Australia through local newsagents or by subscription from Johnsons International Media Services Ltd. (43 Millharbour, London E14 9TR; tel 0171-538 8288; 0171-537 3594), or in Australia through NDD (tel 02 353 9911; fax 02-669 2305).

Another possibility to keep up with UK and international news is to subsribe to the *Guardian Weekly* which is a compilation in English of main articles from *The Guardian, Washington Post* and *Le Monde.* Subscriptions are available from

The General Manager (The Guardian Weekly, 164 Deansgate, Manchester M60 2RR).

Major Newspapers

NSW

Sydney Morning Herald, 235 Jones Broadway, Sydney NSW 2000, tel: 02-282 2833.

The Australian Financial Review, 235 Jones Street, Broadway NSW 2007, tel: 02-282 2833 or 12 Norwich Street, London EC4A 1BH, tel: 0171-353 9321.

The Australian, 46 Cooper Street, Surry Hills NSW 2010, tel: 02-288 3000.

The Telegraph Mirror, 2 Holt Street, Surry Hills NSW 2010, tel: 02-288 3000.

VIC

The Melbourne Age, 235 Edward Street, Melbourne VIC 3000, tel: 03-221 2266.

The Age, 250 Spencer Street, Melbourne VIC 3000, tel: 03-600 4211.

The Herald, 44 Flinders Street, Melbourne VIC 3000, tel: 03-652 1111.

The Weekly Times, 44 Flinders Street, Melbourne VIC 3000, tel: 03-652 1111.

WA

The West Australian, Forrest Centre, 219 St George's Terrace, Perth WA 6000, tel: 09-482 3111.

Sunday Times, Forrest Centre, 219 St George's Terrace, Perth WA 6000, tel: 09-482 3111.

QLD

The Courier Mail, Campbell Street, Bowen Hills QLD 4006, tel: 07-252 6011.

Other Australian Newspapers
Australian Associated Press (AAP Group), GPO Box 3888, Sydney NSW 2001, tel: 02-236 8800 or fax: 02-264 3409. The AAP also has a London office, AAP Pty Ltd, 85 Fleet Street, London EC4Y 1DY, tel: 0171-353 0153.
Australian Chinese Newspapers Pty Ltd, 1st Floor, 357 Sussex Street, Sydney NSW 2000, tel: 02-261 3033.
Australian Consolidated Press Ltd, 54 Park Street, Sydney NSW 2000, tel: 02-282 8000. The ACP produces Australian magazines such as *Women's Weekly*, *Street Machine* etc. and has a London office, the ACP Bureau, 112 Westbourne Park Road, London W2 5PL, tel: 0171-221 3913.

Magazines
The Australian Woman's Weekly is perhaps the most popular Australian magazine (and is also available in good British newsagents). There are also Australian versions of *Woman's Day*, *New Idea*, *Vogue*, *Cosmopolitan* and *Family Circle*. International magazines including *Time* and *National Geographic* are also available. Having shown a recent copy of *The Australian Woman's Weekly* to UK resident, Enid Crossen, an avid magazine reader, Mrs Crossen was impressed by the quality of both the production and articles of the *Woman's Weekly*, which costs £2.00 in the UK and $2.60 in Australia. Most of these magazines are available monthly (even the *Woman's Weekly* which, for obvious reasons, couldn't be called *The Australian Woman's Monthly*), and there are also various sporting, motoring, science and computing magazines available.

Books and Bookshops
UK:
Flinders (Australian Bookshop), 10 Woburn Walk, London WC1, tel: 0171-388 6080

Some Australian bookshops with international stock:

Access Pty: The Dial-a-book Order Service. 615 Hawthorn Road, Brighton East,Victoria; Freephone (in Australia) 008 335 180; tel (03) 576 9033; fax (03) 576 9116. Any book that is in print and in English. Home/Office delivery Australia wide.
All Arts Boc!:shop: 160 Oxford Street, Woollahra, NSW; tel (02) 328 6744. Collectors' reference books on antiques, Australian, Asian and tribal art. Phone and mail order.
Angus & Robertson Bookworld: 625 Hay St. Mall, Perth 6000; tel (09) 325 5622. Australia wide and New Zealand.
Boffins Bookshop: 806 Hay St, Perth 6000; tel (09) 321 5755; fax 321 5744. Technical and specialist books. Computer access to over one million USA, UK, NZ and Australian books in print. Local and overseas special orders.
Koorong: 663 Newcastle Street, Leederville; tel (09) 227 6866;fax 227 5585. Sydney, Melbourne and Brisbane.
Dymocks Booksellers: 705-707 Hay Street Mall, Perth 6000; tel (09)321 3949; fax 481 1964. Interstate franchise with comprehensive range of general, technical and education books. Computer access to over 100,000 titles. Local or overseas orders.

Television
Most British television watchers probably see more Australian television productions than Australians do! Currently, on British television, *Burke's Backyard*, *Neighbours*, *Home and Away*, *A Country Practice* and the *Flying Doctors* are regularly screened. In fact, with a high number of viewers soap operas like

Neighbours and *Home and Away* have to be screened twice a day which gives them a higher profile than in their country of origin. In recent times Clive James and Dame Edna Everage have also had their own shows on British television, and the Australian mini-series, *Come in, Spinner*, was also shown.

Australian television productions are obviously in high demand in the UK. If you ask people why many of them prefer to watch an Australian soap rather than a British one they are likely to reply that they find British ones rather depressing whereas Australian ones depict life in sunnier climes both literally and emotionally.

There are four main channels nationwide in the capital cities. Channel Two, the Australian Broadcasting Commission, is government-owned and does not screen commercial advertisements at all. Advertisements informing viewers of upcoming programmes are only allowed at the end of each programme. The other channels, Seven, Nine and Ten, are all commercially owned and operated, and as a result allow commercial advertisements every ten minutes or so. These commercial interruptions to the programmes are extremely irritating, and last for about three minutes. The interruptions tend to become more frequent as a programme progresses, so by the end of the programme continuity is continually being ruined by advertisements for deodorants or cleaning fluid. In this respect, British television is better than Australian television, as programmes in Britain are not interrupted with anything like the same frequency or for the same length of time by commercial breaks as Australian ones are.

There is also an optional channel which you may be able to receive on your television, or may have to buy a special receiver for. This channel is called SBS and is found on channel eight. It is specifically designed for viewers of other than Australian origin, and foreign language films are regularly shown. The SBS news broadcasts tend to contain far more international news and cover it in more depth than the commercial stations offer. In general, the weather forecasts on any of the channels are more detailed and clear than those of the British channels.

British and American television productions are shown on Australian television. British comedy series *Mr Bean* and *Blackadder* were very popular, and Ben Elton is also an Australian favourite. The old *Carry On* films, *'Allo, 'allo* and *Benny Hill* series are also re-run every so often, but are much less popular than the *Yes, Minister, Rumpole of the Bailey* and *Brideshead Revisited*. Australian television is absolutely brilliant when the ratings are being calculated, when all the channels compete for the highest viewership and screen excellent movies and series. At other times, however, the choice of Friday or Saturday night movies can be described as appalling, and most Australians also own a video! Videos are relatively cheap to hire. A newly released video will cost approximately $7 to hire for 24 hours, and older movies can be rented for up to a week from as little as $2. Many video shops offer a free old movie with every newly-released video hired, or seven old movies for a week for $10.

In remote or rural areas, it is only possible to receive Channel Two and perhaps one other commercial channel specifically aimed at country viewers. Television programmes are advertised daily in local newspapers, including these country channels, and a weekly liftout programme guide is available in the weekend papers.

Perhaps the best feature of television viewing in Australia is that there is no television licensing system. You are required to pay for your own television sets and antennae, but you may have as many televisions in your home or business as you like and you do not have to pay for the privilege of watching them.

Radio

The Australian Broadcasting Commission also owns and runs a radio station, which can be received Australia-wide, and is renowned for its excellent news coverage. It tends to focus on classical music interspersed with interviews and debates about current affairs, and has a reputation for being mostly highbrow. There are literally hundreds of independent stations throughout Australia, run privately by universities, ethnic groups etc; there are even Aboriginal radio stations which service the outback regions. Radio stations are often advertised on car bumper stickers, on television, or in the newspapers, so it relatively easy to choose and tune in to something to your taste.

Popular Music. The Australian music industry is thriving, and local stations will always play a selection of the best home-grown music as well as the best of the international scene. In general, Australians do not go in much for the 'techno' music which has taken over the European pop scene, but for sounds more closely linked to rock. Australian bands have a very distinctive sound, and, judging by the international success of Australia's *INXS* and *Crowded House* (originally from New Zealand, but now living in Australia), this sound is new and worthy of repute. You are not really likely to hear Jason Donovan, Kylie or Dannii Minogue, or even Rolf Harris crooning over the Australian airwaves as they are actually considered rather naff in their home country. Australian music has really developed from the kind of music that was always more popular outside the country than at home.

Post
The Australia Post is owned and run by the Australian Government, and in general provides excellent services. Post offices are open from 9am to 5pm Monday to Friday. Letters between Australia and the UK take between four-seven days to arrive, and parcels take between seven and ten days. The cost of postage for an average letter to Britain is $1.20, and an aerogramme costs 65 cents. Sea mail and Surface Air Lifted mail services are also available at a significantly cheaper cost, but are, naturally, much the slowest services. Most people send parcels SAL or Sea mail, particularly Christmas parcels, and Australia Post issues a list of send-by dates for guaranteed pre-Christmas delivery all over the world. To send parcels back to the UK in time for Christmas, the send-by date is usually at the beginning of October. Australia Post also offers a cheaper rate for Christmas cards, and there is a separate send-by date for international cards, usually four weeks before Christmas. There is no division between first and second class services for local letters, but only one standard service and cost. Local letters cost 45 cents and it usually takes one working day to deliver letters posted within the same metropolitan area, or two working days if the letter is from outside the metropolitan region or is from interstate. Mail is usually delivered once a day Monday to Friday in metropolitan regions, but in remote and/or rural regions the mail may only be delivered once a week and can also often be delayed by adverse conditions such as flooding, torrential rain or even snow.

If you intend to travel extensively through Australia during your stay, it is possible to have letters/parcels sent to you at any Australian post office. Providing it is clearly addressed with your name and Poste Restante followed by the name and address of the post office, the letter/parcel will be held for up to a month during which time you may, upon producing proof of your identification, collect it. If the letter/parcel is not claimed within a month, it is simply returned to the sender. There are also private mail holding and forwarding services available which are useful if you have no permanent address. These services work on a membership basis, you pay a fee to join and are then able to call the service from anywhere in Australia and see if there is any mail for you or if anyone has been trying to contact you. The service will then forward your mail/messages to your present address.

Useful Addresses

A privately owned travellers' mail service is operated by the *Travellers' Contact Point*, 8th floor, 428 George Street, Sydney NSW 2000, tel: (02) 221 8744.

The main Australian post offices are:

SA	14 King William Street, Adelaide SA 5000.
QLD	Shute Harbour Road, Airlie Beach QLD 4012.
	261 Queen Street, Brisbane QLD 4000.
	13 Grafton Street, Cairns 4870.
	25 Caville Avenue, Surfers Paradise QLD 4217.
	22 Flinders Street, Townsville QLD 4810.
NT	33 Hartley Street, Alice Springs NT 0870.
	48 Cavenagh Street, Darwin NT 0800.
ACT	Alinga Street, Canberra ACT 2601.
TAS	Elizabeth Street, Hobart TAS 7000.
	68 Cameron Road, Launceston TAS 7250.
VIC	Cnr Bourke & Elizabeth Streets, Melbourne VIC 3000.
WA	3 Forest Place, Perth WA 6000.
NSW	Martin Place, Sydney NSW 2000.

Telephones

Public telephones in Australia are very similar to those found in Europe and the UK. Local calls cost 30 cents, and STD and international calls are charged according to the rate (determined by the time of day at which you call), distance covered and the length of the call. The telephones accept 10 cent, 20 cent, 50 cent and $1 coins. Many telephones have the facility to accept major credit cards or automatic teller cards for the bigger Australian national banks. Phone cards are also available from newsagents and vending machines in denominations of $2, $5, $10 and $20. STD public telephones are available streetside throughout metropolitan suburbs, outside post offices and in shopping centres. Red telephones are for local use only and are also found in shopping centres, pubs and outside delis.

If you are in Australia temporarily or short-term, it may be useful for you to apply to British Telecom for a BT Chargecard. This card is free and means that all calls you make from Australia are charged to your own British account. Contact BT on 0800-800 893 for an application form and further details.

To call the UK from Australia, you will need to dial 0011-44 and then the number, deleting the first 0 from the area code. To send faxes from Australia, the process is the same, except the international prefix is 0015 followed by the country code, area code (minus the 0) and the number. For example, to send a fax to Oxford, the code necessary would be 0015-44 1865 + number. To call Australia from the UK, dial 00-61 followed by the area code (deleting the initial 0) and then the number. The procedure for sending a fax to Australia is exactly the same as telephoning. The area codes for major Australian cities are given in the previous section, *Setting Up Home, Utilities.*

The emergency number is 000 throughout Australia.

Cars and Motoring

The wide roads in Australia and the mainly rain-free driving make being out on the road generally easy. City traffic, as all over the world, is subject to the problems of congestion and tortuous one-way systems, but the suburban and country roads are usually excellent. In more remote areas the roads can be primitive tracks of dirt or gravel best suited to rugged four-wheel drive vehicles, which are in any case the only vehicle for the tough outback conditions. Even in comparatively populated rural areas, apart from main roads and highways, most roads will be gravel. Generally, it is a good idea to keep your speed down on these roads as your car does not respond so quickly as it does on bitumen, and is liable to slide around a bit. On city and suburban roads, highways and freeways, driving is not a problem, and with many of the major interstate and intercity highways hugging the coast, you can often enjoy some fantastic scenery along the way.

Fuel. Fuel costs vary from one area to another. Even within a metropolitan area, a petrol company can sell fuel cheaper in one suburb than it does in another. Petrol tends to be more expensive in rural and remote areas due to freight costs. As a rough guide, the price of super-grade petrol for the capital cities as at July 1994, in cents per litre, were:

Sydney	68.9	Perth	67.7
Melbourne	66.8	Hobart	73.6
Brisbane	61.1	Darwin	74.2
Adelaide	70.0	Canberra	73.9

Super-grade petrol is the Australian name for four-star, and is usually only between one and three cents per litre more expensive than unleaded petrol. Diesel is also readily available at petrol stations at a similar price to unleaded petrol, and two-stroke petrol is available for lawn-mowers, boat engines etc.

Driving Regulations

Like Britons, Australians drive on the left. There are, however, significant differences in speed-limits, overtaking and other rules. Some of the basic differences between Australian and European driving are therefore worth noting.

Speed Limits. Speed is restricted to 60km/h in built-up areas (defined as those with kerbs and street lighting) and to 100 or 110km/h on freeways or in country areas.

Overtaking. It is legal to overtake in the left (or inside) lane of a dual carriageway/freeway (a.k.a. undertaking). On a three or more lane freeway, it is legal to overtake in any lane. The extreme right lane is not established as a fast-lane, but it is courteous to keep to the left. It is not, however, obligatory to keep to the left, so the British custom of driving up behind a car in the right lane, sitting on its tail and flashing your lights until it moves over to let you pass, is completely inappropriate. This kind of driving is likely to be interpreted as aggressive and may be met by an angry response from Australian drivers.

Road Etiquette. It is imperative that you give way to your right when entering a freeway or dual carriageway from a slip road. It would be considered bad driving to come onto a freeway and expect cars in the left lane to move over to the right in order to let you enter the flow of traffic. Courteous drivers may do this, but it is not common practice, and drivers who do not change lanes to let you onto the freeway/dual carriageway are not considered rude.

The practice of flashing your lights is also different in Australia. In Britain you may flash your lights to indicate to another car that it may enter your lane, that you wish to overtake them or to warn another driver that their headlights are not on. In Australia, you may also flash your headlights to indicate to another driver that their headlights are not on, but you will also see cars travelling towards you flashing their lights in order to warn oncoming drivers that there is a police speed trap ahead. It is, in some states, illegal to warn other cars that they are approaching a speed trap, but the old Australian anti-authority trait from colonial days lives on and most drivers derive satisfaction from helping others avoid the speeding fines.

Highway Code. You can check the rules of the road by obtaining a copy of the Highway Code from your local police station. The Highway Code can vary from state to state, often on minor points, but there can also be differences on crucial points such as priority at intersections. If you wish to drive interstate, it would also be helpful to obtain the Highway Code relevant to your destination as each State/Territory writes its own road laws. Generally, the wearing of seat belts, both in the front and back, is compulsory, and both practices of hitch-hiking and picking up hitch-hikers are actively discouraged, and even illegal in Victoria.

Licence Penalty Points. For minor driving offences, most States have a points system. A driver has 12 points, and a certain number of points are deducted according to the gravity of the traffic offence. Details of the points allocated to a particular offence are outlined in the Highway Code. If all points are lost by a driver within a certain time period, the driver loses his/her licence for a minimum of three months, but this can be much longer if there is serious damage to property and/or persons involved.

Drinking & Driving. In addition to points on the licence, penalties for drink-driving convictions included hefty fines, jail terms and licence suspensions (all of which may result in your acquiring a criminal record). One writer on Australia has described the national obsession of the State and Territory governments to eradicate drink-driving as only surpassed by the fanatical crusades of the Scandinavian and Northern Irish goverments. The Australian government is indeed concerned by the alarming statistics of drink-driving related injuries and fatalities, and has introduced Random Breath Testing (RBT), which means you may be pulled over at any time by the police, who will ask the driver to blow into a breathalyser in order to check the alcohol level of the driver's blood. If the driver is over the limit (which varies from 0.05%-0.08% depending on the state/territory), he/she will be charged accordingly. To describe this concern and practice as fanatical, puritanical or obsessive seems inept in view of the number of tragedies caused by drink-driving in Australia. Statistics show that the RBT system is successful and that the number of road-deaths is falling as a consequence.

Breakdowns and Accidents

Automobile Associations. There are a number of accident and breakdown services in Australia, but the biggest is the RAC (Royal Automobile Club). All companies offer varying levels of cover, but home-start is part of basic cover rather than as an optional extra. Policies change and prices fluctuate, so it is necessary to contact the companies directly to get a brochure. On the whole, accident and breakdown cover costs less than in Britain, and it is the car, not the driver, which is covered. The bigger companies also offer national and international accident and/or breakdown cover free, or at a minimal rate, covering the cost of towing a car from remote areas, or, in the event of a fatality, the cost of flying a body home from overseas. The standard of cover is excellent and membership is well worth the fee, particularly if your car is over five years old. Up to 75% of Australian motorists are members of an automobile association, twice the European rate of membership. As on European motorways, there are telephones every 1km on Australian freeways for the purpose of calling for roadside assistance. Automobiles associations also offer other benefits such as tourist information including hotel guides and maps, and the facility to have one of their qualified mechanics check over a used car a member may wish to buy.

Accidents. Should you be unfortunate enough to be involved in a motor vehicle accident in Australia, whether as a passenger, pedestrian or driver, it is essential that you try to record certain details of the other parties involved such as full names, addresses, phone numbers, driver's licence numbers, the name of the insurance company the other parties are with, the names addresses and phone numbers of any witnesses, and a list of damage to the vehicles involved made at the scene of the accident (if possible). If the total cost of damage caused by the accident exceeds $1,000, you must call the police. In this case, it may be helpful to record the name of any attending officers. In addition, if you sustain any physical injury, no matter how minor, if the accident was not your fault it may be necessary for you to claim for personal injury. You should attend your GP and make clear how your injuries were caused, and the extent of your injuries in detail as medical records can often affect the amount awarded as compensation to a successful claimant.

Driving in the outback. If you intend to drive in the outback, or undertake long distance trips, the Australian Tourist Commission has an information pack called *Hit the Road* which gives details of city-city links, motoring clubs, information on vehicle rental and accommodation as well as essential rules for outback motoring. Drivers are advised to notify friends or relatives of expected times of arrival, and to confirm these upon arrival, to check intended routes carefully, to refuel at every opportunity and to keep an additional week's supply of food, water and fuel in case of a breakdown in remote areas. Many people have died of exposure and dehydration after breaking down in the outback. Finding themselves completely unprepared, they tend to wander away from the vehicle in search of food and water, get lost and die. You are advised to *always* remain with your vehicle if it breaks down in the outback as the vehicle provides shelter from the sun and you are much more likely to be found by rescue teams. The Royal Flying Doctor Service of Australia (RFDS) offers a service for outback travellers which includes advice on touring and emergency procedures, and the hiring of transceiver sets with emergency call buttons. It is advisable to contact the RFDS for information before embarking on a trip into the outback.

Useful Addresses
Royal Flying Doctor Service of Australia Federal Office, Level 6, 43 Bridge Street, Hurstville NSW 2200, tel: 00-61 2 580 9711 or fax: 00-61 2 580 8215. Contact this office for a list of RFDS bases Australia-wide.
Australian Automobile Association, GPO Box 1555, Canberra City ACT 2601, tel: 00-61 6 247 7311 or fax: 00-61 6 257 5320.
Royal Automobile Association of South Australia Inc., 41 Hindmarsh Square, Adelaide SA 5000, tel: 00-61 8 223 4500 or fax: 00-61 8 202 4521.
Royal Automobile Club of Queensland (RACQ), 300 St Paul's Terrace, Fortitude Valley QLD 4006, tel: 00-61 7 361 2444 or fax: 00-61 7 849 0610.
National Roads and Motorists' Association (NRMA), 92 Northbourne Avenue, Canberra City ACT 2601, tel: 00-61 6 243 8826 or fax: 00-61 6 243 8892.
Automobile Association of the Northern Territory (AANT), MLC Building, 78-81 Smith Street, Darwin NT 0800, tel: 00-61 89 3837 or fax: 00-61 89 41 2965.
Royal Automobile Club of Victoria (RACV), 550 Princes Highway, Noble Park VIC 3174, tel: 00-61 3 790 2627 or fax: 00-61 3 790 2844.
Royal Automobile Club of Tasmania (RACT), Cnr Patrick & Murray Streets, Hobart TAS 7001, tel: 00-61 02 38 2200 or fax: 00-61 02 34 8784.

Royal Automobile Club of Western Australia Inc., 228 Adelaide Terrace, Perth WA 6000, tel: 00- 61 9 421 4444 or fax: 00-61 9 221 1887.
National Roads and Motorists' Association (NRMA), 151 Clarence Street, Sydney NSW 2000, tel: 00-61 2 260 9222 or fax: 00-61 2 260 8472.

Driving Licence

Each of the states and territories has a separate authority responsible for the issuing of driving licences and the rules regarding these may vary interstate. However some regulations apply Australia-wide.

The minimum age for holding a licence is either 17 or 18 years, depending on the State/Territory. A Learner's Permit may be obtained by a potential new driver three months before they reach driving age (i.e., at either 16 years and 9 months or 17 years and 9 months of age) provided that they pass a written test on the Highway Code. A learner driver may only be accompanied by one who has a clean driving licence and has been driving for at least seven years. Learners are not permitted to drive on freeways or when it is dark and must always display 'L' plates attached to the car. In practice learners get a lot of driving experience in the presence of a suitably qualified friend/member of the family, but it is compulsory to have lessons with a qualified instructor to prepare for the practical police test. Once the learner feels confident with their driving skills, the driving instructor will make an appointment with a police examiner to take the driving test. Once the test has been passed, usually at the second attempt (unless you are very lucky or proficient) a driver is termed 'probationary' and must display 'P' plates on the car every time they drive. Probationary drivers have certain restrictions as to speed and blood alcohol limits, and face stiffer penalties if caught exceeding these limits. After one year, the probationary driver is considered to be sufficiently experienced to be awarded a full driving licence.

Apart from probationary licences, driving licences can be renewed annually (at an approximate cost of $30), triennially (at an approximate cost of $72) or every five years (at an approximate cost of $96).

If you arrive in Australia with a driving licence issued overseas, the rules are slightly different. If you are considered to be a visiting driver (i.e., you are temporarily in Australia and usually reside outside Australia), you may drive any vehicle, including a locally registered one, provided you hold a current British driving licence or International Driving Permit (issued in your home country) for the class of vehicle to be driven. In Britain, an International Driving Permit can be obtained from the AA, even if you are not a member.

Australian Driving Licence Application. If you intend to become a permanent resident of Australia, you must obtain a driving licence issued by the relevant state/territory authority. Although you may be given a certain period of grace, (which varies from state to state but is usually for three months), you are required to obtain a driving licence as soon as you take up permanent residence. New settlers holding a current valid British driving licence must take a written test based upon knowledge of the State/Territory Motor Traffic Handbook (also known as the *Highway Code*) as well as a practical driving test. In addition, it is necessary in most states to undergo an eyesight test. A driver's licence issued in one particular Australian State/Territory is valid Australia-wide.

Car Registration

Registration fees are payable according to the type of vehicle and the expected wear and tear that vehicle will inflict on the State's/Territory's roads over the course of a year. In most states/territories, temporary residents and visitors are exempt from registration fees as long as the registration of the vehicle continues to be valid in the country of origin. Immediately after its arrival in Australia it must be inspected by the nearest registration authority to ensure it is roadworthy. In addition, you will need to provide the following documents: a *Carnet de Passage* or other evidence that security has been lodged with Australian Customs, evidence that it is covered by Third Party Insurance in Australia, a current registration certificate in the country or origin, and a valid driver's licence from country of origin. Registration payments include Third Party Injury Insurance, and the costs vary between States. The combined cost of registration and TPI of a popular 6-cylinder family sedan ranges from $400-$600. An example of the current costs of motor vehicle licence and third party insurance for a 1988 Mitsubishi Colt 4-cylinder sedan is taken from a bill issued in 1993 for the year 1993/4. There are different rates of fees depending on whether the vehicle is used for business or commercial use (for which standard fees apply) or solely for family or personal purposes (for which family vehicle fees apply). The standard fees and family vehicle fees for the example vehicle are:

	Standard Fees		Family Vehicle Fees	
	12 months	6 months	12 months	6 months
Lic:	$52.75	$26.40	$26.15	$13.10
Ins:	$199.45	$99.95	$199.45	$99.95
Rec:	$10.90	$10.90	$10.90	$10.90
Adj:	$9.00	$9.00	$9.00	$9.00
TOTAL	$272.10	$146.50	$245.50	$132.95

To register your vehicle, contact your local traffic authority (listed below). In New South Wales you must get an endorsed Compulsory Third Party Certificate (The Green Slip) from an insurance company in order to be able to register your vehicle. Payment of the combined vehicle registration and TTPI can be made at any metropolitan Post Office or at the office of the relevant authority, although payment procedures are subject to change and you should check with the proper registration authority. For example,in Western Australia payment of vehicle registration can only be done by cheque or via the metropolitan Post Office branches, and not at the Police Department.

Useful Addresses

NSW — *Roads Traffic Authority:* PO Box K198, Haymarket NSW 2000, tel: (02) 662-5000.

VIC — *Victorian Roads, Vehicle Safety Services:* 60 Denmark Street, Kew VIC 3101, tel: (03) 854-2658.

QLD — *Queensland Transport, Registration Division:* GPO Box 2451 QLD 4001, tel: (07) 253-4700.

WA — *Police Department, Traffic Licensing Centre:* 22 Mount Street, Perth WA 6001, tel: (09) 222-6229.

SA — Registrar of Motor Vehicles: Katena Street, Regency Park SA 5000, tel: (08) 348-9500.

TAS — *Registrar of Motor Vehicles:* 1 Collins St, Hobart TAS 7001, tel: (002) 335-201.

NT — *Motor Vehicle Registry:* Department of Transport and Works, PO Box 530, Darwin NT 5794, tel: (089) 897-664.

ACT — *Registrar of Motor Vehicles:* Department of Territories, PO Box 582, Dickson ACT 2602, tel: (06) 207-7000.

Transport

Air
Domestic travel in Australia is very expensive, due to the huge distances covered between major cities. Tourists will find it is often cheaper to book internal flights from Britain through your travel agent than arrange them in Australia. But obviously this option is not available to anyone who has taken up residence in Australia. There are air passes available which are much cheaper if you are doing substantial travel within Australia; however you need to check this through very carefully as some flights (e.g. Melbourne-Sydney) are actually more expensive on the air pass . For example, Ansett Australia Airlines offers a *G'Day* Pass for air travel within Australia and New Zealand. The G'Day air pass can be used in conjunction with any major airline that flies to Australia and New Zealand and it must be purchased before departure from Britain as it cannot be bought within either Australia or New Zealand. It is only possible to obtain the G'Day pass if one is purchasing at least two flight coupons and the maximum number of coupons available is eight on any one G'Day pass. Fares on a G'day pass are significantly lower than the normal fares, however you can be caught out by actually paying more on the pass than you would if you bought your fare in Australia The fares that are cheaper than the Standard Tariff of £70 or £75 are the very short flights between cities such as Melbourne and Sydney (£63), or Sydney and Brisbane (£66). If you fly with either Qantas, British Airways or Singapore Airlines, you may be eligible for free air travel within Australia. It is worth checking carefully with the airline or your travel agent before you purchase any coupons.

G'Day passes can be bought through Austravel or from Ansett Australia Airlines (20 Savile Row, London, W1X 2AN, tel: 0171-434 4071). Qantas offer discount domestic fares from only £24 per flight and a Qantas Explorer pass from £160 for two flight sectors (up to eight additional coupons are available from £80). Ring Qantas direct or specialist travel agents for Australasia (see list at the end of *General Introduction — getting there*). Ask about Australian Explorer Air Passes sold as coupons.

Rail
Rail travel within Australia is more restricted than air or bus travel as rail lines do not operate all the way around the country. The northern areas of both the Northern Territory and Western Australia do not have railway lines at all (mainly due to the fact that the intense heat would cause them to buckle). Along the eastern coast of Australia there is however, an extensive railway network. Between Perth and Sydney runs one of the great railway lines of the world, *The Indian Pacific* which operates weekly. 4348 miles, 65 hours and two time zones after leaving the Sydney sunrise over the Pacific Ocean, you can enjoy magical Perth sunsets over the Indian Ocean.

There are two passes available with the railways which can be purchased from the UK and booked before you use the railways to travel. Firstly, the Austrailpass enables you unlimited stops on most trains on the Rail Australia Network for a given number of days. As with the air passes, this is a special service for travellers from overseas. First and economy class passes are available, but economy class Austrailpass fares are (note that the conversion is calculated on the current exchange rate of $2.02: £1):

14 days — $435 (approx £215)
30 days — $685 (approx £339)
21 days — $565 (approx £279)
90 days — $1,125 (approx £556)

The Flexipass is more suitable if you are planning extensive travel within a given period. Prices in economy travel within a six month period are:

8 days — $340 (approx £158) not including travel to Perth & Alice Springs
22 days — $700 (approx £325)
15 days — $500 (approx £232)
29 days — £900 (approx £418)

Due to the fact that some rail services only operate weekly, you are well advised to book ahead, particularly if you have a limited travelling time and/or you are travelling within a peak season. Tickets may be booked up to six months in advance. Single tickets are valid for two months and return tickets must be used within six months of using the outbound section of the ticket.

Bookings can be made in the UK through local travel agents, or directly with Leisurail (PO Box 113, Peterborough, PE3 8HY, tel: 01733-335599 or fax: 01733-505 451). Leisurail have useful free brochures available on request.

Bus

Travelling by coach around Australia, while time-consuming, is actually one of the best ways to see the country, and it is also one of the cheapest. There are a number of independent bus companies in Australia, and so there are daily services to almost anywhere in the country from every major city. Prices are competitive and the standards are very high. Long-distance coaches are usually fitted with video and stereo facilities, and the bus drivers often consider themselves to be part of the entertainment, maintaining humour levels should they be flagging in the middle of a long trip. Every bus is fitted with air-conditioning, a toilet and water fountains, and there are frequent stops at road houses for food, drinks, toilets and even showers.

Two of the major bus companies which provide extensive services throughout Australia are Greyhound Pioneer and McCaffertys. Both of these companies have booking agents in the UK, who can be contacted for further details and fares. For Greyhound Pioneer, contact Greyhound International, tel: 01342-317 317, and for McCaffertys and/or Greyhound Pioneer, contact Visit Australia (9 Marine Court, St Leonards-on-Sea, East Sussex, TN38 ODX, tel: 01424-716 544 or fax: 01424-722 304).

The bus companies usually offer bus travel passes and there is a range of passes available. Information about these passes can be obtained from travel agents in Australia, or in the UK if you are travelling with Greyhound Pioneer or McCaffertys. Greyhound Pioneer offers an Aussie Pass which enables you to travel when and where you wish for a number of days within a specified time, e.g.:

7 days travel within a 1 month period $350 (approx £173)
21 days travel within a 2 month period $860 (approx £425)

The Explorer Pass allows the traveller unlimited stopovers within a given time en route to a specified destination. The route is set and there is no backtracking allowed, e.g.:

Sydney to Darwin via Cairns (The Outback and Reef Explorer) is valid for 6 months and costs $425 (approx £210).
Perth to Darwin (The Western Explorer) is valid for 6 months and costs $330 (approx £163).

Depending on how much travel you intend to do, with a bus pass you can make substantial savings. A round-Australia trip stopping at Perth, Adelaide, Melbourne, Sydney, Brisbane, Cairns, Darwin and returning to Perth, would usually cost approximately $1,243 (approx £615).

Combined Road/Rail Travel

New South Wales has a NSW Discovery Pass available for economy travel on all Countrylink rail and coach services (excluding national companies and the Indian Pacific train). Stopovers are unlimited and the pass is valid for one calendar month. The current cost of the pass is $249 (approx £123).

There is also a pass valid for travel between Sydney and Cairns on the Countrylink XPT (train) and Queensland Rail., offering unlimited economy travel between Sydney and Cairns. Remembering that the Gold Coast, Surfer's Paradise and the Sunshine Coast all lie along this route, it is well worth considering, given that the cost is only $199 (approx £98). It costs even less if you only travel to Brisbane, the current price being $76 (approx £37).

In addition, Greyhound Pioneer and Rail Australia offer a combination of their services in the Kangaroo Road 'n Rail Pass which is available in first or economy class. This pass allows unlimited travel anywhere on the road and rail within a given time. The cost of Economy class passes are as follows:

14 days $655 (approx £324)
21 days $900 (approx £445)
28 days $1,150 (approx £569)

The distance chart below gives the distances between towns in miles by the most direct road route.

Adelaide										
966	Alice Springs									
922	277	Ayers Rock								
1238	1880	2157	Brisbane							
1776	1434	1711	1063	Cairns						
764	1731	1757	817	1826	Canberra					
2026	1060	1337	2282	1835	2630	Darwin				
621	1587	1613	1224	2045	561	2647	Hobart			
464	1430	1456	1068	1888	405	2490	157	Melbourne		
1690	2261	2287	2681	3219	2454	2613	2311	2154	Perth	
917	1759	1785	641	1638	188	2545	709	552	2730	Sydney

Urban Transport

In most Australian capital cities, there are good bus and/or rail services. Within the city centre, there are very frequent and cheap buses/trains to service the central business district. In Melbourne, the city transport system consists of trams, reminiscent of older days, which have become a feature and attraction of the city. Trams on a certain city route are free, and it is possible to ride around the city for a couple of hours on a tram, getting to see the city from a different perspective to that usually offered to tourists. Sydney has an underground rail system, and Adelaide offers the O-Bahn. In Perth, the city council provides free bus services within a restricted area of the city. These buses are called 'City Clippers' and the routes are colour-coded. You can catch a clipper at any point along its circular route and stay on as long as you like, without paying a cent. In both Perth and Melbourne, these free transport services are really provided to encourage city workers to leave their cars at home and reduce city traffic congestion, but many tourists and shoppers also take advantage of the excellent services. In common with many European city transport systems (but not in the UK), in many Australian cities the public transport tickets are valid for a certain length of time rather than for a single or return ride. For example, you buy a ticket (which is priced according to how many zones you wish to be able to cover) and that ticket is valid for a specific length of time regardless of how many times you get on and off a bus/train within that time and within the specific zones. In Perth, to get to the city centre from Warwick, you would buy an adult bus ticket from Warwick to the city centre (a distance of about 15 km; two zones), which is valid for two hours, for approximately $1.20. The ride takes approximately 20 minutes from depot to depot along the freeway, and having arrived at the city depot, you could then re-use the same ticket to travel to any other destination within the two zones, providing you got on the bus before the two hour time limit had expired. Zones are considered on a concentric circle basis, so it is possible to travel the same amount of distance again from the city centre over a distance covering two zones to the other side of the city on the same ticket. In addition, in Perth it is possible to use bus and train tickets interchangeably, so you can catch the bus into Perth and then use the same ticket to catch a train to another destination within the zonal distance, or vice versa. You usually pay the driver as you board for your ticket, or there may be a conductor waiting on the platform by the queues for the buses from whom you may buy a ticket before you board. Alternatively, there may be a ticket office at the depot or station from where you may buy your tickets and get general information.

Australian cities tend to be very spread out with long distances in between various areas and in consequence the public transport systems are perhaps not as frequent or as well established as they are in European cities, so most Australians tend to drive their cars to work.

In an attempt to reduce pollution and traffic congestion, there is an an increasing number of Australian 'Park & Ride' schemes which entail driving to a convenient bus/rail depot and taking public transport into the city centre.

Banks and Finance

Banking in Australia is straightforward and the tellers have a reputation for being courteous and friendly. Opening times are consistent across the country, 9.30am to 4.00pm Monday through to Thursday, and 9.30pm to 5.00pm on Fridays. Building societies may open on Saturday mornings from 9.00am-noon, but regional and remote branches may have more restricted opening hours. The four largest nationwide banks are Westpac, the National Australia Bank, the Commonwealth Bank of Australia, and the ANZ which is also available in New Zealand.

Bank Acounts
If you are going to Australia for more than six months,or to work, it is worth opening a bank account either before you leave your home country, or on your immediate arrival in Australia. It is much easier to open an account with an Australian bank when you are actually in Australia, but it can also be arranged through the Commonwealth Bank of Australia in London. The Commonwealth Bank will establish a bank account for you with a convenient branch in Australia and transfer your funds prior to your departure which means that when you arrive in Australia you have immediate and full access to their range of banking facilities (including automatic tellers throughout the country). The Commonwealth Bank can only establish an account for you prior to your arrival if you intend to work in Australia. This means that you have to be able to show them evidence that you have been given the relevant visa. Contact the Commonwealth Bank of Australia (details listed below) for further details or to speak with one of their consultants, 9am-5pm Monday to Friday.

In order to open a bank account, there is a points system operating on any applicant's proof of identification. Different forms of identification are worth different points, and an applicant must have a minimum of 120 points in order to open an Australian account. For example, a library card is worth five points, a driver's licence is worth 50 points, a birth certificate is worth 60 points and a passport is worth 80 points. You will need a combination of these documents with you as proof of identification when attending the branch of the bank with which you wish to open your account. As the points system is subject to change at any time, it is a good idea to take as many different forms of proof of your identification as you can with you.

Details of current interest rates and different accounts available with the different banks are advertised in the newspapers and on television, or you may ask the banks for brochures.

International and Internal Money Transfers

If you wish to send an international money transfer from Britain to Australia, it will cost you approximately £15 regardless of the amount of money you wish to send, and the transfer may only be sent through banks. Relatively recently, the Australian government has introduced legislation which prevents British Royal Mail money orders from being accepted by Australia Post.

In Australia, international money transfers must be made by bank draft, which costs approximately $18, although internal money transfers may be made via the bank by buying a bank cheque, or by sending an Australia Post money order, which costs of which vary according to the amount you wish to send.

Other Banking Services

Credit Cards. Most banks offer a credit card facility. The usual international credit cards: Mastercard, Visa, Diners Club and American Express can also be applied for through your local bank. Alternatively, if you intend to stay in Australia for less than 12 months, it is possible to apply for a credit card in your home country before you leave and then establish a standing order to pay off your monthly credit card bill. It is a good idea to deposit your money in a high interest account because the interest from this account should cover the approximate charge of 2% on cash advances on your credit card in Australia.

Direct Debits. Australian banks also offer direct debit facilities for the payment of regular bills, and many also offer a telephone banking facility which enables you to authorise payment transactions by telephone.

Cheque Accounts. The cheque book facility only applies to specific accounts, and it is important to check whether the account you are considering opening offers this service. There is no system of a cheque card to guarantee a cheque in Australia, so there is also no limit (usually dictated by the British cheque card) as to the amount of the cheque you are able to write. In order to write a cheque, you must usually have your driver's licence or other acceptable form of identification showing your full name and address, which will be noted on the reverse of the cheque. Very few Australian bank accounts offer free cheques. Most cheque accounts charge between 20 cents and $1.00 for each cheque you write. As a consequence, Australians use cheques far more sparingly than their British counterparts, and tend to use cash or credit cards a lot more. Cheques take five working days to clear, but foreign cheques may take up to four weeks to clear and you may be charged a commission on the exchange of cheques made out in a foreign currency.

Money

Australian currency is decimal and based on the Australian dollar, which is made up of 100 cents. In 1993, one and two cent pieces, which were bronze, were withdrawn from circulation as they were felt to be more of an encumbrance in a person's pocket than they were worth. As of 1994, Australian coinage consists of the silver-coloured, cupronickel five, ten, 20 and 50 cent pieces. In addition, one and two dollar notes have also been recently withdrawn, and there are now gold-coloured $1 and $2 coins, made of aluminum-bronze. The $1 coin is about the same size as the 20 cent piece, and has irregular milling which allows it to be easily distinguished by blind people. The $2 coin is noticeably bigger. The notes are in denominations of $5, $10, $20, $50 and $100. The new $5 and $10 notes are made of a kind of plastic which behaves like paper in terms of being folded and even crumpled, but it can't be torn. These new plastic notes bear a transparent seal in the corner (i.e., you can see right through the note), with a stamp and/or hologram in the centre of the seal. This seal was designed to prevent forgery. All notes and coins bear the head of Queen Elizabeth II on the reverse side.

The Australian mint has also coined gold bullion; the coin pieces are known as Australian Nuggets. Each coin has a set purchase price (from $15-$100), but the actual value is determined by the daily fluctuating price of gold and the demand for the coins. The Australian Nugget can be bought Australia-wide at banks as individual coins or as full sets. In addition, at the Australian mint in Canberra, Nuggets and other special investment coins, costing up to $250, can be bought.

You are able to bring an unlimited amount of foreign currency into Australia, but there are regulations which limit the amount of money with which you can leave the country. Currently, it is difficult to leave Australia with more than the equivalent of $5,000. Should you be lucky enough to clean up at that illegal Australian coin game, 'Two-up', you would have to leave your winnings behind or otherwise invest them in Australian business/property. If you intend to take more than this amount out of Australia, you need to contact the *Cash Transaction Report Agency.*

Investment Advice. Expatriates who are not making a permanent move like to have advice on employee benefits, retirement income funding and personal investments and savings provided on an international basis. There are many companies in this field. Godwins International Services (Godwins Ltd., of Briarcliff House, Kingsmead, Farnborough, Hants. GU14 7TE; tel 01252-521701; fax 01252 375721) is part of one of the world's largest Insurance and Advisory Groups.

Useful Addresses
Australian & New Zealand Banking Group (ANZ), 55 Gracechurch Street, London EC3, tel: 0181-280 3100.
Commonwealth Bank of Australia, Australian Financial and Migrant Information Service, Aldwych House, Aldwych, London WC2, tel: 0181-242 4488.
Westpac Banking Corporation, Walbrook House, Walbrook, London EC4, tel: 0181-626 4500.

Taxation

Income Tax
Income Tax in Australia can be quite a complicated business unless like most Australian employees you pay tax through the Pay As You Earn (PAYE) system. If you are self-employed or own your own business and are therefore not PAYE-taxed , the process of assessing whether you are due to pay extra tax or receive a rebate can be confusing. It is possible to complete and lodge your own tax return, and Tax Packs produced by the Australian Taxation Office are available free from newsagents and Taxation Offices Australia-wide. The Tax Pack is continually reviewed, in an effort to make completing a tax return less difficult, but even so the Tax Pack is a formidable publication which currently includes four income tax return forms (for individuals rather than businesses), detailed information and instructions. Both the format and the terminology are quite daunting and for this reason fewer and fewer Australians are choosing to complete their own taxation returns and are turning to chartered accountants, many of whom specialise in minimising taxation liability, to complete their returns, for them.

The Australian financial year begins on 1 July and ends on 30 June, and tax returns must usually be lodged by the end of October. Even if you are not necessarily liable to pay any tax, you are generally required to lodge a tax return in Australia if you are normally resident in Australia, or even if you are a non-resident who has derived an income in Australia. It is obligatory to lodge a tax return at the end of the financial year if any of the following are applicable:

1. You had tax deducted from your pay or other income (including Australian Government pensions, allowances or benefits);
2. You had tax file number amounts deducted from interest, dividends or unit trust distributions (applicable only to residents);
3. You had tax deducted under the Prescribed Payments Scheme (an alternative to the PAYE system);
4. Your 1993/1994 taxable income was more than $5,400 (residents) or $1 or more (non-residents);

5. You incurred a net taxable loss, or are entitled to a deduction for a prior year loss;
6. You were a beneficiary in a trust estate that conducted business in Australia (including farming or mining);
7. You conducted business in Australia (including farming or mining);
8. You paid provisional tax on your previous year's assessment;
9. You were under 18 years of age as at 30 June and your total income from all sources, both within Australia and overseas, was more than $416;
10. You were issued with an assessment under the *Child Support (Assessment) Act 1989*.

Although taxation rules and regulations are subject to continual re-assessment and change, the above points give an indication of the fact that most Australian adults are required to complete and lodge an annual taxation return. It is important to note that despite the necessity of completing a taxation return, most pensions and state allowances are tax-free and should not be included in your taxation return.

Completing A Tax Return

In order to complete a tax return, you need to attach statements (usually issued automatically by your employer at the end of the financial year) of the amount of tax you have paid over the year. These statements are called either group certificates or tax stamps sheets. If you do not receive a group certificate or tax stamps sheet from your employer, you should remind them. If either you or you employer have lost your group certificate or tax stamps sheet, or they have gone missing in the post, you are usually able to get a copy from your employer. If your employer is unable to provide you with a copy, then he/she can give you a letter showing all the details of the original documents. In the unlikely event that you are not able to obtain a letter from your employer, you can fill in a Statutory Declaration for lost or missing group certificates or tax stamps sheets (available from your local Tax Office).

If any information on your group certificate or tax stamps sheet is wrong, your employer must provide a letter showing your correct income and tax details.

Self Assessment If you choose to complete your own tax return, the Tax Office works out your refund or tax bill based on the information you have provided. The Tax Office assumes the information you have provided is true and correct and it is worth noting that after the Tax Office has calculated your rebate or bill and informed you of their calculations in your Notice of Assessment, their computers continue to check for missing or incorrect information. Your tax return may also be subject to an audit and, should the original Assessment be judged incorrect, the Tax Office will change it and send you an amended assessment. In addition to extra tax, you may be liable for a penalty if you fail to show reasonable care in the preparation of your return. Knowing this, it is understandable why many Australians simply don't want to take the risk and pay a professional to shoulder the responsibility.

Professional Assistance. If you would like assistance filling out your own taxation return, you will be able to find chartered accountants or other professional taxation assistance services in the Yellow Pages phone book. It is advisable to phone around as the cost of the service can vary greatly. The Tax Office recommends that if you get someone (other than from the Tax Office) to help you complete your return, you ensure that the person is a registered tax agent. It may be advisable to contact your tax office in order to check the credibility and qualifications of any accountant/firm you may wish to employ to handle your tax returns. Robert Crane, a Chartered Accountant based in

Perth (745 Beaufort Street, Mount Lawley WA 6050; tel 09 370 3981), offers a free initial consultation to give tax advice to individuals and small business owners, and he also offers discounts for pensioners.

You should note that return preparation fees charged by a registered tax agent are tax deductible. In addition, tax help is available for seniors, people from non-English speaking backgrounds, the disabled or those on low incomes who cannot afford assistance with completing their tax returns. Tax Help centres are run by community volunteers, and you should contact your local Tax Office for details of your nearest Tax Help Centre.

The postal addresses and phone numbers of the various state and regional Tax Offices are listed at the back of the Tax Pack or in the government section of the telephone book.

Furthermore, there is a Translating and Interpreting Service (ITS) available to specifically help non-English speaking people with their taxation returns. The TIS offers joint meetings with interpreters and tax officers, and you simply call the TIS to make an appointment. The TIS phone numbers are found in the community information pages of your phone book.

Claiming back tax on expenses If you are audited, you will usually receive written notification at the beginning of the audit, and you should follow the instructions contained in the letter. If audited, you will have to substantiate your work expenses claims, e.g. motor vehicle, other travel, clothing, tertiary studies, tools of trade, reference books and other expenses. It is therefore necessary to keep records of any work-related expenses in order to avoid additional tax and a possible penalty.

If you are an employee and the total of your claims is $300 or less, you must keep a record of how you worked out each of your claims. If the total of your claims is more than $300, the records you must keep are receipts, invoices or similar documentary evidence supported by or on behalf of the supplier of the goods or services. Cheque stubs are not considered acceptable as evidence. The receipt, invoice or documentary evidence must be in English or the language of the country where the expense was incurred, have the date on which the expense was incurred, name the person who or business which supplied the goods or services, show the amount of the expense in the currency in which the expense was incurred, give details of the nature of the goods or services, and show the date the document was made out.

A diary may be used to prove your claims for expenses that are no more than $10 each and which add up to no more than $200, or for which it was unreasonable to expect to get a receipt. The diary should contain all the details that would be required on a receipt or invoice. In addition, you must sign each entry in the diary.

The information outlined above should be kept for a period of three years and six months after lodging your tax return, in the case of salary and wage earners, or for seven years after lodging your tax return if you are self-employed and the claims are for car and travel-related expenses. Records of other business-related expenses incurred by self-employed persons should be retained for five years after lodging their tax return. If you appeal against an assessment, you must retain your records until the dispute has been finalised if that period exceeds the given record retention period.

You can claim for the cost of using your car for work or business purposes, for example travelling directly from one place of work to another, or from one job to another. You cannot, however, generally claim for the cost of travelling from home to work.

Table of Income Tax

There is currently a tax threshold of $5,400 in Australia which is applicable to those stopping full-time education for the first time, those becoming residents of Australia, or those who stopped being residents of Australia. This threshold means that the first $5,400 earned is tax free.

There are many different tables of assessment of tax which depend on personal circumstances and the Tax Pack (see above) gives details about these. However, the tables most likely to be relevant to you have been outlined below.

Table A is applicable if you were a resident of Australia for the full financial year, you did not stop full time education for the first time, and you are entitled to the full $5,400 tax-free threshold.

Table A

Taxable Income	Tax
$1-$5,400	Nil
$5,400-$20,700	Nil + 20 cents for each $1 over $5,400
$20,701-$36,000	$3,060 + 35.5 cents for each $1 over $20,700
$36,001-$38,000	$8,491.50 + 38.5 cents for each $1 over $36,000
$38,001-$50,000	$9,261.50 + 44.125 cents for each $1 over $38,000
$50,001 and over	$14,556.50 + 47 cents for each $1 over $50,000

Table B is applicable if you became a resident of Australia during the financial year. If this is the case, you are entitled to a proportional amount of the $5,400 tax threshold. For the tax year you calculate this amount by adding up the number of months from when you became a resident of Australia (including the month in which you became a resident) to the 30 June. This amount is then divided by twelve (correspondent to the number of months in the year), to give you the proportion of the year spent in Australia and this is then multiplied by $5,400 to give you your tax-free threshold. For example, if you have only been resident in Australia for two months, your tax threshold is assessed as 2/12 x $5,400 = $900, but if you have been resident for eleven months, your tax threshold is 11/12 x $5,400 = $4,950. This reduced tax threshold is known as R in the table of assessment given below.

Table B

For a taxable income of $20,700 or less:

Taxable Income	Tax
$1-R minus $1	Nil
R-$20,700	Nil + 20 cents for each $1 over R

For a taxable income of more than $20,700 S = ($20,700 R) × 20%):

Taxable Income	Tax
$20,701-$36,000	S + Nil + 35.5 cents for each $1 over $20,700
$36,001-$38,000	S + $5,431.50 + 38.5 cents for each $1 over $36,000
$38,001-$50,000	S + $6,201.50 + 44.125 cents for each $1 over $38,000
$50,000 and over	S + $11,496.50 + 47 cents for each $1 over $50,000

Your assessment can take up to eight weeks after lodging your tax return. If you are required to pay tax, you will be given thirty days notice. Tax can be paid by cheque or postal money orders made payable to the Deputy Commissioner of Taxation, in cash or cheque at any Post Office (you must take your Notice of Assessment with you), by mail (cheque or postal order only), at Tax Offices (take your Notice of Assessment), or by direct debit/refund. This last service is available from tax agents who lodge tax returns electronically.

If you cannot pay your tax by the due date, you may be given extra time to pay depending on your circumstances. You will have to provide details of your financial position including assets, liabilities, income and expenditure, and the steps you have taken to obtain funds to pay your debt. If granted additional time, you will be charged interest calculated on a daily basis. This rate is currently 16.7%.

Rebates

There are numerous rebates which may be applicable to different people at different times, and it is certainly worth being aware of them even if you are not eligible at the moment as there may well be a time when, as a resident of Australia, you will fulfil the requirements necessary in order to claim one or more rebates. A brief summary of some of the available rebates is given below:

Sole Parent: If you have the sole care of a child or student, you may be able to claim the sole parent rebate, even if you are not the parent. You can claim a maximum sole parent rebate of $1,116 for the whole financial year if you did not have a spouse (married or de facto), you had sole care of a dependent child or student whose separate net income for the financial year was less than $1,786, and you are not claiming a rebate for either a housekeeper or childminder for any part of the financial year.

Zone Rebate: People living in specified remote areas of Australia can claim a zone rebate. These areas are divided into two zones, Zone A and Zone B, and within each zone there are special areas that are entitled to larger rebates than others. These are called special zones. A special zone is generally a place where the nearest town or centre with a population of at least 2,500 is more than 250 km away.

Medical Expenses: You can claim a rebate of 20% of the net medical expenses you may have incurred over $1,000. There is no maximum amount which you can claim, the rebate is calculated as a percentage only.

Overseas Dependants: If your dependant is overseas, you may be eligible to claim a rebate if they are temporarily away from Australia or are waiting to migrate to Australia. Your dependant must migrate within five years from when you first entered Australia in order to take up residence, and you may be asked to provide evidence in order to substantiate your claim.

Other Taxes

Financial Institutions Duty and Debits Tax. Duties and taxes collected on certain types of bank, building society or other financial institution accounts are called Financial Institutions Duty (FID) and Debits Tax. These are automatically debited from your account by the financial institution which holds your account and will be shown on your statements or in your passbook, whichever is more applicable. If you do not see any sign of FID or Debits Tax deductions having been made on either your statement or passbook, this usually means that your account is not one which is taxable and so no charges have been made. If you can show that the deductions were made against your assessable income, you may be able to claim these as tax deductions in your tax return. This is a fairly complex and confusing point, so it is worth consulting a Tax Officer in order to ascertain whether your account is the type which can be taxed and whether you can claim these as tax deductions.

As mentioned above, some financial institutions charge administration fees. If you are able to show that your account is used solely for investment purposes, it is possible to claim the administration charges as a tax deduction; however initial fees for the establishment of your account are not generally allowable tax deductions. In addition, if your bank account is necessary for your business, you are able to claim any governmental or institutional charges or fees on that account as tax deductions.

Provisional Tax Provisional tax applies to those who earn more than $999 per year in non-salary or wage income from investments, business, primary production (i.e., farming or mining), distribution from a trust or any other source which is not covered by the PAYE system. Provisional tax basically makes provision for the current year's tax in much the same way as salary and wage earners do under the PAYE system. You do not have to pay 1994/95 provisional tax if your taxable income is below the relevant level shown below:

Single	$19,492
Married/de facto	$29,988 (combined income)
Married or de facto and separated due to illness	$37,346 (combined income)

It is important to note that provisional tax must be paid in advance and is based on the earnings of the previous year. If this amount falls short of the amount of tax owed as assessed by the Tax Office at the end of the financial year, the amount owing must be paid within 30 days from the date on which your Notice of Assessment was issued, or on 1 February of the following financial year, whichever is first.

Provisional tax must be paid by self-employed people and is generally paid in quarterly instalments. If, however, you are able to substantiate your claim that more than 75% of your income is received in the last six months of the financial year, the Tax Office may adjust its demands for payment of taxes to bi-annual payments rather than quarterly.

Capital Gains Tax In 1985, the Australian government introduced a system of taxation known as Capital Gains Tax. This means that if you sell or otherwise dispose of any assets or receive any other capital amounts in a financial year, you may be liable to pay Capitals Gains Tax. Examples of capital amounts include a forfeited deposit, premium received for granting a lease, or a capital gain distributed to a beneficiary of a trust. This includes any 'gifts' received, particularly those deemed as 'business' gifts, and the recipient is taxed on the gift at its fair market value.

Assets subject to Capital Gains Tax include:

Listed personal-use assets that you owned for personal use and enjoyment that cost more than $100 to buy, e.g. a rare publication, artwork, jewellery, stamps, coins or an antique.

Non-listed personal-use assets (other than land or a building) that you owned for personal use and enjoyment and which you disposed of for more than $5,000 each, e.g. a lounge suite or a sound system for more than $5,000.

Other assets include shares or units in unit trusts, options or rights to acquire shares or units and real estate (including your holiday home). A series of Capital Gains is available from any Tax Office. It is important to note that there are no Death Duties in effect in Australia. Capital Gains Tax is only applicable if the assets received from a deceased person's estate are sold by an executor or disposed of for money by a beneficiary. There are other exemptions from Capital Gains Tax, including:

The taxpayer's main residence and 'reasonable' land around it, although there is no exemption for houses owned by a family trust or private company and lived in by a trust beneficiary or shareholder.

Superannuation or life insurance policies.

Sale of motor vehicles and other personal-use assets with a disposable value below the amounts given above.

Compensation payments for stolen or destroyed property.

Expenses involved in improving or selling a property are taken into account against the amount of profit made in the sale. Usually, annual expenses such as repairs and interest payments on the asset are excluded from the calculation of the asset's value and any tax which may be owing.

Fringe Benefits Tax The Fringe Benefits Tax was introduced in July 1986 by the government in an effort to control the amount of non-cash (and therefore non-taxable) benefits offered by employers as part of a job package. For example, fringe benefits still offered to certain employees, usually foreign, who may be only temporarily employed to complete specific research or provide an otherwise unobtainable service. These employees may enjoy the provision of occupational health and counselling services, holiday travel, and the education of their children free of charge while in Australia, because the employer may claim these benefits tax-free as part of an employment deal. These deals have become much rarer, however, since 1986 as Fringe Benefits Tax is specifically aimed at companies and employees who were deliberately reducing their tax burden through the exploitation of fringe benefits. Companies are no longer allowed to claim expenses such as business lunches and entertainment costs on behalf of the company, and now any fringe benefits are considered an assessable part of an individual's or company's taxable income.

Taxable fringe benefits include company cars, free or low-interest loans, free or subsidised accommodation or board, goods and services sold at a reduced rate or provided free, and expenses paid on behalf of an employee.

Cars are, perhaps, the most common fringe benefit, and Fringe Benefits Tax is normally paid by an employer when a car is owned or leased by a company and made available to an employee (or family member) for private use. Fringe Benefits Tax does not normally apply to self-employed people or to a partnership if the vehicle is used wholly and exclusively for business. It does not apply to cars owned or leased by an employee, even when the cost of operating the car for business use is claimed as an expense against the taxable income. When Fringe Benefits Tax is chargeable, it applies to all passenger cars, wagons, minibuses, panelvans and utilities designed to carry less than one tonne or a bus with fewer than nine seats. There are many variations and exemptions with the Fringe Benefits Tax and it is well worth consulting a taxation expert in order to ascertain whether you should or shouldn't be paying this particular tax.

Medicare Levy Although mentioned earlier in this chapter, it is worth noting again that you are not required to make any Medicare payments (see the Healthcare System) if your taxable income is less than $12,689 per annum. If your taxable income is more than $12,688 but less than $13,643, you are required to pay 20 cents for every dollar over $12,688. It your income is greater than or equal to $13,643, your Medicare levy is 1.4% of your taxable income.

Higher Education Contributions Scheme. As noted in more detail in the section on Education, any higher education you undertake in Australia can be paid for initially by the government on your behalf, and you are consequently liable to pay a HECS tax out of your salary if you earn more than $26,403 per annum. The rate of HECS tax varies from 3% to 5% of your taxable income. From 1 July 1994, the Australian government instructed employers to deduct additional taxation instalments to cover any possible Higher Education Contributions Assessment Debt in future years. These deductions will only be made if you earn more than $508 per week. For further details on HECS and taxation, you should request a copy of the booklet *HECS; Your Questions Answered*, available from your educational institution or any Tax Office.

Death Duties

At the time of writing, there are no Death Duties payable in Australia. This is likely to be reviewed in the relatively near future by the government, but any attempt to introduce Death Duties is likely to be met with widespread public opposition.

Health Insurance and Hospitals

A recent report, prepared by the Australian Institute of Health and Welfare, states that Australians born in the 1990s can expect to live 15 years longer than those born in the 1920s, and that boys born in 1992 could expect to live to an age of 74.5 while girls would live to an age of 80.4. The Report found that Australia's mortality rate is currently 7.1 per 1,000 people per year, although Aboriginal people continued to have a mortality rate far higher than the national average. Interestingly, the report also compared the mortality rates of migrants and Australian-born residents and found that most migrant groups had death rates significantly lower than the Australian average. Greeks, Italians, Central and South Americans, Vietnamese and those from former Yugoslavia had the lowest rate. In addition, among Australians aged 25-64, the death rate was 15% higher for men living in rural regions, and 9% higher for women in rural areas.

The Report also indicated that multiple births are becoming increasingly frequent which is largely due to the increasing rate of artificial conception (e.g., IVF treatment), that dental health has improved dramatically over recent years to the extent that few people under 35 years of age have lost all their teeth, and that more than 100,000 people were waiting for elective surgery in public hospitals in 1993. Despite this number of people on waiting lists, the report also indicated that recent trends show a continued decline in basic and supplementary private hospital insurance which is likely to drop to 31.1% by 1997. This is perhaps due to the fact that in the year 1992/3, govermental health expenditure was more than $34 billion, working out at an average of $1,944 per person.

Cholesterol continues to be a major cause of health problems in Australia, and 49% of men and 39% of women were estimated to have cholesterol levels considered to show an increased risk of heart disease. In addition, 16% of men and 14% of women were considered to have high-risk levels of cholesterol in their blood. The concern over cholesterol is reflected in the amount spent on drugs. Expenditure on drugs increased to $2.5 billion in the year 1992/3,of which more than $90 million was spent on Simvastatin, which lowers blood cholesterol.

The Report also showed that the nation's health was dogged by a rising suicide rate, with more Australians dying by their own hands than in traffic accidents. For the most part, victims tended to be males between 15 and 24 years old, but this age group was also the biggest risk group among women. The survey indicated strong links between suicide and the socially disadvantaged and the unemployed, particularly among Aboriginals. In recent years, there have been a number of Aboriginal deaths in custody completely disproportionate to the average rate of suicides in prison. So alarming are the statistics, that the goverment has opened an inquiry into the rate of Aboriginal deaths in custody, and numerous investigative documentaries have been produced and shown on Australian and even British television.

Cancer rates also appear to be on the increase, accounting for 27% of Australian deaths in 1992, compared with 15% in 1965. Breast, lung and skin cancers are the most prevalent killers. In response to this many Australian buildings are completely smoke-free zones and Australians protect themselves much better against the sun than they used to with high-factor sunscreens, and hats and T-shirts have become common beach wear.

As the above statistics show, while Australians may have apparently healthy lifestyles, there is a high demand on the nation's health services.

The Health Care System

Using the GP. The first contact for obtaining health care in Australia is the local GP whom you are free to choose yourself. Depending on the doctor, you will either be billed for the consultation, for which you will be reimbursed by Medicare, the Australian national health system, or the doctor will bulk-bill which means they will claim reimbursement directly from Medicare. Doctors who practise in low income areas tend to bulk-bill in order to avoid asking their patients for payment, which is generally considered a gesture of goodwill on behalf of the GP. Medicare covers consultation fees to approximately $18. If GP charges exceed this, the patient is liable for any amount in excess of the $18 threshold.

Should you wish to have a second medical opinion, you simply make an appointment with another doctor. Generally, appointments are made over the telephone, and you can usually see your GP within two days of your call. There is an increasing number of clinics and medical centres opening in the suburbs. These house a number of doctors and usually at least will be female. There may also be a pharmacy housed within the centre, from which you can purchase your prescriptions immediately. Prescriptions are also refundable through Medicare up to a certain percentage of the cost of the medication, depending on the type of medication concerned.

If a GP recommends you see a consultant or specialist, they will usually arrange the appointment for you, and there is generally a waiting period depending on the urgency of your case. You may choose to see a consultant on a private basis, for which you will have to pay yourself, or through the national health care system, for which either you or the specialist (depending on who has paid the cost of your consultation) will be reimbursed.

Using Hospitals. Should you need hospital attention or surgery, you may also choose to go to a private hospital or a public one. If you opt for private hospitalisation, you can choose both your attending doctor/surgeon and the hospital, but naturally you pay large sums of money for this privilege. If you opt for public treatment, you cannot choose your hospital or your doctor, and you may face a long wait for a bed, but you are financially covered under Medicare.

A list of public hospitals, divided by regions, can be obtained from Australia House in London. It is important to note that bills for hospital treatment are always charged directly to the government on your behalf.

Health Insurance Contributions

Every Australian is covered by Medicare. Those who earn taxable wages or salaries automatically make contributions to Medicare (1.5% of the total salary) which is included in normal taxation. Those who are unemployed or dependants have automatic deductions made from the unemployment allowance (dole) or child endowment/dependant allowance. Those who choose to pay for additional private health insurance cover pay their premiums to the private company directly. A standing order can be arranged with the bank, or payments can be made by cheque or in person.

The Australian National Health System

Australia's national health system, Medicare, is generally of an excellent standard, and although many Australians also opt for private medical cover, as mentioned above, this trend is decreasing in popularity. It is funded by the Federal and State governments out of collected taxes. It is necessary to register at a Medicare office in order to be eligible for its cover, although you need not necessarily have registered with Medicare in order to get medical treatment. This entails completing an application form (either before or after you receive medical treatment) which you can get from a Medicare regional office or at post offices Australia-wide. All migrants are covered by Medicare, provided they pay the tax levy (included in their general taxes), and temporary residents who stay in the country longer than six months may be covered by Medicare without having to pay the levy. Medicare covers in-patient and out-patient treatment at public hospitals, and any accommodation in public hospitals. Medicare refunds 85% of scheduled (government approved) fees, whether those fees be for consultations with private doctors, or for eye tests by optometrists. The remaining 15% is called a 'gap' fee which the client is expected to pay. In the case of large scheduled bills for expensive treatment and/or operations, Medicare will only charge the patient a nominal part of the gap fee. If you need constant, expensive treatment, Medicare will cover all of the scheduled fees incurred over the rest of the year after the gap has totalled $150 for any financial year. Prescription drugs and medications are also subject to a Medicare subsidy. Under Medicare cover, pharmaceuticals should only cost a maximum of $10 for the first 25 items per year, after which any perscriptions are fully subsidised.

It is important to note that Medicare does not cover doctor's fees, when these exceed the scheduled fee, or the 15% gap, if the doctor does not bulk-bill the government. You will not be covered for treatment and accommodation at a public hospital if you have been admitted as a private patient, or for treatment and accommodation at a private hospital. Medicare does not cover physio-therapy, chiropractic or dental treatment, although some orthodontal treatment is refundable, particularly if surgery is involved. Neither medical repatriation nor funeral costs are covered, and ambulance costs (including transport and treatment) cannot be refunded through Medicare.

Once you have completed the application forms for Medicare, your application will be processed, and you will be sent a Medicare Card. This card is green and yellow (the national colours) and looks similar to the current British National Insurance Number Card in that it is a plastic card with an embossed account number on the front, together with your name and address, and a signature strip along the back, like any credit card. Upon receipt of this card, you should sign it and keep it in a safe place at home, or in your wallet/purse. Every time you receive medical treatment, you will be required to produce this card and sign a receipt in order to be able to claim any refund for which you may be eligible. You will also be required to produce this card for hospital treatment.

Basically, the message conveyed by the authorities is to get yourself registered with Medicare as soon as possible in order to be able to enjoy the benefits of the national health service and avoid being landed with enormous medical bills in the unfortunate event of sickness or injury.

Reciprocal Agreements

Travellers from the UK, New Zealand, Malta, Italy, Sweden and the Netherlands are also covered by Medicare, and therefore receive medical treatment in the event of an accident or emergency free of charge for the first six months from the date of arrival in Australia, because of existing reciprocal agreements between Australia and these countries. This means that you are not entitled to claim health benefits for a medical condition which existed before you arrived in Australia, including any illness you caught on the way to Australia, or any medication. If you are a short-term visitor and you do not come from a country which has reciprocal health agreements with Australia, it is advisable to take out private medical insurance, which is usually available through your travel agent under travel insurance. It is possible to buy travel insurance valid in Australia for 31, 45, 60, 90, 120 or 185 days, 6 months and 12 months. Insurance is usually purchased by single payment. A typical 12-month insurance package for Australia/New Zealand costs about £200. Although you cannot claim welfare benefits and pensions from the state/federal government if your country of origin does not have a reciprocal medical agreement with Australia, you may be eligible for emergency benefits or other assistance. If you ever feel you are in desperate need of government assistance to pay essential medical bills, you should contact the Department of Social Security (address below). New settlers should be aware that they are fully covered by Medicare (apart from the exceptions noted below). In addition, anyone, regardless of nationality or visa status, is liable for the costs involved with any ambulance services. Even Australians have to cover their own ambulance bills, and the St John's Ambulance Association offers a system of membership for the nominal fee of $14.00 per person per year, which entitles that member to free ambulance services.

Medicare Exclusions. There are two notable exceptions to the above ruling. They are people entering Australia to retire, and those who have been granted permanent residence in the family reunion/migration category, are the parents of their sponsor and are more than 55 years old (men) or 50 years old (women). In the case of retirees, it is necessary to take out travel insurance and private medical insurance (either in your country of origin or in Australia) as you will be liable for all expenses incurred in the case of medical and hospital treatment and hospital accommodation. In the latter case, should any medical/hospital expenses be incurred by the migrant parent (over the stipulated age limit) of a sponsor, that sponsor will be liable to cover all costs. If only one of the sponsor's parents is over the age limit, (e.g., the sponsor's father is 56, but his/her mother is only 49), then the sponsor is only responsible for the medical expenses incurred by that parent whose age is over the limit. In addition, if you enter Australia as a foreign diplomat or as a member of a foreign diplomat's family, you are not covered by Medicare and so cannot benefit from the Australian national health system. It is advisable to take out private medical insurance either before you leave your home country or take out a policy in Australia immediately upon your arrival.

Private Medical Insurance

For the socialists at heart, the situation with private medical insurance can be galling. The current advertising campaign for a leading private health insurance company is based on the premise that if you have private medical insurance, you will receive better treatment more promptly than if you are only covered by Medicare. The idea that only those who can afford private cover get good medical attention really runs against the grain of the principles behind Medicare, but unfortunately in practice public-sector funded medical centres and hospitals tend to be run by comparatively overworked staff and, as a consequence, have much longer waiting lists. As mentioned above, the government has recently increased its health budget considerably in an effort to improve public health facilities and the number of Australians who are taking out private medical cover is decreasing. Having said that, the fact remains that approximately 70% of the Australian population choose to be covered by both Medicare and private medical insurance. It gives most people a sense of security to know that should they be in need of medical attention, they will have the autonomy to choose both the hospital where they will be treated and, to a lesser extent, the doctor/ surgeon who will treat them. In addition, private cover offers refunds for medical services not generally covered by Medicare, such as physiotherapy treatment, prescription glasses and sunglasses, and even some dental work. Like most insurance policies, private health insurance companies offer differing levels of cover, from basic through to comprehensive, and the cost can vary from as little as a matter of cents per person per week to about $5 per person per week. Premiums are usually payable in monthly, quarterly or annual instalments and discounts are usually given for prompt payment and/or for payments made annually.

Children and dependants are usually covered by their parents' private medical insurance, which is also the situation with Medicare.

Private health insurance companies advertise in the local newspapers and on radio and television so there is no difficulty in finding them. Two of the largest are Medibank Private and Hospital Benefits Fund.

Useful Addresses

Department of Health and Social Security, Overseas Branch, Benton Park Road, Newcastle-Upon-Tyne NE98 1YX, tel: 0191-213 5000.
ATI Travel Insurance: 37 Kings Exchange, Tilesyard Road, London N7 9AH, tel: 0171-609 5000.
Columbus Travel Insurance: 17 Devonshire Square, London EC2 4SQ, tel: 0171- 375 0011.

Crime and Police

Australia has many of the crime problems associated with developed nations and big-city life, but on the whole you can feel relatively safe compared with some of the world's more notorious cities, the very mention of whose names is enough to evoke a sense of fear in most tourists and visitors.

The Australian Bureau of Statistics found that the most frequently reported crime in 1993 was unlawful entry with intent (380,000 offences) and relatively few guns were used. Motor vehicle theft was the next most common crime, with 112,500 stolen motor vehicles reported to the police, followed by robbery and sexual assault. In 1993, there were 802 homicides (including 290 murders), 25% of which occured in New South Wales. Dr Ken Polk, associate professor of criminology at Melbourne University, suggested that the relatively low number of guns used in all violent crimes committed last year was because Australia has tough gun laws which make it difficult to buy a gun. Only 20%-25% of homicides involved a firearm in Australia, compared to 65%-75% in the USA.

Of the states, Victoria seems to be the safest statiscally when it comes to volume and severity of crime, followed by Tasmania and Canberra; however the crime patterns differ in all States and Territories. The Northern Territory had the highest per capita rate for homicide and sexual assaults, but the lowest number of armed robberies. Western Australia had the highest number of motor vehicle thefts and burglaries, but its rate of murder and attempted murder were at the national average or below. New South Wales had the highest rate of armed robbery, largely as a result of the state having the highest percentage of heroin addicts in the country. Canberra had the highest rate of kidnapping, which can be attributed to acrimonious marital disputes over custody of children, and South Australia had the highest incidence of robbery and blackmail.

Gone are the days when you did not have to lock your doors and women could go out by themselves after dark. Although in rural areas this is still much the same, in urban areas much more care has to be taken.

The police forces for each state/territory are controlled by a Commissioner for Police, and, depending on the state/territory, may carry guns on duty. Recently, the Queensland and Western Australian forces have been subject to accusations of police corruption, with the result that the forces have been given a thorough cleanout. In general, police enjoy a fairly good public profile and maintain open communications with the community.

Local Government

The local government is usually in charge of a 'shire' or district, and is responsible for the provision and maintenance of public facilities and amenties, including the kerb at the front of your house. Payments for all housing rates and even dog-licensing are made to the local government. In terms of planning permission for building and/or extensions, applications must be made to the local government, and open meetings are frequently held to hear public discussion over topical local issues such as planning and zonal developments. In general, however, most Australians are fairly apathetic and tend not to get terribly involved in local government decisions. Strangely, it is often the migrants and new settlers who become most involved in governmental decisions, perhaps because they most appreciate and wish to preserve what attracted them to reside in that particular community in the first place. Addresses and telephone numbers of local governments are available under the 'Local Government' section at the front of telephone directories.

Social Life

Australian social life is almost inextricably bound up with the nation's sporting life. It is very common to join some sort of sporting team consisting of your social circle or workmates, and compete at a local level. But what happens if you have not been blessed with sporting talents? How can you try to break the ice, meet the locals and both accept and be accepted by them? This section tries to give you a little insight into Australian social life and the kinds of people and attitudes you are most likely to meet.

Manners and Customs

On the whole, Australians are a lot more casual than their British or European cousins. You will find that people, while friendly and courteous, will be a lot more direct in asking questions or telling you what they think. You are much less likely to experience the occasionally chilling British reserve, and are much more likely to know exactly where you stand. When you meet an Australian for the first time at a social gathering, you may find that you are asked a lot of questions about where you are from, what you are doing in Australia, what you do for a living, where you are currently living, what leisure activities you like. Try to bear this with fortitude and at least not show you are taken aback. Australians are generally not sticklers for etiquette or protocol; the quickest and most direct way of doing something is usually the way it gets done. This can also be true for bureaucracy and official red tape. Although it exists, it can often be not as lengthy or as complicated as that of other systems.

It is very difficult to talk about distinct Australian manners and customs, as Australian society is so relatively new and there are no really defined customs. Australia's multicultural society is composed of many customs and traditions, many of which have been brought with new settlers. The overall impression of the culture is somewhat vague and hazy, but the grass-roots view of Australian life is exciting and diverse as the different cultural groups have their own festivals and customs throughout the year.

One custom that seems to be common to many Australians, regardless of ethnic origin, is the tendency to call each other 'mate'. The concept of mateship is a peculiarly Australian phenomenon and has been subject to sociological and anthropological study. Mateship tends to be a specifically male bond and is a very macho kind of friendship, but nevertheless very real and strong. Many Australian men consider their male mates to be just as important as, or even more important than their female partner. The bond of friendship between mates runs deep, and often to the grave. To be described as somebody's life-long mate is a compliment indeed. On the other hand, Australians, and usually Australian males, will call somebody they don't know 'mate' in an ironic way, especially in potentially explosive situations: e.g., 'What do you think you're doing, mate?' or 'You'd better get out of my way, mate'. The tone of voice will indicate whether the term is being used affectionately, neutrally or dangerously. The term 'sport' is also used to indicate male friendship, but is not as common as the term 'mate'. You will hear Australian men, whether they were originally from China, Vietnam, Italy or Greece, calling each other 'mate', which has a pleasing ring to it.

Australians also tend to try anything, and there is an inbuilt sense of respect for anyone who has a go at something new or difficult, particularly if the odds are stacked against the person who is trying. Australians love to see the underdog winning, and perhaps this is a harkening back to the convict past. If you get involved with your work, neighbourhood, sporting team, etc., you will be seen to be giving your new life a good go, and will be respected for it by the locals.

Meeting People/Making Friends

As a new settler, getting out of your new house and into the kind of situations in which you can meet people can be very difficult. This is true whether you are moving from one region in your own home country to another, or whether you are moving overseas, no matter what country you are moving to. Australians are famous for their openness and friendliness, but it is still possible to make life difficult for yourself socially when you get there. First of all, Australians are wary of English migrants in particular, as English new settlers have a reputation for being easily dissatisfied with what they find when they get there. There is nothing more irritating to Australians than to hear new settlers complaining about any or every aspect of Australian life upon their arrival, and the complainers are likely to be met with a fairly hostile reception. It is advisable for any new settler to keep their grievances to themselves, and to offer nothing other than praise for their new home and express only the excitement they feel about the prospect of a new life in Australia. An Australian confronted with enthusiastic new settlers, delighted with his/her country, is much more likely to want to show them around and introduce then to his/her friends.

It can also help to develop an interest in sport, even if you have previously had no inclination to do so. As mentioned above, you will find it easy to meet people and make friends if you get involved in a local sporting club of some sort. It is a really good idea, if invited, to join a sporting team with your workmates as this is a practical and fun way to get to know your workmates out of the normal working situation.

For mothers with small children, there are coffee clubs and craft mornings run by local churches or councils. Technical and Further Education institutions (known as TAFEs) also run both day and evening classes in a wide range of different subjects, from Ikebana (Japanese flower arranging) to panel-beating and drawing. Whether male or female, single or married, working or unemployed, these TAFE courses are enjoyable and inexpensive. A ten-week course can cost as little as $30, depending on what course you choose to do. Local councils also run recreation courses at local community centres, which are slightly less professional than the TAFE courses, but equally enjoyable, in as wide a range of subjects from yoga to badminton and Asian cooking. These courses are also very cheap indeed, and are a good way to meet other people with similar interests in your local community. After-school activities for children are also run at community centres, from crafts and tennis to ballet classes. If your child is attending a school outside the area in which you live, you may find that these activities provide a chance for your child to meet other local children. In addition, the Boys' and Girls' Brigades both operate Australia-wide, as do the Cubs, Brownies, Scouts and Guides, and the Every Boys and Every Girls Rallies. To find out details about TAFE and community centre courses, look up the different TAFE colleges in your local telephone directory, or contact your local council, community centre or library. TAFE and councils also advertise courses, fees and enrolment dates in local newspapers.

Australian suburban back gardens are usually surrounded by six-foot tall asbestos fences, which can mean that the potential for friendly over-the-garden fence chat is prevented. Sometimes it is these chats that can help break the ice and build friendships with your neighbours. It is quite normal for neighbours to invite you around for a coffee or a drink when you first move in, but if they don't do this, you may have to find alternative strategies for getting to know them. Don't be put off if you are not inundated with invitations to visit all your new neighbours, sometimes a particular neighbourhood is not particularly friendly (not every locality is as close and involved as *Neighbour's* Erinsborough). You may need to take the initiative and invite your neighbours around to meet you. In fact, an excellent way to get to know your neighbours is to have a barbecue. Barbies are incredibly social occasions where good food and drink and conversation provide an excellent basis on which to begin friendships. If you host a barbecue, you can provide everything if you want to, but it is more common to provide the salads, bread and some meat and drinks, and to ask your neighbours to bring their own meat and drinks. You must state what your neighbours are expected to bring with them when you invite them, and they will certainly not think twice about being asked to bring something. In fact, this seems to create a real sense of a communal eating/drinking/social occasion, and will go a long way towards making you seem friendly and community-minded in your neighbours' eyes.

Useful Organisations & Addresses

There are a number of ex-pat associations in Australia, including the Chung-Wah Chinese Association. All major cities will have branches of these associations, and the biggest ones tend to be European. The Greek, Italian and Yugoslav clubs are especially well attended. There are numerous Irish clubs Australia-wide, and you should consult your local telephone directory in order to find out more information about an ex-pat club, or contact the Ethnic Communities' Council of Australia (5th floor, 541 George Street, Sydney NSW 2000, tel: 0011-61 2 267 97220).

There is a club specifically for migrants from the UK, The United Kingdom Settlers' Association (PO Box 221, Fitzroy VIC 3065, tel: 0011-61 3 419 3788).

Sport

More than anything, sport is considered to be the Australian national pastime, and is also central to the social life of many Australians. Most Australian children are encouraged to play at least one sport from a very early age. Little Athletics is extremely popular for children as young as five, with regional and national competitions. It is quite prestigious to do well in Little Athletics as this usually signifies that you have real talent and club scouts are very interested in the results of Little Athletics meetings in order to find new talent. In a similar way cricket and football (Australian Rules) are incredibly popular at every age and skill level, and most Australian boys play at some time or another for their local club. Cricket is becoming increasingly in favour with girls, but usually not until secondary age or even later. In addition, an indoor version of cricket is very popular, and is a highly skilled and very fast game. Many different leagues exist in all the different cities and regions, and it is easy (in fact, almost difficult not to) to get involved in a men's, ladies' or mixed team. Sporting centres all over the country also offer volleyball, netball and five-a-side soccer, and single-sex or mixed teams often have their own leagues. Most young working Australians will play in one such team at least one night per week as a way of keeping fit and meeting their friends.

Australian Rules football is the winter game, and is a predominantly male sport. 'Boys' from five to fifty years old love playing this game, but for the older ones the roughness and toughness of the game can be just too much. Aussie Rules football is really a national institution, and is played at the national level. Every state has its own team or teams which play in a national league, the final of which is in September and is always played at the Melbourne Cricket Ground. For the uninitiated, the game can look like sheer madness and total chaos. The rules are, however, fairly straightforward (there simply aren't that many of them) and it only takes watching the game a couple of times with an expert to make sense of the thing and, more importantly, to see the point of the game. Basically, the game consists of two teams of 18 players each who are trying to score goals against each other. The goal posts are four evenly-spaced tall poles, the two outer ones slightly shorter than the inside ones, and there is a goal at each end of the oval (The oval-shaped ground on which they play is about three times the size of a soccer pitch). If you manage to touch the ball over the line between the two middle posts, you have scored a goal, your team gains six points, and the goal umpire (always dressed in a white coat) will make a specific gesture with his index fingers (basically he points with both hands) and wave two white flags in an energetic and semi-ridiculous way. If you touch the ball over the line between a middle and an outer pole, you have only scored a point, and the goal umpire will only make the gesture with one of his index fingers and will wave only one of the flags. The game consists of four quarters, each quarter lasting 45 minutes. You are allowed to kick the ball as well as use your hands to 'handball' it to another player, and to punch it. You are allowed to hold the ball and run, as long as you bounce it every three seconds, otherwise you will be 'caught with the ball'. Bouncing the ball while you are on the run is in itself quite difficult as the ball is shaped like a rugby ball. Although some of the players at the interstate level have started to wear head protection and gloves (to give them a better grip on the ball), Aussie Rules players pride themselves on their extreme toughness and fitness. The game is gruelling and extremely hard on the players. It is long and very physical, but can also be intense and exciting. The best way to see a game is to go to an important interstate match, and to catch the atmosphere of the crowd.

In the eastern states, rugby (both league and union) are also known as football, and Queenslanders in particular are notoriously obsessive about the game. Western Australia, the Northern Territory and Tasmania do not share the same enthusiasm for the game that the others do, but the nation as a whole is very keen on rugby and proud of the excellent standard of its national team, the Wallabies.

Hockey is also very popular, for both sexes, and Western Australia prides itself on its exceptional facilities at Curtin University, and for its track record of churning out most of the players in the national team. The Australian men's and women's hockey teams are respected and feared worldwide and they both compete at the very top of the international circuit.

Netball and softball are also extremely popular sports. Almost 90% of Australian schoolgirls participate in non-school netball competitions during winter, and there are also summer competitive leagues, playing on weekday evenings, which are very popular. Softball is the summer sport which most schoolgirls play. The Australian school curriculum incorporates sport into the normal school day, and each school, whether private or state, usually participates in both an interschool swimming carnival and an interschool athletics carnival each year. In addition, there are interschool cricket, netball, football, and softball leagues and the games are always scheduled during school time or immediately after school. Many private schools, however, only have their interschool sporting matches on Saturdays. In fact, Saturday mornings and afternoons seem to be the national sports times for private clubs as well as private schools, and parents all over the country seem resigned to the fact that for at least five years they will have to get out of bed early on a Saturday morning to deliver their offspring at the relevant sporting venue. Growing up in Australia, I played tennis or netball according to the season on Saturday mornings, and my brother was fanatical about cricket.

Basketball and tennis are widely played throughout the country, and Australia has produced many winners of Wimbledon in the past, and continues to produce many players. Basketball is played at regional and interstate levels, and the national league is relatively new, but extremely well supported and avidly watched on television. In fact, getting a ticket for an interstate match can prove to be very difficult as they are snapped up as soon as they become available. Baseball is an even newer sport to Australia, but there is also a national league which is becoming increasingly popular. The junior equivalent of the baseball league is a game called T-Ball, which involves hitting the ball off the top of a pole, rather than having the ball pitched to you. This is also a game you will frequently see being played by children barely big enough to pick up the bat.

Of course, water sports are also an integral part of Australian social and sporting life. Water-skiing, windsurfing, surfing, boating and diving are all common leisure activities, and are also highly competitive sports. Many Australians own their own pleasure boat, whether that be a yacht or a powerful ski boat, and they delight in either relaxing or getting their adrenalin pumping on the water. There are many competitions for windsurfing, surfing and water-skiing in particular, and when driving along almost any metropolitan coastal road, you will see the water dotted with windsurfers and surfers. Swimming is also part of the school's sporting curriculum, and at both a primary and secondary level, students will swim in either the school or local pool at least once a week. Pupils are divided into classes according to their age and swimming ability, and they are taught the finer points of swimming techniques by qualified instructors.

As part of the school curriculum, the aim of these classes is to allow students to attain swimming qualifications. There are various levels of these certificates and the requirements become increasingly difficult as the levels increase. The first certificate is the Junior, and students can then progress through the Intermediate and Senior Certificates before attempting the Lifesaver qualifications and the Bronze, Silver and Gold medals. Private swimming clubs also abound in Australia, and many young Australians join these at an early age, ending up swimming at a state or even national level. The Australian swimming, diving and water-polo teams are formidable, performing extremely well at the 1992 World Swimming Championships held in Perth, and at the 1994 Commonwealth Games held in Victoria, Canada.

Shops and Shopping

Shopping in the metropolitan centres of Australia is first class. Within the suburbs, large shopping centres offer speciality shops for clothing and goods, as well as supermarkets. The more major shopping centres may also offer a food hall, where one can choose from a wide variety of cheap meals from a wide range of countries, and there may also be cinemas. The city centres, like the European concept of 'high street' shopping, usually house retail headquarters and usually house larger stock than one tends to find the in the suburban or regional branches. Each suburb also has a 'deli' (delicatessen) which is a small, often corner, shop selling bread, milk and other essentials as well as other more exotic foods. Shops are generally open from 9am-5pm, 5.30pm or 6pm Monday to Saturday, and in metropolitan centres the shops stay open till 9pm one night a week (usually a Thursday or Friday). Shops are not usually open on a Sunday, as Sunday trading is still illegal, but there is a push to change this legislation. There are a few shops and shopping centres which have special permission to stay open on a Sunday, but these are rare. Delis and chemists are the only shops which are open after other shops have shut. Delis are usually open 8am-8pm and chemists may operate these hours, or sometimes 24 hours. Each city will have a number of chemists which are open 24 hours a day, 365 days a year. There is an increasing number of 24-hour shops opening in Australia, based on the American 7-Eleven type of shop, and most cities have a handful of these scattered through the suburbs.

The quality of Australian produce and goods is generally good. Goods bearing a green and gold symbol indicate that the goods have been manufactured in Australia, and these consequently tend to be more expensive than the equivalent goods which have been made in south-east Asia due to the higher cost of Australian labour. The excellent standard and quality of Australian-made products is reflected by the higher price you may have to pay. In general, however, Japanese and Taiwanese products, particularly electrical goods, conform to Australia's strict quality standards and are usually very competitively priced.

Many European immigrants feel that the quality of clothing in Australian department stores is not as high as that found in equivalent stores in the EU. Many ex-pats state that clothes found in an EU department store tend to be made of better quality materials, and to higher standards than the same kind of clothing in Autralian stores, which are usually imported from South-east Asian countries. Having said this, the cost of clothing from a cheap Australian store such as K-Mart or Target, as well as other more upmarket stores such as Picnic, Oasis and Esprit, is, depending on the current exchange rate, as much as 50% cheaper than clothing from UK stores of a comparable standard. For example, Mrs Kathleen McGregor was born in Scotland but has been living in Australia for the last 18 years. She returned to the UK for a holiday in July 1994 and found that both clothes and food were virtually pound-for-dollar. Given that the exchange rate was $2.20 per £1.00, the cost of these goods in the UK works out as slightly less than double the cost of the same products in Australia. Mrs McGregor also found that petrol was also more expensive at approximately £0.57 per litre in the UK, compared to approximately $0.67 per litre in Australia.

Alcohol is not allowed to be sold in Australian supermarkets, and so only non-alcoholic or de-alcoholised wines, and soft drinks are available off the shelf at these stores. Alcoholic drinks can only be bought from licensed liquor stores, also known as 'bottle shops'. Drive-in bottle shops are very popular and involve driving your car up to the shop, rolling down the car window and giving your order and money to the attendant in exchange for your cartons of beer or casks of wine, and driving off. Bottle shops are usually open from 10am-10pm Monday to Saturday, and until 8pm on Sunday.

Many of the larger supermarkets, such as Coles and Woolworths, print vouchers on the back of their itemised receipts offering free meal deals (on a buy one, get one free basis) at local restaurants and chains such as Kentucky Fried Chicken, and discounts on anything from carpet cleaning to photo processing. The vast majority of shops accept cheques and major credit cards with adequate proof of identification, and it is possible to use autoteller bank cards at the larger supermarkets to pay by direct debit.

On the whole, in urban Australia, shopping can be an enjoyable experience, with a wide range of products available in modern, well-equipped shopping centres. In the rural and more remote areas, the situation can be very different. The range of choice is much more likely to be limited as shopping centres do not exist on the same scale in rural areas, and prices may be significantly higher due to freight costs. Most country dwellers prefer to wait until a trip to the city before shopping for electrical goods or clothing.

Food and Drink
There are no real regional differences and/or specialities in Australian cuisine; similar to the strange phenomenon that there are no really distinctive differences in accents across Australia. Pumpkin scones may tend to be associated with Queensland, just as Queenslanders tend to have a barely distinguishable accent, but that is really the extent of the regional differences.

Food and drink can be considered an enjoyable part of the Australian lifestyle. Long gone are the days of cremated snaggers (sausages) and other burnt sacrifices offered on the sacramental barbie. Barbecues continue to be an integral part of Australian social life, but the cuisine has dramatically improved. Any respectable barbecue will be laden with tiger prawns, marinated rump steak, chicken, fish as well as the good old burgers and sausages. In addition to this, you may be lucky enough to sample some damper (Australian bread made of flour, salt and water) baked in the coals. In fact, Finlays Fresh Fish BBQ in Kalbarri, Western Australia, makes the six-hour drive north of Perth worthwhile purely for one of their feasts. Tucked away at the back of the town, this literal shack in the sand offers the most unbelievably huge prawns, fresh out of the water fish and enormous steaks which are barbecued for you by Mr Finlay himself. Finlay's mum takes your cash (about $8-$12 depending on what you are having) and prepares a range of about six salads and about ten different sauces for your meal, all of which you help yourself to. Finlay's dad is busy cooking damper (at 50 cents a piece) and you can sit at the rough benches and tables, or on an old saddle around a campfire as you wait for your order to be cooked. The premises are not licensed, so you BYO (bring your own) alcohol. Watching one of the big western sunsets in the vast sky, drinking your favourite drop, smelling your fresh steak, prawns or fish being grilled to perfection over coals, and listening to a group of holidaying youths singing harmoniously around the campfire; what more could you possibly want? Whether you have a barbie prepared by professionals like the Finlays, or your own barbie in your own back yard or in one of the parks on a coin-operated gas barbecue provided by the local council, the food is likely to be great and the fun fantastic. Barbies are just brilliant, and come highly recommended as a way of delighting friends from the homeland who come to visit you. We managed to impress my Scottish grandfather at a barbecue when a particularly cheeky Kookaburra (large kingfisher bird) swiped his burger out of his hand before he managed to get it to his mouth.

As this example suggests, food is relatively cheap in Australia, and what particularly distinguishes it is the general outstanding quality and freshness of the produce. You can expect to eat at an averagely priced restaurant for $10-$15 for a two course evening meal and coffee, excluding wine. The portions you are likely to receive will not leave you hungry. The variety of restaurants available in all major Australian cities is simply incredible, probably comparable to the range available in London. Greek, Vietnamese, Mongolian, various styles of Chinese and Indian, Mexican, Lebanese, Portugese, Italian, Russian, Thai and Polish are just a few of the different restaurants available Australia-wide. Melbourne boasts of being a gourmet's paradise, offering anthing from Armenian to Zulu food, with the whole gamut of national cuisines in between. Sydney also offers nearly as big a range, as does Perth. Japanese food is also becoming increasingly popular, and take-away noodle bars can occasionally be found on street corners.

Australians are particularly fond of fruit and vegetables, and an Australian fruit salad is likely to surpass anything you have previously experienced. In addition, Australians can claim the pavlova as their own invention, created specifically for the ballerina, Anna Pavlova, on an Australian tour. Peach Melba is also an Australian desert, created for the internationally acclaimed Australian soprano, Dame Nellie Melba. In addition, the lamington is an Australian institution. A lamington is a cube of the most incredibly light sponge which has been dipped in a special chocolate sauce and then rolled in coconut. School Parent Associations invariably have 'Lamington Drives' as a way of fund raising. This involves taking orders from students, parents, friends and relatives for at least one dozen lamingtons each, and then a battalion of parents actually making the delicacy. A box of a dozen lamingtons usually sells for about $4.00. Many Australians grow passionfruit vines in their gardens, and passionfruit icing is very popular for sponge cakes and is very easy to make: simply add a teaspoon of melted butter to 150g (5oz) of icing sugar, and then add the juice and seeds of up to two passionfruit until the icing is spreadable.

Australian seafood is generally relatively moderately priced, whether fish or shellfish. Although many immigrants profess themselves disappointed by the general choice of fish, Sydney Rock oysters, Tasmanian and West Australian crayfish, Adelaide whiting, Northern Territory barramundi, sand and mud crabs, and Moreton Bay Bugs (a small delicious lobster from Moreton Bay) are internationally praised. If you buy fish from a fish and chip shop, you are most likely to be served either shark or snapper, both of which are full of flavour. The menu of the average fish and chip shop will also offer crab, prawns or squid (calamari), oysters or mussels.

The most famous Australian take-away food is the meat pie. This is traditionally eaten at Aussie Rules Football matches, or by brickie's labourers, and always with tomato sauce. I personally hate them as I am suspicious about the types of meat used to fill the pies, but they can be extremely tempting on colder winter days.

In the bush, there are many plants and animals which the Aboriginal people have traditionally eaten as being full of nutritional value or as good sources of water. Witchetty grubs are fat, white grubs about three inches long which are dug out of the ground from the roots of a witchetty bush. They are a very good source of water and taste slightly cheesy, but are not for the faint-hearted as they are eaten alive. Buffalo, kangaroo and crocodile steaks are also very popular. Emu steaks are also edible, but apparently not as tasty as ostrich. Goannas (large lizards) are reported to taste remarkably like chargrilled chicken after they have been cooked for a while in the coals of a bush fire. The days of the swagman, camping under the shade of a billabong tree, waiting for his billy to boil and his jumbuck (stolen sheep) to cook seem to be numbered, as the traditional bush foods are now beginning to appear on international menus.

The 'amber nectar' is widely touted in adverts to be Australia's favourite drink, and many Australians would not dispute the claim that lager is a real thirst quencher. Each state has its own beer brewed locally, but available interstate, which are Redback, Matilda Bay, Swan and Emu (WA), Tooheys and Fosters (NSW), Victorian Bitter (VIC), and Castlemaine XXXX (QLD). You will also find that many Australians like international lagers; the Mexican Sol and Corona are extremely drinkable with a couple of squeezes of fresh lemon or lime juice. Beer in pubs is always served ice-cold. Bitter beer or stout is not generally available on tap (draught) in pubs as Australia is an almost exclusively lager-drinking nation when it comes to beer. If you are lucky, you may be able to find Guinness on tap in the occasional pub. Ciders such as Strongbow (dry, sweet or draught) or Woodpeckers are available in most pubs. Pubs often have what is known as a 'sundowner', which is cheap beer and perhaps entertainment available for a limited time, usually around the hours of summer sunset. These are especially popular for workmates on Friday afternoons. Pubs also offer a 'Sunday Session' which is the same kind of set-up as a sundowner, but only on a Sunday afternoon. For many Australians, the sundowner or the Sunday Session are an important part of leisure and social life.

Australian wines are now more than capable of holding their own in the international market. Jilly Goolden, the wine expert from the BBC's *Food and Drink Programme*, is a self-confessed addict of these 'New World' wines, which are readily available from UK and European wine merchants and even supermarkets. Australian Chardonnays and Pinot Noirs are certainly world class, having consistently won international prizes over the last 15 years. Chardonnays from the Hunter or Barossa Valleys are particularly good. An Australian Shiraz or Cabernet Sauvignon (known as a 'cab sav') is also very likely to be excellent. Some of the excellent wine makers and vineyards are the Rosemount Estate, Margaret River Leeuwin Estate, Brown Brothers, Moss Brothers, Woonawarra Estate, James Hardy, Yarra Yerring; and Penfold's Seaview label is also remarkably good at a consistently low price. Quality tawny port is readily available from many vineyards, and white port is becoming increasingly popular. Jane Brook's white port is particularly good as a delightfully refreshing dessert and after-dinner drink. Australian sparkling white wine is the nation's equivalent to champagne, and Minchinbury and Brut are the two major producers. Minchinbury is perhaps a better quality sparkling white than Brut, and this tends to be reflected in the price.

In terms of fast food and chain restaurants, there is pretty much the same selection as you would find in the UK or elsewhere in Europe and the USA. Pizza Hut, Macdonalds and Kentucky Fried each have hundreds of outlets all over Australia. Burger King is also extremely popular in Australia, but it is not known under this name because apparently when Burger King wanted to open the first of their Australian restaurants, they discovered that some tiny burger joint was registered in the name Burger King, so they are affectionately known as Hungry Jack's (or H.J.'s) throughout the nation. You will notice that the cost of eating at the Australian branches of these restaurants is markedly lower than their British and European counterparts, and you easily feed four adults at Hungry Jack's or Macdonalds for $15-$20, at Kentucky Fried Chicken for $18-

$25 and at Pizza Hut for between $20 and $30. There is also a popular restaurant chain known as Sizzlers, where you help yourself to unlimited quantities of salads (there is usually a range of about 15 salads to choose from), pastas (usually a choice of four) and desserts (including create-your-own sundaes). The main meal consists of steak, chicken or fish, or any combination of the three, chips or a baked potato, and bread. For all of this, which leaves you so full that you can only waddle out of the door to your car, you can expect to pay between $7 and $12, not including drinks.

Although Kentucky Fried Chicken is popular, barbecued chicken is also an Australian favourite, and there are a number of national chains specialising in barbecued chicken, such as Chicken Treat and Red Rooster. These chains are generally take-away, and often offer meal deals which can feed a family of four for around $10-$15.

All of the chains mentioned above have recently made additions to their menus specifically aimed at the more health-conscious Australian. A range of fresh salads is available at both Macdonalds and Hungry Jacks, and both KFC and the barbecued chains tend to offer skinless chicken for those who are trying to watch their weight.

Service in any Australian restaurant is likely to be prompt and friendly and, because of the higher rates of pay, tipping is not common. In the more upmarket and positively posh establishments, tipping is more acceptable, but is completely discretionary (at around 10%) and solely for the purpose of rewarding exceptionally good service. Ms Juanita Compton, who used to work as hostess at one of the Hyatt's exclusive restaurants, reported that she was frequently given substantial tips by the 'high flyers' if they felt they had been especially well looked after.

Public Holidays

Each individual state/territory has its own list of public holidays. The long weekend has become a bit of an Australian institution, and is considered to be an ideal occasion to get away from it all and head away from the city. Friday afternoons at the start of a long weekend usually see traffic congestion out of the city caused by excited travellers, and Monday evenings usually see traffic congestion heading back into the city as travellers reluctantly return home. The following dates are, however, public holidays throughout Australia:

New Year's Day — 1 January
Australia Day — 26 January. This is the day on which Australia celebrates its birthday. All around the nation, local councils and authorities put on shows and firework displays to help the parties get started. Fireworks are usually an essential part of the free entertainment, and in Perth the radio station 96FM provides a fantastic Skyshow from the middle of the Swan River. Hours before starting time, the river is lined with happy people carrying their portable stereos, torches (to switch on and wave at the given signal), blankets and refreshments. Two hours of wonderful music, lasers, fireworks and general goodwill follow, and the atmosphere is always wonderfully friendly.
Good Friday
Easter Monday
ANZAC Day 25 April. This is specifically to commemorate the efforts of the men of the Australian and New Zealand Army Corps who died at Gallipoli during WWI, and involves a march through every major city and town by the old soldiers wearing their uniforms and bearing their medals, or as their numbers decline year by year, by their relatives (usually children or grandchildren). There are dawn ceremonies at war memorials as well as a big ceremony at the end of

the march, and this day is considered to be almost sacred in Australia's history. The day can be extremely emotional for both those who march, and those who attend out of respect.It is a good idea to watch the Australian-made film, starring Mel Gibson, *Gallipoli*, which is available on video, to get an idea of the kind of issues and history which surround ANZAC day. It is an excellent film, and extremely watchable as well as being subtly informative. There is a growing number of people who feel that ANZAC day is becoming irrelevant to Australia's new generations who are so removed from times of war, and the Australian play *The One Day of the Year* articulates the darker side of ANZAC day.

Queen's Official Birthday always on a Monday in June (except WA).
Christmas Day 25 December.
Boxing Day 26 December.

Regional Holidays: the dates of some of these holidays may be variable.

Labour Day — 7 March (WA/TAS).	*Darwin Show Day* — 22 July (NT).
Labour Day — 14 March (VIC).	*Bank Holiday* — 1 August (NSW/ACT).
Canberra Day — 21 March (ACT).	*Picnic Day* — 1 August (NT).
Bank Holiday — 5 April (TAS).	*Labour Day* — 3 October (NSW/ACT).
Labour/May Day — 2 May (QLD/NT).	*Queen's Birthday* — 26 September (WA).
Adelaide Cup Day — 16 May (SA).	*Labour Day* — 11 October (SA).
Foundation Day — 6 June (WA).	*Recreation Day* — 7 November (TAS).
Alice Springs Show Day — 1 July (NT).	*Melbourne Cup Day* — 1 November (VIC).

Time

It can be extremely confusing trying to work out the time difference between Australia and Europe/the UK as some states have daylight saving, and others don't. Australian daylight saving occurs between October and March, when the clocks are put forward an hour. Queensland, the Northern Territoy and Western Australia do not have daylight saving. In addition, you need to remember that in the UK the clocks are put forward an hour from Greenwich Mean Time between April and October. Below is a list of the time differences from GMT of the different states and territories:

Eastern Standard Time — 10 hours ahead of GMT: New South Wales, the Australian Capital Territory, Tasmania and Queensland.
Central Standard Time — 9.5 hours ahead of GMT: South Australia and the Northern Territory.
Western Standard Time — 8 hours ahead of GMT — Western Australia.

The time difference between WST and CST is 1.5 hours, between WST and EST is two hours, and between CST and EST is 30 minutes, although this can vary by an hour when daylight saving operates.

Metrication

Australia fully adopted the European metric system in the late 1970. Distances and measurements are invariably expressed as a decimal rather than as fractions. For example, on a road sign you would see 'City Centre 3.5km'. Shoe sizes are also different from those of the UK. In general, Australian sizes are numbered two sizes higher than in the UK. For example, if you are a shoe size 5-6 in the UK, you will be a 7-8 in Australia.

Retirement

Background Information

Australia has traditionally been the destination of young people. New arrivals have tended to be teenage backpackers on Holiday Working Visas or young immigrant families. Indeed it is well known that applicants under 35 are far more likely to be granted a holiday working visa or residency in Australia. This is, perhaps, one of the reasons why the average age of the Australian population has remained relatively low in comparison with other developed countries. In fact, there seems to be a notable absence of Senior Citizens in Australian society. Even activities in society usually dominated by the older generations in European countries, such as church-going, have experienced a reversal of this trend in Australia.

In recent years, Australia has become more accessible in terms of both the cost and length of flights. As a result there has been a gradual increase in the number of older people both visiting Australia and also retiring to Australia. In fact, the Australian government has introduced a visa and residence classification specifically for parents of children who have newly settled in Australia, allowing the children to sponsor their parents and thus give them the status of other residents (see *Residence and Entry Regulations* for details). The warmer weather, cheaper housing and yearning for contact with children and grandchildren are all powerful factors influencing the decision to leave a lifetime's history behind and start a new life on the other side of the world.

Most people moving to Australia find the actual trip is the most daunting element. Many people over 60 find that the flight is too long and expensive to be undertaken without due care and consideration. It is worth noting that travel agents can recommend ways of breaking your journey without adding too much to the expense, which perhaps make the flight more bearable. Alternatively, if you buy a cheap ticket, you are likely to find it is cheap precisely because it is not a direct flight and will stop for up to four hours two or three times during the course of the journey. Many passengers take advantage of these stops to wander around the airport which can be beneficial in terms of avoiding stiffness, cramping and swollen ankles. Airlines can provide wheelchairs and support staff (e.g., to help you collect your luggage) if necessary, providing prior notice is given, and you should also tell your travel agent and/or airline of any special medical conditions or dietary requirements at the time of booking your ticket. A handy hint to know is that if you order special meals for the flight, you are likely to be served first which, in a plane carrying around 300 passengers, can make a big difference to your personal comfort. Besides practical tips like this, this chapter provides information specifically for those wishing to retire to Australia, including the names and addresses of governmental support agencies.

The Decision to Leave the UK

As previously mentioned, many retired people experience 'empty-nest syndrome' most keenly when their offspring have not moved just out of home, but thousands of miles away to Australia. Although the warmer weather, hours of sunshine and lower cost of living are factors appealing in their own right, the deciding factor is usually the pull of the heart strings. The fact that many older Europeans who move to Australia have never actually been there before seems to indicate that it is the people, rather than the place, that are the main attraction. Although it takes tremendous energy and motivation to move to any other country when retired, it requires a significant extra amount to pack up and transport yourself beyond the comforting confines of Europe. The images most Europeans have of Australia have been carefully packaged by marketing experts to encourage tourism, and as a consequence are generally aimed at the young and mobile independent traveller. In order to make sure that Australia is really the place in which you wish to spend the rest of your days, it is highly advisable to take an extended holiday of up to six months in order to get a more accurate impression of what life in Australia as a Senior Citizen is like. A long stay in Australia may, to a certain extent, prevent homesickness (caused by a combination of culture shock and the loss of one's well-established social circle of life-long friends).

There are distinct advantages to be gained by retiring to Australia. Obviously, one does not need to learn a foreign language as one would if one had moved to a European country. There is also no denying that the weather in most inhabited parts of Australia is superb, with warm temperatures and glorious sunshine. Given that most cities are built on or very near the coast, there are health benefits to be enjoyed in terms of the quality of the fresh sea air. In addition, although Senior Citizens are by no means the largest section of the population, they are relatively well looked after in terms of special benefits and discounts for various facilities and services such as public transport, holidays, bills, restaurants, hairdressing etc. At the time of writing, the current exchange rate, combined with the lower costs of living and property in Australia, indicate that moving to Australia from most European countries after retirement, particularly to join children who have already migrated, would certainly not be financially disadvantageous.

Residence and Entry Regulations
Full details of Residence and Entry Regulations for retired people wishing to move to Australia are given in Chapter Two, *Residence & Entry*. To reiterate, there are two possible ways of retiring to Australia. The first method is only applicable if you do not have family already living in Australia. If this is the case and you are at least 55 years of age and have no dependants other than your spouse, you may be able to enter Australia to retire providing you meet financial, health and character requirements. Basically, the Australian Government is only interested in allowing retired people who have no other connections with Australia to enter the country if they can support themselves and have the financial means to make Australian investments. In other words, you will be expected to contribute to, and not drain, Australian resources and so unless you are relatively wealthy or have some sort of family connection, it will be very difficult for you to enter Australia to retire. Essentially, you need at least $A500,000 capital or a combination of at least $A150,000 plus further income of at least $A35,000 per annum.

The other way to enter Australia as a retired person is under the government's family reunion scheme enabling parents to join children already living in Australia. This is the much more common way to enter the country to retire. Details are given in Chapter Two, specifically with reference to 'Class 103, Family Migration'. Basically, this category entitles the parent of any child who has been a permanent resident of Australia for a minimum of two years to permanent residency themselves. Obviously, there is not the same potentially prohibitive financial requirements which need to be met, and there is a distinct advantage in this method of entering the country in that you are automatically granted permanent residency. Your child must, however, agree to sponsor you financially for two years after your arrival in the country.

Obtaining a Residence Permit

If you enter Australia on a Retirement visa, you will never be granted permanent residency. You will enter the country on a six month multiple entry visa which you then need to transfer to a four-year retirement visa. This visa is issued on a renewable basis, so your status as resident is more tenous, perhaps, than other categories of residency as applications for visa renewal can be refused if your circumstances have changed significantly and you no longer meet the financial, health and/or character requirements.

If you enter the country on a Class 103 visa as a migrant, you are automatically granted permanent residency after you have been resident in Australia for two years.

Possible Retirement Areas

Almost every major city in Australia is a possible retirement area in terms of beautiful weather and reasonable housing costs. It must be noted that Darwin, Alice Springs and other cities/towns in Australia's interior or northern regions often experience insufferably hot weather in summer, which many people (both old and young) cannot tolerate. The southern coastal regions also tend to have quite cool winters, but nothing as severe as a typical British or French winter. Many older people love the Mediterranean weather of Perth, Adelaide and Sydney, while others prefer the cooler temperatures of Tasmania or the unpredictable and varied Melbourne weather. A large number of Australians like to retire to Queensland, due to the sunshine and the relatively cheap housing, but others find the tropical, humid weather of Brisbane oppressive and draining.

Retirement Villages. All the cities and major regional towns have special kinds of accommodation for retired people which are not as readily available in Britain or other European countries. These accommodation centres are known as Retirement Villages and offer a three-tiered system of housing for their residents. This means that the villages must, by law, consist of units for completely independent residents, units and assistance, which includes some nursing care and assistance with meals etc., for less independent residents, and rooms with 24-hour nursing care available for the fully dependent residents. There are both government and privately owned and managed Retirement Villages, and many are run by church groups of different denominations.

One enters a Retirement Village by placing one's name on a waiting list and awaiting a vacancy. Once you have bought or leased a unit in the village, you can stay there until death, moving to increasingly assisted accommodation within the village as required. These villages are usually modern, beautifully equipped and are professionally managed with a high standard and quality of care. They are often built close to shopping centres, public transport and police stations, and have contact with the community through local schools and churches.

In general, the Australian attitude to Senior Citizens is to keep them active and independent as long as possible, and the Retirement Villages, purpose-built according to strict legal guidelines, are a reflection of this. Further information about retirement villages and/or other appropriate types of accommodation is available from the relevant organisations under 'Useful Addresses' below.

It must be noted that if you enter the country on the Retirement visa and you wish to buy a house in Australia, you will need to write to the Foreign Investment Review Board, c/o the Treasury, Parkes Place, Parkes, ACT 2600. Due to the fact that you are not considered a permanent resident, you will not be considered eligible for a place in a government Retirement Village and you may also find it more difficult to find a place in a private one.

Pensions (from your country of origin)

Australia does not have any reciprocal pension agreements with the United Kingdom. This means that although you are fully entitled to your British pension even though you now live in Australia, the rate of pension payments will be frozen from the date you left Britain and you will not receive any cost of living increases in pension payment made after this date. Currently, there is a pension upgrade every year to cover the cost of living, but when you become resident of another country you forfeit this upgrade. Although this may seem a nominal sum to forfeit, over the years it may become a significant sum of money and your pension may cease to be adequate. This must be weighed up against the lower cost of living in Australia and the fact that there is no council tax or VAT on electricity and gas.

As reported in the *Australian News*, a British publication, British expatriates in five of the largest Commonwealth countries including Australia, formed an organisation in September 1994 as part of the continuing battle to improve the financial position of pensioners residing in 137 countries where British State pensions are frozen. There are currently 159,235 people in such a position in Australia. However the rule is waived in 33 countries, including European ones, where 230,000 British expatriates receive the same annual increments as pensioners in Britain. Derrick Prance is the UK representative for the British Australian Pensioner Association (BAPA) and the World Alliance of British Expatriate Pensioners, and he can be contacted on tel: 01277-651 795.

If you intend to become a permanent resident of Australia, the process of pension payments is surprisingly simple. All you need to do is go to your local British DSS office and inform them that you are leaving the country. They will then make arrangements, upon your instructions, to have your pension paid to you in Australia, or into a bank account in the UK if you prefer. For further information, you should contact the Overseas Branch of the Department of Social Security in Newcastle (tel: 019122 59459, or the International Operations Branch of the Australian Department of Social Security, GPO Box 273C, Hobart 7001, tel: +61 02 200 333 or fax: +61 02 204 600).

Taxation (from your country of origin)

It is not often that one receives good news from the tax office, and therefore it perhaps comes as something of a pleasant surprise to learn that if you leave Britain and you are currently paid a pension, you will not have to pay any tax on that pension when you leave the country. If you are not currently retired and therefore are not receiving a pension, it is advisable to have a Retirement Pension Forecast made by the Department of Social Security. This is a simple process involving going to your local DSS office and picking up a BR19 form. Upon its completion and return, the DSS will be able to give you some idea of what kind of pension you can expect to receive when you retire and whether you will be paying any tax on it. This kind of information may be extremely helpful if you are considering the financial implications of moving to Australia, and may also help you with your taxation returns in Australia.

It may be advisable to refrain from taking any decisive steps regarding your retirement income until you have consulted a specialist in investment, savings and retirement income funding for expatriates. *Expatriate* and other niche magazines and newspapers carry adverts for such companies. Godwins International Services is part of a large financial services group (Godwins Ltd.,

Briarcliff House, Kingsmead, Farnborough; tel 01252-521701; fax 01252-375721) and can also advise you on savings strategy, prior to retirement.

Australian Pensions & Health Insurance

If you meet the requirements for a Retirement visa and are granted entry into Australia, you will not be covered by Medicare (because the government feels that you have not contributed towards costs as you have not paid tax in Australia), and you will have to make arrangements in your country of origin or take out private health insurance in Australia.

If you enter the country as a Class 103 migrant, your permanent residency entitles you to full Medicare cover two years after you have entered the country. Your sponsor (i.e., your child) is expected to meet any medical expenses you may incur the first two years, although some of this may be refunded. It is important to check with Medicare and/or your private health insurer as to the conditions which are attached.

The full rate of the basic pension at the time of writing is $A312.10 per fortnight for a single pensioner and couples are granted $A260.30 each per fortnight (i.e., $520.60 per couple). If you care for dependent children or students, you may be eligible for extra pension payments. If you live in a remote area (Tax Zone A, see 'Taxation' Chapter Four), you are entitled to an extra $A17.50 if you are single or $A30 per couple per fortnight. If you rent privately, you may be able to claim rent assistance of 75% of the rent paid above $A50 per fortnight. The maximum rates vary, but the maximum rate for a single pensioner or a married couple without dependants is $63.

Pension amounts are calculated by the two separate tests: the income test and the assets test. The test which calculates the lower pension rate is the one used.

The Income Test rules that a full pension must be paid if gross income is no more than $A86 per fortnight for singles or $A152 per fortnight per couple. Pensioners may earn up to $A1,000 a year without jeapardising any pension. If you are eligible for the pension but your spouse is ineligible, you will be paid half the combined married rate.

The Assets Test is more complicated, but basically the full pension is paid if the total net market value of your assessable assets is no more than $A112,500 (for a single home owner), $A193,000 (for a single, non home owner), $A160,000 (for a home owner couple) and $A240,500 for a non home owner couple. A couple's combined assets must be less than $A160,000 if they own their own home for them to qualify for the full pension. If you are on a pension and your spouse is not, you will be eligible for half the combined married rate of the pension. If is worth noting that if you are more than 70 years old, there is no special assets test, and you will be awarded the full pension.

Most of the benefits to which pensioners are entitled in Australia are claimed by showing various cards issued by the Department of Social Security. These give concessions to low-income earners as well as pensioners for a number of different services. *Pensioner Health Benefits and Transport Concession Cards* are issued to pensioners who qualify for fringe benefits (check with the Department of Social Security for the current qualifications as they are continually under review). This entitles you to certain transport and medical services as well as local amenities at a much cheaper cost. Holders of a Retirement visa are generally ineligible for any Department of Social Security Cards, and even Class 103 migrants only become eligible for certain DSS cards after they have been resident in Australia for two years. Some concessions, however, do not depend on a particular DSS or other authorised card, but only on age, so if you are able to produce any identification which states your date of birth, you may also be able to claim certain concessions. It is always worth checking before you pay for anything as to whether you are eligible for a concession due to the number of birthdays you have had. The most common transport, amenities and health concessions are listed below.

Transport:

Some states and territories offer concession travel to people over 60 years of age who are not in receipt of a pension. You should contact your local public transport authority for information. Private bus services also tend to offer concessions to Social Security Card holders, so contact the appropriate company for details. Pensioners receive two vouchers each year for long distance travel within their state which cost just $A10 when used. These are only valid for interstate bus and rail travel. When travelling interstate, you use the voucher to get to the border and then you are charged only half the fare from the border to the capital city destination. These are not valid for interstate country town destinations, only capital city destinations. A 50% discount is offered to holders of a Pensioners Health Benefits Card for the Abel Tasman ferry service between Melbourne and Devonport, Tasmania. In every major city, public bus, rail and (if applicable) tram service will give concessions to holders of a Social Security Card, but even if you do not hold a card (perhaps because you hold a Retirement visa and are not a permanent resident), it is well worth checking with the individual local transport authorities as you may well be eligible due to your age and not pension status.

Amenities:

Pensioners who are eligible for fringe benefits are generally also able to claim a reduction of 50% (to a maximum of $A250) for council rates as well as some other services. Enquiries should be made at your local council. A 50% rebate on water and sewage rates is usually offered to qualifying pensioners and your nearest water authority office will give you further information. If you are eligible for fringe benefits, you should contact your state or territory electricity and gas authorities for any concessions which may be applicable on your electricity and/or gas bills. You may also be eligible to take advantage of a free mail redirecting service from your local post office if you move house within Australia, and also for a $A13.20 concession on each quarterly phone bill. Vouchers for telephone concessions are automatically issued to all pensioners, but further details are available from your local Social Security office. Finally, it is worth noting that many Senior Citizens choose to have a dog both for protection and companionship, and local councils offer registration of seniors' dogs for a nominal fee which is usually around $A2.00.

Health:

Concessions can also be claimed using a Pharmaceutical Benefits Concession Card and Identity Card issued to pensioners who are not eligible for fringe benefits. As a pensioner, you are fully entitled to Medicare benefits, but there are many different health services which are offered at reduced rates to holders of such cards. For example, prescriptions are generally provided at a cost of $A2.60 for each prescribed item up to a maximum of 52 scripts per year. This applies to those who hold either a Pensioners Health Benefits Card, Health Benefits Card, Health Care Card or Pharmaceutical Benefits Concession Card. Emergency first aid and transport provided by ambulances is also free to the holder of any Social Security Concession Card. In addition, free dental treatment is offered at some hospitals and dental clinics to holders of a Pensioner Health Benefits Card, a Health Benefits Card or a Health Care Card. It is worth contacting your local hospital to obtain information on the free treatment to which you are entitled and any treatment for which you would only have to pay a concessional rate. Assistance may also be given for the cost of spectacles from some state government health or community service departments. You should contact your local department for details and you should be aware that this assistance is determined by a strict means test. Free hearing aids, maintenance, repairs and batteries are also available from hearing centres of the National Acoustics Laboratories if you hold a Pensioner Health Benefits Card or a Sickness Benefits Card. For assistance, you should contact your nearest National Acoustics Hearing Centre listed under the Commonwealth Government departments section at the front of the white pages telephone directory.

There are also associations which have been established specifically to deal with particular health problems that tend to affect older rather than younger people. These organisations offer information, advice and assistance, and have branches in every state/territory, the addresses of which can be obtained from the national body listed below:

Useful Addresses
Australian Hearing Services, PO Box 825, Canberra City 2601, tel: 06-257 6530.
Diabetes Australia, GPO Box 149, Canberra city 2601, tel: 06-247 5211.
Arthritis Foundation of Australia, GPO Box 121, Sydney NSW 2000, tel: 02-221 2456.
Stroke Recovery Association Inc., PO Box 673, Petersham 2049, tel: 02-550 0594.
Continence Foundation of Australia Ltd., 59 Victoria Parade, Collingwood 3066, tel: 03-416 0857.
Alzheimer's Disease and Related Disorders Association (Australia) Inc., PO Box 51, North Ryde 2113, tel: 02-878 4466.

Given that there are up to two million Australians who are full time carers, if you move to Australia as a Class 103 migrant, there is a possibility that at some time your sponsoring child will have to either care or obtain care for you as you get older. There is a national body of carers which provides support in the form of counselling and advice, organises respite care or temporary relief, gives advice about benefits and other support services which may be helpful, and also puts your carer in touch with other carers. For further information, contact the *Carers Association of Australia Inc.* PO Box 76, Lyons ACT 2606, tel: 06-282 5730.

Wills and Legal Considerations
This has been discussed in more detail in Chapter Three, but the clear message is that if you move to Australia, you should really make another will as there are variations in the law which may significantly and adversely affect your estate. If you wish to have a will drawn up for you in Australia, it is relatively easy to find assistance as solicitors advertise in telephone directories and also on television and the printed media. The Public Trustee Office specialises in the drawing and storing of wills and it is reassuring to know that their funds are protected by an Act of Parliament. As a consequence, the Trustee's funds are guaranteed by the government and so the office of the Public Trustee can never die, go bankrupt or leave the state. The Public Trustee Office's will-drafting service is free, and this includes any subsequent alterations and storage in a fireproof safe. For further information contact The Public Trustee, GPO Box 7, Sydney NSW 2001.

Hobbies and Interests
In 1987 the New South Wales Department of Health Report stated that more than half of any physical decline in any age group aged over 65 could be attributed to boredom, inactivity and a fear that infirmity is inevitable. Since

that report, there has been a widespread general attempt to provide activities for the more senior members of the community. Of course the weather tends to mean that indoor pursuits such as bingo are less popular than a range of outdoor activities. Many Australian Senior Citizens can be seen, clad in white playing fiercely competitive or mild and friendly lawn bowls in the summer sun. You should contact your local shire/community centre for information of how to get involved in your local lawn bowls club. There is also a variety of associations and clubs which cater specifically for the older, as well as younger, members. Below is a list of such clubs and their contact addresses and/or telephone numbers.

State Cycling Organisations provide organised rides as well as advice on what kind of bike to buy and maintenance. A number of older members have taken up riding because back problems prevented them from playing golf.

Bicycle Institute of NSW, GPO Box 272, Sydney 2001, tel: 02-211 1876.
Bicycle Institute of Queensland, PO Box 5753, West End 4101, tel: 07-899 2988.
Bicycle Tasmania, 102 Bathurst Street, Hobart 7000, tel: 002-34 5566.
Bicycle Victoria, GPO Box 1961R, Melbourne 3001, tel: 03-328 2000.
Cyclists' Action Group (WA), 2 Barsden Street, Cottesloe 6011, tel: 09-384 7409
    (after office hours).

Australian Yoga Masters' Association offers gentle, relaxing exercise often recommended for those in rehabilitation for strokes or operations.

NSW: YMA 02-654 9030 or Iyengar Yoga 02-969 4052.
QLD: YMA Brisbane 07-287 5067, YMA Gold Coast 075-32 2450, YMA Cairns
    070-55 3623, or Iyengar Yoga 07-358 1256.
SA: YMA 08-341 5422 or Iyengar Yoga 08-390 1357.
VIC: YMA 03-846 3704 or Iyengar Yoga 03-347 2949/03-376 6401.
WA: YMA 09-271 0429 or Iyengar Yoga 09-481 6113.

Walking for Pleasure is an organisation which specialises in hiking and camping and is a programme developed by the Department of Sport, Recreation and Racing in New South Wales. Walks are graded Very Easy (which means it is suitable for wheelchairs and prams), Easy, Medium, Medium/Hard and Hard. The benefit of this programme is that you actually get to meet and talk to other people from all walks of life and age groups while you are exercising.

NSW: Department of Sport, Recreation and Racing, MLC Building, 105-153
    Miller Street, North Sydney 2060, tel: 02-923 4305.
ACT: ACT Walking for Pleasure, PO Box 1235, Woden 2606.
SA: Walking for Pleasure, South Australia Keep Fit, 1 Sturt Street, Adelaide
    5000, tel: 08-213 0620.
TAS: Sport and Recreation Tasmania, Southern Regional Office, 152 Macquarie
    Street, Hobart 7001, tel: 002-30 3727.
VIC: Victorian Walking Clubs, Sport and Recreation Victoria, 123 Lonsdale
    Street, Melbourne 3000, tel: 03-666 4200.
WA: Western Australia Walking for Fitness and Pleasure Association, The
    Secretary, 127B Trailwood Drive, Woodvale 6026, tel: 09-409 6194.

In addition, your local swimming pool will almost definitely offer at least one session per week of gentle hydrobic exercise for older people, and will also offer concessions to pensioners. Golf is also an extremely popular pastime for seniors. If you are not sporting, then there are many artistic, musical and theatrical associations and activities throughout every community. You should contact your local community centres for details. If you prefer to be challenged academically rather than physically, most universities and colleges offer part time courses for mature age students, and you should contact the relevant institution for details. There is also the *Australian College for Seniors* (ACFS) which offers education programmes specifically aimed at vintage students. It is not necessary to pass entrance exams or to have any qualifications; the only requirement is that you are aged over 50. The ACFS consists of more than 40 participating colleges, universities and adult education organisations throughout Australia and is run in co-operation with Elderhostel in the United States of America. It offers international learning tours such as a literary tour of England or a trip to Bangkok and Chiang Mai where the information is presented by speakers from leading universities of Thailand. Within Australia, such diverse courses as computer studies, painting, and observing birds in the north of Western Australia are offered. Although the courses are relatively expensive (ranging from $A500 for a local workshop to $A8,000 for the big international trips), it is possible to combine your pension, the concessional travel fares and a tax-free grant from the Commonwealth Government of $A200 to go on such learning holidays. Enquiries should be made through the University of Wollongong (Northfields Avenue, Wollongong NSW 2522, tel: 042-21 3531, 042-21 3484 or fax: 042-26 2521). For registration details or a brochure, call the toll-free registration hotline (from within Australia) on 008-025 473.

If you would like to fraternise with other settlers from your country of origin, you should check your local telephone directory or the Department of Immigration for information on ethnic clubs such as the Italian Club, Chung Wah Association etc. There are also Irish, Scottish, English and Welsh Clubs in most capital cities throughout Australia (check your white pages telephone directory), and there is a United Kingdom Settlers Association in Victoria.

Useful Addresses

Australian American Association, 41 Lower Fort Street, Sydney NSW 2000, tel: 02-247 1092.

Australia-Britain Society, Federal Office, Level 12, 55 Elizabeth Street, Sydney NSW 2000, tel: 02-231 2341.

Australian Irish Society, 263 Miller Street, North Sydney NSW 2060, tel: 02-955 3568.

The United Kingdom Settlers' Association, PO Box 221, Fitzroy VIC 3065, tel: 03-419 3788.8888

Many churches also provide activity groups and coffee mornings during the week, as well as a welcoming service for people new to the area. Most churches advertise in their local newspaper, so you should check your local free newspaper or the telephone directory for further details. In addition, contact the Anglican Church's *Overseas Settlement Secretary*, Board for Social Responsibility, Church House, Great Smith Street, Westminster, London SW1P 3NZ.

Useful Addresses

Below is a list of helpful organisations, any one of which you may need to contact at some point should you plan to retire to Australia:

Councils on the Ageing (COTA): This is a national non-profit organisation designed to provide assistance and independent advice to Senior Citizens on issues such as accommodation, financial management or health. COTA also lobby the government on behalf of older Australians.

Australian Council on Ageing, 3rd Floor, VACC House, 464 St Kilda Road, Melbourne 3004, tel: 03-820 2655 or fax: 03-820 9886.

Australian Capital Territory:, Hughes Community Centre, Wisdom Street, Hughes 2605, tel: 06-282 3777.
New South Wales:, 34 Argyle Place, Millers Point 2000, tel: 02-274 857 or 008-449 102.
Northern Territory:, 18 Bauhinia Street, Nightcliff 0810, tel: 089-48 1511.
Queensland:, Leslie Wilson Youth Centre, Tenth Avenue, Windsor 4030, tel: 07-857 6877.
South Australia:, 45 Flinders Street, Adelaide 5000, tel: 08-232 0422.
Tasmania:, 2 St John's Avenue, Newtown 7008, tel: 002-281 897.
Victoria:, 3rd Floor, 464 St Kilda Road, Melbourne 3004, tel: 03-820 2655.
Western Australia:, 11 Freedman Road, Mount Lawley 6050, tel: 09-272 2133.

Australian Pensioners & Superannuants Federation (AP&SF): This organisation also has a national body and a number of local bodies throughout the country and is helpful on a number of retirement issues. As the name suggests, it is perhaps most informative about financial matters pertinent to Senior Citizens. Only one contact has been given per state or territory, but the national body has a full list of its affiliated bodies.

National body: AP&SF, Suite 62, Level 6, 8-24 Kippax Street, Surry Hills 2010, tel: 02-281 4566.
Australian Capital Territory: Canberra Pensioners Social and Recreational Club Inc., Mrs Win Tate (President), 67c Currong Flats, Braddon 2601, tel: 06-247 3797.
New South Wales: Combined Pensioners and Superannuants Association of NSW Inc., Mr Drew Robertson (Secretary), Suite 6, Level 5, 405 Sussex Street, Haymarket 2000, tel: 02-281 1811.
Northern Territory: Darwin Pensioners and Senior Citizens Association Inc., Mrs Beth Balke (President), GPO Box 852, Darwin 0801, tel: 089-81 9691.
Queensland: Australian Pensioners and Superannuants League Queensland Inc., Mrs Y Zardani (Secretary), PO Box 5/141, West End 4101, tel: 07-844 5878.
South Australia: Retired Union Members Association SA Inc., Mr L Klek (Secretary), Trades Hall, 11 South Terrace, Adelaide 5000, tel: 08-331 8422.
Tasmania: Tasmania Pensioners Union, Mrs E Guy (Secretary), GPO Box 1297N, Hobart 7001 or 156 Elizabeth Street, Hobart 7000, tel: 002-34 8526.
Victoria: Combined Pensioners and Superannuants Association of Victoria, Mrs B Blackmore (Secretary), Box 21 Trades Hall, Carlton South 3053, tel: 03-662 3971.
Western Australia: Pensioners' Action Group WA Inc., Mr Frank Cooke (President), 79 Stirling Street, Perth 6000, 09-220 0656.

Retirement Village Residents Associations: These do not have a governing national body and do not exist in each state or territory. They are, however, worth contacting for information and advice should you wish to live in a retirement village, or if you have any difficulties with the management of your village.

New South Wales: Retirement Village Residents Association Inc., PO Box 1127, Dee Why 2099, tel: 02-971 2981.
Queensland: Mrs Kerwin (President), Unit 5, Sunnybank Gardens Village, McCullough Street, Sunnybank 4109, or Cliff Grimley (Secretary) tel: 07-395 1151.
South Australia: South Australia Retirement Village Residents Association (SARVRA), Mrs Joan Roberts (President), 45 Flinders Street, Adelaide 5000, tel: 08-387 0221.
Western Australia: Western Australian Retirement Complexes Residents Associ-

ation Inc., Ray Brickhill (President), 48/510 Marmion Street, Booragoon 6154, tel: 09-330 2421.

The Accommodation Rights Service Inc. (TARS): TARS was established by the Aged Care Coalition in 1986 in order to provide assistance for individuals resident in nursing homes, hostels, self-care units and boarding houses, specifically in terms of recognising their rights.

Australian Capital Territory: ACT Disability, Aged and Carers Advisory Service, 23/27 Kootara Crescent, Nurrabundah 2604, tel: 06-295 0866.

Northern Territory: Central Australian Advocacy Service, PO Box 548, Alice Springs 0871, tel: 089-52 7511.

New South Wales: The Accommodation Rights Service (TARS), Suite 505, 64 Kippax Street, Surry Hills 2010, tel: 02-281 3600.

Queensland: Older Persons Advocacy Service, 1231 Sandgate Road, Nundah 4012, tel: 07-260 6755.

South Australia: Aged Care Advocacy Service, 1st Floor, 45 Flinders Street, Adelaide 5000, tel: 08-232 5377.

Tasmania: Tasmanian Advocacy Information Service Inc., 192 Macquarie Street, Hobart 7000, tel: 002-24 2240.

Victoria: Residential Care Rights, Ross House, 2nd Floor, 247-251 Flinders Lane, Melbourne 3000, tel: 03-650 5183.

Western Australia: Older Persons Rights Service Inc. and Disability Rights Service, Lotteries House, 79 Stirling Street, Perth 6000, tel: 09-220 0637.

Independent Living Centres: These centres provide information for those with disabilities or limited mobility who live independently and also demonstrate products designed to help such people live more easily. Products include bathroom and toilet aids as well as those which help with communication, eating, drinking, walking and sitting. Transport and lifting equipment is also available. Information on where to hire such products as well as their cost and availability is available from these centres which also publish a quarterly journal called *Independent Living.* Visits to Independent Living Centres are by appointment only.

Australian Capital Territory: 24 Parkinson Street, Weston 2611, tel: 06-205 1900.

New South Wales: 600 Victoria Road (PO Box 706), Ryde 2112, tel: 02-808 2233 or 008-800 523 (toll free).

Queensland: Newdegate Street, Greenslopes 4120, tel: 07-394 7471.

South Australia: 80 Daws Road, Daw Park 5041, tel: 08-276 3455 or 008-800 523 (toll free).

Victoria: 52 Thistlewaite Street, South Melbourne 3205, tel: 03-690 9177.

Western Australia: 3 Lemnos Street, Shenton Park 6008, tel: 09-382 2011.

SECTION II

Working in Australia

Employment
Temporary Work
Permanent Work
Directory of Major Employers
Starting a Business

Employment

Whether you plan to work temporarily on a Holiday Working Visa, or permanently as an immigrant there are certain points you need to consider. Although there is less pressure on the working holiday-maker than the permanent worker, both types will benefit from preparations useful towards finding a suitable job. Many immigrants now strongly advise that you should really try to secure employment in Australia before you leave your own country, as coping with unemployment on your arrival can considerably add to the stress you or your family may experience as a result of the move.

This chapter aims to provide statistical and practical information about the kinds of jobs available in Australia, aspects of employment such as salaries and wages, holidays, sick leave etc., industries which currently have job vacancies, and a regional analysis of the employment situation.

The Employment Scene

More than a hundred and fifty years after the British Government imported largely captive labour in the form of criminals transported from Britain to the penal colonies of Australia, the Australian Government found itself again in need of a large number of workers, so that it offered British immigrants permanent residency and a subsidised one-way sea passage to Australia at an incentive price of only £10. This policy, largely associated with the 1950s, went some way towards meeting the labour demands of Australia's new and rapidly developing economy. However, times have changed dramatically again: the 1980s saw an economic boom during which Australia lived beyond its means. This was followed by the inevitable stock market crash and a long recession. This in turn, resulted in unemployment levels reaching new heights. Such events have had a major incfluence on the nation's immigration policy which has recently seen the introduction of some very strict guidelines. At the time of writing, Australia is showing tentative, but positive, signs of economic recovery. Unemployment recently fell below 10% for the first time in almost three years, but there are still about 851,800 people out of work. The Australian national unemployment rate has shown progressive reduction over the last couple of years which consolidates the theory that steady economic and employment growth are underway. At the time of printing, figures released by the Australian Bureau of Statistics, showed that the unemployment rate is still on the increase in South Australia and Western Australia. Western Australia still, however, has the lowest rate of unemployment for any Australian state. The unemployment rate in other states is however also falling: New South Wales fell to 9.7% from 10%, in Victoria it fell from 11.2% to 10.7%, in Queensland from 9.6% to 9.1%, and in Tasmania it fell to 11.4% from 11.7%.

The employment scene, therefore, remains competitive from the job hunter's point of view. Jobs in certain professions are scarce while other industries are facing the old problem of not having enough labour to meet the demands of the market. Most Australians, however, still contend that if you persevere at job-hunting, take active steps to improve your own qualifications and/or skills while unemployed by attending training courses provided by the government, and are ready to be flexible and try something beyond your immediate skills and experience, you will not have long to wait until you find reasonably good employment.

As present, the Australian employment scene compares favourably with that of the UK, most European countries and the USA in terms of holidays, rates of pay (in relation to the cost of living) and other working conditions.

Residence and Work Regulations

In general, most people eligible to work in Australia have been granted permanent or temporary residence. If you intend to work in Australia, you should make sure that your visa allows you to do so before you depart, as you will be deported immediately if you are found to be working illegally after your arrival. The Australian Government is incredibly strict about illegal workers and immigrants, as it has to be given the high current rate of unemployment, and the penalties are severe if you are caught working without official permission to do so.

Temporary residents eligible to work in Australia

Working Holiday Visa — Class 417 These are normally given to applicants aged between 18 and 25, although the visa is, in certain circumstances, given to those aged between 26 and 31, providing that those applicants convince the Australian High Commission that they have specific skills and/or projects which will benefit both themselves and Australia. The purpose of the visa is to allow young people the chance to tour extensively in Australia, with the option of working for up to three months in any one area. You may stay longer in that particular area, but you are restricted to only three months paid employment in any particular city or town. Therefore, if you are granted this visa, only temporary employment will be of interest to you, as you will have to move on after three months.

Independent Executive — Class 412, Executive (Overseas) — Class 413, and *Specialist (Overseas)-Class 414* These are all generally granted to business and other specialists who have specific skills and experience necessary to establish an Australian branch or office of an existing business, or for a specific temporary project. A specialist is usually brought in by an Australian organisation or company to complete a specific task. However the executive classes are usually organised from overseas by companies or individuals wishing to begin operating in Australia. Usually, the executive will enter Australia to set up the business, get it running, then leave it in the hands of Australian workers and return to his/her country of origin.

Educational — Class 418 and *Visiting Academic — Class 419* visas also allow the holders to work temporarily in Australia, usually for a time specified by the relevant educational institution.

Medical Practitioner — Class 422 allows medical practitioners to work in Australia, but this is usually only granted for specific purposes such as training and teaching. This visa is only granted if the applicant has satisfied the relevant state/territory body that he/she meets all the necessary academic, practical and language criteria.

Permanent Residents

Basically, if you have permanent residency, there are no real additional restrictions or regulations other than those which govern the working practices of all Australians. There may, however, be specific conditions attached to the class of visa by which you enter the country, and there are many different classes of visa available for those who wish to live and work in Australia permanently. As mentioned above in Chapter Two, there are two main categories of permanent residency visas, Family Migration and Skill Migration. Family Migration has been discussed in detail in Chapter Two. Skills Migration is the most pertinent category as it is specifically concerned with employment. In general, Skill Migration visas are only given to those who will be able to contribute to Australia's economy, and one restriction which arises as a result of this is that applicants must usually be under 55 years of age.

Labour Agreement — Class 120 and *Employer Nomination Scheme — Class 121*
Both of these classes have an advantage in that they are not subject to a points test. Both of them do, however, depend on an Australian employer confirming that the applicant has been granted a job. The Labour Agreement visa requires the applicant to be nominated by an employer within a labour agreement (contact Australia House for further information), through which the Employer Nomination Scheme provides the opportunity for Australian employers to recruit overseas for highly skilled people to fill job vacancies which cannot be filled by the Australian workforce. The obvious benefit of entering the country on this visa is that you are guaranteed both permanent residency and a job upon your arrival in Australia.

Independent Entrant — Class 126 and *Business Skills Migration — Classes 127, 128, 129, 130* both require the applicant to complete a points test. The Independent Entrant must show that they are highly skilled in education and/or skills, that they will be able to contribute to the Australian economy and that they are readily employable. The Business Skills Migrant's points test evaluates the size and sector of the applicant's business, the applicant's age and English ability. Extra points are given for any state/territory sponsorship, so it is important to contact the relevant authorities in the state/territory to which you intend to migrate, before you apply for a visa, as such sponsorship could make a significant difference to the outcome of your application.

If you apply for a Business Skills Migration Visa, you will have to provide documentary evidence that you have had an overall successful career which demonstrates a pattern of development and growth. Your most recent business history is extremely important and the net assets held in an actively operating buiness in any two of the last four years should be at least $200,000. This has recently changed as, until May 1994, if you wished to apply for a business migrant visa, you had to show that three of the last four years had been successful. This new ruling means that a lot more people will be eligible for the visa, as you will be able to afford two poorish years out of four as long as two years show net assets of at least $200,000. Calculation of net assets can include shares held in an unlisted company where the shareholdings of the applicant and spouse equal or exceed 10% of total share issue. A special points test applies to all the applicants under the business skills category and the current pass mark is 105 points.

Applicants for this visa need to have been actively involved in the daily management and decision-making affecting the overall direction and business performance of the company. There is a distinction made between the applicant's principal business and other businesses in which the applicant has only passive investment interests.

Since February 1992, the progress of business migrants is now monitored upon their arrival in Australia to determine whether the economic objectives of the immigration programme are being met. If you do not take any significant steps towards establishing or otherwise engaging in business within the first three years of arrival, the immigration minister has the authority to cancel the right to Australian residence of the businessperson and his/her family. Currently, however, the figures are encouraging. Up to May 1993, 41.2% of surveyed business migrants had established 1,862 businesses between them, which employed a total of 6,927 people full-time and 3,663 part-time staff. Approximately 31% had export earnings, including 95 businesses with export earnings of more than $500,000. Two years after arrival, 55.3% of those surveyed had started 2,104 businesses which employed 7,501 full-time and 4,584 part-time staff. Of these businesses, approximately 36% had export earnings in excess of $500,000. Obviously, you will take a considerable risk by choosing to enter Australia on this visa as your permanent residency could be revoked if you do not get involved in business within three years of your arrival, and also you will not be have a guaranteed income. Nevertheless, given the success of businesses started by business immigrants in Australia, it is well worth considering this visa option if you wish to attain permanent resident status, and more relevant detailed information is given below in Chapter Seven, *Starting a Business.*

Skills and Qualifications

The Australian Department of Immigration used to publish a list of occupations for which workers were needed, and a list of skills and qualifications which were required. This was recently stopped as the High Commission states that Australia's own employment market is over-subscribed and the unemployment rate is relatively high. Those who apply to emigrate are, however, expected to have skills and qualifications that will benefit Australia, and this is a deliberate strategy to try to build up a skilled and qualified Australian workforce. The points system of migrant application actually depends to a large extent on the skills and qualifications an applicant has. Points for skill levels are based on your current occupation and whether your qualifications are acceptable or not, based on what is considered necessary to continue that occupation in Australia. Your current occupation is defined as that which you are presently doing, or that which you have performed over the last twelve months and you regard as your usual occupation. Your skill level is assessed by the Australian standards for that occupation, i.e. the requirements necessary to perform the job in Australia, not in your present country. Such requirements may be whether you possess formal qualifications, whether you have had a period of job training or have had experience at that particular job (usually three years), and/or whether you have membership of a professional or industrial association. The table below shows the points awarded for the different qualifications and skills required to perform the job in Australia.

Points awarded for qualifications required for employment in Australia

Qualification	Points
Trade certificate/degree (acceptable) with at least 3 years post-qualification work experience.	70
Trade certificate/degree (acceptable), with 6-36 months post-qualification work experience.	60
Diploma (acceptable), with at least 3 years post-qualification work experience.	55
Diploma (acceptable), with 6-36 months post-qualification work experience.	50
Trade certificate/degree/diploma (recognised overseas aand assessed by Australian authorities as requiring only minor upgrading), with at least 3 years post-qualification work experience.	30
Post secondary school qualifications.	25
Trade certificate/degree/diploma but qualifications are held unacceptable.	25
12 years of primary and secondary education.	20
10 years of primary and secondary education.	10
Less than 10 years of education.	0

You can check you own qualifications and requirements and those considered necessary in Australia in the *Australian Standard Classification of Occupations (ASCO) Dictionary*, available for reference use only (i.e., not for loan) at Australian High Commission, or other relevant overseas Australian Government offices, and at the Department of Immigration, Local Government and Ethnic Affairs in Australia. You can also contact the National Office of Overseas Skills Recognition (P.O. Box 1407, Canberra City, ACT 2601, Australia). In addition to the normal required skills and qualifications, there are 99 jobs listed by the Australian Government which now require immigrants from non English-speaking backgrounds to pass an English 'test'.

Sources of Jobs

Newspapers
UK Newspapers and Directories
Australian News is an Australian newspaper published monthly in the UK and and available by subscription from Outbound Newspapers, (1 Commercial Road, Eastbourne, East Sussex BN21 3QX). It carries much useful information about current immigration procedures, jobs availability and gives potentially useful contact addresses.
The Directory of Jobs and Careers Abroad published by Vaction Work (£9.95) has a section on Australia including specific contacts as well as other sources of job information.
Overseas Jobs Express is a fortnightly publication which lists over 1,000 overseas jobs including professional, non-professional, seasonal, temporary, permanent, long and short term. A year's subscription costs about £28 and is available from OJE (A2, Premier House, Shoreham Airport, BN43).

Australian Newspapers
Jobs are advertised in community, local/regional and national newspapers. Each newspaper will have specific days on which they advertise employment. For example, in both *The West Australian* and the *Sydney Morning Herald,* jobs are advertised on Wednesdays and Saturdays. Competition is fierce for advertised jobs, and you are well advised to purchase a copy of the relevant newspaper the previous night. See the *Cairns Post* or other relevant regional papers if outside the state/territory capital city. See Chapter Four, *Media* for a list of national and state/territory newspapers and their addresses.

Placing Employment Wanted Adverts
'Employment Wanted' advertisements are generally considered cringeworthy if it is the sort that generally advertises somebody's need of a job in any field. These kind of general 'I'm an honest and hardworking person willing to do almost anything' advertisements are usually only placed by students in need of some extra cash, or by people perceived unfairly as in desperate straits. In some specific instances, however it is a good idea to place an 'Employment Wanted' advertisement in the employment section of your community and/or local newspaper, particularly if you can offer services for the individual or domestic reader. The types of services usually advertised are hairdressing, cleaning, gardening, painting and decorating, dressmaking and tailoring, etc. You will not be likely to find much interest shown by large companies or organisations, as they almost always tend to advertise for staff rather than contact any potential staff who choose to advertise their need of a job.
If you do decide to place an 'employment wanted' advertisement, you need

to be very careful not to sound as though you are begging for a job, but that you are a confident and experienced person with a particular skill or service that you know people are prepared to pay for. For example, if you wish to offer childcare services, you could advertise yourself as either a babysitter, childminder or nanny. Be specific and simple. State the service you offer, any relevant qualifications or experience, when you are available, your hourly rate of pay and where and when to contact you. A typical example of such an advertisement might be:

Childminder, qualified, with 10 years experience and references, available anytime, your home or mine, $4.50 per hour. Call Josephine on 233 4435.

These kinds of advertisements are particularly good if you wish to earn some extra money, or if you are really only interested in temporary work. In addition, if you are looking for accommodation. You frequently see advertisements which offer a service or skill in exchange for board and lodging.

In general, however, if you are looking for a permanent, secure job which offers holiday and sick pay etc., then you would do better to look through the 'Situations Vacant' section of community, local and national newspapers, and to consider the other sources of jobs detailed below.

Professional Associations

All Australian professions have an association and membership may be compulsory in order to work in that profession in Australia. If this is the case, membership fees may be tax deductible, and you should check with your accountant or tax consultant. The health, legal, financial, accounting and educational professions all have professional associations, as do the various science professions. The professions usually publish a professional journal which contains relevant news, information, book reviews, and employment, and also organise conferences, seminars and professional development courses. These professions can be found in your local white pages telephone directory.

Specialist Publications

Specialist publications are an important source of information about a particular profession, trade or industry in which you intend to work. Developments in the relevant employment sector are reported, together with job vacancies. In addition, conferences and development courses tend to be advertised in these journals. As mentioned above, all professional associations have their own journals and magazines, and you should also contact your trade union in order to receive relevant newsletters and/or journals. Some employers will actually ask if you subscribe to any specialist publications and it can be useful to mention relevant subscriptions in your CV. If you have ever had an article published in a specialist publication this should definitely be mentioned in your CV.

Employment Organisations

BUNAC The British Universities North America Club (Dept RS1, 16 Bowling Green Lane, London, EC1R 0BD, tel: 0171-251 3472), has a 'Work Australia' programme, which is designed to facilitate finding temporary employment in Australia. The package includes flights, insurance and a working visa, comprehensive orientation sessions in the UK and on arrival in Australia, a group stopover in Bangkok en route, two free nights accommodation in Sydney, and various support services throughout your stay.

A specialist organisation *World Travellers Network Programs* (3 Orwell Street, Potts Point, Sydney NSW 2011; tel 02 357 4425; 02 357 4861), finds work for British, Irish and Dutch passport holders who have been granted Working

Holiday Visas. WTN can also help organise placements on volunteer conservation projects and sports exchange projects and arrange discounted flights to Australia and New Zealand, transfer to hostels from the airport, two nights' accommodation, breakfasts, harbour cruises in Sydney, YHA membership, mail and message service, orientation in Sydney, one month's free luggage storage and many other discounts on travel and accommodation. For further information European applicants should contact WTN's European office (Work & Travel Australia (ATCV, European Administration Office, Postbus 107, 5800 AC Venray (Leunen), The Netherlands; tel +31 04780 88074; fax 4780 11577. WTN plan to have a UK office in 1995 but at the time of going to print the details were not confirmed.

UK-Based Employment Services

Bligh Appointments is the largest employer of working holiday makers in both Sydney and London, therefore if you are looking for temporary work in Sydney, they are probably a very good place to start as they specialise in temporary appointments for British travellers. You are likely to be able to start work immediately as they have a large number of contacts and corporate clients, and they offer good rates. They can be found at 9th Floor, 428 George Street, Sydney NSW 2000, tel: 02-235 3699, or 131-135 Earls Court Road, London, SW5, tel: 0171-244 7277.

Commonwealth Jobsearch is a consultancy providing specialist assistance with both securing employment and obtaining immigrant visas. Dedicated teams of consultants in Australia and New Zealand will market your skills to employers before and after your arrival. In many cases, using state of the art video

conferencing or telephone interviews, they can help you obtain an offer of
employment before you even leave the UK. For further information contact
Commonwealth Jobsearch at Oxford House, College Court, Commercial Road,
Swindon, Wiltshire SN1 1P2, tel: 01793-535300; fax 01973 542554.

Emigration Consultancy Services: De Salis Court, Hampton Lovett, Droitwich,
Worcestershire WR9 ONX; tel 01905 79549; fax 01905 795557. Can help with
preparing and advising migrants on how best to manage a job search according
to their particular requirements.

Leesons Emigration and Demographic Services (LEADS), offer a complete job
service for Australia and New Zealand. For further information write to 4
Cranley Road, Ilford, Essex IG2 6AG, tel: 0181-518 2603.

UK Recruitment Agencies
There are a number of recruitment agencies/search consultants in the UK
which recruit for Australian companies. Many will also consider speculative
applications from those with relevant qualifications and experience. A useful
directory of consultants is the *CEPEC Recruitment Guide* (Cepec Limited, 67
Jermyn Street, London SW1 6NY; tel 0171-930 0322) which lists the Australian
offices of UK consultants where appropriate. The latest edition of the CEPEC
guide is 1995.

Australian State Employment Offices

Commonwealth Employment Services
CES offices are located throughout the metropolitan area of all capital cities and
in all major regional towns. You should check your white pages telephone
directory for your nearest CES, but the addresses of the major offices are given
below. These should really be your first port of call, regardless of whether you
are interested in temporary or permanent, part-time or full-time work, but
particularly if you are looking for permanent work.

Sydney CES, 105 Pitt Street, Sydney NSW 2000, tel: 02-286 7500.
Melbourne CES, 172 Flinders Street, Melbourne VIC 3000, tel: 03-658 2200.
Hobart CES, 175 Collins Street, Hobart TAS 7000, tel: 002-205 011.
Adelaide CES, 55 Currie Street, Adelaide SA 5000, tel: 08-231 9444.
Perth CES, 206 Adelaide Terrace, Perth WA 6000, tel: 09:325 6755.
Darwin CES, 40 Cavenagh Street, Darwin NT, tel: 089-464 877.
Brisbane CES, 23 Adelaide Street, Brisbane QLD 4000, tel: 07-221 0644.

Careers Reference Centres:
These centres liaise closely with the CES offices and offer guidance in terms of helping you analyse your own qualities so that you can target the kinds of jobs likely to be most suited to your own skills and personality. They also offer assistance with composing letters of application and compiling a CV. In addition, many CRCs offer mock interviews for practice, and it is well worth visiting your local CRC to see how they can assist you in your quest for appropriate employment.

Some Careers Reference Centres are:

Level 1, Sydney Central, 477 Pitt Street, Sydney NSW 2000, tel: (02)-379 8099.
Cnr King & Darby Streets, Newcastle Street, Newcastle NSW 2300, tel: (049)-26 0062.
Shop 13, City Link, Burelli Street, Wollongong NSW 2500, tel: (042)-26 5622.
Shop 7, Cascom Centre, Bradshaw Terrace, Casuarina NT 0810, (089)-20 5311.
55 Currie Street, Adelaide SA 5000, tel: (08)-231 9966.
Cnr Elizabeth & Latrobe Streets, Melbourne VIC 3000, tel: (03)-663 8466.
170 Little Malop Street, Geelong VIC 3188, tel: (052)-21 3288.
AMP Building, 83-85 Macquarie Street, Hobart TAS 7000, tel: (002)-35 7102.
263 Adelaide Terrace, Perth WA 6000, tel: (09)-425 4670.
280 Adelaide Street, Brisbane QLD 4000, tel: (07)-226 9266.
16-18 White Street, Nerang QLD 4211, (075)-81 2555.
Australian Association of Career Counsellors, PO Box 781, Strathfield NSW 2135 or Redmyre Street, Armadale NSW 2135, tel: 02-415 3216.

Australian Employment Agencies

There are really four different kinds of employment agencies in Australia, each of which caters for slightly different kinds of workers than the others. These are known as Personnel Consultants, Employment Agencies, Labour Hire Contractors and Student Employment Services. Regardless of whether you choose to use one or all of the different kinds of agencies, the key to your success is to get registered with them as soon as possible, and telephone or visit as frequently as you can. If you make yourself known, almost to the point of being a nuisance, the agency staff are much more likely to call you if something appropriate arises.

If you accept employment offered by an employment agency, you need to be aware that your wages will usually be paid directly to you by the agency rather than your employer. This is because the agency will take a 'cut' of your wages (generally a percentage), so in effect your employer may be paying a lot more for your work than his/her other staff. Many executive positions are negotiated by the agency so that the agency receives 10% of the employee's first year's salary package from the employer. This must be borne in mind as it is inevitable that your employer will be looking for value for money, and therefore will possibly be expecting extra work in accordance with the extra money you have cost him/her.

Personnel Consultants

These agencies tend to specialise in more of the 'white-collar' industries such as sales, marketing, finance, accounting, banking, computing, engineering, office and administration, and hospitality. While many employment agencies will overlap some of these areas, personnel consultants deal mainly with executive placements in these industries, including upper and middle management. Personnel consultants generally offer commercial as well as local government placements, both of which may be temporary or permanent.

Personnel consultants generally advertise in local newspapers, the yellow pages telephone directory, trade and industry publications, and in their office windows.

The most effective way to use personnel consultants is to visit their offices, together with your c.v. and references and a list of the the factors you are looking for in a job, so they will have a better understanding of the kind of placements most suitable for you.

If you do decide that the kind of employment you are looking for will probably be offered by personnel consultants, you should not discount the fact that there are overlapping areas with employment agencies, which often deal with similar kinds of jobs. In fact, some personnel consultants list themselves as both personnel consultants and employment agencies in the yellow pages directories, as do some employment agencies, as there is no strict dividing line between the two types of agencies.

Private Employment Agencies
Employment Agencies advertise in the yellow pages telephone directories, so you should check your local directory for relevant agencies in your immediate area upon your arrival in Australia. One big national agency is *Drake Personnel Ltd*, and it would be a good idea to start with a big company such as Drake when you begin to search for a job. Employment agencies such as Drake tend to have commercial rather than government placements, but will offer both temporary and permanent placements. The jobs offered will tend to be middle-management, secretarial, computing, manufacturing, accounting, engineering and services such as hospitality and perhaps tourism.

Employment agencies tend to advertise vacant positions in their windows, but it is also well worth entering the agency to talk to the staff and see if there are any other more suitable or even newer jobs available. If you are looking for temporary employment, you can afford to be a little less selective about the kind of placement you are prepared to accept, whereas if you are looking for more permanent work you will probably take a little more time and be a little more choosy about accepting jobs. Of course, this needs to be finely balanced with a certain sense of 'beggars can't be choosers' and, given the current economic climate, you need to make sure that you don't back yourself into a corner of long-term unemployment because you are being too selective.

Useful Addresses
AB Secretarial Ltd. 8b Borrack Square, Altona North, Victoria 3025. Arranges both temporary and longer-term office staff jobs in major national and international companies.
Centacom Staff 72 Pitt Street, Sydney 2000. Has over 40 city and local branches and there is a Centacom office in the capital city of every state. Placements include secretarial and computer staff. Temporary and permanent work,
Staffing Centre Personnel Services. Suite 3403, 60 Margaret Street, Sydney 2000 and 155 Queen Street, Melbourne. Office and computer staff, temporary or permanent positions.

Labour Hire Contractors
These agencies specialise in skilled manual labour placements such as the metal and electrical trades, construction, mining, forklift/truck drivers, labourers, storepersons, process workers and factory staff. These kinds of agencies usually do not operate high street offices, but tend to be in more industrial areas. Although they advertise in the yellow pages, it is a very good idea to go into the relevant office, together with any trade or City and Guild certificates you may have. These kinds of jobs are particularly useful if you have limited English or fewer (if any) academic qualifications, as these skills are not normally considered relevant to the actual skills involved in the performance of the job.

Many people from the UK feel that there is some sort of stigma of social inferiority attached to manual labour jobs, and therefore tend to avoid this kind of employment. In Australia, however, the labouring jobs are among the best paid jobs in the nation. Bricklayers, plumbers, and electricians all tend to earn extremely comfortable incomes, while those working in the big mines can earn in excess of $1,000 per week.

Chambers of Commerce

If you wish to find current information about the Australian economy or specific trades, professions and/or industries, it is a good idea to contact the Australian Chamber of Commerce in Australia. Alternatively, you could contact the Australian Chamber of Commerce office in your own country. Chambers of Commerce can also offer advice and specific information about the rules and regulations of employment in Australia, as well as detailed regional summaries. The Australian- British Chamber of commerce aims to promote business growth and development within Australia, and to encourage reciprocal trade between the UK and Australia. You would be well advised to contact the relevant Chamber of Commerce before you arrive in Australia, as their information and advice may influence where you choose to settle in Australia.

Useful Addresses

Australian British Chamber of Commerce, Level 12, 83 Clarence Street, Sydney, New South Wales 2000, tel: 02-299 5474 or fax: 02-299 5483. Contact Jakki Cross, Federal Secretary and Executive Officer, NSW.

Australian British Chamber of Commerce (UK), Suite 10-16, 3rd Floor, Morley House, 314-322 Regent Street, London W1R 5AJ, tel: 0171-636 4525 or fax: 0171-636 4511. Contact: Nick Came, Director.

Australian Chamber of Manufacturers, 380 St Kilda Road, Melbourne VIC 3000, tel: 008-331 103.

Company/Organisation Transfers

If you are currently working for a company which has offices or branches in Australia, you may consider asking for a transfer, either permanent or temporary as applicable. Many banks, finance companies, accounting and marketing firms, advertising agencies, tour companies and restaurant chains which operate in Europe, the UK and/or the USA, are also established in Australia. For example, the restaurant chain *Pizza Hut* operates internationally in many different countries and offers its employees transfer opportunities. Management may, therefore, approve a request to transfer to Australia. Even if a transfer is not approved, you may find that you are much more likely to get a job with *Pizza Hut* in Australia if you have already worked for the company elsewhere as management will usually prefer to employ someone familiar with the company and its system than someone they need to train. Other big marketing and consulting firms such as *McKinsey & Company* specify as part of their recruiting package that employees have various transfer opportunities internationally.

In addition, rather than a transfer, you may wish to discuss the possibility of an Australian exchange. This involves exchanging jobs with someone who does a similar job in Australia. Exchange schemes are very common in the teaching profession, and you should contact your local education authority for further information. Schemes vary in terms of what they include. Some exchanges involve swapping houses, cars and pets for a year as well as the job. Exchanges are most commonly available in academic and educational circles, but you should check with your own company/organisation as to whether such schemes are, or could be, in operation.

Aspects of Employment

Salaries

Recent economic reports show that Australia's national income per head fell in 1992, placing it well behind Switzerland, Sweden, the USA, Germany, France, the UK and other European countries, as the table below, comparing Gross National Product (GNP) per capita, shows.

International Income Rankings

Country	GNP per capita 1991 ($A)	GNP per capita 1992 ($A)	% Changes
Switzerland	33,710	36,230	7.4
Luxembourg	31,860	35,260	10.7
Japan	26,840	28,220	5.1
Sweden	25,180	26,780	6.3
Denmark	23,760	25,930	9.1
Norway	24,090	25,800	7.0
Iceland	23,230	23,670	5.7
United States of America	23,340	23,120	3.5
Germany	20,510	23,131	12.2
Finland	23,930	22,980	3.9
France	20,460	22,300	8.9
United Arab Emirates	22,180	22,220	0.2
Austria	20,200	22,110	9.4
Belgium	19,010	10,880	9.8
Netherlands	18,840	20,590	9.2
Italy	18,580	20,510	10.3
Canada	20,510	20,320	−0.9
United Kingdom	16,600	17,760	6.9
Australia	17,120	17,070	−0.3
Qatar	15,040	16,240	7.9

source: World Book

What must be taken into account, however, is that wages are increasing in Australia at a rate faster than the rate of price increases of food and petrol. In other words, while Australia may lag behind other countries in terms of the Gross National Product per capita, the cost of living in Australia is still approximately one-third to one-half of the cost of living in European, Scandinavian and North American countries. The fact that Australia's GNP figures were lower in 1992 than 1993 is largely due to the country's limited economic growth as it was in a recession. All updated economic reports, however, indicate that Australia is again experiencing real economic growth and wage increases. This can actually be seen in the table of wage increases for various industries and professions, which also gives an indication of the level of wages and salaries in different employment sectors, given below. The wages shown are in Australian dollars and are weekly rates.

Salaries and Rate of Increase

Occupation	May 1989 ($A)	May 1992 ($A)	Increase ($A)	%	Occupation	May 1989 ($A)	May 1992 ($A)	Increase ($A)	%
Child care coordinators	492.80	645.60	152.80	31	Mail sorters	484.20	546.50	62.30	12.8
Real estate salespeople	480.60	623.10	142.50	30	Accountants	581.40	647.60	66.20	11.3
Librarians	480.30	615.10	134.80	28	Painters	426.90	474.90	48.00	11.2

Occupation	May 1989 ($A)	May 1992 ($A)	Increase ($A)	%	Occupation	May 1989 ($A)	May 1992 ($A)	Increase ($A)	%
Invesments/ insurance sales	616.30	767.30	151.00	24.5	Public relations officers	580.90	645.60	64.70	11
Panel beaters	430.20	533.20	103.00	23.9	Chemists	657.00	729.90	72.90	11
Journalists	623.50	768.50	145.00	23.2	Boilermakers	525.60	582.40	56.80	10.7
Geologists	707.20	870.60	163.40	23	Accounting clerks	470.70	521.20	50.50	10.7
Prison officers	648.10	782.00	133.90	20.6	Metal fitters	585.50	646.20	60.70	10.3
Plasterers	516.10	622.40	106.30	20.5	Hairdressers	337.20	371.70	34.50	10.23
Church ministers	445.80	537.50	91.70	20.5	Social workers	567.40	619.10	51.70	9
Registered nurses	587.80	708.50	120.70	20.5	Plumbers	566.40	616.70	50.30	8.8
Police	606.80	730.20	123.40	20.3	Architects	634.80	689.80	55.00	8.6
Secondary teachers	600.70	721.00	120.30	20	Truck drivers	527.50	573.30	45.80	8.6
Tellers	398.80	477.40	78.60	19.7	Cooks	443.50	480.60	37.10	8.36
Fire fighters	618.50	734.50	116.00	18.7	Vehicle mechanics	483.50	523.80	40.30	8.3
Ambulance officers	640.30	749.10	108.80	16.8	Waiters/ waitresses	385.50	416.60	31.10	8
Sales assistants	399.20	465.90	66.70	16.7	Musicians	630.30	677.50	47.20	7.48
Lawyers	639.70	743.70	104.00	16.2	Pharmacists	634.40	675.00	40.60	6.3
Receptionists	409.30	474.40	65.10	16	Pre-school teachers	523.70	554.60	30.90	6
Postal clerks	436.00	505.70	69.70	16	Travel agents	478.80	496.50	17.70	3.6
Cleaners	389.30	451.90	62.60	15.3	Civil engineers	696.30	714.40	18.10	2.6
Primary teaachers	572.10	659.80	87.70	15.3	Announcers	765.50	782.30	16.80	2.2
Air transport support	936.20	1076.30	140.10	15	Electrical fitters	592.90	603.70	10.80	1.8
Electrical powerline trades	538.70	616.50	77.80	14.4	Cabinetmakers	439.10	446.60	7.50	1.7
Computer professionals	660.50	755.10	94.60	14.3					

Source: Australian Bureau of Statistics

Just as the cost of living varies dramatically between states and territories within Australia, so wage rates and incomes can vary greatly. The table below outlines the average weekly earnings of employees within Australia in both the private and public sectors.

Average Weekly Earnings of Employees

	MALES		FEMALES	
	Full-time AWOTE*	All AWE**	Full-time AWOTE	All AWE
Private Sector				
November 1992	$605.20	$571.60	$477.90	$350.20
May 1993	$612.00	$584.20	$489.60	$358.70
Public Sector				
November 1992	$662.80	$665.90	$593.20	$506.10
May 1993	$677.50	$680.60	$603.70	$516.90

AWOTE* = Average weekly ordinary time earnings.
AWE** = Total average weekly earnings.

The 1994 Autumn Salary Update indicated that executives received payrises between 4% and 25% while senior auditorscommonly received payrises of up to 20% for the period January to June 1994. In addition, the accounting profession in general experienced increases in salaries of between 5% and 10%, which some states offered increases of between 15% and 20%.

Cullen Eggen Dell estimated that companies would pass on salary rises of, on average, 4% for 1994, which, given the above figures, validates their predictions to a certain extent, while some professions could expect significantly higher pay rises of up to 25%. In general, following the recession, researchers and economic analysts feel that the Australian market is much more conservative than it was prior to the recession, and that there is now much more accountability for job performance. Organisations are clearly demonstrating that employees can no longer expect pay increases unless they are earned through improved productivity and performance. The main beneficiaries of pay rises will be senior management (likely to receive 4.9%), finance and administration (4.4% rise estimated), human resources (4% rise estimated), information technology, and production and supply executives (likely to receive 3.8%), and engineering and science, and sales and marketing (3.6% rise estimated). The biggest pay increases were likely to occur in the pharmaceutical industry, while the finance industries received the smallest.

Both Federal and State governments fix so-called Award Wages (the minimum wage rate), for various trades and industries, although many employers pay above the award wage. You should find out what the current Award Wage is so that you are able to negotiate reasonable terms with your employer, if appropriate.

Benefits and Perks

In April 1994, the taxation rules regarding fringe benefits tax and other employee perks were changed and, in consequence, many employers reduced the number of fringe benefits hitherto provided. For example, entertainment expenses are now subject to a tax of 48.4% instead of the previous 33% for entertainment provided by the employee on expenses to corporate clients. Whereas if the employee holds a corporate credit card and the entertainment costs are charged directly to the employer, the effective tax remains at 33%. It therefore is to the employee's advantage to use the employer's corporate account, rather than his or her own for client entertainment expenses.

Popular benefits such as cars and superannuation contributions are still generally being offered as part of salary packages to new employees, but tend to be on a reduced scale in order to allow for increased taxes on fringe benefits levied at employers. A report in the April edition of *Australian Outlook* showed that the tax will effectively mean a sacrifice of salary for employees who currently enjoy fringe benefits such as a car. For example, if an employer offers an overall remuneration package of $80,000 which includes a $30,000 car and $7,000 superannuation contributions, the salary sacrifice may be calculated as follows:

Gross remuneration	**$80,000**
Less: Superannuation	$7,000
Motor vehicle lease	$11,000
fees, registration, insurance	$5,065
FBT on motor vehicle	$23,065
Net annual salary	**$56,935**

An important benefit which will remain untaxed is child care provided by the employer on the business premises. This benefit is, however, offered only at the discretion of individual employers. Child care is not yet considered as important a benefit as entertainment expenses or a car by Australian employers.

In general, if you hold an executive position in a company, you can expect to have additional superannuation payments made by your employer on your behalf, and to be given a company car. In most other jobs, however, there are no real expectations of benefits and perks, although it is very common for employers in various employment sectors to offer to pay more than the required 3% of an employee's salary in superannuation payments. Many will offer between 4% and 6%.

Working Hours, Overtime and Holidays

Generally the maximum number of hours in an Australian working week is 35-40 hours over a five day week. You will not usually be required to work more than eight hours per day, but some industries, such as nursing or hospitality, have special requirements which cater for flexible hours. Minimum working pay and conditions are set by either Federal or State Authorities. You should be aware of these conditions in order to ensure that your employer is not an exploiter.

If you work on a Sunday or public holiday, you should be paid at twice the normal rate. If you work overtime at any other time, you should be paid at 1.5 times the normal rate. You are entitled to a minimum of four weeks of paid leave with a 17.5% 'holiday loading' (i.e., extra 17.5%) on holiday pay. Many industries and professions, however, offer employees four weeks holiday in his/her first year and six weeks thereafter and some professions offer as many as nine or more weeks' holiday per year. An interesting point to note is that Australian employers are much more likely to allow their staff to take their annual leave as a block rather than split it into two or three periods to be taken over the course of a year. Ms Louise Keogh, a chemist for Western Mining at their Perth branch, was recently allowed to take fully paid leave of nine weeks in order to travel to Europe. She has been working for Western Mining for just over two years.

Furthermore, after seven to ten years consecutive service (the government stipulates that long service entitlements begin to accumulate after ten years service) with one particular employer, an employee is usually entitled to long service leave of up to six months (full pay) or twelve months (half pay). Long service leave arrangements do, however, depend very much on the employer, and different companies/organisations will have different conditions. There does not appear to be an equivalent system in any profession in Britain except perhaps the system of sabbaticals offered to academic staff at higher education institutions.

Trade Unions

Recent research has shown that fewer Australians are choosing to join trade unions than ever before, and this may be primarily due to the fact that the Australian strike rate has now reduced to less than the rate it was 50 years ago. Most people who do join trade unions feel that they may require the influence and support of the union if they should ever need to make a claim against their employer or if their employer ever brings a claim against them. The Australian Council of Trade Unions (ACTU Australian Workers' Union, Head Office, 245 Chalmers Road, Redfern NSW 2016, tel: 02-690 1022) is the national body which is extremely powerful, although many feel that its power has been recently diminished as the result of lower membership. If you gain employment, whether temporary or permanent, full-time or part-time, and you wish to join a trade union, you should contact the ACTU for information on the specific trade union relevant to you. Alternatively, you should also be able to find out this information from your union representative at work. Membership is not generally compulsory, but some trades put a lot of pressure on their members to join the union. Membership fees are usually minimal, and members receive newsletters, negotiations for better pay and working conditions on their behalf, legal and often medical assistance in work-related cases.

Employment Contracts

Employment contracts are extremely important and should be read thoroughly before signing. They are an agreement between you and your employer about your working conditions, and you need to make sure that you are happy with all the specified conditions before you sign. For example, how much paid and unpaid sick leave are you allowed? Is there any child care? Are you going to receive a company car? If so, who will pay for its insurance, maintenance and repairs? How many hours are you expected to work? Do you have to take compulsory holidays (as teachers generally do) or are you free to request holidays when it suits you? How many holidays are you allowed in a year? Are you allowed to take them in a block or are they split into units? Are there any restrictions about taking holidays during the Christmas and New Year periods? Do you have to comply with a dress code? Are there any uniform or clothing allowances? Is overtime compulsory when your employer requires extra work to be done?

Your contract should also specify how long your probationary period is (if applicable) and how much notice either you or your employer needs to give of termination of employment. In addition, if your employer wishes to terminate your employment, your contract should clearly specify the process of termination, e.g. first verbal warning, second verbal warning, first written warning, second written warning, interview with the board/governors etc. You should perhaps make a point of asking whether documentation of these warnings is kept, including the date and content of the warning, and the incident which caused a warning to be deemed necessary. This kind of documentation means that you always know where you stand, and that your employer must have a justifiable and sufficient reason for terminating your employment.

An employment contract should also clearly specify whether your position is temporary or permanent. If temporary, there still may be a probationary period, and your contract should state the length of both the probationary period and the contract. If your position is permanent, you must ensure that your contract says so. It should also state your payment period, i.e., whether you are paid monthly, fortnightly, weekly, daily or upon completion of the project/contract.

Basically, your contract outlines the regulations, conditions and any benefits of the job, and once you have signed it, you are legally obliged to fulfil your part of the agreement for as long as the employer upholds his/her part of the agreement. As soon as the contract is broken, by either party, the injured party is able to effectively sue the other party for a breach of contract through industrial/trade tribunals. For this reason, it is essential that you read, understand and agree with everything on your contract before you sign it, because if you break it for any reason, you may suffer financial loss and legal prosecution. For example, you may not give your employer sufficient notice of resignation, in which case he/she is not strictly legally required to pay you any wages owing for the period of time equal to the period of notice you should have given. In some cases, this may mean a loss of up to one month's salary.

Work Practices

Different industries have different codes of work practices, and you should be made aware of these by your employer at your interview or at the commencement of the job. Examples of such work practices are: no smoking in designated areas, the wearing of steel-toed boots and/or hard-hats, long hair being tied up or secured in a hair net, no jewellery other than a watch, etc. Usually these work practices are in accordance with health and safety regulations, and it is important that you follow them, particularly if you need to make a worker's compensation claim at any stage.

Women in Work

As the first table of this chapter suggests, working women in Australia tend to experience what is known as the 'glass ceiling', which prevents them from earning at the same rate as men do for the same work, despite the fact that equal pay legislation and centralised wage fixing have been in operation since the early

1980s. In fact, *Australian Outlook* recently reported that women seemed to be losing the battle for equal pay as the rate of men's wages was increasing at almost twice the rate of pay for women. The Australian Bureau of Statistics has recently released figures which show that men's wages experienced an increase of 5.2% in the year to May 1993 while women's earnings experienced only 2.7% growth. The result, as can be seen from the table of average weekly earnings of employees given above, is that women's total average weekly earnings actually fell in relation to men's earnings. In 1992, women earned 85.8% of what men earned, but in 1993 this fell by 1.4% to 84.4%.

It is important to note that there are various reasons for this discrepancy in the average weekly earnings of men and women in Australia. Firstly, women are over-represented at the bottom of pay scales. The result of this is that there are relatively few women in management positions; for example only 4% of managers in the public service are female. The survey by the ABS found that 74% of all managerial positions in both the private and public sector were held by men. Women managers in the private sector earned $708.40 per week while men earned $929.20 per week for the same work. Professional women earned approximately $707 per week, while their male counterparts earned $866.20 per week. Para-professional women earned on average $666.60 per week compared with para-professional men who were paid $738.80.

In addition, only 1% of women earned $1,000 per week, while 7% of men earned $1,000, and women were twice as likely as men to earn less than $400 per week. Even the most highly paid women in non-managerial positions, e.g. mining engineers, earned substantially less than men. For example, the highest average weekly earnings for women employed full-time in the mining industry was $715.10 compared with $1,026.20 for men.

Significantly, the only jobs which allowed women to earn more than men were announcers, authors and kitchen hands. The highest paid women were mining engineers, community service workers and those in the communication industries, while the worst paid were those who worked as shop assistants, in construction, recreation, personal or other services.

The survey found that women are disadvantaged in terms of pay scales at all levels of employment in all industries, and that women earn less due to comprising 75.7% of the part-time workforce which effectively prevents them from earning as much overtime as men do.

In terms of job distribution, the medical, legal, financial, construction and labouring, information technology, and tertiary education sectors are still very much male dominated and women are very much under-represented at top levels in these employment areas. In fact, the University of Western Australia was recently reported in *The West Australian* as trying to redress the imbalance by actively recruiting female lecturers. The traditionally female employment sectors such as nursing, primary teaching, and hospitality still tend to be dominated by female workers; however again the top management is much more likely to be male.

Basically, as a woman, you are not less likely to be employed unless you are applying for a top executive or upper management position. However even if you are readily employed at a lower level of the industry pay scale, you are still likely to be paid much less than your male counterparts. It is worth subtly asking about a company's attitude to equal pay in an interview or before you sign a contract of employment.

Maternity Benefits, Parental Leave and Employment Rights

Maternity Benefits:
At time of writing, maternity benefits depended very much on the sector in

which you work, i.e. whether it is public or private. Almost all of the female workers in Australia are entitled to twelve months unpaid maternity leave. However in the public sector, female workers are currently entitled to twelve weeks paid maternity leave while very few private sector women receive paid maternity leave. The government's employment outlines are, however, currently under review and it is expected that some time after the Federal Budget in May 1995, all Australian female workers will be entitled to some sort of paid maternity leave up for a period of up to twelve weeks. This maternity pay agreement has been negotiated by the Australian Council of Trade Unions (ACTU) with the government and is based on the International Labour Convention 103, which dictates payment over twelve weeks funded by the government rather than employers. In addition, the ACTU and the Australian Government have arrived at an agreement on wages policy over the next two years which could lead to low-paid workers receiving pay rises of up to $24.00 per week, although this will be implemented in two separate tranches of up to $12.00 per year.

Parental Leave:
Currently, only the mother is allowed to take up to twelve months unpaid leave in the event of giving birth and there is no paternity leave, either paid or unpaid, to which fathers are entitled. Usually, employers are very understanding about the birth of a child, particularly a first child, and are likely to grant either paid or unpaid holiday (to be negotiated between the employer and employee) in the event of a child's birth. This period is unlikely to extend beyond two weeks. There do not appear to be any governmental or ACTU plans to push for paternity leave as a basic worker's right at the time of writing. In addition, there is no tax relief or government subsidy for child care, and this must be taken into account should you or your spouse decide to return to employment after the birth of a child, as you will have to calculate the salary which would be earned against the amount which would be spent on child care, and consider whether you think it is worth returning to the workforce.

Employment Rights:
There are all sorts of different rights which employees have, but the most common right from which the other rights derive is the basic right to a fair and reasonable working environment and conditions. If, for example, you suffer injury at work due to your employer's negligence or unsatisfactory working conditions, you have the right to claim worker's compensation for any injury, discomfort, and loss of earnings you may incur as a result of that injury. Sexual harassment is also considered to be a fundamental denial of the right to a fair and reasonable working environment, and there have been cases of employers being taken to court because they allowed offensive and/or pornographic posters and pictures to be displayed in common staff areas.

   You have the right to be paid for the amount of work you complete, in accordance with your contract. Unless specifically stated otherwise in your contract, you should be paid for any overtime you do at the national rate, which is either time-and-a-half or double-time, depending on the day, time and the amount of overtime you have done. You are also entitled to a certain number of sick days per year, for which you should be fully paid. If you use up all your sick days, you will be expected to provide a medical certificate and you will need to negotiate with your employer as to payment. Various trades and industries will have certain periods which they agree to allow their staff to be sick for (either paid, unpaid or a combination of both) before the employer is allowed to dismiss the sick member of staff. Many employers, particularly if you are a valued employee, will have compassion and hold your position for you until you are well enough to return to work, provided that you have not contracted a very lengthy illness such as ME or a terminal illness. During the time you are ill, you have the right to claim Sickness Allowance from the Social Security, (see section below). You should also make sure you know exactly what your limit of sick days is and how long your employer is legally obliged to hold your position for before you can be dismissed. This should be part of your employment contract. The government has stipulated that employees have a minimum of ten days fully paid sick leave per year. Unlike holidays, however, sick leave cannot accrue if it is not used during the course of the year.

As an employee, you also have the right to a fair dismissal, and each trade and industry has its own rules regarding what does and what does not constitute a fair dismissal. If you are employed and feel that you are being treated unfairly by your employer directly, or by other members of staff, it is worth contacting your trade union in order to ascertain exactly what your rights are and whether any action can be taken to redress the problems you are experiencing. Many cases are heard at union tribunals every year of unfair dismissal, and it is actually illegal for employers to sack employees on grounds other than those stipulated by governmental and union agreements.

Perhaps most importantly, you need to remember that you have certain basic *human* rights which are still applicable when you are at work. That is, you have the right not to be discriminated against because of your ethnic origin, your gender, your religious or political beliefs, or your nationality. If you feel that you are being discriminated against, even at the job application stage, you should contact your local Department of Employment, Education and Training office in order to find out the relevant procedure for complaint.

Useful Addresses

Australian Industrial Relations Commission, 80 William Street, East Sydney NSW 2001. For state award enquiries tel: 02-226 0688 or federal award enquiries tel: 02-282 0888.

Department of Industrial Relations, Employment, Training & Further Education, 1 Oxford Street, Darlinghurst NSW 2010, tel: 02-266 8111 or fax: 02-266 8321 for infomation about the awards for different industries, the Long Service Leave Act, Annual Holidays Act, Parental Leave etc.

Social Security and Unemployment Benefits

Australia's Social Security system is excellent and provides cover for Australian citizens and permanent residents almost from their arrival/birth until death. It is not difficult to obtain social security payments and services in Australia, but payments are means-tested according to both annual income and total assets owned (see Chapter Five 'Pensions' section for further details about means-testing). Payments can usually be posted to your residential address or automatically credited to your bank account. You do, however, have to prove your identity by showing substantial evidence, and you also have to be able to demonstrate that you are entitled to services or payments.

In order to prove your identity you will be required to show at least three documents which show your name, your address and your marital status. You can use any combination of an Australian Passport or Certificate of Australian Citzenship, a current overseas passport stamped for entry into Australia, an Australian birth certificate or extract issued at least twelve months ago, an Australian birth certificate issued for your child at least twelve months ago, citzenship papers, a proof of identity document from the Department of Foreign Affairs, a real estate title, deed or mortgage papers, school reports and examination certificates, a driver's licence (showing the same address as is on your claim), motoring organisation membership papers more than one year old showing the same address as on your claim, paid motor vehicle registration papers with the same address as your claim, hire purchase agreements, a rental contract with the same address as your claim, a letter from a government department with the same address as on your claim, an employer's reference, a gas, electricity or Telecom account in your name showing it was paid to your current address, legal documents and motor vehicle registration papers, bank, credit union or building society books at least twelve months old, insurance renewal papers with the same address as on your claim, a tax assessment notice, an Australian marriage certificate issued by a government department, or divorce papers.

A birth certificate or extract issued within the last twelve months, a marriage certificate issued by a Church or non-government body, learner's permit/provisional driver's licence, employer ID card, student card, baptismal certificate, credit card, a bank, credit union or building society accounts less than twelve months old, or an electricity, Telecom or gas account which shows a different address to that on your claim are all unacceptable as evidence to prove your identity.

Unemployment Benefit

Australia has no 'dole' system as such, but unemployed people are given payments under either the Jobsearch or Newstart allowance. It is important to note that if you do not have a job to go to in Australia, you will have to wait for at least 26 weeks before you can claim any kind of unemployment benefit. In addition, this 26-week waiting period does not start from the date you arrive in Australia, but from the time you 'sign on' with the Commonwealth Employment Services. You should, therefore, contact and register with your local CES office as soon after your arrival as possible. All Social Security payments are made fortnightly and are usually paid directly into the recipient's bank account.

Job Search Allowance

In order to be eligible for the Job Search Allowance, you must be unemployed, under 18 years of age, or over 18 years of age and registered with the CES for twelve months or less, have permanent resident status, and be actively searching for work. You will also have to satisfy the CES and the Department of Social Security that you are spending your time actively looking for a job or are striving to improve your employability by attending training schemes and courses. The CES may request you to undertake or engage in specific activities in order to satisfy them that you are attempting to end your period of unemployment. You must report to Social Security on your job searches and any other activities you have undertaken in relation to your employability every fortnight on a form in order to receive payments.

It is important that you register with the CES as soon as possible. The CES may have job referrals and be able to help you gain immediate employment. If this is not the case, you will be given a form which you must take to the DSS within 14 days or else you will lose some of the payments to which you are entitled. You and your partner (if applicable) will be interviewed by the DSS in order to check that you meet all the requirements, including the income and assets test rules. The amount to which you are entitled is entirely dependent upon your individual circumstances. You will need to take proof of identity, your Employment Separation Certificate and Tax File Number to this interview. You may not get paid from the day you claim if there are any non-payment

178 *Working in Australia*

periods which apply, such as the 26-week period mentioned above which applies to new settlers. You need to check with the DSS when you lodge your claim.

If you remain unemployed for over a year, you will need to apply for the Newstart Allowance, from the day after the Job Search Allowance stops.

Newstart Allowance
In order to be eligible for the Newstart Allowance, you must be unemployed, over 18 years of age, registered with the CES for more than twelve months, have permanent resident status, and be actively searching for work. Similar to the 'activity test' required by the CES and DSS to claim the Job Search Allowance, in order to claim the Newstart Allowance you need to sign an agreement with the CES which is an action plan outlining things you can do to improve your employment prospects. When you sign the agreement, you agree to do the things outlined in your agreement. If you do not sign an agreement with the CES, it is unlikely that you will be paid the Newstart Allowance.

If the CES is satisfied with your attempts to find work, you will be given a Newstart Allowance claim form to take to the DSS. Like the Job Search Allowance, this form must be taken to the DSS within 14 days or you could lose some of the payments to which you are entitled, and again, the payments are entirely dependent upon individual circumstances and you will have to take proof of identity, your Employment Separation Certificate and Tax File Number. You will have to take a form outlining information about your income and assets back to the DSS every fortnight in order to receive payments.

Regardless of whether you are eligible for the Job Search Allowance or the Newstart Allowance, if you and your partner are both under 21 and have no children, you will both have to claim the relevant allowance.

Sickness Allowance
If you fall ill and are unable to carry out even light work for a short period (i.e., eight hours or more) each week, you may be eligible for a special sickness allowance. To qualify for Sickness Allowance, you must be aged between 16 and 59 for women or 16 and 64 for men, have permanent residency or be an Australian citizen, have lost income as a result of an injury or illness, and be temporarily unable to work. You must also provide a medical certificate.

Sickness Allowance is usually only paid for up to 52 weeks, but payment can sometimes be made for up to 104 weeks. It is paid for the period on your medical certificate, and you should ask your doctor for the Special Sickness Allowance Medical Certificate and ensure that the DSS receives your new Special Sickness Allowance Medical Certificate before the old one expires or you could lose some payments to which you are entitled. You should make your claim within five weeks of your illness or injury in order to receive full payment, including back-pay. If you become ill while you are receiving the Job Search or the Newstart Allowance, you can be transferred to Sickness Allowance if you can produce a doctor's certificate.

The form for Sickness Allowance is obtained from any DSS regional office as well as some hospitals and doctors' surgeries and you can either return your form to the DSS in person or by post. You will have to prove your identity, give your Tax File Number and details of your usual income which, if you are self-employed, means that you will have to show your last tax return. If you are in receipt of worker's compensation or other employer payments, the amount of your Sickness Allowance payments could be affected.

In general, you cannot claim for the first seven days of the illness or injury in your claim, but if you have more than $10,000 in liquid assets ($5,000 if you are single without dependent children), then you may not receive payment of

Sickness Allowance for four weeks. Below is a table of rates of payment for the Job Search, Newstart and Sickness Allowances.

Rates of Payment

Age, residential and family situation	Maximum fortnightly rate ($A)
Single, no children under 18, at home	132.30
under 18, independent or homeless	218.40
18-20, at home	159.10
18-20, away from home	241.50
21 years, or over	294.10
60 or over, after 6 months	318.10
Single, any age, with children	318.10
Couples (combined) any age, with children	530.60
both over 21, with or without children	530.60
One partner under 21, without children for partner 21 and over (each)	265.30
for partner 18-20 (each)	241.50
for partner under 18 (each)	218.40

In addition, payments are made for children. People in receipt of an allowance automatically get Basic and Additional Family Payments (plus Guardian Allowance if applicable). See the table of Family Payments below for further details. The above allowances are dependent upon income and assets test, and a table of the assets limits is given below.

Assets Limits

Family/homeowner situation	Assets limit ($A)
Single homeowner	112,750
Single non-homeowner	193,250
Partnered, homeowners (combined)	160,500
Partnered, non-homeowners (combined)	241,000

Family Payments

Family Payments are made by the government to assist parents and guardians with the costs involved in maintaining basic standards of living for children in their care. Like other DSS payments, Family Payments are also subject to income and assets tests, unless the parents receive a DSS pension, benefit or other allowance. Usually, these payments are made every fortnight (normally into the mother's bank account). However if you have large expenses such as school books or uniforms, it is possible to have part of the Family Payment paid in lump sums in advance twice yearly, in January and July. The maximum amount you can be paid using this system is $138.45 which is half the amount you would normally be paid for one child for six months. The Basic Family Payment is $21.30 per child per fortnight if your income is below $60,000 per year, and you are allowed to earn a further $3,000 per year for each additional child without losing any of your payments. If you are in rented accommodation, you may be eligible for further payment, although this will depend on your income.

Additional Family Payments are made in accordance with the age of the child and the parent's income. For families with one child, the combined income must be less than $21,350 per year in order to receive Additional Family Payments of $64.20 per child under 13, $90.60 per fortnight per child aged 13-15 and $34 per fortnight per child aged 16-18 or a student. For each successive child, the parents' annual income is allowed to increase by $624 per year without affecting payments, but any amount in excess of $624 will result in the annual rate being reduced at the rate of 50 cents in every dollar.

Children under 16 are considered dependent if the child is wholly or mainly in the care of the person claiming the Family Payments, and the child is not a full time student, but has an income of less than $114.85 per week. A child of 16-17 is dependent if the child is a full time secondary student, the child is not eligible for a study grant, the student's income is expected to be less than $4,200 if living at home or $6,300 if living away from home. Family payment cannot be paid for students after completion of their secondary studies or they turn 18, whichever occurs first. Below is a table of the rates of Family Payment.

Rates of Family Payment

Basic Family Payment

Number of children	Rate per fortnight ($A)	Not paid if income* exceeds $A per annum
1	21.30	60,000
2	42.60	63,000
3	63.90	66,000
4	92.30	69,000
5	120.70	72,000
each extra child	28.40	3,000

Additional Family Payment

Child's Age	Rate per fortnight ($A)
Under 13	64.20
13-15	90.60
16-18, student	34.00

For *Part Payment*, parents' combined annual income* must be less than:

Child's age	Limit for one child ($A)	For extra children, add ($A)
Under 13	26,688.40	3,962.40
13-15	26,061.20	5,335.20
16-18, student	24,118.00	2,392.00

* Income includes taxable income, foreign income and the value of certain employer provided benefits.

These limits will be higher if you are receiving Rent Assistance or Guardian Allowance.

Pensions

Throughout Australia, men and women reach state retirement pension ages at 65 and 60 respectively. Pensions are currently paid fortnightly at a maximum rate of $318.50 per fortnight for a single person and $265.30 each per fortnight for a married couple. Applicants for the Age Pension are usually required to be residents of Australia and to have been living in Australia for the last ten years continuously. It is important to note, however, that a reciprocal agreement between the Governments of Australia, New Zealand and the UK allows new settlers to claim pension without delay upon reaching pensionable age. Australian age pensions are also subject to income and assets tests.

Restrictions on UK Pension Funds

Basically, there are no restrictions on UK-managed pension funds except those mentioned in Chapter Five, *Retirement*.

If you presently receive a pension paid by the UK government, it will be frozen from the time you leave Britain, which means you will not be eligible for any pension rate increases awarded after your departure from Britain. You will, however, be entitled to full payment of your current pension after your departure, and you should make arrangements with the Department of Social Security in Britain prior to your departure to have your pension paid to you in Australia.

If you reach pensionable age in Australia and you have been awarded permanent residency, you should inform the DSS in Britain in order to claim your UK pension entitlement, together with your Australian pension if you are eligible for the latter. Your UK pension will, however, be frozen at the rate current when you reach pensionable age and will not be indexed to increase in line with any pension rate increases awarded in the UK.

If you are entitled to a large superannuation or other pension fund payment upon your retirement, you must remember that if you are transferring funds of $5,000 or more into Australia, you will be obliged to report this transfer to the Cash Transactions Reports Agency, (c/o The Treasury, Parkes Place, Parkes ACT 2600, tel: 06-263 3762).

Short Term Employment

One important point to note, and one which travelllers have been made aware of while looking for work, is that anyone on a Holiday Working Visa would be well advised to avoid jobs advertised which paid 'commission only' and state 'travellers welcome'. These jobs generally involve selling (paintings, books etc) and appear to generously offer 'free travel'; however the free travel really means a one-way trip to the middle of nowhere from which you have to sell enough to pay your fare back to civilisation!

Agriculture

There is harvesting work to found all year round in Australia due to the wide variety of crops grown and the different climatic regions in the country. For example, one could pick bananas in Carnarvon, Western Australia, then move to the Barossa Valley to pick grapes and end up in Cairns, cutting sugar cane.

In addition, there is often more general work available on farms and stations in more remote regions, such as roustabouting, shearing and cooking. The best way to find such work is to go to temporary employment agencies or regional CES offices, and scan local and community newspapers in relevant regions.

Useful Address

International Agricultural Exchange Association (NFYFC Centre, National Agricultural Centre, Kenilworth, Warwickshire CV8 2LG arranges working visits to a range of countries including Australia. Applicants should be single, aged between 19 and 30, with at least a year's practical farming/horticultural experience. Participants receive wages at the local rates.

Fishing

Fishing, including crayfishing and prawning, is available in many coastal towns around Australia, for up to six months at a time. It usually pays extremely well but involves being at sea for extensive periods. See the regional analysis below for further details.

Au Pair/Nannying

Australians do not generally have au pairs or nannies, and they certainly tend to avoid those terms. Au pair work has traditionally involved housekeeping as well as looking after children, and most Australian families do not require the services of an au pair. Australians will, however, employ a cleaner for a specified number of hours per week (e.g. two hours twice weekly), and then a babysitter/ childminder as required. As a childminder, you will not generally be required to clean, wash or iron, and likewise, as a cleaner, you will not generally be required to look after children. Having said this, many families in remote areas often advertise for nannies for their children. In these cases, the nanny is usually required to tutor and otherwise look after the children. Nannying and cleaning work tends to be advertised in local and national newspapers as well as at employment agencies, but such work is not generally well paid. *Dial-an-Angel* is an agency with branches in most big cities, otherwise look under domestic services in the yellow pages for listings of other agencies that might be able to find you domestic work.

Teaching English

There are many students, tourists and professionals in Australia currently enrolled in English language classes, and there are many English language schools around the country. Until recently, these were largely unmonitored by the government, but then the financial collapse of several colleges caused the government sufficient embarrassment to impose more stringent controls and requirements. As a result, it is very difficult indeed to pick up work teaching English at a registered primary, secondary or tertiary institution, even if one is fully qualified. If you do not have teaching qualifications which conform to the standards of the British Royal Society of Arts, you will simply not be considered for employment by institutions. You can, however, advertise at tertiary institutions, in local newspapers and at various ethnic clubs and societies as an English tutor, and earn a considerable income. Usually, depending on your qualifications, you can ask for between $15 and $25 per hour for English tutoring. If you target the Japanese market, you are likely to do very well indeed as the Japanese are normally keen to learn both written and spoken English, to acquire a good accent and are able to afford private tuition.

If you have any other skills, e.g., musical or academic, you should also perhaps consider advertising in community newspapers or at educational institutions as a private tutor. Get an idea of the hourly rates from advertisements of other tutors and the kind of information you should include in your advertisement. Many secondary school students require extra tuition in maths, sciences, English and languages, so if you have recently graduated from university or have tuition experience, you will be able to do well. Some universities and colleges also require tutors, so you should also contact the relevant institutions and enquire about the possibilities.

Music lessons are also very popular, particularly the piano and guitar. If you are of a sufficient standard to teach, you should consider tutoring. It may be useful to take a guitar with you if you think there is a possibility of teaching while you are in Australia. Obviously it is more difficult to transport a piano, but generally this won't prevent you from teaching as you will be able to arrange to teach at the students' homes on their pianos. In addition, many talented musicians do reasonably well busking in busy city centres, and you could possibly consider this if you have the nerve. Do consult the relevant city council, though, as you may be required to obtain a licence to busk (usually costing around $15) and you should also find out if busking is banned at any particular times or in any particular areas. You do not want to lose all your hard-earned cash in payment of a fine!

Tourism
Being one of Australia's main employment sectors and also being generally seasonal, you are likely to be able to pick up some sort of temporary work in the tourist industry, whether it is washing dishes in the kitchen of a major resort or leading dives on the Great Barrier Reef. Your employability largely depends on your skills, qualifications and personality. You should remember that big hotels need all sorts of skilled workers, including childminders, chambermaids, porters, bar and casino staff. In order to pick up this sort of work, you need to be persistent. Do not wait for jobs to be advertised, but politely pester local hotels, motels, boat charters, windsurfing and waterskiing schools etc. If you get knocked back, don't give up, go back a week later and see if anything has turned up in the meantime. That way, employers are likely to remember your name and face, to see you are extremely keen to work for them, and to think of you if anything turns up.

Useful Addresses
Contiki Travel (UK), Wells House, 15 Elsfield Road, Bromley BR1 1LS; specialises in travel by coach including tours in Australia. Needs tour managers and qualified PSV Drivers from April to October.
Showbusiness Australia, Hay Street, Perth WA 6000, tel: 09-481 1156. Useful for temporary work in the bar/nightclub scene.

Voluntary Work
It is not only admirable, altruistic people who undertake voluntary work, although most voluntary workers are, to a certain degree, self-sacrificing and dedicated. If you are experiencing difficulties obtaining permanent employment, it is sometimes beneficial to do some voluntary work in a relevant field in order to gain experience which will make you more employable. It is important to think laterally about the possibilities of doing voluntary work. Most people only think of health and other care industries being keen for volunteers, but many companies and industries are happy to have an extra pair of hands working for them, particularly if those hands do not get paid.

The vast majority of Australian high schools operate a 'Work Experience' scheme for their 15-year-old students. This is the chance for students to think about what they would like to do in the future, and to experience working in that field for at least one week. This work is completely unpaid, so in a way these students could be considered as voluntary workers during this period. There is no real reason why anybody else who is keen to gain experience in a particular field should not be able to offer their services free of charge in exchange for experience. Send letters out to a number of relevant employers stating who you are, what your qualifications are, what services you are offering and that, if there are no job vacancies available, you would like to offer these services in exchange for experience. You will probably gain skills and experience which will make you more employable, and you may also be likely to get offered a job if any vacancies arise as employers generally prefer to employ someone who does not need training.

There is also the more conventional, but equally valuable, voluntary work to be found with established organisations such as the Red Cross and the Salvation Army. Most charitable foundations are eager for volunteers to help in different areas involved in the running of that organisation. You may, for example, contact the Spastic Association of Australia and learn that they require an extra volunteer riding instructor to take part in their Riding for the Disabled programme over summer. Organisations often require drivers, cooks, assistants, and friendly faces. This kind of work can also be of benefit on a CV as it indicates to prospective employers that you have a kind and caring character. Voluntary work will sometimes be advertised in community newspapers, but you should also check your local yellow pages telephone directory under 'Charitable Organisations'.

Useful Addresses

Australian Trust for Conservation Volunteers ATCV Headquarters, POB 423, Ballarat, 3353, Victoria. Places volunteers in work teams all year round. Work includes fencing, collecting seeds, tree planting, trail constructing. Prospective volunteers have to make a contribution to costs of about A$600 for six weeks to cover board, lodging, and internal travel expenses.

WWOOF (Willing Workers on Organic Farms) is a worldwide organisation with an active Australian branch (Mt Murrindal Reserve, W Tree, Via Buchan, Victoria 3885; 051-550218) with over 200 member farms in Australia needing short and long-term volunteers. Further details from the above address.

Training & Work Experience Schemes

There are many training and work experience schemes available in all Australian states and territories. These are generally provided by the Commonwealth Employment Services, by employers, or by educational institutions. Technical and Further Education (TAFE) Colleges continually offer skillsbased training schemes, and you should contact your local TAFE college for further details, or scan local and community newspapers as TAFEs regularly advertise upcoming courses. The CES offices are the best source of work experience schemes in Australia, but if you are younger and on a temporary Working Holiday Visa, you should perhaps consider a scheme such as BUNAC (see *Sources of Jobs* above), or contact your organisations in your country of origin to see if there are any exchange programmes in operation between your country and Australia. Rotary Clubs are particularly popular in Australia and they offer international exchanges for young people, usually under 25 years of age. You should contact your local Rotary Club for further information.

Permanent Work

Automotive

There are two major car manufacturers in Australia, Ford Australia and General Motors Holden. According to a report in *Australian Outlook*, Australian car sales experienced a 13.1% increase in the first five months of 1994. Ford Falcon sales were up 69.9% since January, and Holden Commodore sales increased by a massive 95.4%. It is perhaps surprising that Ford has retained leadership of the automotive market over the last few years and that Holden is actually second. In addition, Mitsubishi, Mazda, Nissan and Hyundai all rank highly in market sales.

Jobs in the automotive industry shifted from mechanical and manufacturing to sales, and although perhaps not expanding their workforce as rapidly as one would expect with such growth figures, the automotive industry does generally have a constant need for good salespeople. South Australia has just benefited from a decision by Mitsubishi Motors to invest in a ten-year, $500 million plan which will guarantee 5,000 jobs.

In addition to car manufacturers, the automotive spares and accessories market is a major Australian industry worth over $A2 billion per year.

Banking and Finance

In 1993, the ANZ bank monitored recruitment advertising and noted that the index of job adverts in banking and finance had increased by 18.7% in February 1994 over the previous six months. Approximately 140,000 jobs were created in this time in banking and finance service industries, and this index can be taken as an indicator of employment trends.

Executive Employment Prospects

Executive job prospects are generally good with smaller, rather than larger companies. Small companies are expanding whereas large established ones are rationalising and therefore in the process of laying off large numbers of staff. A recent survey of Australia's top 200 private sector companies showed that at top levels, the chief executives were in an earning bracket far beyond those of senior sales executives, senior manufacturing executives, senior information systems executives and senior personnel executives.

Food and Agriculture

Traditionally, Australia's economy has been very much wool and wheat based, but this is changing rapidly.

The food processing industry is Australia's largest manufacturing sector, employing 70,000 people. Domestic and international sales exceed 20% of manufacturing turnover at more than $A28 billion. The average investment in plant and equipment is expected to grow by 10% in the immediate future, and jobs are predicted to shift away from factories to sales, research, development and marketing.

The value of imported foodstuffs into Australia is more than $2 billion per year. It is highly competitive market, and there has been a shift in preference away from convenience to healthy and fresh foods. This trend is expected to continue.

Economic experts predict that the food, agriculture, wood and transport industries will all experience a decrease in available employment. It is expected that as these industries will become more mechanised, and, as Australia's economy shifts to become more technology-based, employment will be more difficult to gain in these areas. There does, however, seem to be a growth market for high-value-added gourmet foodstuffs.

Information Technology

Jobs involved with computing enjoyed dramatic expansion and development in the decade ending in the late 1980s and growth has levelled off somewhat. There is however, potential in computing jobs as skills are becoming increasingly specialised. The current salary rates are about $28,000 for graduates, $50,000 for experienced professionals, and between $70,000 and $100,000 for those with more than 15 years experience. Information technology in telecommunications and media is particularly in demand. A UK management consultancy that handles jobs for computer specialists is James Baker Associates (Park House, Wick Road, Egham, Surrey TW20 0HW).

Medical
Doctors from overseas are required to complete an internship year as part of the requirements which allow them to practise in Australia. Health therapists, such as physiotherapists, occupational therapists and speech therapists need to have their qualifications approved by the Australian authorities before being allowed to work in Australia.

In general prospects for many health practitioners are curtailed by the national surplus of medical graduates. There is however a shortage of nurses and as there are many private and public hospitals in Australia, jobs are relatively easy to find. The jobs that are most likely to be vacant however are those for night-shifts and other less desirable nursing jobs as these are the ones which the authorities are having difficulty in filling.

Petrochemicals
There has been massive investment in oil and gas exploration, particularly in the North West Shelf Project off the coast of Western Australia. British supply companies have reaped the benefits from the demand for tried and tested North Sea technology. Future developments in the main areas of the petrochemical industry should result in continuing opportunities for British companies, particularly those which are able to successfully undertake joint-ventures with Australian companies.

Retailing
As mentioned above, the larger businesses are not currently employing more staff, but tending to cut back on middle-management and other executive positions. There are, however, some larger retail chains that are planning to increase staff members in the near future, but only when sales have reached such a level as to make opening new stores feasible.

The retailing industry is still suffering the effects of the recession, during which most Australians simply did not have enough money to spend. The 1980s boom years were really the decade of the credit card, and it is only in the last couple of years that there have been more bankruptcies caused by unemployment rather than credit card debt. Although credit cards are still popular and used by the general population, Australians these days are far more conscious and careful of how much they spend. You would be likely to do well if you manage to find work with a retailer who specialises in information technology, computer hard and/or software, or telecommunications.
and marketing.

The value of imported foodstuffs into Australia is more than $2 billion per year. It is highly competitive market, and there has been a shift in preference away from convenience to healthy and fresh foods. This trend is expected to continue.

Economic experts predict that the food, agriculture, wood and transport industries will all experience a decrease in available employment. It is expected that as these industries will become more mechanised, and, as Australia's economy shifts to become more technology-based, employment will be more difficult to gain in these areas. There does, however, seem to be a growth market for high-value-added gourmet foodstuffs.

Petrochemicals
There has been massive investment in oil and gas exploration, particularly in the North West Shelf Project off the coast of Western Australia. British supply companies have reaped the benefits from the demand for tried and tested North Sea technology. Future developments in the main areas of the petrochemical

industry should result in continuing opportunities for British companies, particularly those which are able to successfully undertake joint-ventures with Australian companies.

Retailing

As mentioned above, the larger businesses are not currently employing more staff, but tending to cut back on middle-management and other executive positions. There are, however, some larger retail chains that are planning to increase staff members in the near future, but only when sales have reached such a level as to make opening new stores feasible.

The retailing industry is still suffering the effects of the recession, during which most Australians simply did not have enough money to spend. The 1980s boom years were really the decade of the credit card, and it is only in the last couple of years that there have been more bankruptcies caused by unemployment rather than credit card debt. Although credit cards are still popular and used by the general population, Australians these days are far more conscious and careful of how much they spend. You would be likely to do well if you manage to find work with a retailer who specialises in information technology, computer hard and/or software, or telecommunications.

Monash University's Centre for Policy Studies and Syntec Economics Services recently published results of a study which show that employment in wholesale and retail sales are likely to rise by 3.9% per year as the economy begins to develop again. This is significant when compared with the national rate of 2.1%. It is expected that strong rates of return, expanded demand and increased imports and exports will promote a rate of job growth of 5% per year in wholesaling, and 3.25% in retailing, until the year 2001.

Steel and Non-ferrous Metals

Australia is not so much a steel manufacturer as an exporter of iron ore to other countries which process and refine the ore into iron products such as steel. Mining is, therefore, a significant employment sector and is expected to display the most potent growth over the next eight years in economic terms. The Australian mining industry is one of the most high productive in the world and is a significant investor in capital equipment. Black coal is the most mined product and British equipment suppliers enjoy a large share of the underground coal mining market. The main underground coal mining activities are located in New South Wales and Queensland.

Australia is also rich in other natural resources such as manganese, uranium, diamonds, zirconite, mineral sands, lead, zinc, copper, gold, silver, alumina and bauxite. These mining industries also operate on a large scale in the country and are large employers.

Teaching

The demand for teachers, at almost all levels of education, currently outstrips the supply of highly qualified teachers in Australia. In all state schools, at both primary and secondary levels, teachers must be qualified in terms of holding a three-year Diploma of Teaching/Education or a one-year Graduate Diploma of Education (equivalent to a UK PGCE). In the private school system it is not necessary to hold a specific teaching qualification; particularly good university qualifications are sufficient although this is now changing towards an education qualification biase too. To work for the state system you will need to apply to the revelant Ministry of Education in the state or territory where you wish to work. For jobs in private schools comb the education section of local newspapers, and possibly national newspapers and you could also send your CV to local schools offering your services as a relief (supply) teacher.

Textiles

The textiles workforce is expected to diminish at a rate of 2.7% into the next century, due to increased technology and mechanisation of the industry.

Regional Employment Guide

In addition to the basic summary of major employment sectors given below, please refer also to the *Regional Guide* given in Chapter One as it contains further details about the economies of the various states and territories.

Western Australia

Permanent: With the nation's lowest unemployment rate, it is probably easier to find work in almost any industry and profession in Western Australia than elsewhere. Oil and gas industries, and the service companies which supply them, are particularly successful in this state due to the existence off the North West Shelf, of one of the world's largest deposits of natural gas. Western Australia is currently enjoying a boom in the search for oil and gas and the North West Shelf Project has been implemented in two phases, domestic production and Liquified Natural Gas export. The domestic phase is two-thirds Australian owned, one sixth British and one sixth American, with $2.2 billion invested. The LNG phase has about $9.8 billion invested and is approximately half Australian owned and one sixth owned each by the UK, USA and Japanese interests. From mid-1994, seven international companies associated with the petroleum industry decided to establish their South East Asian regional headquarters in Perth. These recent months have seen the arrival of the US-owned Western Geophysical, Norway's Nopec, Canada's Drillex International, Britain's W.S. Atkins, and from Scotland's North Sea industry, E.S.D. Simulators. Global Drilling is in the process of relocating its Jakarta (Indonesia) operations to Perth and government negotiations are in advanced stages with the French based Coflexip Group for the establishment of a regional headquarters and a $55 million flexible pipe manufacturing plant near Perth to serve the Asian region.

Western Australia is incredibly rich in natural resources, and it is a leading producer of iron ore, gold, industrial diamonds, alumina, nickel, mineral sands products, wool, wheat, salt and forest products. ALCOA of Australia has an investment of approximately $5 billion, and is a 51% American and 44% Australian company which operates three refineries and three mine sites, employing 2,700 people. Worsley Alumina is 50% American, 37.5% Australian and 12.5 % Japanese owned. It employs 780 people with an investment of $1.2 billion. Dampier Salt is 65% Australian and 35% Japanese, and employs 300 people with $94 million invested. Dyno Industries is a 50/50 operation of Australian and Norwegian interests. It manufactures resins for the timber and plastics industries. Kalgoorlie, a gold-mining town 600km east of Perth is currently riding the crest of a boom due to improved gold prices and technology, and there is at present no shortage of jobs in most sectors in this growing town, although the major demand is in the mining industry for skilled workers.

Major new plants have been established for ceramic powder, titanium dioxide, silicon metal, turbine blades, wool scouring, pure wool quality apparel, pharmaceuticals for the Asian market, alumina and timber processing. Western Australia already has the world's largest zirconia plant.

The main products of the Western Australian fishing industry are rock lobster, prawns, shrimp and scampi which are mainly processed for export, principally to the USA and Japan.

There are nearly 3,000 manufacturing establishments in Western Australia, producing an annual turnover of more than $10 billion. Industries in the food and beverage sector and basic metal products areas have dominated in recent years.

Western Australia's financial sector has grown strongly since 1983, with the deregulation of much of the Australian financial system. There are now 20 banking groups represented in the state. Traded services is the fastest growing component of world trade and the government is intending to concentrate on this area for development and expansion. The state offers expertise through overseas consultancy services in mining, engineering, forestry, agriculture and conservation. The state's high standard of expertise and facilities has seen it develop as an exporter of medical services and technology and is increasingly a destination for visitors seeking specialised medical services.

Temporary: Harvest work is available all year round and is mainly found in the south-west corner of the state. Casual work in the fishing industry around the region of Carnarvon can be found between March and October. Roadhouses often require cooks, and cattle and sheep stations are often looking for workers, particularly at shearing time. Hospitality industries in any of the major tourist towns are generally looking for workers during the tourist season, which in Broome is between May and September. Work on the mines is also relatively easy to pick up, as well as other indoor jobs such as clerical, cleaning or catering, as mines often have a high turn-over of staff due to the harsh, remote conditions. Mining work is, however, gruelling as it usually involves shift work and the shifts are usually of twelve hours.

Northern Territory

Permanent: The Northern Territory is also rich in natural resources, and as a result its mining industries are a substantial component of the employment sector. The mining sector contributes 21.8% to its Gross State Product, and it has 14 operating mines. Minerals continue to dominate overseas merchandise trade, including alumina, manganese, gold, bauxite and uranium. Manganese is produced on Groote Eylandt, one of the world's four major mines producing high-grade ore, bauxite is mined at Australia's third largest mine at Gove, zinc lead and silver are mined at Woodcutters mine, McArthur River. Alligator Rivers uranium province produced $212 million in 1991 and the territory's main gold mines are located in the Adelaide River/Pine Creek region, the Tanami Desert and Tennant Creek. Exports of oil and gas accounted for approximately 35% of exports. Oil and gas production occurs mainly onshore from Mereenie and Palm Valley in the Amadeus Basin, and offshore mainly from the Jabiru and Challis fields in the Timor Sea. There are currently both private and governmental initiatives underway to ensure that Darwin becomes the national oil/gas capital, and the Sumitomo Corporation is examining the possible use of the Petrel and Tern gas fields in the Bonaparte Gulf for an export oriented Liquified Natural Gas project.

Tourism is also a major employment sector of the territory with Alice Springs, Darwin and Kakadu National Park being the centres of the tourist and hospitality industries. The territory also has a strong defence industry.

Temporary: The hospitality industry provides the majority of temporary jobs during the main tourist seasons which are May to December in Darwin and all year at Alice Springs. Remote resorts also tend to have a high staff turn-over, and are likely to have short-term work available, and some ranch work is available if you can either ride a horse or a motorbike.

South Australia
Permanent: Prominent existing industries in South Australia include wine making, motor vehicle and component manufacture, defence electronics, computer software, microelectronics, information processing, mineral processing and tourism. Businesses include food processing, aquaculture, natural fibre and textile processing, petrochemicals, biotechnology and pharmaceuticals, transport and space industries.

Various large international companies have recently chosen to establish operations, or make significant investment in current operations in South Australia. As mentioned above, Mitsubishi Motors are major employers in South Australia, at the Clovelly Park plant, and it is likely that the new $500 million investment will provide long-term security for approximately 30,000 jobs in the automotive parts industry, and, as previously mentioned, 5,000 new jobs are likely to be created in the near future. The Adelaide-based Kinhill Engineers Pty Ltd has also recently launched a recruiting drive as a result of a significant increase of base-load work and project commissions, and the company expects to recruit approximately 100 engineering and associated staff in the immediate future. This indicates that there will possibly be national growth in the engineering industry, so more jobs may be available in other engineering companies in other states/territories.

The giant US corporation Motorola, one of the world's leading suppliers of electronic and mobile telecommunications equipment, recently commenced operations in Adelaide to establish the Motorola Australia Software Centre which will be a major technology centre. By the year 2000, the Centre will employ 400 research and development engineers, and will involve investment, technology transfer, research and development, and exports from Australia valued at over $A240 billion. The world's largest subscription television operator, Telecommunications Incorporated, supports Australis Media Ltd which has recently announced it will open its national Customer Services Centre in Adelaide. This centre will employ 700 staff by 1998/99 and is expected to increase its workforce to over 1,000 by the year 2000.

In addition, Doug Elkins, of *Australian Outlook*, reported in April 1994 that there was a shortage of toolmakers and nurses in Adelaide, and that the Manager of the Immigration Promotion and Settlement Unit in South Australia, Nick Scarvelis, would be most happy to assist new settlers with employment.
Temporary: From February to April, there is grape picking available in the Barossa Valley and Adelaide Hills. There is also harvesting work available from June through to February. There is also some hospitality work available in Adelaide, particularly at the time of the Adelaide Grand Prix.

Tasmania
Permanent: It is important to note that at the time of writing, Tasmania has the highest rate of unemployment, so permanent jobs are more likely to be harder to find than elsewhere in Australia. For example, the mining industry is facing a crisis as it requires massive investment in exploration by the year 2000 or most mines will face closure. Having said this, there are employment sectors which have enjoyed recent growth, and jobs may be more likely to be available in the areas of agriculture, retailing, and manufacturing. Tasmania has recently diversified its agricultural industries to include a wide variety of grains, fruit and vegetables to include poppies, blueberries, grapes, essential oil crops, pyrethrum, goats and deer in an effort to corner a niche in the agricultural market. The state's retailing sector has continued to experience growth, though perhaps not at the rate of other states/territories, and approximately 30% of the retail establishments are food stores, which employed 37% of people employed in retailing. Tasmania's manufacturing industry accounts for approximately 20%

of the state's Gross Product and pays just over 23% of the state's total wage and salary bill. Recently, however, there appears to have been a steady decline of the number of persons employed in Tasmania's manufacturing sector. The largest sectors of the manufacturing industry are food, beverage and tobbacco, which contributed 30% of total Tasmanian turnover. Other important sectors were the wood, wood products and furniture, textiles, clothing and footwear, paper and paper products, chemical and petroleum products, basic metal products, fabricated metal products and transport equipment industries.

In general, it would perhaps not be advisable, at present, to migrate to Tasmania unless you had a firm offer of employment as you may be likely to experience more difficulty in finding a job in this state than others. It may be better to settle initially in another state/territory and then try to secure employment from within Australia when you can investigate the Tasmanian employment situation for yourself.

Temporary: Hospitality work available in Mount Field and Ben Lomond Ski Resorts from June to August, and harvest work of apples, grapes and hops is available from December to early April around Launceston, Kingston and Glenorchy.

Victoria

Permanent: 34% of Victoria's manufactured exports are in the food processing industry, with an export value of $A1.5 billion. International corporations among the 1,000 food processing companies in Victoria include HJ Heinz, Kraft Foods, Cadbury Schweppes, Mars and Bunge.

40% of the national production of aluminium is located at the Victorian primary aluminium smelters of Portland and Point Henry. 12% of Victoria's manufacturing is involved in chemicals, plastics and rubber, including ICI, Chemplex and Hoechst which are all based in Melbourne.

Approximately 45% of Australia's $2 billion communications industry is accounted for in Victoria, as Telecom Australia has its research laboratories and much of its head office functions in Melbourne. In addition, the Victorian software and services industry accounts for about 33% of the nation's consumption. There is still room for development, however, in providing services to the financial sector and specialist services such as systems integration and facilities management.

The largest employer in Victorian manufacturing, accounting for 17% of the state's employment, is in textiles, clothing and footwear. Growth is expected in the areas of wool processing and niche footwear and clothing production. Over half of Australia's automotive industry production occurs in Victoria, and Fords, General Motors and Toyota are all based in Victoria, together with more than 500 components producers.

Melbourne was originally a port, and there is much employment to be found in port services, as Melbourne handles 44% of Australia's overseas container trade, almost double the volume of containers of Adelaide, Brisbane and Fremantle combined. Significant private sector developments in the port and port services in 1992/3 included the upgrading of the Tasmania Passenger/Freight terminal at Station Pier by TT Line and the upgrading of the Coastal Express Line terminal at Webb Dock. Pacific Terminals have started a project to install seven new food grade storage tanks at Coode island and utilisation of the dry bulk berth at 26 South Wharf was improved with investment made by Melbourne Cement. The two terminal operators at Swanson dock, Australian Stevedores and Conaust are committed to developing their facilities to operate at international best practice performance levels. Major investment for redevelopment of these terminals over the next 20 years will exceed $300 million.

Geelong is Australia's eleventh largest city and was once known by Britons as 'the Bradford of the South' because of its major role in the country's textile industry. Today, however, although wool production and textile manufacture still play a major part in the prosperity of the 200,000 strong city, its future lies more in high-technology industries, education and research. Geelong now boasts one of the highest concentrations and diversity of the manufacturing industry in the country such as textiles, clothing, footwear, petroleum and coal products, chemicals, basic metal products and transport equipment. It is also the centre of Australian aerospace activity which will continue to develop into the next century, at Avalon Airport, together with major assembly and maintenance plants operated by ASTA and Hawker de Havilland in Melbourne. In addition, the Ford Motor Company, Shell Oil Company of Australia and the aluminium giant ALCOA of Australia are the largest among the hundreds of small to large industries that have chosen to expand in this region.

Temporary: There is plenty of fruit picking around Mildura and Shepperton from January to April, and around Echuca and Lilyfield from September through to February. The Northern Victoria Fruit-growers' Association in Shepperton, Victoria, and the Victorian Peach and Apricot Growers' Association in Cobram, Victoria, are two organisations generally able to offer jobs during the harvesting season. There is also limited hospitality work during the ski season in the Snowy Mountains. City work such as temporary secretarial, office and administration work is also relatively easy to obtain in Melbourne.

New South Wales

Permanent: More than 70 international businesses currently operate in New South Wales, in such diverse areas as information technology, telecommunications, computer hardware and software, aerospace, medical equipment, pharmaceuticals, environmental industries, industrial textiles, shipping and railways, construction and mining equipment, metal and minerals processing, processed foods, paper and pulp, greeting cards, banking, travel services and hotels, advertising, motion pictures and audio products. Most of these businesses are from the UK and USA, and European and Japanese companies are also represented.

Two of the major British organisations which now operate in New South Wales are British Airways and British Telecom. British Airways recently acquired 25% of Qantas, Australia's only international airline, and British Telecom was the successful tender for the NSW State Government communications network. Significantly, this was the biggest single private network investment British Telecom has ever made outside the UK.

New South Wales is Australia's leading state in basic metals, heavy engineering, chemicals, electronics and communications, finance and business services, and international tourism. Sydney is the head office location of the Reserve Bank of Australia, the Australian Stock Exchange, the Australian Export Finance and Insurance Corporation, and the Sydney Futures Exchange. The city is a leading developer of derivative financial products and provider of advanced financial services. Most of the foreign banks in Australia have their headquarters in Sydney, and Sydney's foreign exchange market caters for 8% of the world turnover. The six largest international accounting firms are located in Sydney, as are law, management consulting, data management and marketing firms. Major telecommunications companies that have located their Australian and Asia-Pacific operations in Sydney include Vodafone, Optus Communications, BT Australasia and the government-owned Telstra Corporation. As a result of the telecommunications expertise, major international users of information technology have chosen to establish their operations in Sydney, including Cathay Pacific's data-processing centre, the Australasian and South Pacific regional management office of the international airline database SITA, and the Asia-Pacific Field Data Centre of the giant US computer company Data General.

In addition, Sydney will be host to the Olympic Games in the year 2000, and there are many employment opportunities which will arise as a result. In Sydney, the 760-hectare Olympic Park being established over the next five years is providing many opportunities for private enterprises involvement, including the construction of an Olympic Village for more than 4,000 people to be later used as private housing. In addition, new public transport systems are proposed. For example, feasibility studies have been completed for an $800 million rail connection between the Sydney Central Business District and the international and domestic air terminals. There has also been a recent agreement with British and French companies for four water utilities for major new housing areas in Sydney, which will require finance of up to $600 million.

Temporary: It is possible to find office, factory and hospitality work in Sydney, but Christmas work can be difficult as students on their summer holidays tend to get much of the holiday work. Harvesting work can be found throughout the years in different regions of NSW, you just need to follow the crops.

Australian Capital Territory

Permanent: Most of the permanent jobs in the Australian Capital Territory are located in Canberra, and as it is the political centre of the country, the Federal Government is the biggest employer and service industries associated with political life are also important in the territory's economy.

Temporary: There is not much temporary work to be found in this area at all, although the odd job is always available for bar/café staff.

Queensland

Permanent: Agriculture was the original foundation of Queensland's economy, with grains, beef and wool as the most important industries. While these commodities are still important, other agricultural industries such as sugar cane, tropical and citrus fruits, dairy products, vegetables, cotton, livestock and tobacco are also competitive. Queensland's fishing industry is second only to Western Australia's and there are currently 4,487 commercial fishing vessels and 6,161 personal fishing licences operating in Queensland. Prawns, crustaceans and fin fish are the main catches exported to Asia, Europe and the USA.

The state is also rich in natural resources and its economy has thrived on developments of mineral mining such as gold, copper, lead and zinc. Currently, the Mount Isa mine is one of the world's leading producers of lead and silver, and is ranked in the world's top ten for copper and zinc production. The state's coal and bauxite reserves are also among the largest in the world and are generally high grade and easily accessible, and magnesite, phosphate rock, and limestone are also mined. The mining industry is expected to continue to flourish due to the availability of economical, coal-generated electricity, and the fact that large resources of magnesite, oil, shale, uranium, tin, mineral sands, clay and salt are as yet untapped. Queensland is the largest Australian producer and exporter of black coal. The primary industries of agriculture and mining presently account for about 5.4% of the Gross State Product, 6.4% of the state's employment and about 25% of Australia's total primary production.

Maufacturing industries in Queensland have developed to support the energy intensive mineral processing and agricultural industries. The manufacturing industry is dominated by four major industries, food, beverages and tobacco, basic metal products, basic metal products, fabricated metal products, and chemicals, petroleum and coal products. Processed foods is Queensland's largest manufacturing industry with a 1989/90 turnover of $6.9 billion generated by 690 establishments employing 35,700 people. The manufacturing sector currently accounts for approximately 12.0% of the state's Gross State Product, 11.3% of employment and about 12.0% of Australia's total manufacturing production.

Queensland's tourist industry is currently operating at an all-time high, due to its climatic advantage and many natural attractions such as the Great Barrier Reef, rainforests, extensive beaches and islands, and its Tourist Commission's higly successful international marketing campaign.

The state's service industries which were initially developed to support the mining and agricultural industries, have expanded to cover industries such as construction, wholesale and retail trades, communications, business and financial services, and industries servicing the tourism sector. The state's tertiary sector, including construction and tourism, currently accounts for about 75.1% of the Gross State Product, 80.5% of employment in the state, and about 15.0% of Australia's total production of services.

Temporary: There is a lot of fruit and vegetable picking work available throughout the state, particularly at Stanthorpe, Bowen and Warwick. Hospitality work at resorts is available during the main tourist seasons, and work on prawn trawlers can often be found at Cairns and Karumba. Mining and cattle station work is to be found in and around Mount Isa.

Directory of Major Employers

Australia's top 60 companies are listed below. Many of these companies have dozens, or in some cases hundreds of subsidiaries with diverse operations completely unrelated to their principal activity.

Companies whose revenue is predominantly earned overseas and/or reported in a currency other than A$ have been excluded. It must be noted that only publicly listed companies have been listed below. Information given includes a summary of operations together with addresses, phone and fax numbers of the main registered office. Most of the companies below also have numerous Australian and international offices, and you should contact the company directly for information of other offices.

Banking, Insurance & other financial services

Advance Bank Australia Limited, 182 George Street, Sydney NSW 2000, tel: 02-964 5000 or fax: 02-964 5111. Retail banking, home loans, commercial lending, financial services, treasury, property investment, funds management, and provision of life insurance services. The bank has branches in NSW, ACT and QLD.

Australia and New Zealand (ANZ) Banking Group Limited, 13th Floor, 55 Collins Street, Melbourne VIC 3000, tel: 03-658 2955 or fax: 03-658 2909. Wide range of banking and financial services to corporations and individuals worldwide.

Commonwealth Bank of Australia, 1st Floor, 48 Martin Place, Sydney NSW 2000, tel: 02-227 7111 or fax: 02-227 3317. Many subsidiaries include electronics, shipping and and investment and banking worldwide. Also the Commonwealth Development Bank which services the small business and rural sectors.

FAI Insurances Limited, FAI Insurance Building, 422 Collins Street, Melbourne VIC 3000, tel: 03-221 1155 or fax: 03-223 1144. General insurance for motor vehicles, consumer credit, fire, houseowners, marine, accident and loss, boating and general commercial risks. Life insurance, accident compensation fund, health benefits, reinsurance and professional indemnity and other financial services are also available.

GIO Australia Holdings Limited, 2 Martin Place, Sydney NSW 2000, tel: 02-

228 1000 or fax: 02-235 3909. General and corporate insurance services, personal insurance and investment products. There are 100 retail outlets, mainly in VIC and NSW, but also in other states.

National Australia Bank Limited, 24th Floor, 500 Bourke Street, Melbourne VIC 3000, tel: 03-641 3500 or fax: 03-641 4916. Worldwide operations and many subsidiaries.

National Commercial Union Limited, 8th Floor, 485 La Trobe Street, Melbourne VIC 3000, tel: 03-605 8222 or fax: 03-605 8410. Underwriting various classes of general insurance investment funds, and development, ownership and occupation of property.

QBE Insurance Group Limited c/o Phipson Nominees Pty Ltd, 10th Floor, Darwin Place, Canberra City ACT 2600, tel: 02-235 4444 or fax: 02-235 3155. General insurance and reinsurance risk underwriting services, investments in listed equities and properties.

St George Bank Limited, 4-16 Montgomery Street, Kogarah NSW 2217, tel: 02-952 1111 or fax: 02-952 1000.

Westpac Banking Corporation, 60 Martin Place, Sydney NSW 2000, tel: 02-226 3311 or fax: 02-231 2661.

Tooth & Company Limited, Level 44, 225 George Street, Sydney NSW 2000, tel: 02-258 711 or fax: 02-247 8919.

Brewing & Wines

Foster's Brewing Group Limited, 1 Gardent Street, South Yarra VIC 3141, tel: 03-828 2424 or fax: 03-826 9310. Manysubsidiaries many of them very remote from brewing (e.g. a horse breeding stud). International brewing company with interests in Australia and the Asia Pacific region. The company holds 50% of the Australian beer market through wholly owned subsidiary Carlton and United Breweries, whose products account for more than 70% of all Australian beer exports. Brands include Foster's, Victoria Bitter and Crown Lager.

Chemicals & Pharmaceuticals

ICI Australia Limited, 1 Nicholson Street, Melbourne VIC 3000, tel: 03-665 7111 or fax: 03-665 7937. Industrial and specialty chemicals, plastics and olefins, agrichemicals and fertilisers, pharmaceuticals, paints, explosives, ceramics, building materials and scientific instruments.

F H Faulding & Company Limited, 160 Greenhill Road, Parkside SA 5063, tel: 08-372 1500 or fax: 08-373 3120. Comprises the operations of Faulding Pharma Group and Faulding Pharmaceutical Group. The Faulding Pharma Group is involved in research, development, manufacturing and marketing of pharmaceuticals and high technology scientific and medical equipment.

Incitec Limited, Paringa Road, Gibson Island, Murarrie QLD 4172, tel: 07-867 9300 or fax: 07-867 9310. A subsidiary company is Grow Force Australia Ltd specialising in the manufacturing and marketing of fertilisers.

Foods & Beverages

Arnotts Limited, 11 George Street, Homebush NSW 2140, tel: 02-394 3555 or fax: 02-394 3500. Manufacture and distribution of biscuits, cakes, confectionery, bread, formula and dietary food.Brands include Arnott's Brockhoff's, Sunshine and Swallows.

Burns Philp & Company Limited, Bridge Street, Sydney NSW 2000, tel: 02-259 1111 or fax: 02-251 3254. International food/fermentation manufacture and supply with the head office in California, USA. The company provides yeast and bakery ingredients, industrial processors/ingredients and services, retail and consumer foods, antibiotics, hardware and also has investments in shipping agencies, bulk liquid storage facilities and motor vehicle distribution networks.

Coca-Cola Amatil Limited, c/o Deloitte Ross Tohmatsu, 11th Floor, 461 Bourke Street, Melbourne VIC 3000, tel: 02-259 6666 or fax: 02-259 6623.

Foodland Associated Limited, 18 Miles Road, Kewdale WA 605, tel: 09-350 2400 or fax: 09-353 2624. Western Australia's largest grocery and associated merchandise wholesaler, distributing more than 53% of the state's groceries through four warehouses.

George Weston Foods Limited, c/o Mallesons Stephen Jacques, 10th Floor, 60 Marcus Clarke Street, Canberra ACT 2601, tel: 02-439 1499 or fax: 02-438 1281. Manufactures and markets bread and other flour products in all Australian states. Brands include Tip Top, Sunblest and Kelly's. Also produces epoxy resin adhesives for paint brush and roller manufacture, hot foam felts for motor vehicle construction, disposable diapers and laminated foil.

Goodman Fielder Limited, Level 42, Grosvenor Place, 225 George Street, Sydney NSW 2000, tel: 02-258 4000 or fax: 02-251 5839. Has approximately 48% of its market in Australia. Operations include baking and milling, including brands such as Buttercup, Fielders, Vogels, Riga, Pampers, Country Fair, Home Style, Sunshine and Reiaentsteins. A vast range of processed foods is also produced.

National Foods Limited, Level 22, Royal Exchange Building, 56 Pitt Street, Sydney NSW 2000, tel: 02-240 6777 or fax: 02-252 1816. Operates food processing and household consumer products, primarily dairy products, fruit juices, food wrapping and storage products, stockfeeds and birdseed.

Freight, Transport & Security

Brambles Industries Limited, Level 40, Gateway, 1 Macquarie Place, Sydney NSW 2000, tel: 02-256 5222 or fax: 02-256 5299. Has 57 subsidiaries including materials handling services such as pallet, pallet cage and unit load container pooling and specialised containers; industrial and mining equipment services forklift truck rental and maintenance, fleet management, ancillary services, crane, truck, earth moving and related equipment, heavy haulage, metals recovery and logistics management; waste management; maritime services; security services; removals and storage of household and office contents; freight forwarding and transport; textile rental and laundry services.

Howard Smith Limited, 7th Floor, 474-482 Flinders Street, Melbourne VIC 3000, tel: 02-230 1777 or fax: 02-251 1190. Transporation for the timber, coal and other mining industries, rail maintenance and stevedoring services.

Mayne Nickless Limited, 21st Floor, 390 St Kilda Road, Melbourne VIC 3004, tel: 03-868 0700 or fax: 03-867 1179. One of Australia's largest transport and security companies. Operations include transport, distribution and warehousing, security, and health care services. (Healthcare of Australia is now the largest manager of private hospitals in Australia).

TNT Limited, Suite 1, Level 7, 12 Moore Street, Canberra City ACT 2601, tel: 02-699 2222 or fax: 02-699 9238.Provides land and air freight transport services specialising in express freight.

General Industrial

Alcan Australia Limited, 31 Market Street, Sydney NSW 2000, tel: 02-287 1411 or fax: 02-261 4770. Has a smelter division, sheet division, extrusion division, Alcan Foil Products division, Alcan Aluminium Centres division, Home Improvements division, window manufacturing subsidiary, trading division, and a subsidiary which constructs aluminium road tankers.

Australian National Industries Limited, Level 5, The Merlin Centre, 235 Pyrmont Street, Pyrmont NSW 2009, tel: 02-552 2600 or fax: 02-660 1395. Contracting

(shipbuilding and repair services), distribution of steel and other metals, manufacturing of general commercial forgings, castings, extruded products, specialised metal and steel products, and investment in associated companies.
Metal Manufacturers Limited, Level 33 Gateway, 1 Macquarie Place, Sydney NSW 2000, tel: 02-240 0555 or fax: 02-247 4155. Manufacture of electrical wires, cable, copper, copper alloy, plastic tubes, and electrical equipment for coal mining.
Tubemakers of Australia Limited, 23rd Floor, 1 York Street, Sydney NSW 2000, tel: 02-239 6666 or fax: 02-251 3042. Structural and engineering products, fluid conveyance products, precision products, metals merchandising and telecommunications products. Revenue: $1,155,232,000. Net Profit: $26,151,000.

Manufacturing, Building & Construction
AMCOR Limited, Southgate Tower East, 40 City road, South Melbourne VIC 3205, tel: 03-694 9000 or fax: $03-686 2924. The major Australian businesses are Containers Packaging, Amcor Fibre Packaging (AFP), Australian Paper Manufacturers (APM) and Kimberly-Clark Australia.
Boral Limited, 20th Floor, Norwich House, 6-10 O'Connell Street, Sydney NSW 2000, tel: 02-232 8800 or fax: 02-233 6605. Provision of building materials throughout Australia, manufacturing and energy production. Boral Bricks Inc is one of the largest US brick manufacturers, and production of masonry, concrete, fly ash and lightweight aggregate occurs in the UK.
BTR Nylex Limited, 15th Floor, 390 St Kilda Road, Melbourne VIC 3004, tel: 03-823 5700 or fax: 03-867 4103. Company Groups include polymer products, engineering and industrial design, construction products and resources, packaging (manufacture of glass, plastic bottles and other containers), building products, glass distribution and textiles/commercial interiors.
CSR Limited, Level 24, 1 O'Connell Street, Sydney NSW 2000, tel: 02-235 8000 or fax: 02-235 8555. Building and construction materials, timber products, sugar and aluminium.
Email Limited, Joynton Avenue, Waterloo NSW 2017, tel: 02-690 7333 or fax: 02-699 3190. Manufacture and distribution of domestic appliances (whitegoods) and air conditioners. Commercial and industrial products include air conditioning and refrigeration equipment, electric ranges, gas cookers, wall ovens, dishwashers, washing machines, and dryers. Also special purpose production machinery and tooling is designed and manufactured by Simpson Automation.
James Hardie Industries Limited, 65 York Street, Sydney NSW 2000, tel: 02-290 53333 or fax: 02 262 4390. Has many subsidiaries. Manufacturing and retailing construction and retail goods.
Leighton Holdings Limited, Level 5, 472 Pacific Highway, St Leonards NSW 2065, tel: 02-925 6666 or fax: 02-925 6005. Building, civil, mechanical and electrical engineering, contract mining, waste and environmental management, project management services and property development.
Pacific Dunlop Limited, Level 41, 101 Collins Street, Melbourne VIC 3000, tel: 03-270 7270 or fax: 03-270 7300. Hashundreds of subsidiaries manufacturing consumer products such as clothing, footwear and sporting goods. Clothing brands include Holeproof, Berlei, Red Robin and Bonds. Footwear brands include Grosby, Winstock and Dunlop. Sporting goods include Adidas, Dunlop, Slazenger, Repco, Speedwell, Malvern Star, Raleigh and Cyclops. Also has interests in foresty, processed foods, distribution engineering, mining, medical products, tyres and building and construction materials.
Pioneer International Limited, Level 20, 580 George Street, Sydney NSW 2000, tel: 02-364 4000 or fax: 02-364 4009. Manufactures and distributes pre-mixed

concrete, asphalt, bricks and clay products, masonry and concrete roof tiles, plasterboard and cement. It is also involved in petroleum refining and marketing.

Spicers Paper Limited, 44 Raglan Street, Preston VIC 3072, tel: 03-487 8888 or fax: 03-484 2577. Manufactures and markets envelopes, stationery, playing cards and other paper products; a paper merchanting group which distributes specialty papers, paperboard, packaging and carbonless and business form papers; and an office products division.

Media & Communications

The News Corporation Limited, 121 King William Street, Adelaide SA 5000, tel: 08-288 3000 or fax: 08-288 3292. Subsidiaries include publishing interests in the USA and the Uk and Twentieth Century-Fox Film Corporation and Sky Television Plc. The company publishes and prints a national newspaper, *The Australian*, and newspapers in all Australian states.

Mining

The Broken Hill Proprietary (BHP) Company Limited, BHP Tower, Bourke Plaza, 600 Bourke Street, Melbourne VIC 3000, tel: 03-609 3333 or fax: 03-609 3015. Mining, engineering, transport and financial services.

Caltex Australia Limited, 167-187 Kent Street, Sydney NSW 2000, tel: 02-250 5000 or fax: 02-231 6427, Oil refining and wholesale and retail of petroleum products, and coal mining.

Coal & Allied Industries Limited, c/o Price Waterhouse, 19 Moore Street, Canberra ACT 2600, tel: 02-233 4122 or fax: 02-251 3019. The company mines for coal in the Hunter Valley of NSW, operating two large open cut mines, three underground mines and three coal preparation plants. Operates its own coastal vessels serving the Sydney industrial coal market.

Comalco Limited, 31st Floor, 55 Collins Street, Melbourne VIC 3000, tel: 03-658 8300 or fax: 03-658 3707. One of the world's leading suppliers of bauxite.

McIlwraith McEacharn Limited, Level 12, 32 Walker Street, North Sydney NSW 2060, tel: 02-956 4000 or fax: 02-954 1445. Coal mining, mine contracting, coal recovery and marine activities, but it is also involved in shipping.

Petroleum and Gas

The Australian Gas Light Company, AGL Centre, Cnr Pacific Highway & Walker Street, North Sydney NSW 2060, tel: 02-922 0101 or fax: 02-957 3671. Operations include the sale of gas and gas appliances, natural gas and oil exploration and production, operation of natural gas and oil pipelines, property development, financing and rental, extraction and sale of liquefied petroleum gas and ethane.

Property

Jennings Group Limited 350 Wellington Road, Mulgrave VIC 3170, tel: 03-566 8888 or fax: 03-566 8360. Specialises in housing, providing home designing and building services, home improvements, residential land development, residential housing project development, and order housing.

Lend Lease Corporation Limited, 46th Level, Australia Square, George Street, Sydney NSW 2000, tel: 02-236 6111 or fax: 02-252 2192. Residential, retail and commercial property development, interior office development, property management services, retail financial services, and corporate services.

Retail

Brash Holdings Limited, 276 Collins Street, Melbourne VIC 3000, tel: 03-654 6544 or fax: 03-650 3998. Brash Holdings operating areas are: Angus & Robertson Bookworld which has 118 company and 55 franchised bookshops; Consumer Electronics which retails 1,500 brand name products in the superstore network; Recorded Music, Video, Music and Accessories which retail CDs, tapes, records, video and associated products such as sheet music and instruments. Also computers and related products.

Coles Myer Limited, 800 Toorak Road, Tooronga VIC 3146, tel: 03-829 3111 or fax: 03-829 6787. Australia's largest retail organisation operating supermarkets, discount stores, department stores and specialty retail outlets. Brand names include Coles, Bi-Lo, K-Mart, Myer and Grace Bros. Revenue: $15,177,800,000. Net Profit: $370,700,000.

David Jones Limited 86-108 Castlereagh Street, Sydney NSW 2000, tel: 02-266 5544 or fax: 02-267 3895. One of Australia's leading department store retailers with a one-third stake in Woolworths, owned by Industrial Equity Ltd. Other operations and investments include Clark Rubber, Eastman Corporation, automotive and general engineering.

Vox Limited, 505 Abernethy Road, Kewdale WA 6105, tel: 09-353 0590 or fax: 09-353 2160. Retails household appliances, home entertainment products, furniture, bedding, curtains and blinds, pre-recorded music, and extended warranties. Operates through three business units: the Vox Retail Group, Vox Financial Services and the Kresta Group. Revenue: $823,917,000. Net Profit: $11,491,000

Tobacco Products

Rothmans Holdings Ltd Level 42, Northpoint, 100 Miller Street, North Sydney NSW 2060, tel: 02-956 0666 or fax: 02-956 7442. Manufacture, processing, importing and distribution of cigarettes, cigars and other tobacco products.

W D & H O Wills Holdings Limited, Wills Pagewood Park, Westfield Drive, Pagewood NSW 2035, tel: 02-344 1500 or fax: 02-344 1188.

Miscellaneous

The Adelaide Steamship Company Limited, 123 Greenhill Road, Unley SA 5061, tel: 08-258 8833 or fax: 08-235 3700. Subsidiaries include: Sellers Atkins Ltd, Pioneer Property Group Ltd, WA Realty Pty Ltd, Markheath Plc. Operations include retail and investment, meat, office supplies, building supplies, building and property development, energy and resources, manufacturing and distribution, marine towage, and real estate.

Independent Holdings Limited, 410-450 Findon Road, Kidman Park SA 5025, tel: 08-352 9595 or fax: 08-354 0111. Warehousing, distribution, property management, the wholesaling of groceries, general merchandise and liquor.

SA Brewing Holdings Limited, Level 23, State Bank Centre, 91 King William Street, Adelaide SA 5000, tel: 08-239 7777 or fax: 08-231 0886. Beverage and goods group, a packaging group, an appliance group, and an international group which manufactures drums and buckets.

Wesfarmers Limited, 11/40 The Esplanade, Perth WA 6000, tel: 09-327 4211 or fax: 09-327 4216. Coal mining and production; gas processing and distribution; fertiliser and chemical manufacture; building and forest products,; transport; retailing; rural merchandise and agency business; dairy activities; and insurance.

Starting a Business

Australia used to be considered the 'Lucky Country' or the 'Land of Opportunity' and businesses seemed to mushroom and thrive nationwide. Until relatively recently, it was not necessary to be a multi-million international conglomeration to survive, and small businesses such as plumbers, caterers, painters and decorators, landscapers, hairdressers and beauticians, and pottery studios not only found space for themselves in the Australian market, but remained buoyant and generated fairly prosperous incomes.

With the recession, however, came a much more depressed business climate, and large and small businesses collapsed in dramatic profusion. Although the Australian economy is now showing slight signs of recovery, it has on the whole become far more difficult for new businesses to survive their first year. A recent survey conducted by the Family Business section of the Australian Business Development Office found that 30% of family-owned businesses survive to the second generation, 15% to the third generation and only 3% beyond the third. Business economists are now, however, predicting growth due to new governmental guidelines specifically designed to protect new and young businesses in their first years of operation. The Australian government also offers various tax incentives, which both protect and assist small businesses, helping them to be more efficient.

The manufacturing and services industries are currently the most successful, and this is largely due to the devaluation of the Australian dollar. The need to become more competitive internationally has forced small businesses to provide higher quality products and services at costs which can compete with international businesses. The result of this is that these particular sectors have experienced outstanding growth compared to other sectors of Australia's economy. Economic and business experts believe that this trend is likely to contine for some time.

Despite the fact that the Australian economy has been suffering the effects of recession for the past several years, it would be wrong to suggest that business is depressed. In fact, the British newspaper, *Overseas Jobs Express*, recently reported that business in Australia is picking up and that Australia is third only to the USA and Switzerland as a destination for top executives in pursuit of new and potentially lucrative business opportunities and personal development. Indeed, Australia is the preferred destination for Asian executives, who seem to feel that there is more chance of realising personal dreams there than in their own countries.

In the Family Business survey, 51% of responders identified the level of taxes and costs as being major inhibitors of business growth. 36% felt that lack of funding restricted their business's growth, while 32% attributed this to economic conditions. 20% found that the lack of suitably qualified employees prevented their business from performing as well as it could/should, and 15% found that the lack of skills among family members involved in the business was a significant factor in inhibiting the business. This chapter aims to give practical advice about starting a new business as well as suggestions as to what kinds of businesses may do well in Australia in order to help your business avoid being one of the above statistics. In addition, it can be used as a source of information regarding the taxation, rules and regulations relevant to creating a new business and also the procedure involved in buying an existing business. The *useful addresses* section at the end of the chapter may be particularly helpful in providing contact names and addresses of advisors and authorities who may be able to help you get off the ground.

Preparation From Scratch

Once you have ascertained that you have the necessary qualifications, it is essential to make the right decision regarding the product/service you wish to sell. Most important is your complete familiarity with the product, including detailed technical knowledge. Next, you must ensure that the market for this product exists and you should identify the size, geographical and sociological distribution of that market. Research is really the key to success and you would be well advised to find out as much as possible about your target population and your competition. This kind of information can be gained from government statistics (contact the Australian Bureau of Statistics, address below), universities and institutes of technology, advertisements in the media, and telephone directories (both the yellow pages and the business directory). In addition, you should find out whether there is a trade association which deals with the product or service you are offering as this might be a source of information, advice and assistance.

Product Protection You may wish to protect your product by a patent. A patent can only be granted for a new, tangible product and is generally used for products and processes in the industrial or agricultural fields. According to the Patents Act 1952, patents are granted for products and processes that are new, novel, non-obvious, inventive and have utility. Inventions that are contrary to the law and/or are unrelated to manufacturing processes are not patentable. A patent entitles the holder to manufacture the product and receive all the profits on its sale. The product must be defined in the patent specification and it is therefore necessary to consult a patent attorney to prepare your application for you. There are two major kinds of patents available in Australia: the standard patent, which expires after sixteen years (from the date it was filed) if the patent renewal fees (payable at the end of the second year) are paid annually; and the petty patent, which is granted for a year from the date of the filing, with a possible extension of up to six years. The petty patent is primarily intended for products with short commercial lives. The Patent Co-operation Treaty (PCT) allows companies to file an international patent application, with the effect that the product is protected in all participating PCT countries. There are 74 countries participating in the PCT, including the USA, Canada, Mexico, the UK, Austria, Belgium, Switzerland, Germany, Denmark, Spain, France, Greece, Ireland, Italy, the Netherlands, Norway and Sweden. There are also many other participating countries from eastern Europe, Africa and the Asian-Pacific region. The patent application consists of several forms and a detailed set of drawings, and the cost of submitting an application is dependent upon the complexity of the drawings. A schedule of fees is available from the Australian Industrial Property Organisation, Patent Trade Marks and Designs Office (address below) and applications are submitted to this office. There are Patent Offices in every PCT country, and the address of the UK office is also given below should you wish further information before you leave Britain.

If your product is competing with others of a similar type, you may wish to register a *trademark*, which is essentially a distinguishing word or symbol displayed on your product. Once this word/symbol is registered, at an initial

202 Working in Australia

cost of $A200, in accordance with the Trade Marks Act, the mark can only be used by you. A trademark is registered indefinitely providing renewal fees are paid seven years after registration and every fourteen years thereafter. A trademark must also be registered with the Patent Trade Marks and Designs Office in Australia. Processing time for applications is currently quite lengthy at twenty months, and this must be allowed for in the overall time schedule of your planning for the new business. Once your trademark has been accepted, its acceptance is published in an Official Journal, after which objections may be filed within three months. If there is no opposition, registration occurs within twelve months. Therefore, the overall time taken to register your trademark, from date of application, can be as long as 32 months. If there are any objections raised about your application, you will obviously face a much longer wait and possibly have to amend your application.

Besides protecting your product by having it patented, it is also possible to protect the *design* of that product in terms of its shape, colour or pattern. Protection of the design usually occurs in conjunction with a patent, and registration of designs are governed by the Designs Act 1906. The maximum period of registration for a design is sixteen years (an initial six-year term with two renewable five-year terms), and it will cost approximately $A150. You will need to include full details of the design and the goods which the design applies to in your application to register your design at the Patent Trade Marks and Design Office.

If your product has not been tested in the market, it is beneficial to have it tested by the Standards Association of Australia which provides specifications for a large number of products. Their approval of your product means that you are able to use the SAA mark on your product which could be beneficial in terms of product credibility. In addition, you should consult local universities in case research is being undertaken in the same area. If this is the case, mutual co-operation can be extremely advantageous in terms of expert assistance in the development and testing of the product.

Choosing an Area

Obviously, if you decide to buy an existing business your area will generally be predetermined, but if you are starting your business from scratch, the decision of where to locate your business, including the type of premises you require, can be vitally important to its future. The needs of your business should determine its location. Various factors, such as whether you expect frequent deliveries from suppliers or visits from customers and whether you need to attract passing trade (thus choosing premises which are highly visible) can influence your decision as to which area is better than another, but you also need to consider the needs of your staff, particularly if they are dependent on public transport to get to work, and whether there is sufficient parking space for those who drive.

Renting Business Premises

The rents of commercial property vary greatly across Australia. Perth currently has a fairly substantial amount of vacant industrial and office space and so the rents offered (calculated in dollars per square metre) are low compared to similar properties in Sydney, Melbourne or Canberra. Similarly, the rates of leasing commercial property in Darwin, Adelaide, Brisbane and Hobart are markedly lower than that of comparable properties in the central business districts of Sydney, Melbourne and Canberra.

Whether leasing or purchasing, you need to make sure that the premises have adequate facilities such as security, access, essential services (including electricity, water, waste collection, energy efficiency, sound and thermal insulation), flexibility of design should you wish to expand at a later date, and that the dimensions in terms of height and floor space are sufficient. Furthermore, you need to ask your solicitor to check that your type of business will not breach any environmental laws if you conduct that business in those particular premises. The buildings must comply with fire and safety regulations, town planning and other regulations, and the Health Act and Shops and Factories Act (obtainable from the Government Printer or various technical publishers) applicable in your state/ territory.

If you choose to lease premises, ensure that the lease is perused by a solicitor and, if possible, an accountant. The terms of the lease are always negotiable, and your solicitor/accountant will advise of ways to negotiate terms and conditions to give you a better deal. You should attempt to negotiate a rent free period, a lower initial rental, reduced annual escalations, payment by the landlord or any improvements or refurbishments to the property and payment by the landlord of any outgoings associated with the property. You should identify who is responsible for insurance, property taxes and maintenance, what your rights are to make alterations or renovations, and whether the lease permits sub-letting of the premises. Your negotiating power will depend on that state of the property market at the time, which at the time of writing is certainly advantageous to lessees.

The term of the lease can be significant in that a long lease may reduce flexibility. A shorter lease with the option to renew is sometimes preferable, depending on the current economic conditions and your choice of premises. When considering a lease, it is helpful to ask for a plan which clearly states the extent of the premises being let, and make sure that the proposed use of your building does not breach any terms of the lease. Before you sign, you should also compare the rent, rates and service charges (usually given on a dollar per square metre basis), annual escalations and rent review clauses with those of other premises. You should also be aware that a verbal lease, which is binding on both parties, is recognised by law and should therefore be avoided as they are fraught with difficulties.

Your choice of premises can also have tax implications as payments for rent of business premises are tax deductible. For buildings constructed or improvements commenced after 26 February 1992, depreciation is an allowable tax deduction at the rate of 4% per annum. Business premises constructed from 19 July 1982 to 22 August 1984 and from 16 September 1987 to 26 February 1992 are subject to a depreciation rate of 2.5% per annum, while buildings constructed between 21 August and 15 September 1987 can be depreciated at 4% per annum. Moveable furnishings and equipment within the buildings are subject to higher rates of depreciation for taxation purposes.

Raising Finance

You can have the best ideas, products and service in the world, but if you cannot manage to raise the finance to put all of your plans into practice, your dreams (not to mention potential profits) will remain unrealised. The most important thing to do before you approach any of the many different finance organisations, is to ensure that you are prepared to explain your business concept fully and to answer any questions about your proposals. In order to do this properly, you need to formulate a business plan that is thorough and logical.

You need to demonstrate that you have thought of and allowed for every eventuality, thus making you seem less of a financial risk. It is possible to divide planning ideas into two categories; estimated figures and assumptions. Estimated figures include estimates about sales, cost of sales, administration expenses etc., whereas assumptions include the expected level of inflation, the expected rate of taxation, the expected trend of interest rates, capital expenditure and its timing, stock turnover, debtors' collection period and creditors' payment period. It is very important not to be overly optimistic in making estimates and assumptions as it is all to easy to try to paint a rosy picture for the benefit of the financial institution from which you wish to borrow money. The truth is, however, that the institutions will see this as naivety at best and deception at worst, and either way will be less likely to approve your application for financial assistance. Experts suggest that being as conservative as you can is much more likely to help your application for financial assistance. When preparing your business plan, you need to consider whether there will be any seasonal variations, whether your set up costs are adequate, and whether you have correctly assessed the period of time you are likely to be without income and/or profit.

One of your first steps in drawing up a business plan is to consider the different sources of finance available to you. The Commonwealth Bank of Australia strongly recommends that business owners should look much more carefully at maximising the business's ability to generate internal funds in order to avoid relying too much on external sources for the funding of its operations. Although a new business is hardly likely to be in the position to generate enough internal funds in order to become self-sufficient for at least three years, you should think very carefully about trying to borrow as little as possible from outside sources in the long term, and incorporate self-sufficiency into your long-term business proposal. Once you have done this, you need to look very carefully at all the different financial institutions and the options available to you in order to choose one or a combination that is most appropriate to the needs and goals of your company, and your repayment capacity.

As mentioned in *Daily Life*, there is a large number of different financial institutions in Australia. Deregulation of banking has led to increased competition and, as a consequence, more innovative and sophisticated banking techniques have been introduced. In addition, opportunities to obtain loan funds have greatly increased and there are now many more options available in terms of structuring loan agreements. In an effort to encourage the growth and development of Australian industry and resources, a number of industrial banks have been established, including the government-owned Australian Industry Development Corporation (AIDC) which provides development finance, equity funding and financial advisory services.

Types of Finance

Equity, long term loan finance and working capital finance are basically the three types of finance available for starting a new business in Australia. Equity is usually contributed by the owners of the business. The Commonwealth Bank of Australia claims that this option is not considered seriously enough and state that many rejections of applications for finance occur precisely because the owners of the business have not made what is termed 'adequate personal contribution' which is, in turn, seen to be a lack of commitment. This means that if the owners of the business make substantial and often sacrificial contributions to the business, that business is far more likely to attract financial backing from other sources. If you wish to use finance for long term projects, such as your business or plant and machinery for your business, you will be more likely to apply for long term loan finance. In many cases the loan will be secured against the business started or machinery bought. In addition, the financial institution will generally require personal guarantees from the business owners. There is usually a substantial difference between the amount of the loan and the value of the asset in order to allow for risk and the costs involved should the business fail. Long term finance is available from diverse sources such as your own personal financial resources. It is important to calculate how much of your own personal contribution can be used as share capital and how much can be used as loan capital. The calculation of this can affect your taxation, see *Taxation* below for further details. Cash subscription from your family and friends can also be used as long term finance, as can cash received from any other sponsor or venture capital. The more conventional and, perhaps, expensive ways of raising capital in terms of a long term loan are through a bank or finance company loan, or through leasing or hire purchase finance. It must be noted, however that leasing or hire purchase finance generally have interest rates which are significantly higher than other sources.

Government Backed Finance.

It is important to note that the Australian government, at both Federal and State levels, provides various forms of assistance, technical as well as financial. Financial assistance can include direct cash grants, subsidies and tax concessions, and the technical assistance includes professional and technical advice. At the time of writing, the chance of participating in Government guaranteed projects is high, and there are substantial benefits which can be claimed by both large and small businesses involved in the schemes. Federal Government assistance is varied. The Export Market Development Grant (EMDG) scheme provides a grant of 50% of exporters' eligible expenditure incurred between 1 July 1990 to 30 June 1995. The minimum qualifying expenditure is $A30,000 and the maximum grant is $A250,000. 'Eligible expenditure' means the costs which were incurred in the promotion of Australian goods and services, skills or industrial property rights. It also sometimes includes market research, advertising, the preparation of tenders and company representation overseas.

Given that the government imposes significant tariffs on imported products, it offers *bounties*, which are direct cash payments to certain Australian manufacturers (operating within Australia), in lieu of, or supplementary to, assistance provided by means of tariff or customs duty. This means that the manufacturer is then able to sell the product at a lower price and thus be able to compete with the imports. Industries eligible for bounties include manufacturers of books, shipbuilders, textile yarns, robots, metalworking machines, computers and microprocessor-related equipment. You should contact the Australian Customs Service in your capital city for further information.

Rebates and subsidies are also offered to employers as an incentive to provide employment and to encourage them to provide training (including allowing employees to dotrade/development courses) by giving the employer compensation. Closely related to this are employment schemes such as the CRAFT scheme and the Traineeship System which give wage subsidies to employers who employ apprentices, school leavers and the long term unemployed. For further information about employment incentives, you should contact the Commonwealth Employment Service in your capital city.

As an employer or owner of a small business, you may be eligible for Marketing and Trade Assistance provided by the Department of Industry, Technology and Commerce. This assistance often involves specialist laboratory and advising services for packaging, design and materials. If your business is involved in exporting goods from Australia, AUSTRADE (The Australian Trade Commission) will be able to provide marketing advice and assistance. The Grants for Industry Research and Development (GRID) scheme is designed to help new businesses companies that have not yet incurred any tax liability, or other companies that are not able to take advantage of tax concessions. The Federal Government offers tax incentives which are detailed below in the 'Investment Incentives' section. For further information about general assistance, you should contact the relevant capital city branches of the Industry and Research and

Development Board, the Australian Trade Commission, the Department of Industry, Technology and Commerce, or the National Industry Extension Service (NIES).

In terms of State Government assistance, most states and territories provide financial assistance in the forms of loan funds or guarantees to businesses. This assistance is generally only provided as a final resort. Other assistance includes transportation and freight subsidies and advice on diverse areas such as effective business operations, production processes, technological development and export market opportunities. State Government assistance is generally given to encourage the establishment of new businesses, or the expansion of existing ones within the state or territory and, in order to receive such assistance, businesses must demonstrate that they are viable, both in the short and long term, and that they can provide assessable, real benefits to the state. The government will be likely to favour enterprises that can create new, permanent jobs, provide new skills, increase the state's technology or production capacity, tap new markets outside the state, and offer diversification of the state's industrial base or range of products. For further details about State Government assistance, you should contact your Federal or State Member of Parliament, your state's Small Business Development Corporation or similar body, the Federal and State Industry Development bodies and the state's Commonwealth Employment Service.

Summary of Financing

Although a potential financer will want a thorough plan, they will not want a long report, so you should try to keep your proposal down to between ten and twelve pages. You must ensure that you state and/or describe your product, the premises from which you intend to operate, relevant information about each member of the management team, your marketing strategy, your competition, past performance (if any), financial projections and assumptions relating to them, the financial resources required and what changes will be necessary if your assumptions prove to be either pessimistic or optimistic, and your assessment of the risks involved in the project. It is a very good idea to use a personal or micro computer in the preparation of a proposal as it not only makes it relatively easy to adjust calculations if there are any changes to estimates or assumptions, but to assess the effects of these changes. Furthermore, the finished product is likely to look professional, and you must consider the proposal's presentation as an important factor. Finally, it is important to get professional advice when preparing a business plan, but you need to be fully involved as ultimately it will be you that is expected to be able to answer questions on every aspect of it.

Accountants

Finding a good accountant is essential to the success of your business. You will find that the process of creating a new business or buying an existing one is so complex and involved, that you will not be able to complete it without expert assistance. Your accountant should be registered with one of the industry associations, and you must check this at the outset. Accountants have different rates and charges, so it is useful to contact a number of different firms for brochures, quotes and information before you make your decision. Basically, your accountant will act as your financial and, at times, legal adviser, often fulfilling duties which could also be done by a solicitor. If the advice you receive is false or misguided, it could mean the failure of your business and possibly even fines and legal costs. For this reason, you will want to make sure that the accountant you decide to use is reliable and reputable. It may be worth investing in one of the larger accountancy firms as when it comes down to it, your accountant is really another business investment you will have to make and you will want to reduce the element of risk. It is advisable to consult your accountant on every initial business decision you make as they will tend to give you more independent advice than a real estate agent or business broker, and it is wise to keep the accountant informed of all business activities.

Useful Addresses

The Australian Copyright Council, 245 Chalmers Street, Redfern NSW 2016, tel: 02-318 1788.

Australian Industry Development Corporation, Level 33 Maritime Centre, 201 Kent Street, Sydney NSW 2000, tel: 02-235 5155, or for Investor Services tel: 02-252 2700.

Australian Industrial Property Organisation, Patent Office, PO Box 200, Woden ACT 2606, tel: 06-283 2225 or fax: 06-285 3929.

Australian Quality Council, Level 1, 80 Chandos Street, St Leonard's NSW 2065, tel: 02-906 4677.

Department of Business & Employment, Minister for Industry & Employment, 228 Victoria Parade, East Melbourne VIC 3002, tel: 03-412 8000; Minister for Small Business & Youth Affairs, 100 Exhibition Street, Melbourne VIC 3000, tel: 03-655 3300.

The Institute of Patent Attorneys of Australia, 2 Railway Parade, Camberwell VIC 3124, tel: 03-882 8041 or 008-804 536. You should also check the yellow pages under 'Patent Attorneys' for further information.

Inventors' Association of Australia, 40 Winmalee Road, Balwyn VIC 3103, tel: 03-836 9927.

Investment Centre Victoria, Level 29, 120 Collins Street, Melbourne VIC 3000, tel: 03-655 8999.

New Enterprise Incentive Scheme, Level 27, 80 Collins Street, Melbourne VIC 3000, tel: 03-655 8999.

United Kingdom Patent Office, Cardiff Road, Newport, Gwent, NP9 1RH, or filings by hand may be made at 25 Southampton Buildings, London WC2A 1AY, tel: 01633-814 586 (for international applications), 01633-812 151 (for international preliminary examinations), 01633-814 000 (operator service) or fax: 01633-814 444.

Accountants

In addition to the specialised consultants listed below, it is possible to find an accountant simply by scanning the yellow pages telephone directory. Alternatively, you could contact the Institute of Chartered Accountants, the Australian Society of Accountants in your capital city or the National Institute of Accountants.

Australian Accounting Group, 56 Neridah Road, Chatswood NSW 2067, tel: 02-411 4866.

Australian Association of Independent Business Ltd, 200 Alexandra Parade, Fitzroy VIC 3065, or 2/28 Prospect Street, Box Hill VIC 3128, tel: 03-418 3922 or 008-804 781.

Ernst & Young, The Ernst & Young Building, 321 Kent Street, Sydney NSW 2000, tel: 02-248 5555 or fax: 02-248 4962.

Institute of Chartered Accountants in Australia, 37 York Street, Sydney NSW 2000, tel: 02-290 1344.

PJ St Clair & Co, Chartered Accountants, Level 8, 235 Macquarie Street, Sydney NSW 2000, tel: 02-221 4088 or fax: 02-221 7498. To arrange for a free 'Buy a Business Seminar' contact Ann Taylor on 02-221 4088.

Ray Eastgate, Spectrum Consulting, operates from the Toowoomba Management & Accounting Services which specialise in the preparation of professional

profiles and resumés, independent accountants and business consultants Australia-wide. Contact him at 4 Little Street, Toowoomba QLD, tel: 076-391 969, 076-327 866 (after hours) or fax: 076-383 708.
Business Reports & Values, tel: 09-275 5572, mobile: 018-916 752 or fax:09-276 7886, offers valuation for Family Court Proceedings, valuation for litigation including misrepresentation, tenancy, or loss of goodwill, valuation of minority shares, valuation for buyer or seller, retiring partners or insurance claims.

Banks
Trading Banks:
ANZ Banking Group Ltd, 20 Martin Place, Sydney NSW 2000, tel: 02-227 1911.
Commonwealth Bank of Australia, 108 Pitt Street, Sydney NSW 2000, tel: 02-227 7111.
National Australia Bank Ltd, National Australia Bank House, 255 George Street, Sydney NSW 2000, tel: 02-237 1111.
Westpac Banking Corporation, 60 Martin Place, Sydney NSW 2000, tel: 02-226 3311.

See also the banking section of Chapter Four for the British branches of these banks.

Merchant Banks:
BA Australia Ltd, 167 Macquarie Street, Sydney NSW 2000, tel: 02-221 2855.
Barclays Australia Ltd, 25 Bligh Street, Sydney NSW 2000, tel: 02-238 4789.
BNP Pacific (Australia) Ltd, 12 Castlereagh Street, Sydney NSW 2000, tel: 02-232 8733.
BT (Bankers Trust) Australia Ltd, Level 38, Australia Square, Sydney NSW 2000, tel: 02-259 3555.
Chase AMP Bank, Qantas International Centre, International Square, Cnr Jamison and George Street, Sydney NSW 2000, tel: 02-250 4111.
Lloyds Bank NZA Ltd, 35 Pitt Street, Sydney NSW 2000, tel: 02-239 5555.
Macquarie Bank Ltd, 20 Bond Street, Sydney NSW 2000, tel: 02-237 3333.
Standard Chartered Bank Australia Ltd, 345 George Street, Sydney NSW 2000, tel: 02-232 6599.

Finance Companies:
Australian Guarantee Corporation, 130 Phillip Street, Sydney NSW 2000, tel: 02-234 1122.
Avco Financial Services Ltd, 910 Pacific Highway, Sydney NSW 2072, tel: 02-498 0222.
Custom Credit Corporation Ltd, 10 Bond Street, Sydney NSW 2000, tel: 02-229 2222.
Esanda Finance Corporation Ltd, 68 Pitt Street, Sydney NSW 2000, tel: 02-237 9777.
Australian Finance Advisory Service, 9 Redman Street, Canterbury NSW 2193, tel: 02-718 4548 or mobile: 018-268 654.

Real Estate:
Australia Wide Realty Pty Ltd, 355 Homer Street, Earlwood NSW 2206, tel: 02-559 3333.
Real Estate Services Council, tel: 02-287 9000.
Real Estate Institute, tel: 02-264 2343.
J Macgregor Dunn & Son, Licensed Real Estate Agents & Property Managers, 22 Conway Street, Lismore NSW, tel: 066-215 088.
Raine & Horne, Real Estate Agents, Auctioneers, Property Managers, Marketing Consultants, Valuations & Business Sales, 71 Marine Drive, Tea Gardens

NSW 2324, or PO Box 13, Tea Gardens NSW 2324, tel: 049-970 126 or fax: 049-970 749.

Realtors of Distinguished Properties Brisbane Commercial, PO Box 1440, Toowong QLD 4066 or Level 1, 64 Sylvan Road, Toowong QLD 4066, tel: 17-870 2425 or fax: 07-870 3979.

Taylor & Cook Real Estate, Business, Commercial & Industrial, Westpac House, 3276 Beaudesert Road, Browns Plains QLD.

Thomas O'Brien Real Estate, 81 Sanger Street, Corowa NSW 2646, or PO Box 51, Corowa NSW 2646, tel: 060-332 044 or fax: 060-333 349.

Troystar Business Real Estate, Suite 2, Level 2, Ocean Central, 1 Ocean Street, Maroochydore QLD 4558, or PO Box 504, Maroochydore QLD 4558, tel: 074-791 722 or fax: 074-791 717.

In addition to the above, the yellow pages telephone directory will contain further estate agents in your state/territory which may prove to be more helpful.

Useful Publications

Books and Information Packs

Australian Bureau of Statistics, 3rd Floor, St Andrews House, Sydney Square, Sydney NSW 2000, tel: 02-268 4111, 02-268 4611 or fax: 02-268 4668. The ABS publish yearbooks which contain the results of every recent survey and research projects, and can be particularly helpful in terms of finding statistics regarding population and consumption in order to identify markets for particular products or services.

Australian Financial Review Books, 81-1/2 George Street, Sydney NSW 2000, tel: 02-241 5385.

Doing Business in Australia is a detailed and very informative handbook which functions as a useful introduction to how business is done in Australia. It is published by Ernst & Young as part of their *International Business* series and is available from their Australian office listed above under *Accountants*. They also have many international offices which generally stock copies and you should consult the telephone directory in your country's capital city for further information. Ernst & Young also publish *A Guide to Audit Committees, A Guide for the Company Director, A Guide to the Corporations Law, A Prospectus Guide, Business Stress Index* (Corporate Recovery & Insolvency), *Due Diligence, Financial Futures: The Ernst & Young Guide, How to Prepare a Business Plan, How to Raise Finance, Options: The Ernst & Young Guide, Swaps and FRAs: The Ernst & Young Guide*, and *Tax Facts*, all of which provide relevant information and advice on more specific areas of business.

Starting Up or Running Your Own Business: Commercial Banking is produced by the Commonwealth Bank of Australia which has state/territory administration offices within Australia and also has an London office at 3rd Floor, No 1 Kingsway, London WC2B 6DU, tel: 0171-379 0955.

In addition, you can contact publishers direct for further information.

Commonwealth Government Bookshops sell books published by the Australian Government Publishing Service, 32 York Street, Sydney NSW 2000, tel: 02-299 6737.

Australian Professional Publications, 220 Pacific Highway, Crows Nest NSW 2065, tel: 02-922 6833.

Periodicals

Australian Business for Sale News is a magazine produced every two months which gives information and details about franchises, distributors, investments, dealerships and partnerships for sale. It is available from Australian

Business for Sale News, PO Box 586, Darlinghurst NSW 2010, tel: 02-281 4599 or fax: 02-212 6925 and a year's subscription will cost $36.50. Alternatively, the periodical is available in the UK as a volume for £4.95 from the Subscription Department, Australian Outlook, 3 Buckhurst Road, Bexhill-on-Sea, East Sussex, TN40 1QF.

Australian Economic Analysis Pty Ltd, 21 Holbrook Avenue, Kirribilli NSW 2061, tel: 02-959 4123.

Australian Economic Report, 1/263 Alfred Street, North Sydney NSW 2000, 02-264 2000.

Australian Financial Press, 179 Harris Street, Pyrmont NSW 2009, tel: 02-552 4688, 02-552 3787, 02-552 3775 or 02-552 3925.

The Australian Financial Review, 235 Jones Street, Broadway NSW 2007, tel: 02-282 2833 or 12 Norwich Street, London EC4A 1BH, tel: 0171-353 9321.

The Business Register is a free monthly business listing produced by and available from Business & Investment Realty Pty Ltd, 22 First Avenue, Maroochydore QLD 4558, tel: 074-438 061.

The Franchisees Guide ($A5 per copy) and *The Franchisors Manual* ($A25 per copy) offer professional advice and are available from the Franchisors Association of Australia and New Zealand, Unit 9, 2-6 Hunter Street, Parramatta NSW 2150, tel: 008-804 317 or 02-891 4933.

Industry & Trade Reference Publications, 224 George Street, Liverpool NSW 2170, tel: 02-601 7499.

Ernst & Young also publish a number of periodicals, all of which are available from any of their Australian offices and these include *Accounting Brief*, *Business Alert* (Corporate Recovery and Insolvency), *Corporation Topics*, *Customs & Trade News*, *E&Y Corporate Adviser*, *Extract* (Natural Resources), *Federal Budget Brief*, *Indirect Taxes Brief*, *Key Issues* (Banking and Financial Services), *Mini-Budget Brief*, *Profit Line*, *Tax Alert*, *Tax Brief*, *Topics for Lawyers*, and the *Trans-Tasman Brief*.

In addition, general periodicals such as *Australian Outlook* and *Australian News*, published in the UK, should be consulted as they often contain information on taxation or legal changes which may affect businesses.

Relocation Agencies and Business Services

As mentioned in *Setting up Home*, the major international relocation firms tend to specialise in executive and corporate relocations rather than the private individual, due to the large costs involved. The services offered as part of executive or company relocation tend to include pre-departure briefings, information about housing, education and spouse careers together with steps taken to secure these, individual and family counselling and training in cultural awareness. It is possible to commission an agent from a relocation company who will attempt to prepare you as much as possible for executive/company life in Australia, and find appropriate housing, schools and employment for any members of your family who will be travelling with you. Some relocators may also offer the service of finding you a suitable car, although most exective salary packages tend to include a company car, so you must be careful to check this with your company before you make any agreements with a relocator. You must also check who is responsible for payment of the relocator before you make any binding agreements, as Australian companies often tend to contract their own relocators within Australia, or have their own relocation services within the company (particularly if it is a multi-national conglomerate). If you are being employed by a large international company, you should be careful to ask as part of your salary package what services you are likely to receive in terms of a relocation bonus. Many companies simply offer a cash bonus for relocation purposes, and you should make sure that the amount offered will be adequate to cover your relocation needs.

Most relocation firms within the UK advise that you should contact Australian relocation firms if you are moving from the UK to Australia as the Australian offices will simply be more likely to offer you a better service. Having said that, most large UK relocators tend to have offices overseas or are have business agreements with certain firms in Australia, so it is possible to go through the yellow pages telephone directory (under 'Relocators') and call firms within the UK in order to find out if they either do a service to Australia or whether they can recommend a company that does. It is important to note that most UK relocators actually provide services for those relocating to the UK from other countries.

Besides making housing, education and employment arrangements on your behalf, many of the relocation companies also specialise in finding appropriate business premises and relocating complete companies, including plant and machinery.

Useful Addresses
Below is a list of relocators which advertise as specialising in the relocations of executives, company personnel and their families.

Allied Pickfords, 19-21 Rowood Road, Prospect NSW 2149, tel: 02-636 6333 or fax: 02-631 3055.

Ashton Relocations Pty Ltd, 38 Park Place, South Yarra VIC 3141, tel: 03-820 3295 or mobile: 018-393 515.

Australia-wide Relocations Pty Ltd, 414 Toorak Road, Toorak VIC 3142, tel: 03-826 0001 or fax: 03-827 0762.

Corporate Relocation Management Pty Ltd, 187 Marion Street, Leichardt NSW 2040, tel: 02-564 3244 or fax: 02-564 3277. This company offers complete office relocation services.

Corporate Relocations, 3rd Floor, 74 Pitt Street, Sydney NSW 2000. This company is a member of the Relocation Group in Australia and the International Relocation Associates, and you should contact the Managing Director, Margaret Kelly, on tel: 02-231 3222 or fax: 02-232 7545.

Coyle & Hitchcock International, Relocation and Migration Services, 502 South Tower, Chatswood Plaza, Railway Street, Chatswood NSW 2067, tel: 02-412 1505 or fax: 02-411 2155.

Coyle Wendy & Associates Pty Ltd, 21 Elamang Avenue, Kirribilli NSW 2061, tel: 02-957 2314 or fax: 02-954 0247.

Eggerton & Associates, International and Interstate Executive Relocations, 1 Bydown Street, Neutral Bay NSW 2089, tel: 02-953 9685 or fax: 02-953 9685 (same number).

Executive Relocations, 383 Malvern Road, South Yarra VIC 3141, tel: 03-827 4668.

Expat International, 207 George Street, East Melbourne VIC 3002, tel: 03-419 9351 or fax: 03-416 0786. Expat International are affiliated with the Migration Institute of Australia and the Employee Relocation Council (USA).

Grace Removals, Executive and Commercial Relocations, Carter Street, Lidcombe NSW 2141, tel: 02-648 4244.

Relocation Information Services, 160 London Road, Croydon, Surrey CRO 2TD, cater more for companies that wish to relocate to the UK and specialise in finding business premises for such companies. They do, however, have Australian connections, and are happy to give further information upon request by telephone (0181-681 3692) or fax (0181-686 4061).

Ideas for New Businesses

Basically, to find ideas for a new business, it is a good idea to research the current economical climate and see what kind of businesses are doing well. The main sectors of industry that seem to experience consistent growth are manufacturing and tourism. If you want to capitalise on this, then you need to try to find a business that will draw upon these sectors. You may wish to start up a new kind of tourist resort/caravan park for a specific type of tourist, e.g. the European tourist or the retired tourist, or you may wish to provide a service in the form of a tourist assistance agency which helps tourists in the event of an accident, stolen money or passports.

Some other possibilities are:

Leisure. Australians greatly value leisure, so you would be likely to do well if you started a business that was either involved in supplying existing leisure centres with a superior new product/concept or providing some sort of service associated with leisure, such as a squash club, swimming club etc.

Information Technology. Information technology is a new and expanding international industry, and although you would have to be careful about assessing the existing competition, you could also do well in either the product or service side of this industry.

Agriculture. Agriculture is also an important and essential part of Australia's economy, and you may wish to start up a market garden which supplies a suburban region with fresh fruit or vegetables, or you may wish to head for more remote areas of Australia and try your hand at emu farming, a new and potentially highly lucrative industry.

Import Export. Alternatively, you could try importing and exporting. Given the high numbers of immigrants, careful research could identify any products new settlers particularly yearn for from their home countries. For example, many British immigrants miss Marks & Spencers' products, both food and clothing, and use return trips to build up supplies. In addition, before you leave your country, identify the Australian migrants there and assess whether there are any particular products which Aussies away from home particularly crave. In terms of beer, wine and Vegemite, Australians are catered for very well in Britain, but there are other home comforts we long for. In the clothing line, it is important to note that Australians generally wear brighter colours, largely due to the weather, and in itself this could be a potential business in terms of exporting from Australia to Britain, aimed at the Australian in Britain. In addition, there are particular Australian brands of clothing which seem to be as yet almost impossible to obtain in Britain, including the designer company *Jag* or the surf/beach wear companies *Billabong*, *Rip Curl* or *Hot Tuna*.

As stated above in 'Starting From Scratch', the key to success in a new business is research in terms of your potential market and competition.

Business Structures and Registration

Buying an Existing Business

Franchises

Alternatively, you may feel that you have the skills and personal qualities necessary to start your own business, but you are undecided as to what sort of business to go into. If you do not wish to start from scratch on your own and you would like a little more direction, you should possibly consider being a franchisee. This means that you run a business of your own, but you sell somebody else's product.

Fast food chains are well known franchise operations, but there is a wide range of other products and services franchises available. A recent volume of the *Australian Business for Sale* lists no fewer than 64 diverse franchise opportunities ranging from *Magic Seal Magnetic Insect Screens*, the pet grooming service *Aussie Pooch Mobile*, and a bouncy-castle hire service *Jolly Bouncers* to more conventional franchises offered by *BP Australia*. As an example of the kinds of costs involved in these franchises consider the following two examples:

Aussie Pooch Mobile offers all new equipment and a trailer, fully paid training, computerised backup, a central personalised booking office, constant support, secure cash flow, repeat work, constant advertising campaigns and a guaranteed minimum income of $A500 per week, for a total franchise investment of $A15,000. *Jolly Bouncers* offers five designs of bouncy castles for a unit price of $A4,500 per castle.

One advantage of the franchise is that starting one is not as risky as starting on your own and you may also have the advantage of not needing to identify and establish a market for your product. The basis of any franchise operation is the franchise agreement. This must be considered very carefully and it is advisable to consult your accountant/solicitor before signing anything. Before you enter into any franchise agreement, you need to consider whether you are technically able to deal with the product or service and the extent of the competition. This is particularly important if the franchise is one involving changing technology, and you need to assess whether the franchisor also has the expertise and resources to be able to compete successfully in the market. If your product is manufactured overseas, or is composed of parts made elsewhere, you must identify delivery times and calculate the risk of delays and the potential for foreign currency losses. In addition, you will have to ascertain whether there are any import duties or regulations which have an impact on the price of the product. You should also be clear on how much assistance is given and control exercised by the franchisor, and you would be well advised to investigate the franchisor's financial credibility and stability. It can be beneficial to talk to other franchisees about the business and the franchisor's methods of operation. It is imperative that you understand what the duration of the franchise is, what costs and fees are involved, whether you have to pay any royalties to the franchisor (and if so, how much), and what the arrangments are for termination. Information about available franchises can be obtained from business brokers, your local Chamber of Commerce, business and trade fairs, and both local and national newspapers. If you require specialist legal advice regarding franchises, Richard Spencer offers advice for prospective buyers of franchises at GPS Solicitors, 1st Floor, Central Park One, 36 Park Road, Milton QLD 4064, tel: 07-268 2577.

Non-franchised Businesses

Most businesses for sale advertise with real estate agents, business brokers, trading associations and in the national and local newspapers.

A successful acquisition depends on a thorough study of the business or company from many different angles. Your accountant should check out the value of stock and the cash flow of the business. Profit should be calculated after the fair working salaries of proprietors or partners have been deducted. Your accountant should also advise you on the stamp duty and tax implications of the purchase of a particular business. The last three years' accounts of the company (audited if possible) should be examined, together with current management accounts and projections (if available), particularly in terms of the valuation of assets, contingent liabilities and the company's tax position.

Finally, you need to ensure that you will be able to raise the finance required before committing yourself to the purchase, and this applies to the purchase of either a business or a company. See the section *Raising Finance* above for further details.

Some examples of businesses for sale Australia wide in 1994:

Victoria.
1. Automotive repairers, Airport West, Melbourne. Fully equipped with reception area and office. Specialist in Honda repairs holding contracts with Telecom, insurance companies and fleet customers. 1993 turnover was $345,000. Asking price was $95,000.
2. Charter boat, Oceana Charters, Melbourne. Established six years. Includes 48-foot charter boat licensed to carry 34 passengers. Includes all permits and full liquor licence. Substantial advance bookings. Existing skipper will stay if required. Asking price $246,000.

Northern Territory
1. 'The Nook' caravan park 29 km south of Darwin. Consists of the owner's four-bedroom residence, 30 powered sites, six new mobile units for tourists, and 11 permanent on-site vans let at $110 per week. There is also an amenities block, kiosk, office and pool. Asking price $395,000.
This business has been established for 27 years and is located in a busy main tourist shopping mall. All fixtures, fittings and necessary equipment are included. Well-established overseas client base and enjoys an excellent reputation with both passing and regular trade. Unique jewellery and gifts are both made and sold on the premises.

Tasmania
1. Commercial leasehold laundry in Hobart. Coin-operated laundry close to city centre in a busy shopping area. Comes with established contracts for commercial laundry and expanding personal/service wash and nappy service. Trading six days a wek. Premises in excellent condition. Asking price $125,000.

South Australia
1. Retail Chicken, Fulham. A family business established for 27 years and is the original charcoal chicken shop of Adelaide. Trading seven days a week on a busy street. Weekly turnover $4,000 (at 30% profit). Asking price of $85,000 negotiable.

Western Australia
1. Replica Company Manufacturing, Kellerberrin. Australia's best known Cobra manufacturer, sold throughout Australia and internationally in both right and left hand drive configurations. Based on a five year average, the annual turnover was $A480,000. The owners suggested that relocating the business to one of Australia's more populated states would promote even higher profits. Asking price of $190,000 includes approximatley $30,000 of stock.

Queensland
1. Advertising Business, Shalier Park. Suitable for operator who could work from home or office. It won a Logan Chamber of Commerce award for being the most successful business less than two years old. Advertising and office equipment are included in the asking price of $50,000.
2. Beach Takeaway, Hamilton Island. Only takeaway shop on the resort side of this incredibly popular and beautiful island. Open seven days a week and would

suit an owner/operator. The annual turnover is currently $160,000 and the owner is willing to train. Asking price $39,000.

New South Wales
1. Beauty and Nail Clinic, Merrylands. Established seven years. Located in shopping centre. Very limited competition and good regular and passing trade. Spacious premises. Annual turnover $125,000 plus. All fixtures and fittings included in the asking price of $80,000.

Australian Capital Territory
1. Earth moving and Excavation, Canberra. Plant includes 1980 Mack R600, 350 Motor with two-axle dog trailer, SDK8 Toyota bobcat, seven tonne Yanmar 1989 excavator with rock hammer, borer etc., 14 tonne Sumitomo excavator with rock grab etc. Advertises in the Yellow Pages. The annual turnover is over $A200,000 and also includes a work utility truck and mobile phone. Asking price $195,000.
2. Bottle shop (drive-in), Hawker. Established 17 years.Turnover of $700,000 from a trading week of seven days from 12 noon to late. Part of soccer club complex and a motel, which guarantees regular trade, and passing trade. Currently employs two permanent staff and two weekend casual staff. Asking price $210,000.

Establishing a Company

The formation of a company is usually conducted through solicitors, company registration agents or your accountant. Your advisers should supply you with the numerous necessary forms as part of their standard procedure.

Proprietary companies are generally cheaper and easier to register than a public company. A private company only needs to have a nominal share capital to commence operating. Directors and a company secretary must be appointed and as soon as is practically possible after incorporation, a public officer has to be appointed for taxation purposes. For proprietary companies, there must be at least two directors, one of whom must be an Australian resident. Public companies must have at least three directors, two of whom must be residents of Australia.

Directors are not necessarily actively involved in the daily management of the company, but they are responsible for the actions of the management of the business. In accordance with the Corporations Law, a director must act with the utmost good faith towards the company and its members and must not obtain any benefit for him/herself from the activities of the company other than remuneration. A director is also expected to excercise skills which reflect his/her qualifications and experience. Although a director is responsible for the keeping of the statutory records and the books of account, this duty is usually delegated. The Corporations Law is very specific about the kinds of books and records which must be kept and it is advisable to initially contact professional advisers for assistance with this. A director may accept a loan from the company providing that loan has been approved by the shareholders. It must be noted that such loans must be shown in the accounts in accordance with statutory requirements. A director has the power to appoint an alternate director who has the full powers and duties of a director. If the business becomes insolvent, the directors become personally liable for any debts contracted by the company during the period of insolvency.

Within one month of the first and every annual general meeting, companies must provide the ASC with their directors' names, ages, addresses, company shareholding and other public company directorships. The appointment of additional or new directors, the company secretary, and an auditor (if required) should be made at this time. Banking arrangements and the end of the company's financial year (normally 30th June) should also be determined. Shares should be allotted and transfers of subscribers' shares should be approved. Arrangements should also be made for keeping statutory books such as the Register of Members, Register of Directors and a Minute Book, and the company's registered office should also be specified. In addition, a Public Officer should be appointed for income tax purposes.

The company secretary is responsible for statutory duties and must be a resident of Australia. Public companies must have at least five members, while proprietary companies need only have two. Wholly owned subsidiaries, public or proprietary, have no minimum requirement. A proprietary company must have between two and fifty shareholders, whereas public companies must have a minimum of five shareholders and have no maximum limit. Shares may be sold for cash or otherwise issued, but details must be reported to the ASC. For both public and proprietary companies, the minimum capital derived from shares is one share per subscriber. The minimum time required to establish a company is three to four days and the ASC fees must be paid during registration.

The formation of a company from scratch can take between one to two weeks from application and will cost approximately $A750 plus solicitor and/or accountant fees. The creation of a brand new company involves choosing and agreeing to an appropriate name, compiling suitable Memorandum and Articles of Association (i.e., a company's constitution documents), lodging these and other documents with the ASC and obtaining a Certificate of Incorporation. All companies which operate in Australia are allocated an Australian Company Number (ACN) which functions as a company identifier. Your company registration agent will usually complete and process all this documentation for you.

If you need to establish the company quickly, agents and solicitors often have 'ready-made' comapanies which can be bought off the shelf. Shelf companies can be purchased for approximately $700-$800 from company registration agents. In most cases the name of such shelf companies will be unsuitable and amendments may have to be made to its Memorandum and Articles of Association. A change of name usually takes approximately four weeks to be processed and approved, and the ASC must issue a *Certificate of Incorporation on Change of Name*. The additional cost of changing the name of the company and the Memorandum and Articles is around $150. If you do choose to buy a shelf company, you should consult with your advisers to consider whether the Articles of Association need to be amended. You need to consider whether the existing constitution allows for: the rights of directors to decline to register a future share transfer; the requirements if a shareholder ceases to be a director or employee or dies; the chairperson's casting vote; the shareholder/director's voting rights; and who controls the company, as different levels of shareholding confer different rights and there may also be different classes of shares conferring different rights.

When you purchase a shelf company, you should receive a complete set of first board minutes and statutory books. If you do not receive these, it would be advisable to check with the previous owners as they can often contain important information and you are expected to hold them.

Regardless of whether you have created your company from scratch or whether you have bought a shelf company, you cannot commence business in the form of trading until you have been issued with a Certificate of Incorporation. If it is a shelf company, the Certificate will have already been issued but trading can only commence immediately if the name of either the shelf company or your registered business name is used.

If you are starting the business as a partnership or sole trader, there are no legal formalities involved other than the notifications required for tax purposes. In the absence of a partnership agreement, the partnership will be governed by the Partnership Act of the relevant state/territory which specifies how a partnership should adminster its affairs, but most partnerships prefer to have their own agreement to meet their own particular needs. Partnership agreements are usually drawn up by a solicitor and should include details of the arrangements for partners' capital, banking accounts, profit-sharing, salaries (if relevant), drawings, change or termination of partnership and voting rights. This agreement is particularly important if a dispute between partners arises, but business experts claim that the more important course of action is to avoid such potential disputes by choosing the right partner/s in the first place. In this way, partnerships are often parallelled with marriage.

Running a Business

Once you have had your business plans approved, you have secured financial backing, formed a company/partnership/sole trader, chosen and registered its name, and have obtained premises from which to operate your business, then it is time to consider how to go about the daily operations of the business. The most important factors here are probably your staff and your taxes. If you manage to get both of these areas right, it is highly likely that your business will run smoothly and be a success.

Taxation

Australian business taxation law is extremely complex and if you are starting a new business there are a certain number of things you will have to do and decisions you will have to make. The taxation is even more complex if you have been employed in Australia prior to setting up your business. Furthermore, the structure you choose for your business may have significant tax consequences, so it is important to investigate taxation thoroughly when planning its structure. There is simply no avoiding the tax maze and Australians just live with it. What is of the ultimate importance is that you get professional advice from the early stages of your business.

Sole traders and partnerships have very different taxes to companies or trusts. Essentially, for a sole trader or partnership, any profit earned from the business is added to any other income that you have and you are taxed on the total. Your level of taxable income is determined by the financial statements you produce, however there are some adjustments that are made to the income shown on the statements in order to arrive at a taxable income. You may, for example, be allowed to claim special deductions such as those available for research and development costs. In fact, the government provides a grant for costs incurred in relation to research and development in the form of a tax subsidy to the extent of 125% and in certain circumstances, when a company cannot take advantage of the tax concession, a cash grant may be made. Generally, the 125% allowance applies to any wages, salaries and any other labour costs incurred exclusively for research and development if those costs total more than $A50,000. Partial benefits are available for amounts less than $50,000. Taxable grants are also payable on eligible export market development expenditure in respect of any goods, services, industrial property rights or knowledge which are substantially of Australian origin. Anyone conducting business in Australia is entitled to apply for a grant which covers 70% of all eligible expenditure incurred by new exporters and established exporters trying to develop new markets, although there are certain limits. Some of the income you receive may not be subject to tax such as the rebates paid to you under the CRAFT scheme (apprenticeship training scheme). In accordance with the Australian government's Economic Statement of 1991, you are now also allowed to claim depreciation on all of your plant equipment and other business fixed assets, and items valued at less than $300 or with an effective life of less than three years can be written off in the year of acquisition.

Companies are taxed differently because they are considered to be separate legal entities from their owners. A company is subject to income tax on its taxable income whereas the partners in a partnership are taxed on their share of partnership taxable income even though a tax return must be lodged for the partnership. An important difference to note is that there is no variation according to income of the tax rate for companies as there is for individuals. Both resident and non-resident companies are subject to corporate income tax of 39%.

The calculation of a company's or family trust's taxable income is roughly the same as that use to assess a partnership or sole trader, but there are some significant differences. Firstly, providing it is at a reasonable level, the remuneration of the company's directors (or owners in the case of a family company) is a deductible expense in determining the company's taxable income. Secondly, there is a complicated system known as 'Dividend Imputation' which refers to the distribution of a company's dividend income. Dividend imputations distributed by Australian resident companies have a tax advantage attached to them if the dividends are paid from profits which have been taxed in the company's hands at the company rate. Basically, this means that the system allows shareholders a tax rebate to the extent of the difference between personal and corporate income tax rates. Any excess rebate may be offset against any other income tax of the shareholder, including capital gains and these dividends which have been relieved of tax are known as 'franked'. If the company holds on to its dividend, it will generally be subject to credit under the 'Dividend Imputation' system. This jargon can be mystifying, and it is well worth asking your accountant or tax adviser to explain the system to you. Your adviser will also be able to explain the system of tax payment as companies must pay instalments of tax by certain dates.

If you decide to take over an existing company, you should ask your accountant to help you draft taxation warranties and indemnities which should appear in the purchase agreement as these will protect you from any unexpected tax liabilities that may arise as a result of the acquisition. Also, the capital gains tax exempt status of assets owned by a company may be lost when ownership of the company is changed.

As the owner of a business, whether new or already in existence, you will be expected to pay Sales Tax, Fringe Benefits Tax, PAYE deductions and Prescribed Payments Tax. Sales Tax is a Federal Government tax which is intended to be paid only once on goods going into use in Australia. It usually applies to wholesalers on sales to retailers, but some manufacturers and importers may have to pay it. This tax is collected and administered by the Australian Taxation Office. It is calculated on the last wholesale price of the goods and generally applies only to new goods and not to services or second-hand goods, apart from imported second-hand goods which have not been previously used in Australia. At the time of writing, the general rate of sales tax is 20% while other categories of goods are taxable at either 10%, 15% or 30%, so it is advisable to check which sales tax rate (if any) will apply to the product you wish to sell. Some goods, including clothing, food and medicines are always exempt from sales tax and others may be conditionally exempt from sales tax because of the status of the person who uses them (eg, a Government department) or the use to which the goods are put (eg, as manufacturing equipment). Patents and copyright are not subject to sales tax as is also the case with services unless the cost of the service effectively forms part of the selling price of goods. If your company is liable to pay sales tax, you need to register with the Taxation Office in order to be allocated a Sales Tax Registration Number. In accordance with the law, this number can then be quoted to suppliers to acquire tax free goods. Your business will then be expected to make a self-assessment, complete and lodge a monthly sales tax return, although if your business's annual sales tax liability is less than $50,000 quarterly sales tax returns need only be made. The Federal Government has recently announced that small businesses with an annual sales tax liability less than $10,000 do not have to pay sales tax on the goods they sell.

If you employ staff, you are responsible for deducting taxation installments (PAYE) from your employees and paying it to the Commissioner of Taxation. In order to do this, you must register as a group employer with the Commissioner of Taxation and each employee must submit to you their personal particulars, including his/her tax file number, on an income tax instalment declaration form. PAYE must be deducted from wages, overtime pay, commissions, fees, bonuses, gratuities, lump sum payments and any other allowances.

The Australian tax year ends 30 June, and for companies that also end their financial year on this date, tax returns must be filed by the following 15 March or, in certain circumstances, 15 December of following the end of the tax year. If an alternative financial period has been adopted by the company, its tax returns must be filed at the earliest by the fifteenth day of the sixth month following the year-end, with a maximum extension to the earlier of the fifteenth day of the ninth month or 15 June following the end of the alternative financial year. Tax returns of individuals, partnerships and trusts must generally be filed by 31 October each year and an extension may be granted if the return is to be filed by a registered tax agent. It is important to note that penalties of up to 200% of tax underpayment may be imposed for filing an incorrect return, together with interest charges and penalties for the late filing of returns or payment of tax are strictly enforced.

If you are self-employed or run a small business, TAFE colleges and the Tax Office have joined forces to create a course (possibly tax deductible) which explains the tax system and provides guidance on how to complete tax returns. The Tax Office does not provide addresses of the centres, but phone and fax numbers are outlined below:

NSW & ACT:	TAFE-PLUS-Commercial Development Unit, ph: 02-965 6075 or 008-817 507, or fax: 02-965 6095.
NT:	Darwin, ph: 089-439 121 or fax: 089-439 151.
QLD:	Brisbane, ph: 07-213 5505 or fax: 07-313 6656.
	Chermside, ph: 07-213 8612 or fax: 07-213 8950.
	Townsville, ph: 077-537 518 or fax: 077-537 277.
	Upper Mount Gravatt, ph: 07-213 3649 or fax: 07-213 3650.
SA:	Adelaide Small Business Training Centre, ph: 08-410 0000, 008-882 286, or fax: 08-420 0633.
TAS:	Hobart, ph: 002-210 327, 13-2861 or fax: 001-210 560.
VIC:	Melbourne, ph: 03-275 250, 008-136 874 or fax: 03-275 4109.
WA:	Perth, ph: 090-268 5155, 13-2861 or fax: 09-269 5168.

Useful Addresses
AUSTRADE (Australian Trade Commission), AIDC Tower, Maritime Centre, 201 Kent Street, Sydney NSW 2000, tel: 02-390 2000.

Australasian People Training Systems, 7 Ryde Road, Hunters Hill NSW 2110, tel: 02-816 3623.

Australian Asset & Insurance Valuers (NSW) Pty Ltd, 23A Stuart Street, Langley Vale NSW 2426, tel: 02-418 9058.

Australian British Chamber of Commerce, Level 12, 83 Clarence Street, Sydney, New South Wales 2000, tel: 02-299 5474 or fax: 02-299 5483.

Australian Bureau of Statistics, 3rd Floor, St Andrew's House, Sydney Square, Sydney NSW 2000, tel: 02-268 4111, 02-268 4611 or fax: 02-268 4668. The ABS also have a Dial-a-Statistic recorded message service available from within Australia, tel: 0055-26400.

Australian Business Control, STE 4.32 Colbee Court, Phillip ACT 2606, tel: 06-285 4888 or fax: 06-285 4889.

Australian Business Economists, 123 Clarence Street, Sydney NSW 2000, tel: 02-200 2610.

Australian Business Education Council Ltd, 21 Berry Street, North Sydney NSW 2060, tel: 02-957 6515.

Australian Business and Fax Directory, 37 Bundall Road, Bundall QLD 4217, tel: 008-074 009.

Australian Business and Personal Contacts, 46 Barker Avenue, Lidcombe NSW 2141, tel: 02-748 1786.

Australian Chamber of Commerce (UK), Suite 10-16, 3rd Floor, Morley House, 314-322 Regent Street, London W1R 5AJ, tel: 0171-636 4525 or fax: 0171-636 4511. Contact: Nick Came, Director.

Australian Chamber of Manufactures, 380 St Kilda Road, Melbourne VIC 3000, tel: 008-331 103.

Australian Customs Service, Head Office 447 Pitt Street, Sydney NSW 2000, tel: 02-213 2000.

Australian Industrial Registry, 80 William Street, East Sydney NSW 2001, tel: 02-332 0666.

Australian Industry Development Corporation, Level 33, Maritime Centre, 201 Kent Street, Sydney NSW 2000, tel: 02-235 5155.

Australian International & British Ltd, 275 Alfred Street, North Sydney NSW 2060, tel: 02-929 5700.

Australian Securities Commission (ASC), Level 8, 55 Market Street, Sydney NSW 2000, tel: 02-911 2500 for general enquiries, document lodgment and searches. Business Centre, Level 8, 55 Market Street, Sydney NSW 2000, tel: 02-911 2570. Corporate Regulation & Investigations, Level 10, 135 King Street, Sydney NSW 2000, tel: 02-911 2200.

Australian Small Business Association, 28 Mary Road, Auburn NSW 2144, tel: 02-649 8298.

Australian Small Business & Investing, 180 Bourke Street, Alexandria NSW 2015, tel: 02-353 6666.

Australian Stock Exchange Ltd, 20 Bond Street, Sydney NSW 2000, tel: 02-227 0000.

Australian Trade Commission (AUSTRADE), Australia House, Strand, London WC2B 4LA, tel: 0171-438 8535.

Australian Tradelinks Pty Ltd, 65 Berry Street, North Sydney NSW 2060, tel: 02-957 5792.

The Australian and New Zealand Trade Advisory Committee, Suite 10/16, 3rd Floor, Morley House, 314-322 Regent Street, London W1R 5AE, tel: 0171-637 3992.

Australian Patent, Trade Marks and Designs Office, Scarborough House, Phillip ACT 2600, tel: 06-283 2211.

Australian Trade Commission, Stockland House, 181 Castlereagh Street, Sydney NSW 2000, tel: 02-581 2555.

Department of Business and Regional Development, Office of Small Business, 3rd Floor, Enterprise House, 1 Fitzwilliam Street, Parramatta NSW 2150, tel: 02-895 0555 or fax: 02-635 6859.

Department of Immigration and Ethnic Affairs, Benjamin Offices, Chan Street, Belconnen ACT 2617, tel: 06-265 1111.

Department of Industry, Science and Technology, Small Business Section, Canberra ACT 6000, tel: 06-276 1384 or fax: 06-276 1685.

Department of Industry, Research & Development, Central Office, Canberra City ACT 6001, tel: 06-276 1000.

Department of Trade Industry, Australasia Section, Room 544, Kingsgate House, 66-74 Victoria Street, London SW1E 6SW, tel: 0171-215 5321 or fax: 0171-215 4398.

Exhibitions and Promotions. Held in association with the Commonwealth Bank of Australia and the NSW Business and Regional Development Office is the Annual Business Opportunities Expo. For information about their services and the next expo, contact PO Box 7035, Gold coast Mail Centre, QLD 4217, or tel: 075-924 266 (QLD), 02-955 6963 (NSW), 09-221 1718 (WA) or fax: 075-924 606.

Foreign Investment Review Board, c/o The Treasury, Parkes Place, Parkes ACT 2600, tel: 06-263 3762.

FT Profile, PO Box 12, Sunbury-on-Thames TW16 7UD, tel: 01932-761 444 or fax: 01932-781 425.

Reserve Bank of Australia, 65 Martin Place, Sydney NSW 2000, tel: 02-234 9333.

Securities Exchanges Guarantee Corporation Ltd, 87 Pitt Street, Sydney NSW 2000, tel: 02-227 0400.

Standards Association of Australia, 1 The Crescent, Homebush NSW 2140, tel: 02-746 4700.

Technical Requirements, Technical Help to Exporters, Linford Wood, Milton Keynes MK14 6LE, tel: 01908-220 022 or fax: 01908-320 856.

Export

The Australian Institute of Export, 320 Sussex Street, Sydney NSW 2000, tel: 02-264 9322.

Export Intelligence, Prelink Ltd, Export House, 87A Wembley Hill Road, Wembley, Middlesex HA9 8BU, tel: 0181-900 131 or fax: 0181-900 1268.

Export Market Information Centre, Ashdown House, 123 Victoria Street, London SW1E 6RB, tel: 0171-215 5444/5 or fax: 0171-215 4231.

Export Marketing Research Scheme, The Association of British Chambers of Commerce, 4 Westwood House, Westwood Business Park, Coventry CV4 8HS, tel: 01203-694 484 or fax: 01203-694 690.

Overseas Promotions Support, Dean Bradley House, Horseferry Road, London SW1P 2AG, tel: 0171-276 2414 or fax: 0171-222 4707.

Business Brokers

AAA Business Sales, 1st Floor, ANZ Bank Building, 49 Horton Street, Port Macquarie NSW 2444 or PO Box 401, Port Macquarie NSW 2444, tel: 065-841 555.

Australasian International Brokers Pty Ltd, Market Plaza, Flemington Markets NSW 2169, tel: 02-764 3700.

Australian Society of Real Estate Agents & Valuers Ltd, 6 Union Street, Parramatta NSW 2151, tel: 02-635 8144.

Australiawide Realty Pty Ltd, 35 Homer Steet, Earlwood NSW 2206, tel: 02-559 3333.

Century 21 Real Estate, Business Brokers, 3/74 Grafton Street, Coffs Harbour

NSW 2450, or PO Box 1445, Coffs Harbour NSW 2450, tel: 066-513 322, 066-533 355 (after hours) of fax: 066-513 575. Contact Dave McInnes.

Chris Couper & Associates, Business Brokerage, PO Box 1603, Broadbeach QLD 4218 or 93 Surf Parade, Cnr Surf Parade and Victoria Avenue, Broadbeach QLD 4218, tel: 075-920 687 or fax: 075-315 978.

Clayton's Realty, 544 Ruthven Street, Toowoomba QLD, tel: 076-385 955, mobile: 018-795 668, after hours: 076-382 2536 or fax: 076-391 270. Contact Lew Harberger, Business Broker.

The Professionals, Cnr Maud Street & Aerodrome Road, Maroochydore, Sunshine Coast QLD, tel: 074-433 300 (Monday to Friday) or 018-793 355 (after hours and weekends). Contact Dallas Hopping, Specialist Business Broker.

Resort Brokers, Motel & Resort Consultants. Contact Ian R Crooks, tel: 07-878 3999 or fax: 07-878 1199.

Talberg Pty Ltd are licensed real estate agents who specialise in investors and investments, and businesses from $18,000 to $1,000,000+. For a free information brochure contact PO Box 429, Gympie QLD 4750, tel: 074-827 708 or fax: 074-828 804.

Wilsons Business Brokers Pty Ltd, 59A Stewart Avenue, Hamilton South NSW 2303, tel: 049-623 388, mobile: 015-252 222 or fax: 049-695 682.

Taxation

Australian Financial Investment and Taxation Services, 25 Belmore Road, Randwick NSW 2031, tel: 02-399 8333.

Australian Sales Tax Consultants Pty Ltd, 38/401 Pacific Highway, Artarmon NSW 2064, tel: 02-906 7477.

Australian Taxation Office, 2 Constitution Avenue, Canberra ACT 2600, tel: 06-275 222.

Australian Tax Planning Consultants, 122 Dutton Street, Yagoona NSW 2199, tel: 02-707 1833.

Australia Wide Taxation Accountant, 93 Argyle Street, Parramatta NSW 2150, tel: 02-633 9444.

Employment

The Australian Employers' Federation, 313 Sussex Street, Sydney NSW 2000, tel: 02-264 2000.

Australian Industrial Relations Commission, 80 William Street, East Sydney NSW 2001. For state award enquiries tel: 02-226 0688 or federal award enquiries tel: 02-282 0888.

Department of Industrial Relations, Employment, Training & Further Education, 1 Oxford Street, Darlinghurst NSW 2010, tel: 02-266 8111 or fax: 02-266 8321 for infomation about the awards for different industries, the Long Service Leave Act, Annual Holidays Act, Parental Leave etc.

The Institute of Personnel Consultants, National Administration Office, 6th Floor, 521 Toorak Road, Toorak VIC 3142, tel: 03-827 9000.

New Zealand

SECTION I

Living in New Zealand

General Introduction
Residence and Entry Regulations
Setting Up Home
Daily Life
Retirement

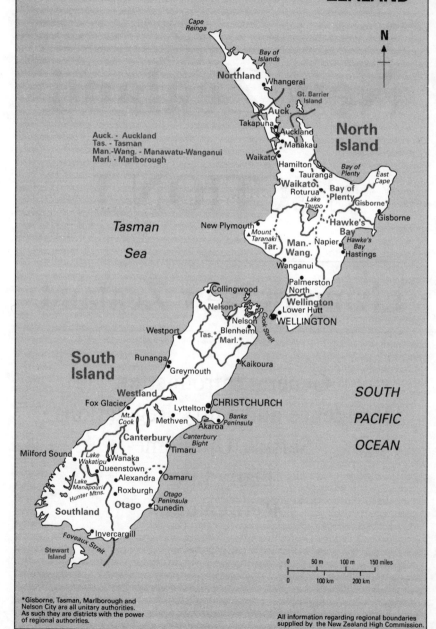

NEW ZEALAND

N

Cape
Reinga

Bay of
Islands

Northland

Whangerai

Gt. Barrier
Island

Auck.

Takapuna

Auck. - Auckland
Tas. - Tasman
Man.-Wang. - Manawatu-Wanganui
Marl. - Marlborough

Auckland

**North
Island**

Manakau

Waikato

Hamilton

Tauranga

Bay of
Plenty

East
Cape

Waikato

Roturua

Lake
Taupo

**Bay of
Plenty**

Gisborne

Gisborne

Tasman

New Plymouth

Mount
Taranaki

Tar.

**Man.-
Wang.**

**Hawke's
Bay**

Napier

Hawke's
Bay

Hastings

Sea

Wanganui

Palmerston
North

Wellington

Lower Hutt

Collingwood

Nelson *

Cook Strait

WELLINGTON

Nelson

Westport

Tas. *

Blenheim

Marl. *

Runanga

Greymouth

Kaikoura

**South
Island**

Westland

Fox Glacier

Mt.
Cook

Lyttelton

CHRISTCHURCH

Methven

Banks
Peninsula

Akaroa

Canterbury

Canterbury
Bight

Milford Sound

Lake
Wakatipu

Wanaka

Timaru

Queenstown

Lake
Manapouri

Alexandra

Oamaru

Hunter Mtns.

Roxburgh

Otago
Peninsula

SOUTH

PACIFIC

OCEAN

Southland

Otago

Dunedin

Invercargill

Foveaux Strait

Stewart
Island

0   50 m   100 m   150 miles

0   100 km   200 km

*Gisborne, Tasman, Marlborough and
Nelson City are all unitary authorities.
As such they are districts with the power
of regional authorities.

All information regarding regional boundaries
supplied by the New Zealand High Commission.

Introduction

Destination New Zealand

New Zealand has a reputation for being similar to Britain but with a slower pace of life, fewer social problems and a lot more sheep. While there is some truth behind this impression (there are eighteen sheep for every human), New Zealand is not just a little England in the South Pacific. It is still true that the majority of New Zealanders are of British descent, but a significant and growing minority of New Zealanders are Polynesians, either descended from the original inhabitants, the Maori, or more recently, immigrants from the surrounding islands of the South Pacific.

New Zealand political traditions derive from Britain, but constitutionally it has often been several steps ahead. New Zealand gave women the vote in 1893, twenty-five years before they were enfranchised in the UK. In 1938 it was one the first countries in the world to set up a comprehensive system of social security, from child care benefits through to pensions, and including a national health system that provided a model for the British NHS.

Since European settlement first began in the early 1800s, links with Britain have been close. The first generation of settlers grew up regarding England as 'home'. New Zealand foreign policy was basically an extension of British policy and 'where England leads, we follow' as one New Zealand prime minister put it, led New Zealand into a number of wars as a British ally. When Britain joined the European Community in the early seventies, New Zealand found its own path in the world and its own identity as a Pacific country, rather than a piece of Europe that somehow got transplanted to the Antipodes. There is a degree of residual colonial defensiveness in dealing with expatriate Britons but in most cases, it does not go much beyond a bit of teasing about pommy accents. In general visitors and immigrants get a warm welcome. New Zealanders deserve their reputation as amongst the friendliest people in the world — when they invite you to come and stay they really mean it.

Newcomers will find that while elements of the culture owe something to Europe (the national obsession with sports revolves around two British exports, cricket and rugby) New Zealand has its own distinctive character. Polynesian, particularly Maori culture is a growing influence. Auckland, the largest New Zealand city has the biggest Polynesian population in the world. There are new immigrant communities from various Asian countries as well as a long established Chinese community. The different groups make for an interesting and at times volatile cultural mix. New immigrants will find that it is important to respect the cultural traditions of different groups, particularly Maori traditions, as they were the first inhabitants of the islands. The Maori word for themselves is the *Tangata Whenua*, which means the people of the place.

In other respects New Zealand will seem quite familiar to Europeans, particularly British immigrants. The main language is still English, the system of government, schools, health care are all similar. European style arts and culture can be found in the big cities. If you are looking for a country with fewer social problems than Europe, where the environment is cleaner and the pace of life is more relaxed, New Zealand could be the place for you.

Pros and Cons of moving to New Zealand

Despite having a comparatively low GDP per capita compared to other developed countries, New Zealanders enjoy a high standard of living. Income per head of population figures compare unfavourably because of the exchange rate: you will find that the pound goes a long way in New Zealand. Other attractions for immigrants are the non-quantifiable factors that make for a high quality of life: clean air, clean water, miles of unspoilt beaches, and some of the most spectacular scenery in the world. If your idea of the good life is a city where rush hour lasts for five minutes and the nearest beach is no more than 30 minutes away, then you will enjoy the New Zealand lifestyle. About 240,000 Brits agree with you as according to the 1991 census that was the number of people born in the British Isles resident in New Zealand.

New Zealanders enjoy a wide range of outdoor activities: climbing, hiking, swimming, surfing, canoeing or mountain biking in their spare time. Aucklanders own more yachts per head of population than any other city dwellers in the world. Two great attractions of the country are the parks and reserves and the sea. Even New Zealand's biggest cities are within 20 or 30 minutes of hills and forest largely untouched by human habitation and all the major cities apart from Hamilton are on the coast. With a lifestyle revolving around outdoor pursuits, the nightlife in smaller towns is not exactly lively. In the big cities the scene is more interesting. European style cafés and bars have multiplied in the last decade and there is always the traditional Kiwi pub — watering holes more noted for the cheapness of the beer than the ambience. Licensing laws are are liberal and some pubs and cafés in the big cities are open 24 hours.

Working practices are similar to the UK. The standard working week is five days, 40 hours, although many people increase their earnings by extra work and overtime. Professionals on salaries can expect to work quite long hours, particularly at the start of their careers. Wage workers used to enjoy a high level of employment protection: national pay rates and conditions were set down in awards, legal documents which bound employers. Most bargaining was done by unions at a national level. Employment protection has been considerably weakened over the last decade and in some areas of the labour market, particularly casual work in catering, horticulture and agriculture, pay rates and conditions can be very poor. The social security system, once relatively generous, has also been cut back. On the other hand personal tax rates on high incomes are lower than in many European countries; there is no capital gains tax, GST (the equivalent of VAT) is 12.5% and the highest income tax rate is 33%. Unemployment dropped to 8% in 1995 after peaking at 11% in 1991. The labour market is more promising than the statistics suggest though as the number of jobs on offer has grown significantly in the last year. Unemployment has remained high because of increased labour market participation. The strongest growth was in the manufacturing and construction sectors, and continued strong expansion in these sectors is expected.

Rented accommodation is not hard to find, although it can be expensive in Auckland and Wellington. Rental agreements can either be on a renewable basis where the tenancy continues untill either side gives notice, or for a fixed term, usually one year. Houses are usually let unfurnished, while apartments and townhouses may let furnished or unfurnished.

Pros: Economy on the up after a long recession — predicted to have the strongest growth in the OECD in 1995/6
High quality of living
Diverse ethnic mix
Cheap cost of living
Relaxed lifestyle
Easy access to beautiful areas of countryside
Friendly locals
No language problem

Cons: Small economy
Can be parochial and inward looking
Climate in some parts similar to Britain
Not much sophisticated nightlife or the range of arts and culture familiar to Europeans.

Political and Economic Structure

The original inhabitants of New Zealand were the Maori, a Polynesian race who arrived by canoe from the central Pacific around 1000 AD. They lived a nomadic lifestyle initially dependent on hunting a large flightless bird called the moa, which is now extinct. More permanent settlements followed based on cultivating the kumara, a type of sweet potato and harvesting the seas. By the time the first Europeans arrived in the 18th and 19th centuries, the Maori had settled throughout the warmer North Island. They had developed a strongly tribal and family based society with a complex oral tradition. They were skilled craftspeople, particularly in woodcarving and weaving, and also in warfare. War between tribes was common, part of the competition for status and authority.

The first Europeans to sight New Zealand were the members of a Dutch East Indies Company ship led by the explorer, Abel Tasman. They anchored off the coast of the North Island in 1640, at a place they called Murderer's Bay because four of their crew were killed by local Maori. Tasman gave the country the name Niieeuw Zeeland after Zeeland, an island in the Baltic sea. The Maori name for the country is 'Aotearoa', the land of the long white cloud. Other explorers followed Tasman's lead. James Cook arrived in 1769 and returned again twice in the 1770s. Members of his second expedition were the first Europeans to make landfall in New Zealand. As with Tasman's first contact with local tribes, there were misunderstandings at first, the Maori interpreting the arrival of the strangers as a hostile force. Ten of his men were killed and eaten in one incident. Other meetings were more favourable, local Maori for the most part being curious to meet the strangers and to trade.

Trade and commerce provided the impetus for the first semi-permanent European settlements. Whalers and sealers arrived in the 1790s. They set up bases along the coasts but generally did not make permanent homes in the new country. Next to arrive, in the early 1800s, were the missionaries, who established stations around the Bay of Islands, on the north east of the North Island. They began preaching the faith amongst the tribes as well as introducing European cultivation techniques, literacy and other useful skills. They were the first to write down the Maori language so that they could translate the scriptures into Maori. Other settlers with more worldly ambitions soon arrived. They were interested in exploiting natural resources such as timber and flax. Local Maori tribes began cultivating wheat and maize to trade with the new arrivals. New Zealand's export trade in agricultural produce began in the 1840s with the export of potatoes, wheat and pigs to Australia. The bulk of the produce was grown by Maori farmers. Contact between Europeans and local tribes was confined to the small areas which the settlers were based in, the whaling bases around the coasts of the South Island and the lower North Island, the mission stations in north and the trading settlements at various points. For most of the first half of the 19th Century, the balance of power between the settlers and the tribes was still very much in favour of the Maori as the early settlements were dependent upon the goodwill of local tribes for their survival. However this was about to change. The Maori population was declining as a result of the introduction of new diseases, and firearms which transformed the ritualised inter-tribal wars into massacres. By the 1840, a balance of firepower had led to a virtual halt in inter-tribal warfare, the cost in lives being too high. The legacy of the warring period was large scale of loss of life, disruption to land holdings and social dislocation.

The decline in the Maori population alarmed the missionaries. They were also concerned about the rough, lawless lifestyle of the early settlements. Accordingly, back in Britain, the Church Missionary Society put pressure on the British Government to annex New Zealand as a Crown Colony, and to establish the rule of law. In 1840, New Zealand became part of the Empire. A treaty was signed at Waitangi, a little settlement in the Bay of Islands between the new Lieutenant-Governor, Captain William Hobson and representatives of local Maori tribes. Hobson then sent copies of the treaty around the country for other tribes to agree to, but some important tribes failed to sign. The terms and significance of the Treaty of Waitangi have been a source of controversy ever since 1840. Under the English text, the tribes ceded sovereignty to the British Crown and gained the rights of British citizens. The Maori text, hastily translated by local missionary, Henry Williams, is considerably vaguer in its terms. In particular, Williams used the unfamiliar term 'kawanatanga' a transliteration of the English word governorship to express the concept of sovereignty. It is doubtful that the first signatories understood that they were handing over rule over the land to the newcomers.

During the late 1830s plans for widespread colonisation were developed under the auspices of Edward Gibbon Wakefield's New Zealand Company. Wakefield intended the settlements to mimic the pre-industrial class structure of England but the actual settlements bore little resemblance to his plans. Prospective immigrants were attracted by the promise of cheap land but the company and its agents did not always acquire the land legitimately from the tribes, especially as the pressure to provide more land increased. Maori land tenure is complex as land is not owned by individuals but by the tribe as a whole. Company agents were not particularly scrupulous about whose signatures they obtained on sale documents and as the increasing numbers of new settlers demanding more land put pressure on them to provide it, their methods became more dubious.

New Zealand was directly governed by the British Crown between 1840 and 1852. After pressure from the settlers, self government was granted in 1852. As European settlers increased in numbers and started to demand more land, conflicts occurred with the Maori people over land tenure. The tribes disputed a number of dubious deals undertaken by New Zealand company agents. Resistance movements to further land sales developed. The settler government ignored its responsibilities to protect the rights of the Maori under the Treaty. Skirmishes between the government and the tribes began in the 1860s and full scale war broke out. It took nearly 15 years for the forces of the government, reinforced by troops from Britain to overcome Maori opposition. Even at the end of hostilities in the 1870s Maori tribes in the centre of North Island still held out against government control. The wars further decimated the Maori population and resulted in the confiscation of the land of the 'rebellious' and 'loyal' tribes alike. The loss of the land and the resulting social breakdown, probably contributed more than any other factor to the decline in the Maori population at the end of the 19th century.

Meanwhile European numbers were increasing spurred on by the discovery of gold in the South Island in the 1870s, and the invention of refrigerated shipping in the 1880s which made it viable to export meat and dairy products to Europe. The gold soon dried up but the agrarian economy founded in the late 19th century has remained the basis of New Zealand's economic prosperity. Economic security brought on social reform, at least for the European population. First the extension of the vote to women (1893), then a new system of industrial relations, based on minimum wage rates for every industry (1894) and one of the earliest pension schemes (1898). Maori were legally equally able to vote but property owning, which was based on European patterns of individual tenure, rather than Maori communal tenure effectively disbarred many of them until its abolition in the late 19th century.

New Zealand was involved in both world wars as a British ally. The disastrous World War One campaign at Gallipoli in Turkey proved to one of the defining moments in forming a separate national identity. New Zealand lost more soldiers as proportion of its population than any other allied country: nearly one in three men between the ages of 20 and 40 were killed or wounded. The interwar years brought the election of the first Labour government which continued the tradition of pioneering social policy programmes started by the Liberals. The 1938 Social Security Act established a national health service and a universal social security system. Public education to secondary level was free to all. World War Two saw New Zealand participating again as a British ally, but in the post-war years it began to rely less on Britain for defence and to form closer relations, with Australia and the United States. Britain's entry into the Common Market in the 1970s confirmed the loosening of colonial ties. At the same time closer links were being developed with other countries in the Asia-Pacific region.

Economic restructuring resulting from the increasingly poor performance of the economy since the late 70s and race relations have been the major policy issues over the last two decades. Economic change is discussed in the section below. The prevailing belief that relations between the races were harmonious was challenged by a number of Maori political movements in the last twenty years, ranging from radical groups calling for the restoration of Maori sovereignty to tribal leaders taking a more conciliatory stance. Two common concerns unite the diverse strands of Maori protest movements: a call upon the government to honour the terms of its original treaty with the Maori people and a concern with the inequality between Maori and European living standards. Income, life expectancy, health, and education standards differ markedly between the two groups. The Treaty became central to government policy towards the Maori as a result of Court of Appeal decision in 1987. The government's obligations towards the Maori as an equal partner under the Treaty were acknowledged. Maori is an official language (English being the other) and knowledge of Maori culture is increasingly required by Government departments and stressed as an equally important cultural heritage. Tensions remain between the Maori and the Government over historical injustices, particularly the large scale acquisition of Maori land by Europeans in the 19th century through confiscation, extortion, blackmail and theft, and the Government's neglect of its duty to protect Maori rights under the Treaty.

Economy

Agriculture has always been the basis of New Zealand's economy. The temperate climate is ideal for growing grass suitable for rearing farm animals cheaply, but it took a century and a half of effort to cultivate the ten million hectares of arable land currently in production. Much of it was initially unsuitable for agriculture being heavily forested, while the mountainous terrain has provided a challenge to develop alternative cultivation techniques. Nearly two-thirds of farmland is too rugged to be fertilised and sown by tractor. Instead New Zealand farmers pioneered the use of light aircraft to spread fertiliser and seed.

New Zealand was able to exploit its agricultural potential with the development of refrigerated transportation in the 1880s. Meat and dairy products joined wool as the basis of exports to Europe. At the end of the 19th century, New Zealand was one of the richest countries in the world. As a former colony, it enjoyed close cultural and economic links with the UK. For most of the following century, three-quarter of New Zealand's exports went to the UK. Britain was also the major source of imports.

By the 1950s New Zealand was an efficient producer of wool, meat and dairy products which could compete successfully in northern hemisphere markets. The success of the export industry allowed New Zealanders to enjoy a similar standard of living to the industrialised countries of Europe and America. The relatively high standard of living attracted a constant inflow of immigrants. In the early 60s as a result of a worldwide boom in commodity prices, it enjoyed amongst highest living standards in the OECD. However even during this relatively prosperous period, it was recognised that future economic security depended on diversifying the export base, both in terms of markets and of the range of goods being exported. New Zealand's traditional market, Britain, was not growing as fast as other countries and there was the possibility throughout the sixties that it would eventually join the European Economic Community (EEC).

The golden years ended in the 1970s. Several factors were influential such as the entry of Britain into the EEC in 1973 and the first oil price-shock in the same year. Britain's entry into the EEC led to the restriction of access for New Zealand exports. In combination with the rise in the price of oil which had a severe effect on the New Zealand economy, as it was extremely dependent on importing oil to meet its energy needs, the loss of most the British export market contributed to a sudden decline in economic performance. The cost of imports rose sharply while exports receipts dropped and the Balance of Payments deficit plummeted to 14% of GDP. Arguably however the effect of these two events only exposed the underlying weakness of New Zealand's economy rather than causing the economic decline. The government of the time decided that the best solution to the problem of New Zealand's dependency on fuel imports was to embark upon a series of major investment projects to develop domestic energy sources. Unfortunately the viability these projects was based on the price of oil continuing to rise more than it did. Most of the so-called 'Think Big' projects turned out to be expensive white elephants.

By the early 1980s, the economy was performing badly. Inflation was high, and at the same time, unemployment was rising rapidly. Subsidies protected inefficient sectors of the economy and discouraged innovation. Years of borrowing to cover the trade deficit and the cost of the 'Think Big' experiment had increased New Zealand's foreign debt. The National government tried to control inflation by imposing a price and wage freeze in 1982. The freeze succeeded in controlling inflation, but money supply continued to grow throughout the two and half years it was in place. In 1984 a Labour government was elected. At the time of the election there was no indication that the new administration would introduce a period of radical economic reform. The Labour party mainfesto made no mention of many of the central policy changes they enacted. The programme of economic liberalisation included removal of price and wage controls, deregulation of financial markets, the floating of the dollar, the introduction of a sales tax, the reduction of agricultural and industrial subsidies, the removal of employment protection, and the weakening of the collective bargaining power of unions. This was accompanied by tight monetary policy and the selling of a number of state assets, including the railways, forests, the national airline and the telecommunications section of the post office.

Against these short term swings in government economic policy, a longer term process of economic adjustment has been occurring. New Zealand's export industry has diversified both in product and export markets. A free trade agreement was signed with Australia in 1983 which is now New Zealand's main trading partner, with the balance of trade being slightly in New Zealand's favour. The development of new markets in Asia has been a significant development over the last ten years. Japan is the third largest source of export income after Australia and the USA. Europe, which in the late 1960s provided two-thirds of New Zealand's export revenue, now accounts for less than 20%. The range of exports has also diversified to include forestry, horticulture, wine and manufactured goods. The dependence upon meat, wool and dairy exports has declined considerably as a result. In the 1960s, these three sectors accounted for over 80% of export revenue; they now make up less than 50%. Although the range of products has diversified, the economy as a whole is still reliant upon exporting agricultural and horticultural commodities. As a result the economy remains sensitive to changes in worldwide commodity prices. It is also vulnerable to climactic and environmental factors.

The adjustment process to the restructuring has been long and difficult. Unemployment rose from under 4% in 1985 to over 10% in 1990, levels not seen since the Depression years, as economic activity declined due to tight monetary policy. Farmers' gross incomes dropped by nearly half when government subsidies were removed. A large number of manufacturing industries went to the wall, unable to compete with cheap imports once tariffs were removed. The abolition of financial controls caused a brief speculative boom in the mid-eighties but the stock market crash in 1987 exposed much of the increased activity as paper wealth. The dollar rose as high interest rates attracted overseas investment which reduced returns from exports, critical to the overall health of the economy.

Whether the social costs of economic restructuring outweigh the efficiency gains is still being debated. Some sectors of the economy have adjusted better to deregulation than others. Despite predictions that many farms would not survive the removal of agricultural price supports, there were only a few casualties. The agricultural sector has become more efficient. Manufacturing has not been as fortunate and the shedding of jobs in this sector along with the restructuring of previously inefficient government industries largely accounts for the rise in unemployment. The gap between high and low income earners has grown and poverty has emerged for the first time since the war as a visible social problem. For a country which used to pride itself on its egalitarian ethos and comprehensive social welfare system, these developments have caused much public concern.

Future economic predictions are more encouraging. The economy emerged from recession halfway through 1992 and current growth trends are strong. Unemployment is still predicted to stay above 7% however, despite the growth of new jobs, as the number of people looking for work is also rising. Discouraged job-seekers are being attracted back into the labour market by the improving economic position and some groups are increasing their labour market participation rates, notably women and older people.

Government
The system of government in New Zealand is very similar to the British system. It is a parliamentary democracy within the Commonwealth with the Queen as

the titular head of state represented in New Zealand by the Governor General. The current inhabitant of Government House, Dame Cath Tizard is a feisty former Labour party politician, known for her informal style and blunt opinions. New Zealand shows no signs of following the current Australian enthusiasm for republicanism. There is no equivalent to the British House of Lords. The upper House was abolished in the 1950s and there are no plans to reinstate it. Legislation is consequently easier to pass in the New Zealand parliament as it only requires the approval of one body. Parliament used to be dominated by the ruling party and party discipline was the tightest of any Westminster-style parliament.

As a result New Zealand has one of the most centralised systems of executive government in any western country. While levels of local government exist, they do not provide a countervailing force as their powers and responsibilities are comparatively weak. Radical policy programmes can be introduced relatively quickly as is demonstrated by the case of the fourth Labour government, who transformed the country between 1984 and 1990. The problem has been that the electorate has not universally welcomed change as is demonstrated by the electoral backlash against both the major parties in the 1993 election. Neither of the big parties gained the confidence of the electorate, and small parties got a record number of seats. The result on the night was a hung parliament, but a recount in some of the most marginal seats resulted in a narrow victory for the ruling National party.

In conjunction with the election was a referendum on whether New Zealand should change its method of electing representatives to a proportional representation (PR) system similar to those used in Europe. PR which is the voting system in most European countries, and in fact in democracies with the exception of New Zealand and the UK, uses the percentage of votes a party gains to work out their strength of numbers in parliament or the equivalent legislative body. There are many types of PR and in the referendum, the New Zealand voters were given a choice between a variety of systems. A majority backed MMP, a proportional representation system similar to the one used in Germany. But the support for MMP seems to stem from a reaction against conventional politics and the mainstream parties rather than from any widespread support or even understanding of the consequences of changing the electoral system.

At the time of writing, the first election under MMP has yet to occur. But the electoral upheavals consequent upon changing the system of voting have already started to destabilise the major parties. Under MMP there will be fewer constituency seats so some sitting MPs will find that their electorates will disappear before the next election. They are already looking around for new fields to conquer but with 96 MPs and only 65 seats, more than a few are going to be left without a chair when the music stops. As well as pitting MPs in the same party against each other in the undignified struggle for selection, MMP will make it much easier for small parties to gain representation than is currently the case. Existing small parties who have struggled in the political wilderness for years are looking forward to the first PR election. So are some current MPs who have decided that the best way to get on the new world of PR is leave the big parties to founder and to found a party in their own image. The result is a proliferation of new parties with programmatic titles such as the 'Right of Centre' party. For a brief guide to the growth industry that is currently the party political scene, see the section below.

Political Parties

For most of the second half of this century, the New Zealand political scene has been dominated by two major parties, National and Labour. National is a conservative party, traditionally the party of farmers and business people. It has been the dominant political party in New Zealand politics, holding office for the majority of the post-war period. Labour has some elements in common with the British Labour party. Like the British labour party it arose out of the labour movement, but the New Zealand Labour party has subsequently had greater independence from the trade unions. It has often been the innovator of radical social policies, even when these have gone against its own political traditions. The 4th Labour Government which held power from 1984 to 1990 was responsible for introducing anti-nuclear legislation which stopped American warships from entering New Zealand ports. It also deregulated the economy, ran a tight monetary policy along Thatcherite lines and sold off a number of state assets-not exactly socialist policies. For those who like their political spectrum neatly divided into left and right, New Zealand politics currently present a confusing spectacle. Since losing power in 1990, Labour have sacked their old leader, elected a left winger, Helen Clark, the first woman to lead a political party in New Zealand, and are going through a period of rediscovering their social democratic roots, although it remains to be seen if the public will be convinced. National, since being elected to government had a brief experiment with introducing even more extreme free-market policies.

Up till now, as in Britain smaller parties have been kept out of power by the first past the post electoral system. Parties have been able to gain power holding less than a majority of votes and small parties whose supporters were spread around the country would not even gain sufficient votes in any one electorate to elect an MP to Parliament, even though their overall share of the vote could be substantial. As a result of a referendum in 1991, New Zealand is about to move to a European style system of proportional representation for the next election in 1996. The political landscape is likely to change quite dramatically before the election as smaller parties will become electorally viable. This process has already begun. Two smaller parties now have seats in Parliament, New Zealand First, a populist party led by rebel National MP Winston Peters, and the Alliance, a coalition of left wing parties led by former Labour MP, Jim Anderton.

Geographical Information

Area
New Zealand is an island chain, consisting of two major islands and a number of smaller ones with a total land area of 103,515 sq miles/270,534 sq km, slightly larger than the United Kingdom. It is nearly 1600 km long stretching across 13 degrees latitude from 34 degrees S to 47 degrees S, only 420 km wide at its widest point. Most of the country is mountainous. The snow-capped Southern Alps dominate the South Island dividing the land between the wet rain forests of the West Coast and the dry pasture lands of the Canterbury, Marlborough and Otago. Fiordland, the south-west corner of the South Island is almost all national park and as its name suggest consists of deep sounds or fiords carved into the bush covered mountains. The North Island still bears the marks of the volcanic activity which formed it. A chain of occasionally active volcanoes runs from White Island sending up clouds of steam off the east coast, through the central volcanic plateau where snow and hotpools coexist, to Mt Egmont on the west coast. There are active thermal areas where mud pools literally bubble and geysers send up streams of boiling water.

National Parks

Thirty percent of New Zealand's land area is in protected conservation sites, in a network of national, maritime and forest parks. Many of these wilderness areas are untouched by human habitation, although unfortunately the effect of the animals introduced with the arrival of humans has been harder to control. The Department of Conservation which looks after the parks aims to preserve the flora and fauna as far as possible, while allowing people recreational access. They look after an extensive network of tracks and huts for hikers (known in New Zealand as trampers, as in to tramp). There is a small fee for using the huts. The walking tracks vary in difficulty from family strolls of less than half a day to serious two or three day hikes up hill and down. Most New Zealanders go tramping at some point in their lives, whether they are dragged reluctantly along on a school trip or are keen walkers every weekend.

Keep in mind though, that although the New Zealand bush looks welcoming on a warm day, it can be a very hostile environment. The weather can change unexpectedly and in some areas of New Zealand's national parks, you can be far away from any inhabited areas if something goes wrong. It is important to take precautions before venturing into the bush, such as bringing warm clothing and emergency food supplies, and informing someone of your plans.

Regional Divisions and Main Towns

The following regions correspond to the territorial divisions of local government, with the exception of some of the smaller districts such as Gisborne which have been grouped with larger neighbours.

North Island:
Northland, Auckland, Waikato, Bay of Plenty, Gisborne/Hawkes Bay, Taranaki, Manawatu-Wanganui, Wellington.

South Island:
Nelson/Marlborough/Tasman, West Coast, Canterbury, Southland and Otago.

There are four main cities:
North Island: Auckland, Wellington
South Island: Christchurch and Dunedin.

Population

At the last census the New Zealand population numbered just under 3.45 million, a half million increase since the early 1970s. Growth rates have been declining since the mid-seventies as a result of downward trends in birth rates, as is the case in most Western countries, the current rate of increase is less than one percent. The other major factor affecting population change is migration patterns which have been particularly volatile over the last twenty years. New Zealand has a very low population density compared with European countries, at 12.7 people per sq km. (the UK by comparison has 235.5 per sq km and Taiwan has 576.5)

Despite New Zealand's reputation as a largely rural society, 85% live in cities. Auckland, the biggest city, has a population of just under one million, nearly one third of the population. It is a relatively youthful society — children under 15 comprise just over 23% of the population and those of working age account for about 60% of the population.

Nearly three-quarters of the population are of European descent (known as Pakeha from the Maori word for non-Maori). New Zealand Maori make up the next largest group forming nearly 10% of the population. The next largest group are Polynesians from the Pacific Islands, such as Samoa, Tonga, and Fiji who form nearly 4% of the population. Other ethnic groups represented amongst the population are New Zealanders of Chinese and Indian descent.

Climate

New Zealand has an oceanic climate, without extremes of hot or cold. The seasons do not vary as much as in Britain, and are the opposite to the northern hemisphere, January and February being the warmest months and July the coldest. New Zealand's long thin shape results in considerable climactic variation between regions. The far north of the country has an almost sub-tropical climate, with mild winters, hot summers and quite a lot of rain. In the south of the South Island, the country can be frozen over for three months during the winter and the summers are hot and dry. Whatever the region, New Zealand summers are generally hotter than British summers. The sun is also stronger in the Southern Hemispere resulting in a higher risk of sunburn. Unfortunately the ozone hole over the Antartic has a tendency to drift north over New Zealand during December, which makes the risk of burning higher. Along with Australians, New Zealanders have one of the highest rates of skin cancer in the world.

Average Maximum Temperature, Sunshine and Rainfall

	Mean daily maximum Jan C/F	Jul	Bright sunshine hours	Mean annual rainfall mm/in
Auckland	23/73	14/57	2102	1185/47
Wellington	20/68	11/52	2019	1230/48
Christchurch	22/72	11/52	1974	655/26
Dunedin	19/66	10/50	1676	785/31

Regional Guide

Most New Zealanders live in the North Island, nearly one third of them in the greater Auckland region. The two major North Island cities, Auckland, the largest city, and Wellington, the capital, provide the closest New Zealand equivalent to the culture and lifestyle of big cities in the rest of the world. There is amicable rivalry between the two cities, Auckland being bigger, brasher and more commercial, Sydney for beginners, according to some people. Wellington takes itself more seriously as befits a capital city. It is the headquarters of most national cultural institutions such as the national ballet company and symphony orchestra and the seat of government. The South Island is more sparsely populated but attracts more visitors because of the splendours of the scenery. Christchurch, the biggest city in the south is very English in appearance and has a rather staid, conservative feel, perhaps because of the architecture. In the south of the South Island, the influence of Scottish settlers is very strong. About the only distinctive regional accent in New Zealand is the rolled 'r' of the Southlander. Groups of new immigrants often used to settle in particular regions. The area just up north of Auckland is full of family vineyards run by Dalmatian immigrants who arrived last century from what is now the country of Croatia. British expatriates are now fairly evenly spread around the country.

Information Facilities

The New Zealand Tourism Board runs a network of Visitor Information Centres throughout the country, where you can obtain maps of the area, information, public transport timetables, and have your queries answered. Information Centres can be found in most large towns. The Tourism board is also beginning an accreditation scheme for the tourism industry. You can recognise accredited establishments by the Taste New Zealand and Kiwihost signs.

Northland
Visitor Information Centre: Whangarei Visitor's Bureau, Tarewa Park, Otaiki Rd; tel (09) 438 1079.
Main city: Whangarei
Northland is one of the larger regions but is one of the least densely populated with only 131 000 inhabitants, just under 4% of the total population. It stretches from north of Auckland to the very tip of the North Island, Cape Reinga, where according to Maori legend, departing souls in the form of birds pause on the tree at the very end of the land before setting off for the oceans. Northland has a semi-tropical climate, miles of isolated beaches, and undisturbed rainforests. The Bay of Islands on the east coast was one of the earliest sites of European settlement. The Treaty of Waitangi under which the British Crown gained sovereignty over New Zealand was signed at Waitangi on one side of the Bay of Islands, and on the opposite side of the bay is Russell which was the capital of New Zealand for the first twenty years of British rule. These days one of the main areas of economic activity is tourism. It is a popular destination for New Zealand and overseas visitors. Aside from the historical attractions, it is a centre for big game fishing enthusiasts, sailors and divers.

Auckland
Visitor Information: Auckland Visitor Centre, 299 Queen Street, PO Box 7048, Auckland; tel (09) 366 6888.
Main city: Auckland.
The Auckland region is dominated by the city from which it takes its name, the largest in the country with a population of 885 000 and the financial and manufacturing centre. Two natural harbours, one on the Pacific coast, the other on the Tasman, bite deep into the land, and the island consequently is narrow at this point. The city covers the width of the island between the harbours. Although Auckland has the highest population concentration in the country, it is not densely populated by the standards of European cities. Most Aucklanders live in detached single stories dwellings in the suburbs which stretch further into the surrounding countryside each year. The city centre is situated beside the Waitemata harbour and although it has a number of modestly tall high rise buildings, it's not exactly Manhattan. In fact one of Auckland's most attractive aspects is the parks and reserves that are dotted throughout the urban area. Many of these reserves are volcanic hills — there are over sixty extinct volcanoes in the city area. Another attractive feature is the beaches within walking distance of the city centre. Auckland is the main industrial and financial centre and dominates the rest of the country through its size and concentration of economic activity. Nearly one third of the population live in the greater Auckland region and it is likely to be the fastest growing area of economic activity for some time.

Waikato
Visitor Information: Hamilton Visitor Centre, Angelsea St, PO Box 970, Hamilton; tel (07) 839 3360.
Main city: Hamilton.
The Waikato region stretches from the Bombay hills just south of Auckland to Lake Taupo in the centre of the North Island. The lake is the source of the river for which the region is named. The Waikato river is the longest in New Zealand.

Along its 425 km length there are nine hydro-electric dams which provide alarge partof the country's electricity requirements. The Waikato is the main dairy farming region in New Zealand. The Coromandel pennisula in the north-east corner of the region is a centre for forestry production. The Coromandel is also a popular holiday destination. Its rugged bush clad mountains protect almost deserted beaches. Other attractions include the thermal regions around Wairakei, where steam is harnessed to drive turbines producing electricity, and the limestone caves at Waitomo. Hamilton, the largest city has a population of nearly 150,000 people but the atmosphere of a small town. It has one of the more dynamic universities in the country (whose new vice-chancellor, Bryan Gould is a Kiwi who returned home after a long sojourn in British politics). The Waikato is also the headquarters of the King movement, one of the Maori cultural and political movements responsible for the renaissance of Maoridom in the 20th century. The King movement is based at Turangawaewae marae (Maori meeting place and cultural centre) at Ngaruawahia, the home of the Maori queen. Like many marae, it is open to groups of visitors by arrangement.

Bay of Plenty
Visitor Information: Tauranga Information & Visitor Centre, The Strand, PO Box 1070, Turanga; tel (07) 578 8103.
Main Towns: Tauranga, Rotorua.
The Bay of Plenty is one of the main horticultural regions in the country. It is located on the east coast of the North Island above East Cape. The area around Te Puke is the kiwifruit growing capital of the country. If you are fond of the small, furry, brown fruit, you can find them on sale at roadside stalls at ridiculously cheap prices during the season, sometimes when export cargoes are held up for any reason, growers practically give them away. The Bay of Plenty region is a good place for finding casual fruit picking work in season. Rotorua is famous for its geysers and mudpools and for the distinctive sulphuric smell of the thermal activity, reminiscent of rotten eggs. The beaches around Tauranga and Mount Manganui are particularly pleasant and attract crowds (by New Zealand standards) during the summer months.

Hawkes Bay/Gisborne
Visitor Information: Napier Visitor Information Centre, Marine Parade, Private Bag, Napier; tel (06) 835 7579.
Eastland and Gisborne District Information Centre, 209 Grey St, PO Box 170, Gisborne; tel (06) 686 6139.
Main towns: Napier, Hastings, Gisborne.
Gisborne and the East Cape region are very sparsely populated with only 44 000 inhabitants, 31 000 of whom live in the main town Gisborne. Dairy and sheep farming are the dominant industries although wine-making is small but growing activity. In this remote area, Maori influences are strong and the lifestyle of local Maori is relatively unaffected by European culture. Hawkes Bay, located on the east coast, below East Cape is another primarily agricultural and horticultural region. It has a mild climate with long sunshine hours and low rainfall. The area around Napier and Hastings is particularly known for its vineyards, producing a number of excellent wines, particularly Chardonnay and Sauvigncn Blanc. Napier has some of the most striking architecture in New Zealand. Totally flattened by an earthquake in 1931 it was rebuilt in the art deco style then fashionable around the world. Most of the original buildings survive undwarfed by modern tower blocks.

Taranaki
Visitor Information: New Plymouth Public Relations Office, Cnr Liardet & Leach St, New Plymouth; tel (06) 758 6086.

Main town: New Plymouth.
According to Maori legend, the North Island of New Zealand was originally a giant fish which the hero Maui hooked from his canoe, the South Island. If you consider the shape of the North Island as a flattish sort of fish, with a fin on each side, Taranaki occupies the western fin. The dominant feature of the Taranaki landscape is Mt Egmont (also known as Mt Taranaki), a perfect volcanic cone, topped year round with snow. Taranaki is dairying country and is also the centre of the petrochemical industry. Off the coast of New Plymouth is the Maui natural gas field and a number of small oil fields. The region around Mt Egmont is a national park and there are a number of hiking paths.

Manawatu-Wanganui
RVisitor Information: Palmerston North Information Centre, The Square, tel. (06) 358 5003.
Wanganui Information Centre, 101 Guyton Street, PO Box 637; tel (06) 345 3286.
Main towns: Palmerston North, Wanganui.
The Manawatu-Wanganui region stretches from just above Wellington up into the centre of the North Island to the central volcanic plateau. The main river in the region is the Whanganui, ('wh' is pronounced like 'f' in Maori). The town which is situated on its banks, should correctly be known as Whanganui as well, but established usage prevails. According to Maori myth, the Whanganui was first explored by the great navigator Kupe. The town was one of the earliest established by European settlers who recognised the navigable properties of the river. While other cities have expanded, Wanganui has retained the atmosphere of a quiet country town. Tourist attractions include jet boat rides on the Whanganui river. The main industry is sheep and dairy farming. Tongariro National Park, in the north of the region has within its bounds the highest points in the North Island, the snow-capped volcanoes, Mt Ruapehu, Mt Ngaruahoe and the shortest of the three, Mt Tongariro. Mt Ruapehu is the main North Island skiing destination. The whole area is popular centre for outdoor activities., from climbing to fly-fishing. In the thermal region nearby there are hot springs, and a dip in a naturally heated pool is a popular end to a day's skiing. The largest town is towards the south of the region. Palmerston North, is the home of Massey University, one of the two original specialist agricultural colleges.

Wellington
Visitor Information: Wellington City Information Centre, Cnr Wakefield & Victoria Streets, PO Box 2199, Wellington; tel (04) 801 4000.
Main City: Wellington.
The Wellington region covers the southern tip of the North Island. It is named for its largest city, Wellington, the capital of New Zealand. The House of Representatives is currently located in temporary quarters over the road from the old Parliament buildings which are being upgraded to proof them against the earth tremors that are feature of life in Wellington. The city spreads across steep hills overlooking a harbour shaped like a natural amphitheatre. Wellington is infamous for its winds which must easily rival those of that other windy city, Chicago. A favourite cheap thrill amongst inhabitants is watching airplanes battle their way into Wellington airport on a windy day. Being a passenger on a plane trying to land at Wellington is less fun. The city itself is quite small, with a population of around 150 000 in the main urban area but despite its size it is suprisingly lively. There are a host of late night cafés and bars, many of which feature local bands, and a thriving theatre scene. Wellington hosts an arts festival every two years which attracts international musicians and performing artists as well as local artists. Most of the other towns in the region provide commuter fodder for Wellington, and as such lack much personality. The exception perhaps

are towns along the edge of the harbour opposite Wellington. Most of these are scarcely more than villages as the steep hills drop almost into the sea at this point leaving only a narrow strip of land to build on. A regular ferry service takes about 25 minutes to cross the harbour to Wellington from Days Bay.

Marlborough/Tasman
Visitor Information: Nelson Visitor Centre, Cnr Trafalgar & Halifax Street, PO Box 194, Nelson; tel (03) 548 2304.
Main Cities: Nelson, Blenheim.
The Marlborough and Tasman districts cover the top of the South Island. It is the largest wine making region in the country. The climate is pleasant, hot without being as humid as northern parts, with more sunny days and less rain than Auckland. The area around Nelson is a centre for artisans and craftspeople, particularly potters, which may account for the slightly alternative feel to the town. It is a relaxed, laid-back place (as are most South Island towns) with easy access to some beautiful wilderness areas and beaches. Over the Takaka hills to the west lies the aptly named Golden Bay. There are a number of national parks in the Tasman distirct. East of the city of Nelson lies the Marlborough district, the largest wine making region in the country. Blenheim is the main town.

West Coast
Visitor Information: Buller Visitor & Information Centre, 1 Brougham Street, Westport; tel (03) 789 6658.
Main Town: Greymouth.
The West Coast is a wet and wild part of the South Island with its own distinctive breed of New Zealanders. The Coast is accessible by a few roads most of which climb up through the Alps in a series of hairpin bends through spectacular scenery. The routes through the centre of the island are occasionally cut off by weather which may account for the remote feeling of the Coast. Or it may be the independence of its inhabitants resultings from the area's historical legacy. Mining, gum digging and possum trapping were the main industries for much of this century and the last; all solitary occupations. In the south of the region there are spectacular glaciers and views of the mountains (when the weather permits) including New Zealand's highest, Mt Cook.

Canterbury
Visitor Information: Canterbury Information Centre, Cnr Worcester Street & Oxford Tce, PO Box 2600, Christchurch, ph (03) 379 9629.
Main City: Christchurch.
The Canterbury region is mostly sheep farming country, miles of pasture land stretching from the foothills of the southern Alps to the coast. The main city Christchurch is the largest in the South Island with a population of more than 300,000 It was founded by an idealistic bunch of Oxford graduates and named for their old college. These days it is known as the Garden City, for its botanic parks, trees and green spaces. It is set on the Avon river and is a popular destination for Japanese tourists who like the slightly English flavour Christchurch retains. The Christchurch skyline is dominated to the west by the Southern Alps. Mt Hutt, a major ski resort is only an hour's drive from the city. Just below Christchurch is Banks Peninsula, a collection of bays and hills jutting out into the Pacific. Lyttleton harbour is the deep water port for the city of Christchurch and is connected to the city by a 1.6 km tunnel running through the Port Hills. Akaroa, the main settlement on the Peninsula was orginally founded by the French who had ambitions to colonise New Zealand but were beaten to it by the British. These days the French influence does not extend much beyond the street names and the architecture. The Canterbury plains are

prime crop-growing land. Further west on the foothills of the Alps, the land is most used for sheep farming.

Southland
Visitor Information: Gore Information Centre, Cnr Medway and Ordsal Streets, PO Box 1, Gore; tel (03) 208 9908.
Main towns: Invercargill, Gore.
Southland, as the name suggests is the southernmost region of the South Island. Stewart Island at the very bottom of the South Island is the southern most inhabitated point of the country. It is off the coast of Southland, below Invercargill, the largest town in the region. At Bluff nearby Invercargill is the country's only aluminium smelter. In the western part of the region is Fiordland national park. It contains some truly awe inspiring scenery: fiords or sounds carved out by glaciers, cut deep channels into the land. The surrounding cliffs are covered in bush and traced by waterfalls. One of the best known parts of Fiordland is Milford Sound, the destination of the Milford track, a popular walking trip for tourists. Most of Southland is beef and sheep farming country, with some dairying around Invercargill.

Otago
Visitor Information: Dunedin Visitor Centre, 48 The Octogon, PO Box 5457, Dunedin; tel (03) 474 3300.
Main city: Dunedin.
The Otago region covers the south-eastern part of the South Island. Land use is mostly for dairy farming and crop growing. The central Otago basin enjoys surprisingly hot dry summers despite its latitude and is a centre for horticulture, particularly stone fruit orchards. The southern most city, Dunedin was founded by Scottish settlers. Perhaps the most characteristic buildings in Dunedin are those of the University which reflect the importance of education to the early settlers: founded in 1869, the University of Otago is the oldest in New Zealand. Fueled by the discovery of gold in the 1860s Dunedin grew to be one of biggest towns in colonial New Zealand. The gold largely ran out after the initial boom, and Dunedin's growth rate fell behind the northern cities. It has remained much the same size since the early days of the 20th century, and many of its historic buildings have been preserved as a result. It has also retained the somewhat austere character of its Presbyterian forefathers, although every year a new intake of students at Otago University tries to reverse this. It is the only truly 'student' town in the country, university life dominating the town during term time while students provide much needed revenue for local businesses. Further north, Queenstown is a major tourist mecca. Set on Lake Wakatipu against a spectacular mountain backdrop, it is close to ski resorts and other outdoor attractions.

Getting There

Travel Agents
If you do not have a regular travel agent, it may be worthwhile considering the advantages of using an agency which specialises in long haul flights or in Australian and New Zealand destinations. They should be in touch with any discounted or cheaper fares that may be available, although the drawback of these deals is usually that the tickets have restrictions and can be hard to change once booked. Some antipodean travel agencies offer other services which may be useful, for example, organising temporary accomodation when you first arrive.

The cheapest flights are via London, so if you are travelling from another European destination it may be worth checking if it makes sense to go via Heathrow or Gatwick. From London, you can either fly east or west to get to New Zealand, with a refuelling stop either in Asia or the USA. It is slightly quicker to go via Asia, but if you fly via the States, the baggage allowances are much more generous. (see below). Going west also minimises the jetlag because you are following the path of the sun so your body clock is not so disorientated. There are other ways of minimising the effects of jetlag while on the flight. Drink plenty of water, avoid acohol, and try and stretch your legs every so often. This may sound like boring advice but the jet lag after a thirty-hour flight across twelve time zones is considerable. Avoiding the free airline alcohol is not such a big price to pay for being awake and alive your first few days in your new country. Another idea is to arrive in plenty of time for your flight so you can ask for bulkhead or exit row seats which have extra leg-room.

You are only allowed to take 20 kilos of luggage with you on the aircraft if you travel economy class via Asia to New Zealand. If you travel via America you can take two suitcases, neither of which may exceed 32 kg in weight. Airlines are strict about sticking to these limits and as the excess baggage charge works out at about $72 per kilo you will need to make sure your luggage is within the limits. Should you arrive at the airport and discover that you are over the limit, the best option is unaccompanied baggage. Your luggage will go on the next available flight, and usually reaches your destination a couple of days after you do. You will have to clear it through Customs at the other end and there may be storage charges as well. The usual charge for unaccompanied baggage is about $9 per kilo.

Useful Addresses

Ausflights, 102 New Street, Birmingham B2 4HQ; tel 0121-633 3232; fax 0121-633 4081.

Auspac Travel, Suite 71/2, 3rd Floor, 87 Regent Street, London W1R 7HF; tel 0171-437 2328; fax 0171-437-2339.

Connections Travel: 93 Wimpole Street, London W1M 7DA; tel 0171-495-5545; fax 0171-408 4450. Connections brochure gives fares and tours pricing for different seasons and offers ideas as how best to build itineraries.

Cresta World Travel, 44/46 George Street, Altrincham, Cheshire WA14 1RH; tel 0161-927-7177; fax 0161-929 0433.

Golden Wings Worldwide, 29 Kent House, First Floor, 87 Regent Street, London W1R 7HF; tel 0171-734 3070; fax 0171-494 3936.

Modern Air Travel, 61 Reform Street, Dundee DD1 1SP; tel 01382 322713; fax 01382 201079.

Southern Cross Travel: Best Beech Hill, Wadhurst, TN5 6JH; tel 01892-783869.

Travel Mood: 246 Edgware Road, London, W2 1DS; tel 0171-2580280.

Insurance

Working travellers and those on speculative job searches in New Zealand are advised to take out comprehensive travel insurance.

Useful Addresses

Atlas Travel Insurance Service Ltd (ATI) 37 Kings Exchange, Tileyard Road, London N7 9AH; tel 0181-579 3700; fax 0171-609 5011.

Downunder Insurance 24a Bristol Gardens, London W9 (Warwick Ave. tube); tel 0171-286 2425; fax 0171-289 6562.

Golden Wings Worldwide 29 Kent House, First Floor, 87 Regent Street, London W1R 7HF; tel 0171-494 3936; fax 0171-437 6379.

Residence and Entry Regulations

The Current Position

Throughout New Zealand's history, population growth has been boosted at various points by government policies designed to attract immigrants. The main source of the new arrivals for most of the first century of European settlement was the British Isles. Aside from the British, the other major source of European immigrants was the Netherlands. Sadly New Zealand missed out on achieving some of the ethnic diversity Australia enjoys by not actively encouraging immigration from other European countries in the post World War Two period. The last major campaign to attract immigrants was in the 1950s. These were the days when the New Zealand government paid for the passage on the condition that the would-be immigrant stayed for two years. When this scheme ended, a more restrictive immigration policy was introduced, based on occupational quotas. Most prospective immigrants had to have a job waiting for them before they applied for residency.

In 1991 the Government changed the occupational quota scheme for a points system similar to the Canadian and Australian schemes. A job offer is no longer a requirement for gaining residency. Applicants for residency are ranked by the number of points they score for attributes such as age, qualifications, and work experience. Those who reach the target number set by the New Zealand government automatically receive provisional approval. At the same time the annual target number of immigrants was increased to 25,000 and the immigration service began a campaign in the UK to promote New Zealand as a destination for those considering emigration — the first such campaign since the old days of assisted passages. As a result, applications for residency have increased markedly and the number of immigrants has increased by a fifth. The UK is the largest single source of new migrants, followed by South Africa then South Korea.

Applying for New Zealand Residency

If you qualify for permanent New Zealand residency you are entitled to work in New Zealand without any restrictions. Besides the general category which is based on age and employablility criteria, there are three other ways of qualifying for permanent residence: Business Investment, Family, and Humanitarian. Whatever category you are applying under, there is a lot of paperwork to be got through. You will be required to provide medical certificates and character references. You will not be accepted if you have ever been convicted and served a sentence of five years or more, or a sentence of one year or more in the last ten years. These days because of the sensitivity of race relations and concerns over the political affiliations of the growing number of South African immigrants, you will also be required to declare that you have never been a member of a white supremacist organisation. Like the American immigration requirement to declare that you have never participated in genocide, the point is not that anyone would declare themselves to be racist but that if you make a false declaration, it is an offence under the Immigration Act and you can be deported forthwith. None of this paperwork comes cheaply — New Zealand is the pioneer of charging for the privilege of filling out official forms. See the table below for the cost of the different types of visas.

Immigration Consultants

You may consider employing the services of an immigration consultant. The number of organisations offering advice on emigrating to New Zealand has grown substantially since the new immigration policy was introduced in 1991. Most consultants offer help with all aspects of the immigration process. They will provide general information about New Zealand to help you decide whether you want to make the move. Some consultancies will organise special tour packages to New Zealand so you can visit the country before deciding whether to emigrate. As emigration is a major life step it may be worthwhile to consider a reconnaisance trip and you can make an application for permanent residency while in New Zealand on a visitor's visa or permit if you decide you like the place. The main function of the immigration consultant is however to help you negotiate your way through the immigration requirements. Once you have made the decision, an immigration consultant will guide you through the maze of paperwork and residency regulations which can appear daunting.

Using a Consultant

Bear in mind though, that using a consultant to help you through the application process is not a guarantee that you will be successful. They cannot make the paperwork disappear and having a job offer does not necessarily guarantee acceptan ce by the authorities. Consultants will probably ask for a list of documents then do most of the client's paperwork on their behalf which can make the whole process easier and less stressful. You should be wary of any consultancy which appears to promise that they have a special relationship with the New Zealand Immigration Service. All applications are considered equally regardless of whether a consultant has been involved or not. However a competent consultant can help to maximise the client's chances of qualifying: Mark Holden, of Macleod Immigration Services Ltd., says that statistics show that persons applying without being represented by an agent have an approximately 70% chance of qualifying; while the success figure for those who use a consultant is over 95%.

The other very useful service consultants provide is help with settling in once in New Zealand. To summarize: most good consultants should provide you primarily with assistance in dealing with New Zealand immigration and also with deciding where to live, looking for a job, finding a house and other aspects of organising your new life.

If you do not have a job and a home to go to in New Zealand, the other important aspects to consider are the practical help consultants can offer in addition to helping you deal with the immigration authorities. Do they have a job search branch in New Zealand? What kind of contacts do they have in promoting your employment chances?

According to the New Zealand Immigration Service, the major consultancies they deal with regularly are all above board. If you are uncertain about whether a consultancy is bona fide, you can contact the Immigration Service to check them out. It is worth shopping around and making sure you get value for money.

Useful Addresses

Ambler Collins: Riverbank House, Putney Bridge Approach, London, SW6 3JD; tel 0171-3719191; fax 0171-7368841.

Emigration Consultancy Services: De Salis Court, Hampton Lovett, Droitwich, Worcestershire WR9 0NX; tel 01905-795949; fax 01905-795557.

Malcom Consultants: 1 Hay Hill, Berkeley Sqaure, London, W1X 7LF; tel 0171-2673575; fax 0171-2840080.

Network Migration Services: Oxford House, College Court, Commercial Road, Swindon, Wiltshire, SN1 1PZ; tel 01793-612222.

New Zealand & Australia Migration Bureau: Oranje Nassaulaan 25, 1075 AJ Amsterdam, The Netherlands; tel 31-20-6717017; fax 31-20-6760065.

OZ-Link-UK: Personal and business migration agents. Higher Elstone Cottage, Elstone, Chulmleigh, Devon EX18 7AQ; tel/fax 01769-580318.

Ranfurly Residency Services: 40 Bow Lane, London EC4M 9DT; tel 0171-4898827; fax 0171-2366325.

Useful Publication

New Zealand Outlook published monthly by Consyl Publishing Ltd. (3 Buckhurst Road, Bexhill-on-Sea, East Sussex TN40 1QF). Aimed specifically at migrants and is a useful way of keeping up with NZ migration policy and entry regulations.

Residence Categories

General residence category: To qualify in this category you must be under 55 years old and have sufficient understanding of English to conduct a conversation, and to read and respond to questions about yourself and your family. Applicants under the general category are assessed through the new points system. Points are awarded in three different areas: employability, age and settlement factors. If your score is above the pass mark then your application is provisionally approved, subject to meeting normal immigration requirements such as a clean bill of health and not having a serious criminal record. The pass mark has been set at 28 points since the new system was introduced in 1991. Below 20 points is an automatic fail. Between 20 and 27 points, your application will be put in a pool. Each month a certain number of applications may be drawn from the pool, those with the highest numbers first. The number taken from the pool depends on how many are required to meet the annual immigration tally. Your application will stay in the pool for four consecutive months. If you are not chosen in this time, your application lapses, although you may apply again. You do not get your application fee refunded if you do not qualify.

The system favours young people with tertiary qualifications. However older people with work experience and qualifications can also gain enough points to pass. If you have work experience but no formal qualifications, then your experience only counts if your occupation is on the approved occupations list. Copies of the list can be obtained from the New Zealand Immigration Service. An offer of a job adds to your chances but is not required. It makes no difference which country you apply from. The points system has the advantage that it is completely neutral: if you have sufficient points to make the grade your application will be provisionally approved, it is not up to the discretion of an individual officer. You can check your eligibility in these areas by applying for a self-assessment guide from the New Zealand High Commission. To give you an idea of how the system works here is the points table from the most recent self assessment guide:

A. Employability factors	Factor	Points
1. Qualifications	Successful completion of 12 years schooling	2
	Diploma or Certificate at least 1 year and less than 2 years full time study	4
	Diploma or Certificate from 2 yrs to 3 yrs full-time study	8
	Bachelor's degree in any area of study not mentioned below or a Trade Certificate or Advanced Trade Qualification	12
	Post graduate Degree or a Bachelor's degree in any science, technical or engineering area of study	15
2. Work Experience	Two years	1
	Four years	2
	Six years	3
	Eight years	4
	Ten years	5
	Twelve years	6
	Fourteen years	7
	Sixteen years	8
	Eighteen years	9
	Twenty years	10

Maximum points for employability factor: 25

3. Age	18-24 years	8
	25-29 years	10
	30-34 years	8
	35-39 years	6
	40-44 years	4
	45-49 years	2

Maximum age limit: 55 years
Maximum points for age factor: 10

4. Settlement factors	NZ $100,000 settlement funds	2
	Family sponsor	2
	Community sponsor	3
	1 point for each additional settlement funds up to a maximum of $300 000	3
	Offer of skilled employment	3

Maximum points for settlement factors: 5

MAXIMUM POINTS: 40
PASS MARK: 28

Points to watch out for:
You can only claim points for your highest qualification.
Only one person in a family need qualify. Partners and dependent children under 20 will be granted residence as well.
You do not have to have a job offer although you will score more points if you do.
Years of work experience are rounded down, so if you have nine years and eight months of work experience, that will count as eight years or four points.
You can apply for residence under the general category if you are between 50

and 55 but you will receive no points for your age. You are not eligible if you are 55 years or older.

Medical requirements are not clearly spelled out anywhere but the criteria seems to be whether you would be a burden on the New Zealand health system. Chronic managable syndroms such as epilepsy would not disqualify you, but having a terminal disease probably would.

If at any point a large number of applicants score over 28 points and therefore automatically qualify, the Immigration Service will not draw any applicants from the pool. This was the case for most of 1993 and 1994. If you are unsuccessful in the pool after four months your application lapses and you do not receive a refund. If you are in the 24-27 point area, you should look carefully at the settlement factors to see if you can find the critical extra points to take you to 28 points. Sponsorship is one area to look into. Sponsorship imposes no formal obligations on the individual or group concerned. It is just an indication that you have some kind of support system when you arrive, a family member or organisation able to help you settle in. A family sponsor must be an adult brother, sister, parent or child of the principal applicant and must have be a New Zealand citizen or resident who has been living in the country for the three years prior to your application. Family sponsorship is worth an additional two points and community sponsorship, three. Community sponsors are organis-ations approved by the Immigration Service. Most approved organisations are ethnic or religious organisations and they will usually require some evidence of your ethnic or religious background. Their obligations as sponsors are to provide food, clothing or shelter should you fall on hard times within the first 12 months of residency so they may also want to know about your financial stability and career prospects. The organisations currently approved by the Immigration Service are listed below. You should contact them directly to find out whether they will be prepared to sponsor your application. Securing an offer of skilled employment is worth three points. Skilled employment means that the job must either be relevant to your qualification or on the list of occupations approved by the Immigration Service. Note that the list of approved occupations only applies to this situation and for people claiming job experience with no qualifi-cations.

Finding the extra points to raise you above the pass mark is an area where a good immigration consultant may be able to help. Most of them offer a job search service. You could also consider visiting New Zealand and looking in person. Remember you can apply for permanent residency from within New Zealand. First hand experience of any country is still the best way of deciding if you want to live there.

Business Investment: This category is aimed at potential migrants who have professional or business skills and a lot of money to invest in New Zealand. You can qualify for residence under this category if you bring a minimum of NZ $500, 000 and to invest it for at least two years in an active business venture. If the venture is in the Auckland and Wellington regions, the minimum amount is NZ $625,000. In the case of investment in stocks, bonds or a bank account, the minimum figure rises to NZ $750, 000. The money has to have been earned from your own business or professional work and you will be required to meet a minimum of seven points from the employability section of the general category points test. You will also have to meet the same English language requirements as in the general category. If you meet the criteria and have the necessary funds to invest, approval in principle will be given. The residence visa is not issued until after the investment is made. Unconditional residence is not granted until the money has been invested for two years.

Family Reunification: You are entitled to apply for residence under this category if you have a partner or close family member who is a New Zealand resident or citizen. Spouses, de facto and homosexual partners all qualify but in the case of de facto or homosexual partners you have to go to greater lengths to convince the Immigration Service that the relationship is 'genuine and stable'. The relationship has to have been of at least two years duration for de facto and four years in the case of homosexual relationships. Approval is not automatic for any of these cases including spouses, and the Immigration Service will probably require an interview with both partners.

You can also qualify under family reunification if you have a close family member who is a New Zealander. Dependant children (under the age of 17, unmarried and childless) may qualify to be reunited with their parents if they were declared on their parents' residence application. Single adults may qualify for reunification with a New Zealand brother, sister or parent. Parents may be reunited with adult children provided all their adult children live outside their country of origin, or if they do not have dependant children, more of their adult children live in New Zealand than in any other country, or if they do have dependant children, they have a greater or equal number of adult children living in New Zealand than in any other country.

To qualify under any of these categories you will need to provide evidence of your relationship to the family member and that they are New Zealand citizens or residents.

Humanitarian Category: Applicants under the humanitarian category have be suffering some kind of persecution in their home country and have to have a New Zealand sponsor who is a close family member.

Approved Community Sponsors

Auckland Chinese Community Centre
Auckland Indian Association
Auckland Irish Society
Auckland Welsh Club
Bayanihan Club Of New Zealand
British Isles Club of Wellington
Combined Council of Scotish Societies
Commission for Latin American Refugees
  and Migrants
Croatian Club in Wellington
Croatian Cultural Society of New Zealand
Czechoslovak Club in New Zealand
Dalmatinsko Kulturno Drustvo

Federation of New Zealand Netherlands
  Societies
Korean Sports and Cultural Society
New Zealand Arab Association
New Zealand Malaysian Society
New Zealand Tamil Society
Odysseus Brotherhood
Stowarzyszenie Polakow
Turkish New Zealand Friendship Society
United Synagogues of New Zealand
United Sri Lanka Association
Wellington Indian Association
Wellington Tamil Society

The Application Process

If you are applying under the general category, you should be able to tell from having completed a self-assessment form whether you are likely to qualify automatically or go into the pool. Having obtained an application for visa form from a New Zealand embassy or High Commission, completed it along with the required documentation, you return it to the High Commission. A major cause of delay in having your application considered is incorrect documentation. Make sure for example that you send the full birth certificate (not short birth cerficates) for all family members included in an application for residency. Part of the medical requirements are that you have certain blood tests and the results for these must be sent in. Once you have sent the correct documents, your eligibility will be checked by Immigration Service staff. Processing time has been lengthy in the past at the Immigration Service in London. You should begin the application process about a year before your intended date of migration.

Fees:

Visitor's visa	£25	Residence visa (business)	£875
Work visa	£50	Student visa	£75
Residence visa	£275	Returning resident's visa	£20

Citizens from Japan, Iceland and Finland are not charged for any type of visa. Citizens of Austria, Greece, Israel, Italy and Turkey are not charged for residence visas. Citizens of the USA are not charged for Work and Student Visas.

New Zealand Citizenship

If you have resided legally in New Zealand for three years you can apply for New Zealand citizenship. This will entitle you to vote and to carry a New Zealand passport. You will no longer require a returning resident's visa when you travel outside New Zealand. Children born in New Zealand to non-New Zealanders are New Zealand citizens. They can have dual nationality and are entitled to a New Zealand passport.

For citizenship inquiries you should contact: Helen Jarroe, Director of Citzenship (Department of Internal Affairs, PO Box 805, Wellington).

Entry and Work Permits

If you want to visit New Zealand and you are not a citizen or permanent resident then you will need a visitor's visa or permit. You apply for a visa from the New Zealand embassy in your home country before you travel. The initial period of a visa is usually three months but you can extend it by a further six months once you are in New Zealand by applying to local offices of the New Zealand Immigration Service. It is becoming more common though for travellers not to need to obtain a visa as New Zealand has negotiated visa-free agreements with a number of countries. If you have a passport from one of the countries on the following list, you will not require a visa, you simply apply for a visitor's permit at the airport. You will be required to show that you have sufficient funds to support yourself while you are in New Zealand and a return or onward ticket. Like the visa, the visitor's permit is issued for three months initially and can be renewed by a further six months within New Zealand. Sufficient funding is deemed to be NZ$1000 for every month you intend to stay. If you have a friend or relative prepared to sponsor your visit, the amount is reduced to $400. They will need to fill in a form *Sponsoring a visitor* which they can get from New Zealand Immigration, and to send it to you.

Visa-free Countries:
Austria, Belgium, Canada, Denmark, Finland, France, Germany, Greece, Iceland, Indonesia, Ireland, Italy, Japan, Kiribati, Liechtenstein, Luxembourg, Malaysia, Malta, Monaco, Nauru, Netherlands, Norway, Portugal, Singapore, Spain, Sweden, Switzerland, Thailand, Tuvalu, USA.

Australia: Australian citizens are free to travel to New Zealand without a passport and can work in New Zealand without requiring a work visa under the terms of the Closer Economic Relations agreement which creates a free labour market accross the Tasman.

Britain: British citizens do not need to apply for visas and will be issued visitor's permits for an initial period of six months.

Applying for a longer visa:
If you know before you travel that you want to stay for longer than three months it is worth applying for a visa even if you are from a visa-waiver country. You can apply for a maximum of 12 months.

Studying in New Zealand:
In order to study in New Zealand you will need to apply for a student visa before you set off. You apply for the visa after you have been accepted by the educational institution in New Zealand. Information about New Zealand universities and polytechnics is available from the Trade Development Board of New Zealand which is in New Zealand House. You must be studying an approved course and have sufficient funds to cover tuition fees and maintenance (see Chapter Four, *Education* for an idea of the cost of courses). The Trade Development Board at New Zealand House has information on tuition fees and maintenance costs. (2nd Floor, New Zealand House; tel 0171-973 0380).

Working in New Zealand:
If you wish to work in New Zealand for a short period and you are not a citizen or resident you will need to apply for a temporary work visa. You can either apply for one before you travel if you already have a definite employment offer, or if you find a job while visiting New Zealand, you can apply for a visa there. If you are applying for a work visa before travelling, allow at least four weeks for the application to be processed. Your prospective employer will need to provide details of your job title, responsibilities, qualifications required, conditions and duration of employment and pay, as well as proof that they have unsuccessfully tried to recruit New Zealanders to fill the position. You can apply a work visa for up to three years, if you have a job offer before you arrive in New Zealand. If you apply for a work visa in New Zealand, the maximum period you will be granted is nine months. The employer will be required to provide the local Immigration Service with the information outlined above. For further information you can get a leaflet called *Getting a Work Visa* from the New Zealand Immigration Service.

Working Holiday Visa: Like Australia, New Zealand has a working holiday visa scheme for young British visitors. British citizens between the ages of 18 and 30 inclusive can apply for the visa which will enable them to take casual work without requiring a separate work visa, while on holiday in New Zealand. The maximum period of the visa is one year and you must be resident in the UK at the time of application. Only 500 are issued each year. You apply to the New Zealand Immigration Service in London, showing evidence that you have NZ$4200 to support your visit, and a return travel ticket or enough money to purchase one. The 500 successful applicants are chosen through a random draw. Applications are usually opened in May and the draw is one month later

Useful addresses:

New Zealand Information, Immigration and Visa Inquiries in the UK:
The New Zealand High Commission: 80 Haymarket, London, SW1Y 4TE; tel. 0171-930 8422.
The New Zealand Immigration Service: 3rd Floor New Zealand House; tel. 0171-973 0366/8/9.
NZIS information line: 0891 200288 (calls charged at 39p/49p per minute).
The New Zealand Trade Development Board: 2nd Floor New Zealand House, tel. 0171-973 0380.

Information for British Citizens in New Zealand:
British High Commission: 44 Hill Street, PO Box 1812, Wellington; tel (04) 472 6049; fax (04) 471 1974.

Setting Up Home

New Zealand house prices are cheap by British standards. Typical prices can be ascertained from the property section of some New Zealand newspapers. The main New Zealand newspapers can be read at New Zealand House in London (80 Haymarket, London, SW1Y 4TE; tel. 0171-930 8422) between 9am and 5pm weekdays. More detailed advertisements can be found in New Zealand real estate magazines. You can order these through *New Zealand Outlook* and *Destination New Zealand* the UK newspapers for intending immigrants. (Pick up copies outside the Visa Inquiries desk on the third floor of New Zealand House or order them from the addresses listed in Chapter Six *Employment — UK Newspapers and Directories*). Immigration consultants will also offer advice on buying properties. The property market in New Zealand's main cities is currently quite lively as a result of low interest rates and improving economic prospects. Auckland and Wellington are the most expensive places to buy houses. Outside the main cities, property prices are between 30-40% cheaper. Average prices in different regions are set out below in Table 1.

Most New Zealand houses are detached, single storey houses on individual plots of land known as 'sections' (The term bungalow to describe such a house is not common). Conveyancing is a less complicated business than in the UK because most houses are detached dwellings with no cross leases, and because, with a smaller total population, the house buying 'chains' are typically not as much of a problem as in the UK.

The standard size of the New Zealand section used to be a quarter of an acre, but as urban property prices have risen in recent years, subdivisions have become more common and new houses are being built on much smaller sites. The average size of new houses is just under 150 sq m. Although the vast majority of houses are still separate units, in recent years multi-unit developments have become more common, particularly in the big cities.

Deciding where to live for most people, is influenced first and foremost by employment prospects. The areas where new immigrants are most likely to buy houses are Auckland and Wellington. In both cities the areas where people live are mostly suburban and it is most common for people to commute by car into city centre to work. Each suburb has its own particular character and prices can also vary considerably between areas for reasons as diverse as mere fashion or, in the case of hilly areas, related to the amount of sunshine that different parts tend to enjoy. It is worth looking at the less fashionable areas; if you are aiming at the cheaper end of the market, you will get more house for your dollar.

If you have children, your choice may be influenced by proximity to schools. The location, however, does not make a lot of difference to the standard of education on offer. Inner city schools perform as well as suburban schools on the whole. Rural schools achieve slightly lower academic results than city schools but have the advantage of smaller class sizes and better pastoral care. The best idea is to go along to schools in the area and see what you think of the atmosphere. Now that school zoning has been abolished, you are free to select the school of your preference, within the limitations of getting the children there every morning.

How do New Zealanders Live?

New Zealand has a high level of home ownership, with nearly three-quarters of dwellings being owner-occupied. (The equivalent figure for the UK is 66%) They tend to be quite house-proud, and spend a lot of time on home improvements and gardening. The average standard of housing is high. Household services such as water, electricity and sewerage are almost universal. Most houses have TVs, over 60% have videos, and nearly a quarter have dishwashers.

Of those who are living in rented homes, a quarter live in state houses rented from the Housing Corporation, while the majority lease housing from private landlords or companies. Rental accommodation is usually provided unfurnished except for ovens, fridges and sometimes washing machines. Local authorities do not play a major role in providing housing.

The majority of households are made up of just one family. Amongst Maori and Pacific island communities, where extended kinship links are important and because average incomes amongst these groups are lower, households are more likely to include more than one family. Even amongst Maori and Pacific island homes though, one family households are the most common. The average number of occupants per dwelling is 2.8 people.

Levels of second home ownership are also quite high. Many New Zealand families own what is known as a bach or crib (bach is the North Island term, and crib, the South Island), a small holiday cottage on a lake or by the sea. Bachs are a great New Zealand institution. They are unpretentious dwellings usually furnished with furniture and kitchen-ware discarded from the family home, comfortable to live in, not always kept immaculately clean because when the family is on holiday, the chief cook and cleaner deserves a holiday too.

Buying a House

Non-New Zealanders can buy property of less than one acre without any bureaucratic formalities, but property purchases over an acre require the permission of the District Land Registrar or the Land Valuation Tribunal. However as most immigrants buy a house once they have been granted permanent residency, this restriction is not normally relevant.

Finding a property

Most people begin either by approaching a local real estate agent or searching in free weekly property newspapers in their desired location. Daily newspapers also carry property advertisements. There are many types of property on offer, although the variety is not as great as in Europe where architecture of many periods co-exists. European style architecture only has a short history in New Zealand and you do not find many thatched cottages. The typical period house is a wooden Victorian villa. This type is very popular with the do-it-yourself set as a renovation project. Most older houses were made of wood because of the risk of earthquake. The standard New Zealand house of the post War period is a three-bedroom, brick bungalow with a large section. Formerly, houses were generally built with a northern hemisphere model in mind and thus did not always make the most of the New Zealand climate. Modern houses are designed to capture the sun and to make the most of outdoor living during the New Zealand summer. Because of rising inner city land prices there is a growing

trend towards building town houses and apartment blocks. Town houses are compact units, often multi-level, usually built as part of a group on one site. In the suburbs, where land is cheaper you can find modern mansions with swimming pools, en suite bathrooms, separate lounge and dining room, all on a huge site. At the other end of the budget spectrum, you will find houses advertised as 'the handyman's dream' or 'needing TLC' (tender loving care), which is real estate speak for a dwelling in dire need of repair. This type of property is Mecca to the home handyman who seems to lurk under the skin of most New Zealand males and quite a few females. If your experience with nails is confined to those on your digits, then you should probably avoid this type of thing and look for something a more immediately habitable. On the other hand, inner city Victorian villas can still be picked up cheaply if you are prepared to do the work on them and, once renovated, they make charming homes.

Useful Addresses
New Zealand Real Estate Agents:

Auckland
Harcourts Real Estate: PO Box 99549, Newmarket, Auckland; tel (09) 520 5569; fax (09) 524 7059.
United Realty: PO Box 37074, Auckland; tel (09) 377 6843; fax (09) 377 6845.

Hamilton
Harcourts Real Estate: PO Box 9325, Hamilton; tel (07) 839 5085; fax (07) 834 1000.
Challenge Realty: PO Box 9141, Hamilton; tel (07) 856 0200.

Wellington
Harcourts Real Estate: PO Box 151, Wellington; tel (04) 472 6209; fax (04) 473 3380.
United Realty: PO Box 5117, Wellington; tel (04) 472 9323; fax (04) 473 4902.
Challenge Realty: PO Box 30125, Lower Hutt, Wellington; tel (04) 569 9139; fax (04) 568 3581.

Christchurch
Challenge Harding Real Estate: POB 31-204, Christchurch 4; tel/fax +64-3-358-4063.
Harcourts Real Estate: PO Box 1625, Christchurch; tel (03) 379 6596; fax (03) 379 2241.
United Realty: PO Box 29146, Christchurch; tel (03) 351 7665; fax (03) 351 7665.

Dunedin
Harcourts Real Estate: PO Box 5267, Dunedin; tel (03) 477 5334; fax (03) 477 3445.
United Realty: PO Box 221, Dunedin; tel (03) 477 0044; fax (03) 474 0484.
Challenge Realty: PO Box 1655, Dunedin; tel (03) 477 4303; fax (03) 474 4303.

Miscellaneous Useful Addresses
Consyl Publishing: (3 Buckhurst Road, Bexhill-on-Sea, East Sussex TN40 1QF) produce a monthly newspaper *New Zealand Outlook* which is aimed at those planning to emigrate to New Zealand. The newspaper carries details of housing there. A complimentary copy can be obtained by sending a 43p s.a.e.
Emigration Consultancy Services: De Salis Court, Hampton Lovett, Droitwich, Worcestershire, WR9 ONX; tel 01905-795949; fax 01905-795557. As well as helping emigrants deal with immigration, Emigration Consultancy Services provides help with the practical aspects of migration including accommodation.
Relocations International: POB 6112, Wellesley Street, Auckland; tel +64-9 378 9888; fax +64-9 376 1882; Wellington office: tel +64-9 473 9463; +64-9 473 9404.

Table 1: Average House and Apartment prices by Region

District	House	Unit/Apartment	Section
Northland	$112 000	$85 000	$42 500
Auckland	$169 063	$60 000	$70 500
Waikato/ Bay of Plenty	$15 750	$117 000	$40 000
Hawkes Bay	$115 000	$97 500	$54 000
Manawatu/Wanganui	$98 000	$95 000	$35 500
Tabanaki	$95 000	$105 334	$33 750
Wellington	$134 000	$105 000	$64 500
Nelson/Marlborough	$123 500	$102 000	$51 750
Canterbury/Westland	$117 500	$116 000	$48 500
Otago	$95 000	$101 750	$34 750
Southland	$76 000	$139 500	$65 000
Average for New Zealand	$125 600	$130 000	$52 500

Source: Real Estate Institute, quoted in *NZ News UK* July 6, 1994.

Purchasing and Conveyancing Procedures

Buying a property is less complicated in New Zealand than in many countries. Establishing clear title is generally straightforward because there are fewer complications like cross leasing and lease-hold properties. As a result you do not get chains of prospective buyers waiting for the next person in the chain to organise the sale of their house which is a feature of the market in the UK. Nor are there problems of establishing who actually owns the property in question which can occur in some other European countries.

It is not mandatory to have a lawyer do the conveyancing of property but it is a sensible idea to leave it to the professionals. Most house sales are handled in the first instance by real estate agents. As in the UK they act on behalf of the vendor and so you should bear in mind that they are not required to tell you about the negative points of a property you are considering, although they are not allowed to wilfully mislead you. Real estate agents may try to pressure you to sign a standard property-sale contract early on in the negotiations, before you have consulted your own lawyer. This is the equivalent of the exchange of contracts stage in the UK process and is the point where you are bound to purchase the property, usually subject only to finding finance. It is not advisable to sign a contract before your lawyer has checked whether the title is clear and that there are no local government requisitions on the building or land. However pressure to sign early is a particular problem at the moment because the property market is booming. If the real estate agent tries to persuade you to make an offer on a house before someone else steps in then you can get your lawyer to do the necessary title search quickly. Alternatively your lawyer can draft a special clause in property sale agreement to protect you if the title turns out to be not straightforward.

Professional Assistance

As noted above, although it is not mandatory to hire a lawyer to do the conveyancing of property, it is nevertheless a sensible precaution. In New Zealand, there is no distinction between barristers and solicitors, a lawyer may act as either, although most usually specialise in one particular role. The cost of hiring a lawyer to do your conveyancing may add $1000-$2000 to the cost of the house but it could save you from making an expensive mistake.

Finance

Mortgages with New Zealand Banks

Mortgages are the standard method of financing house purchasing in New Zealand. Until recently interest rates were low (about 7-8%) but at the time of going to print had just been hiked to 11% which may reduce the number of people taking out mortages. Banks are the main lenders. Building societies used to be separate institutions from banks but since deregulation in the 1980s they have been allowed to provide the same services and most have now converted themselves to banks. The banks have responded to the competition over providing mortgages by offering more flexible repayment terms.

Up to 80-90% of the purchase price can be borrowed, but if you borrow more than 80% the bank may require some form of mortgage insurance (see below). The maximum amount you may borrow is not always directly related to your salary but you will be expected to provide information on your monthly income as part of a hypothetical budgeting exercise and repayments would not normally be expected to be more than 30% of your income. If you are borrowing more than 60% of the purchase price, the bank may require a valuation. For some low income households, mortgage assistance is available from the Housing Corporation if they are unable to get a commercial loan but this is becoming less common.

Mortgage and Associated Costs

Your bank will charge mortgage application costs of around 1% of the value of the mortgage. The Land Transfer Registration fee is $150, although if a lawyer acts on your behalf this fee will come out of general legal disbursements. There are two types of insurance. Mortgage protection insurance is more comprehensive, it repays the mortgage in the event of your death. Mortgage risk insurance will pay the mortgage for a fixed period if you lose your regular income. There is no government benefit to help you pay the costs of a mortgage.

Repayment Conditions

Repayments are usually made on a monthly basis, but can be fortnightly. The usual term of mortgage used to be twenty- five years, but it is increasingly common for people to arrange shorter term mortgages with commensurately higher monthly repayments. Most banks will not approve of a mortgage arrangement which requires you to repay more than one third of monthly income. Interest rates can be either fixed or floating. There are three main types of mortgage: Table, Straight Line or Interest Only. In a table mortgage you pay equal monthly (or fortnightly) payments of interest and capital over the whole term of the mortgage. In a straight line mortgage, monthly payments start high because you pay fixed amounts of principal, plus the amount of interest you have accrued that month. At the beginning, there will be a lot of interest to pay off, but this decrease as the principle is repaid resulting in decreasing monthly payments. The third type is an interest only mortgage which is exactly what it sounds like — you pay a higher rate of interest on a monthly basis, which tends to add up to the same sum, more or less, as a repayment mortgage, but at the end of the whole term the original sum borrowed is effectively written off. The banks are quite flexible about changing the repayment conditions once you have entered into the mortgage, for example increasing or decreasing the size of monthly payments or switching to fortnightly payment intervals. You can even alter the type of mortgage or transfer it to another property.

Renting Property

Most immigrants rent property while they look for a house. You can arrange to rent a furnished apartment before you arrive in New Zealand through an immigration consultant or through some of the newspapers for intending migrants (*New Zealand Outlook* and *Destination New Zealand*, see Chapter Six *Employment* for subscription details). Some travel agents will also provide assistance in finding accomodation. This type of accommodation tends to be more expensive than finding a rental house yourself but has the advantage of being ready and waiting for you as soon as you get off the plane. It will certainly be cheaper than staying in a hotel while you are house hunting.

The cost of rented accommodation is quite moderate, although you can expect to pay quite a lot if you want something more than just a run of the mill three bedroomed house. Cheaper houses can be hard to find, particularly in towns with a large student population. If you are looking at the cheaper accommodation, the start of the university year, February/March, is a bad time to look because you will be competing with students looking for flats. Most privately let houses are unfurnished. Real estate agents are good places to inquire about furnished property.

Tenancy Agreements

There are two types of tenancy agreements, fixed term and periodic. Most houses are let on a periodic basis. This means that the tenancy runs until either side gives notice. In standard letting contracts, the tenant must give at least 21 days written notice that they want to end the tenancy, and the landlord 90 days notice. The landlord is allowed to give only 42 days notice if they are moving into the house themselves or if they have sold the house. In a fixed term tenancy the duration is fixed at the start of the letting period and cannot by changed except by agreement of both parties. Most tenancy agreements are sorted out between the landlord and the tenant using a standard tenancy agreement available from bookstores. A standard agreement is also available from the Tenancy Services section of the Ministry of Housing. It is not usually necessary to have a lawyer check the agreement. Tenancy Services are there to help in case of disputes between landlords and tenants and they will also give you information about your rights and responsibilities as tenants. The landlord is required to maintain the premises but tenants are responsible for any damage caused by misuse or abuse.

Rental Costs

Tenants are usually required to pay a bond or deposit to the landlord in case of damage to the property. It can be up to four weeks rent. Bonds used to be held by the landlord but as a result of disputes between tenants and landlords over the witholding of bond money, the bond is now passed on to the Bond Processing Centre, part of the Tenancy Services division of the Ministry of Housing. Tenancy Services act as arbitrators between tenants and landlords in disagreements over bonds.

Useful Phone Numbers

Tenancy Services

Auckland tel (09) 357 5450.
Hamilton tel (07) 834 1569.
Wellington tel (04) 471 6900.
Christchurch tel (03) 371 2100.
Dunedin tel (03) 479 3880.

Insurance and Wills

Wills

If at the time of your death you have a permanent place of residence in New Zealand or you are living in New Zealand for more than half the year, you are considered by New Zealand law to be a resident. This means that any property you own in New Zealand is subject to New Zealand laws if you die intestate. It makes sense therefore make a will, after you have bought a house. Property disposed under a New Zealand will is not subject to inheritance tax. If you are retaining assets in the UK, you should check with your solicitor to see that your

New Zealand will is recognised in the UK. Property in other countries is normally subject to the inheritance laws of those countries.

You do not have to use a lawyer or trustee company to draw up a will in New Zealand but it does not cost much and may save problems later. Certain procedures must be followed for a will to be valid, and it must be signed by the testator in the presence of two witnesses who cannot be beneficiaries. Trustee companies (including the Public Trust Office) will draw up a will for free , although you must name them as executors. They will claim a certain proportion of the estate as executors' fees. Alternatively you can get a will drawn up by a lawyer for a fee of around $50 — $80.

Insurance

Taking out insurance on a new property is a sensible precaution. Most mortgage lenders will probably require you insure your new house. As in the UK there are different types of cover available. Multi-risk policies (called accidental damage policies) provide blanket cover for all losses unless specifically excluded. Defined risk policies, as the name suggests, list what risks the policy provides cover for. This type of policy is less costly but accidental damage policies are probably a better option. Your house can either be insured for its indemnity value, or replacement value. The indemnity value is the depreciated or current market value of your house, excluding the value of the land. It would not cover the cost of rebuilding but you should be able to buy a similar house. The replacement value can be open-ended or fixed sum. The difference between this and indemnity value is that there is no deduction for depreciation. Open-ended replacement value means the insurer will pay the full cost of repairing or rebuilding as new. Fixed sum replacement value means that the insurer will pay up to the agreed sum. Typical premiums on an accidental damage policy range from $100-$150 per annum for an average size house with a replacement value of around $100 000. (Remember, this excludes the value of the land).

It makes sense to take out household contents insurance with the same firm as you have your house insurance with. According to *Consumer* magazine, you should get a discount for having both types of insurance with the same company and it will save arguments over who is responsible for a claim. Again you can either get a multi-risk or a defined risk policy for either indemnity or replacement value. If you have a accidental damage policy you can sometimes buy an extension to cover your possessions outside of your house, for example for personal sports equipment.

One unique feature of buying household insurance in New Zealand is earthquake damage insurance. Because New Zealand is prone to earthquakes, a special government scheme exists to provide insurance cover against them. When you take out a household insurance policy that includes cover against fire (ie a total replacement policy) you also automatically gain cover in the case of earthquake damage. In fact, it is the New Zealand Government that underwrites the risk of earthquakes because the potential cost of a major earthquake in a big city is too great for commercial insurance companies to handle. Your insurance company will charge you a compulsory disaster insurance premium which they pass on to the Earthquake Commission. The maximum amount the Commission will pay out is $100,000 or the amount for which you have insured your home, (whichever is lower) and $20,000 for personal belongings or the amount for which you have insured them. (Again they will pay out the lower amount). The premium works out at about 5c for every $100 insured, and the maximum yearly premium is $67.50. The coverage is fairly basic and does not extend, for example, to motor vehicles, boats, jewellery, works of art. Nor will the Commission pay for any indirect costs arising out of an earthquake such as, for example, the cost of having to stay in rented accommodation. It may be a good idea to take out top-up cover with an insurance company. It will cover the items noted above which EQ cover does not cover, and will also cover you for the value of your house above the $100, 000 covered by the government.

Utilities

Services such as electricity, telephones, water and sewerage are just about universal in New Zealand. Holiday cottages in some far-flung corners of the islands may not be on mainline electricity and commonly will have a septic tank rather than being on mainline sewerage, but the average family home comes provided with a similar level of services as its UK equivalent. Most government departments providing commercial services were turned into State Owned Enterprises (SOEs) in the late 80s. They were set up like commercial companies, although as the name suggests they remained publicly owned, and given commercial targets. The change in performance between the new SOEs and the old government departments was dramatic. When telecommunications were run by the Post Office, average installation time was at least six weeks. Now it seldom takes more than two days.

Electricity
Most of New Zealand's electricity supply is generated through hydro-electric schemes on New Zealand's main rivers. Hydro energy has the advantage of being cheap, clean and renewable. Most of the power is generated in the South Island on the rivers draining the mountains of the Southern Alps. It is a long standing grievance between South Islanders and the North that despite providing most of the electricity for the country, southerners pay the same. The bills come every two months. An average bill for a three-bedroom house would be around $160-200 for two months supply.

Electricity supply in New Zealand is 230 volts and 50 hertz. Most UK electrical equipment will work in New Zealand. However there is no point bringing televisions or videos as the transmission systems are different. UK video tapes will work in New Zealand video machines. Electricity sockets are three pin but a different shape from the UK so any appliances you bring will need new plugs. Appliances in New Zealand are sold with plugs attached. Electricity is supplied by local electricity companies which are publicly owned.

Gas
Household gas supply is not universally available. Natural gas is produced off the Taranaki coast and piped to most areas of the North Island. It is available as far north of Auckland as Whangarei, in Wellington and on the east coast in Gisborne, Napier and Hastings. In areas which do not have a household supply, bottled gas is available. In the South Island most gas is of the bottled variety except in Dunedin and parts of Christchurch. The local supply company can be found in the front of the *Yellow Pages* under the useful numbers section. Before they will connect your property the gas company will require you to fill in an application for the supply of gas and to pay a bond of around $100.

Water
New Zealand water is clean and quite drinkable, although it tastes better in some areas of the country than others. In Auckland and Hamilton it has an unpleasant chlorine taste. Most people seem to put up with it, though, as

evidenced by the fact that the bottled water market is not particularly large in New Zealand. Water shortages are a not normally a problem in most areas of the country, although at the time of writing Auckland is suffering a major drought as a result of historically low rainfalls. In most of the rest of the country supply is plentiful and guaranteed. In some areas local councils charge for the water supply and your supply will be on a meter, in others the cost of water connection and supply is included in your annual rates bill.

Telephone

Telecommunications technology is relatively advanced as a result of a billion dollar investment programme in the late 80s. Telecom, the state owned enterprise which took over running telecommunications from the Post Office, was sold off in 1990 to a consortium of two US phone companies and two local companies. The investment programme was part of the process of revamping the company prior to selling it. As a result New Zealand's rather antiquated phone system got a much needed overhaul. Prior to the investment programme, manual exchanges were not uncommon. At the same time the industry was deregulated to allow competitors into domestic supply and provision of phone units. Deregulation has led to improvements in customer service.

After Hong Kong, New Zealand has the highest percentage of digital connections per head of the population. It also has one of the highest densities of telephones in the world, with 432 lines per thousand of the population. The down side of privatisation is that despite being a private company, Telecom, because it owns the network, has an effective monopoly in many areas of telecommunications services. There is no industry regulator to check that the prices Telecom charges consumers are fair. Competition in the long distance calling market exists in the form of Clear Communications, and as a result toll prices have dropped. But Telecom remains the dominant player and sets the terms on which others join the market. As a result some industry commentators argue that toll calls are still too expensive.

You are obliged to hire your phone line from Telecom as they retain a monopoly on the provision of the network, but you no longer have to hire the phone itself as well. Despite this, 90% of domestic users still pay $4 a month to hire a Telecom phone. You may find it worthwhile shopping around to see what other models are available. To get your phone connected, Telecom will require proof of who you are, name, date of birth, postal address, physical address of the phone, previous address, employment history and next of kin. It takes about 48 hours to connect a new number. The connection fee is $61.88 to reconnect an existing line and an additional $33.75 for a new connection.

Local calls are free for domestic customers. The costs of toll calls are explained at the start of the phone directory. The ten charging steps depend on distance and the four call rates depend on the time of day. Peak time is 8am to noon Monday to Friday. Long distance calls are slightly cheaper on Clear Communications, the rival long distance calling company. You do not require any special equipment or numbers to use Clear. To route a call through Clear you prefix the number you are dialling with 050.

Removals

Packing up your possessions and getting them to the other side of the world is an expensive business. Most household removals are done by sea freight which takes from six weeks to three months. The likely cost of shifting the contents of an average three bedroom house is in the region of £2500-3000, not including insurance. At these sort of prices you will want to think twice about what you really want to take with you. When deciding what to bring, remember that the New Zealand electricity supply is considerably different from a European supply, and slightly different from British supply. It is not just the voltage that differs, the supply frequency or hertz rating in New Zealand is also different. Although electrical goods are more expensive in New Zealand, having your existing appliances adapted to suit New Zealand supply may work out more costly in the end and not worth the trouble. TVs and videos for example, use a different transmission system. Appliances incorporating an automatic timing device, designed to operate on a different supply frequency will require expensive modification. Your removal company should be able to advise you on these points. On the other hand, good quality household furniture, fine china and glass will generally be worth bringing with you. You can get a free hints leaflet about moving abroad by sending a SAE to The British Association of Removers (277 Grays Inn Road, London, WC1X 8SY).

Be careful when chosing a removals company. The company who were so helpful when it came to moving you from Swindon to Surrey may not be experts in international removals. Look out for companies that specialise in packing and shipping internationally. If you know of anyone who has had their household shifted, ask them about their shipping company or if you are dealing with an immigration consultancy find out which company other emmigrants have used successfully. You should check if they are members of an international removals trade association and if the association offers a payment guarantee scheme if the removals company goes bust while your goods are still in transit. Two well-known ones are the British Association of Removers, and the Association of International Removers. When it comes to comparing quotes from different companies, be sure to get quotes in writing based on the same list of goods. Freighting costs are worked out by volume either on the basis of a shared container, or a full container. In the case of the former, the quote will be based on the cubic volume of your goods, so it is essential to make sure the removals estimator knows exactly what you want to take as any last minute extras will cost more. In the case of a full container quote, the price per container is standard, but you should get a quote for the costs of any excess goods in case they do not all fit in one container. Make sure you know the type of container they are quoting you for, as volumes differ between insulated and non-insulated containers. If the quote is based on a shared container load, make sure it includes an estimate of total volume of your goods. If you have only a small amount of effects to move, it will probably be cheaper to pack them yourself. There are few important points. You should pack your possessions in stout containers, using a material such as woodwool or paper. Most removals companies will provide suitable containers. Goods packed with straw or chaff will not pass New Zealand agricultural quarantine regulations. You should label baggage carefully, inside and out. Most removals firms require about two weeks advance notice before the date you want your possessions moved.

Insurance: Insuring your possessions during the move is critical. Shipping firms will usually offer marine insurance as part of the service but you need to check the small print carefully. Make sure that the policy is all risks and that it covers any storage period either in the UK or in New Zealand. If the insurance company has offices in New Zealand, any claims are likely to be settled much more quickly than if they have no New Zealand base. There are several different types of marine insurance with varying exclusions so make sure you obtain a copy of the terms and conditions and compare them carefully. The cost of insurance is based on the value of your belongings and is usually around 2-3% of their value.

If you have a lot of fragile goods, such as china or glassware, the premium may be as high as 4-5% of value.

Useful Addresses
Abels International Movers: tel 0800-626769
Avalon Overseas International Movers; tel 0181-4516336.
Brewer and Turnball: Admail 457, Harrow, Middlesex; 0500-749126.
Chaffeys International Removers Ltd: tel 0800-318164.
Davies Turner: Overseas House, Stewarts Road, London SW8 4UG; tel 0171-6224393.
Double E Overseas Removals Ltd: Movements House, Ajax Works, Hertford Road, Barking, Essex, IG11 8BW; tel 0181-5916929.
Econopak Removals Ltd: Unit K, Abbey Wharf Industrial Estate, Kingsbridge Road, Barking, Essex IG11 0BT; tel 0181-5913434.
John Mason: 2 Mill Lane Industrial Estate, Mill Lane, Croydon, Surrey CR0 4AA; tel 0181-6671133.
Personal Shipping Services: 8 Redcross Way, London Bridge, London SE1 9HR; tel 0171-4076606.
Pickfords: tel 0800-243687.
Scotpac: Head Office Kilsyth Road, Kirkintilloch, Scotland; tel 0141-7767191.

Customs Regulations
Information regarding the importation of household, personal effects and cars into New Zealand can be found in a series of almost incomprehensible leaflets from New Zealand Customs. New Zealand embassies and high commissions should have copies available. The basic principle is that if you are coming to New Zealand to take up permanent residence, you can import your household goods and car duty free. The goods must be used and not be intended for sale or commercial use. If you are a returning resident, coming back to New Zealand after an absence of more than 21 months, your household goods qualify for the duty free concession, but in the case of cars, you can only qualify for the duty free concession on the first occasion you arrive to take up residence. You are also entitled like any visitor to New Zealand to bring in personal effects duty free.

Import Procedures
Provided that you qualify for the duty free exemption outlined above, importing your household goods ought to be straightforward. The complicating factor is that you and your possessions will most likely be travelling separately, you by plane and your worldly goods by sea, a process taking six weeks at minimum. You can either send off your goods well before your departure and hope their arrival in New Zealand coincides with yours, or send them off when you leave and manage without for your first few weeks in your new country. You should make sure that your insurance policy covers any storage time, either before shipping or delivery at the other end. If your car and possessions arrive in New Zealand before you do, you can avoid paying port storage charges by arranging for a nominee to clear them through customs for you. The Collector of Customs at the port will require evidence of your nominee's authority to act for you and evidence that you are arriving in New Zealand for the first time to take up permanent residence, plus, in the case of a car, documents proving that you have owned it for at least a year, prior to departure (see below for the documentation required). Your nominee will be required to pay a deposit equivalent to the cost of duty on the vehicle and/or goods which will be refunded in full once you arrive.

Whether you are picking up your goods yourself or have authorised a nominee, you need to provide customs with an inventory of your belongings. There are certain imports that are prohibited, most obviously drugs. Firearms require a police permit to be imported. You should be careful to thoroughly clean any garden tools or furniture, hiking boots, or anything else that may have traces of mud or dirt on it as your goods will be inspected by the Ministry of Agriculture and Fisheries before being released to you, and they may require such items to be steam cleaned or fumigated to kill off any pests or diseases. MAF inspection charges vary from $100-300 per consignment. If you have any queries about what types of goods you can import and the procedures contact the Collector of Customs at the port of destination, at the addresses below:

Auckland: Box 29; tel (09) 377 3520; fax (09) 309 2978.
Auckland International Airport: Box 73003; tel (09) 275 9059; fax (09) 275 5634.
Christchurch International Airport: Box 14086; tel (03) 358 0600; fax (03) 358 0606.
Dunedin: Private Bag 1928; tel (03) 477 9251; fax (03) 477 6773.
Invercargill: Box 840; tel (03) 218 7329; fax (03) 218 7328.
Napier: Box 440; tel (06) 835 5799; fax (06) 835 1298.
Nelson: Box 66; tel (03) 548 1484; fax (03) 546 9381.
New Plymouth: Box 136; tel (06) 758 5721; fax (06) 758 1441.
Tauranga: Box 5014, Mt Maunganui; tel (07) 575 9699; fax (07) 575 0522.
Timaru: Box 64; tel (03) 68 9317; fax (03) 688 4668.
Wellington: Box 11746; tel (04) 801 5007; fax (04) 384 2232.
Whangarei: Box 873; tel (09) 438 2400; fax (09) 438 2225.

Importing Pets

Getting your pets to New Zealand is going to cost as much as getting yourself there, and require every bit as much paperwork, and a lot more vaccinations. Requirements for importing animals into New Zealand are extremely stringent. However, if you fulfil all the pre-flight veterinary requirements, your animals will be able to go home with you when they arrive in New Zealand. However, they are subject to a quarantine period of thirty days at their owner's home. There are a number of firms which specialise in the air-freighting of pets (for names and addresses see below). As this involves organising an IATA approved air travel container which has to be sealed by a vet, as well as an examination immediately prior to departure, it is probably best to hand over your pets to the professionals. You will need to contact a firm at least six weeks before you depart as they will apply for an import permit from New Zealand on your behalf, and it takes at least six weeks for one to be issued and sent over. You will need to organise some of the veterinary procedures yourself as some vaccinations have to be done at least a month prior to departure, and there are a number of tests which have to be done and the results must travel with the animals. Most firms will suggest that you leave the animals with them for the night prior to departure. In most cases they will collect the pet from anywhere in the UK. The cost of all of the above is likely to be around £400 for a cat and £900 for a dog.

Useful Addresses

Airpets Oceanic: Willowslea Farm Kennels, Spout Lane North, Stanwell Moor, Staines, Middlesex, TW19 6BW; tel 01753-685 571.
Ladyhaye Livestock Shipping: Hare Lane, Blindley Heath, Lingfield, Surrey RH7 6JB; tel 01342-832161; fax 01342-834778.
Par Air Livestock Shipping Services: Stanway, Colchester, Essex; tel 01206-330332.
Pet Emigration: 43 London Road, Brentwood, Essex, CM14 4NN; tel 01277-2311611.

Pinehawk Livestock Shippers: Church Road, Carlton, Newmarket, Suffolk, CB8 9LA; tel 01223-290249.
Transpet: 160 Chingford Mount Road London E4 9BS; tel 0181-529 0979.
Worldwide Animal Travel: 43 London Road, Brentwood, Essex CM14 4NN; tel & fax 01277-231611 & 0181-552 5592.

Importing a Vehicle

If you are considering importing your car, there are a number of firms who specialise in organising the sea freighting of motor vehicles. You will obviously want to consider whether the original value of the car plus the cost of freight, port handling costs and insurance is lower than the replacement cost of the car in New Zealand. In general, European cars cost more to replace in New Zealand than the their original value plus shipping costs, assuming the vehicle qualifies for duty free entry (see below for conditions). Japanese and Asian cars are cheaper because of the commercial importation of second hand vehicles from Japan. One source of information on second-hand car prices in New Zealand is the classified section of newspapers. You can order New Zealand motor trade magazines from *Destination New Zealand* and *New Zealand Outlook*. Some car shipping companies will also provide lists of recent New Zealand prices for common models of car.

If you are emigrating to New Zealand for the first time, you can import your car into New Zealand free of duty provided you satisfy Customs that you are importing the vehicle for your own use, that you have owned it for at least a year prior to your departure, and that you arriving in New Zealand to take up permanent residence for the first time. You will be required to sign a deed of covenant agreeing that if you sell the car or boat within two years of importing it, you will be retrospectively liable for the duty and sales tax (GST). If your car does not qualify for duty-free entry, duty is levied at 20% of purchase price for UK made vehicles, and 30% of purchase price for other foreign cars, less depreciation. The exchange rate used in calculating the New Zealand dollar value of your car will be based on the current exchange rate at the time you clear your vehicle. The costs of shipping an average size car are between £1200-£1400 depending on the size of the car and which port in New Zealand your car is being shipped to. It usually takes about six weeks. Some companies offer a cheaper option where the vehicle is not shipped in a container, but the risks of damage or theft in transit are higher. You should arrange insurance for your vehicle, whichever option you choose. Average premiums are around £15-£20 per £1000 insured value, which should be calculated on the New Zealand value of the car. Most companies advise that you do not pack personal belongings in the car for the journey. There is a risk of pilferage particularly if the car is not containerised during the journey and the contents of the car will have to be declared to customs by the shipping company or you will risk a fine.

Procedures for clearing your car through customs in New Zealand are as follows. You will need to provide documentary evidence to the collector of customs that the car is yours and if you are applying for a duty free entry, that you have owned it for at least one year prior to importing it, in the form of a dated receipt of purchase showing the date delivery was taken, registration papers, and evidence of the date on which you gave up the vehicle for shipping to New Zealand. Next the vehicle will be inspected by the Ministry of Agriculture and Fisheries (MAF). All used vehicles must be steam cleaned before MAF will pass them. You can have your car commercially steam cleaned before shipping but remember to keep the receipt to show to MAF in New Zealand. Some shipping companies will steam clean your car as part of the service. MAF's object is to prevent any pests and diseases which could endanger livestock being brought in to the country and their standards therefore are stringent. We know of one recent immigrant who was required by MAF to have his car steam-cleaned a second time because the shipping company's clean had not removed mud from under the wheel arches. Your car will be required to comply with New Zealand safety regulations, some of which differ from European standards. Your vehicle must have front and rear seatbelts, and a high mounted rear stop light. It is a good idea to have these fitted before you leave because you will not be able to drive the car in New Zealand until it complies with local safety standards. Left hand drive vehicles require special import permission. Apply to the *Land Transport Safety Authority:* (Box 27459, Wellington; tel 04- 382 8300). You cannot drive the car legally until it has a warrant of fitness and is registered, so you will need to arrange for it to be transported from the port to the nearest vehicle inspection test centre to obtain a vehicle inspection certificate. These used to be called warrants of fitness, and in some places testing centres still advertise them as warrants. Once it has passed its warrant, you take the certificate to a post office, along with the ownership documents and the importation documents, and obtain a registration certificate, sticker and number plates. All of this is likely to take a couple of days and cost from $450-$600 depending on whether you need to have the vehicle cleaned.

Useful addresses include *Interconti Forwarding Ltd:* PO Box 1, Landmark, Main Road, Salcombe, Devon, TQ8 8LB; tel 01548-843191 and *Karman Shipping Services:* tel 0181-8588268. In addition, a number of shipping companies will also organise freighting your car. See Personal Shipping, Anglo Shipping, Econopak, and Double E, listed under Removals firms above.

Buying a Car

Having found out the cost of importing your car to New Zealand you may decide that the best option is to leave it behind. New cars are are comparatively expensive but the second hand market in Japanese and Asian cars is competitive. European cars tend to be quite pricey and are can be difficult to get parts for. Familiar models may go under slightly different names in New Zealand. There is no domestically owned brand, but most cars are locally assembled. Buying second hand is a viable option. Cars have to be sold warranted as road worthy so you have some minimum level of protection. There are a number of companies offering pre-purchase checks including the AA who will check a car without charge if you are a member. If you want to organise car hire before you arrive, there are agencies who will arrange your rental for you with a New Zealand company. (Kiwi Kar Rentals, UK agent for McDonalds car hire; tel 01633-400997; fax 01633-400060).

Insurance

You are not legally required to get insurance in New Zealand, however it is sensible to get at least third party coverage. If you are involved in an accident and cause harm to another driver, you will not be personally liable for the injuries you do to them because of the no-faults compensation for personal injury provided by the Government through the Accident Compensation Corporation (See Chapter Four-*Daily Life*). But if you write off their car and you have no insurance then, like anywhere else in the world, you will be paying the bill. The premiums for full insurance coverage vary according to your age (under 25s pay a lot more), sex (some firms offer females a discount because they are statistically less likely to have accidents) and driving history. A no claims record entitles you to discounted premiums. You should bring evidence of your claims record with you because a claim free UK or European insurance record will qualify you for the bonus. Some firms may not be prepared to insure you until you have a New Zealand drivers licence. See Chapter Four *Daily Life* for requirements for getting a New Zealand drivers licence.

Daily Life

One of the most disconcerting aspects of emigrating to a country where the locals speak the same language is that there is a tendency to underestimate the cultural differences. New Zealand, for all its superficial reminders of England, is a foreign country. Some of the streets may be named after English counties, the towns after British soldiers, but the daily lives of New Zealanders are very different from the lives of people in the UK. It is obviously not possible to explain all the peculiarities of life in New Zealand in one short chapter and individuals are unlikely in any case to experience any major form of culture shock. This chapter therefore aims to prepare you for some of the main, every day differences between New Zealand and the UK.

The Languages

New Zealanders speak their own distinctive version of English. Newcomers may be forgiven for thinking that New Zealanders use one vowel sound, although locals do not seem to have any problems distinguishing between words. 'New Zealand' as pronounced by the locals sounds like 'Nu Zilind'. As well as the subtle distinctions between vowel sounds, further problems for the newcomer arise from the rapid pace at which New Zealanders speak. Probably more of an obstacle than the accent to understanding New Zealanders is the use of uniquely Kiwi expressions. A 'dairy' is a corner store (open till late and selling most of the essentials), a 'crib' in the South Island or 'bach' in the North is a holiday home on the coast or beside a lake. Some of the slang is similar to Australian, for example 'pommy' for an English person, 'bush' for forest, 'shout' for buying a round in a pub. A number of Maori expressions have become part of everyday usage, for example *Pakeha* for a person of European descent.

Maori is the other official language although it is not in everyday use in most regions. Official signs are bilingual as are Government documents. The number of Maori speakers is growing and there is a active campaign to preserve the language (in Maori *Te Reo*). Pronunciation of Maori is not difficult to learn even if at first glance some to the place names seem impossibly complex. It is a good skill to master though, as correct pronunciation of Maori is a sign of courtesy and also indicates that as a newcomer, you are prepared to integrate into the local community.

There are five vowel sounds each of which may be short or long:

short a:	like u in 'but'	long a:	like a in 'father'
short e:	like e in 'pet'	long e:	like ai in 'fairy'
short i:	like i in 'pit'	long i	like ee in 'meet'
short o:	like or in 'port'	long o	like ore in 'pore'
short u	like u in 'put'	long u	like oo in 'moon'

Diphthongs (double vowel sounds) retain the sound of the second vowel clearly. Consonants are as in English with the following exceptions:

wh   is pronounced f
ng   is like ng in the middle of 'singer', ie the g is never hard
r   is slightly rolled

Word stress is rather too complicated to reduce to a few simple rules here and you would do better to learn by listening to a Maori speaker. It is worth noting that many Pakeha pronounce Maori words, particularly common place names, embarrassingly badly. Do not follow their example. In recent years radio and TV announcers have been learning to pronounce Maori correctly and in general their pronunciation is a good guide.

Schools and Education

The New Zealand education system is dominated by the state sector which educates 95% of the population. The Ministry of Education spends $4.8 billion yearly on education, nearly 16% of the national budget. Schooling is compulsory from ages five through to 15. The school year has three terms, beginning in early February and running through to December with holidays in May and August. Four term school years are being trialled at some state schools. Schooling is largely free although schools are beginning to charge 'optional' fees to cover extra equipment and facilities.

There is no tradition of streaming into academic and not-so-academic schools, so while the average standard of education at a New Zealand high school is probably higher than at its equivalent, the British comprehensive school, the academic standards achieved by the brightest pupils are not as advanced. Generally New Zealand students do well in international tests, particularly in reading comprehension. Their mathematics skills compare less favourably particularly with the standards achieved by Japanese and other Asian students. Most schools have good cultural, academic and sporting facilities. Even inner city schools have extensive playing fields. There is a strong tradition of team sports, (not just rugby although soccer used to be banned at some particularly strong rugby schools lest the boys be lured away from chasing the oval ball to 'inferior' versions of football) and many state schools offer outdoor activity programmes where pupils learn abseiling, canoeing, and go hiking in New Zealand's national parks.

Schools are becoming ethnically more diverse particularly in Auckland with its substantial Polynesian population. Increasingly the new immigrants are Asian. As a result foreign language instruction which used to be predominantly in French and German is being replaced by Japanese and other Asian languages, reflecting the change in focus in New Zealand's trade from Europe to the Pacific rim. The language of instruction, except in a few Maori language immersion schools, remains English.

In general New Zealand state schools are safe and well disciplined learning environments. Nevertheless, some parents choose alternatives to the state system for their children. Most private schools have religious links, either to Anglican or Catholic churches. Many Anglican schools offer a single-sex, English style boarding education and a traditional approach to learning and discipline. They manage to be more English than their models or perhaps just a few decades out of date as they are both stricter and more spartan than independent schools in the UK. Boarding fees vary from $3500-$5500 per term. A number of state schools also offer boarding facilties. Usually these are rural schools whose students come from a widely dispersed population so boarding is the only practical way of overcoming the distance from home to school. Not all state boarding schools are in the country. Nelson College and Christchurch Boys are city schools with a long tradition of providing a state boarding school education. As state schools their boarding fees tend to be cheaper than the private sector.

The Structure of the Education System

Preschool: This is divided into playcentres whch tend to be run by volunteer groups of parents, and cater for children from a young age kindergartens, usually for the over twos, and private crèches catering for anything that walks, waddles or wees. Kindergartens are usually free while playcentres may charge a nominal sum. Crèches on the other hand can be quite expensive, although the government subsidises the running costs of all registered childcare centres with qualified staff. More than 90% of four-year-olds are in some kind of preschool programme. A growing number of children, Pakeha and Maori, attend *Kohanga Reo* or Maori language nests where they learn *taha maori* (Maori language and culture).

Primary: Primary schools cater for children aged five to ten years old. The curriculum includes reading, writing, science, mathematics, and social studies. Teaching standards are high. The teaching of reading skills is particularly strong and New Zealand reading programmes are being copied in British and North American schools.

Intermediate: Most children spend two years at intermediate school between primary and high school. Some primary schools however, are beginning to keep their senior students for a further two years as the interlude is thought to be disruptive rather than helpful. In country regions, 'area' schools have always included years six and seven (usually called forms one and two). At intermediate school pupils begin studying foreign languages (traditionally French, now increasingly Maori), and move between specialist teachers rather than being taught by one person for every subject.

Secondary: Secondary education begins in the eighth year of school, at around age 13. In pre-recession New Zealand when jobs were easy to find it was quite common for students to leave school as soon as it was legal at age 15, but retention rates have improved as the economy has declined. The core curriculum consists of English, Maths, General Science, Music, Arts and Craft, Social Studies and Physical Education, all of which are compulsory for the first two years. Students sit national examinations, School certificate at the end of their fifth form year (the third year of secondary education) and University Bursary at the end of their final year.

Further Education

Further education is divided into three areas, universities, polytechnics and colleges of education (teacher training colleges).

Universities: New Zealand universities offer degree programmes in a similar range of subjects to British universities. Most bachelor degrees are three year courses with an option of taking a four year honours programme. There are seven universities, located in the four main cities and three smaller regional towns. Standards are uniform, none of the seven being particularly older or more established, Auckland's size probably makes it the leader in more fields but 20,000 plus students on a crowded inner city campus has its downside as well. Teaching in arts subjects is mostly done in large lecture streams with weekly tutorials of about a dozen students. Admission procedures vary depending on the institution and the course. Some high demand courses such as medicine, law and business administration have restricted entry usually based on University Bursary results. Other courses are open to anyone who meets the general university entrance requirement.

Polytechnics: As the name suggests New Zealand polytechnics remain by and large the specialists in technical and applied subjects. There is less cross over with universities in subject area, although some programmes (for example business studies and accounting) can be studied either in a polytechnic for a certificate or diploma or in a longer degree programme at university. The majority of polytechnic students however either study part-time while working or are on short full-time courses.

Student Finances: Tuition fees for New Zealand students, whch used to be free, now cost between NZ $2000-$10,000 a year, depending on the course and the institution. Reductions are available for students from low income families. The possibility of fees being doubled in the next few years has been recently mooted by a task force, looking into tertiary education. Students from families whose annual income is less than $27,800 are eligible for the means tested student maintenance grants, called student allowances. Students 25 and over are not subject to the family means test. Those who do not qualify for student allowances may borrow money through the government run students loans scheme to pay for maintenance and tuition.

Foreigners at New Zealand Universities

Foreign students (that is, non-New Zealand residents) get hit even harder in the wallet than New Zealand students. Fees vary across courses and by university, from $9500 per annum for an arts or humanities course, to $18,000-25,000 for medicine or dentistry.For information on studying at New Zealand universities or polytechnics as a foreign student, contact the Trade Development Board at the New Zealand High Commission, (2nd Floor, New Zealand House; tel 0171-973 0380).

International Schools

There are no schools in New Zealand specifically set up for international students. However some schools offer senior students preparation for International Baccalaureate which is an entrance qualification for most European universities. To find out more about this contact the Trade Development Board (see address above).

Useful Addresses

Schools offering the International Baccalaureate:

Scots College: PO Box 15 064, Wellington 6030; tel (04) 388 7177 (Boys only, private boarding and day school).
Waitaki Girls College: Trent Street, Box 42 Oamaru; tel (03) 434-8429 (Girls only, state boarding and day school).

Media and Communications

Newspapers

New Zealanders read as many newspapers as the British do and a lot more than do North Americans. Unfortunately the standard of the newspapers does not justify this dedication to newsprint. Regional papers were established last century when provincial government was more powerful than national government and communication networks between the scattered European settlements were poor. These regional papers have all survived and as a result New Zealand has a high number of daily newspapers, but there is no truly national paper. The so-called *New Zealand Herald* is not widely circulated in the South Island. Most of the major papers are of the size and quality of a large provincial paper and betray their provincial loyalties by their selection of news stories. There is only one tabloid style newspaper, *The Truth* which appears weekly and does not approach the shock, horror, sheer awful appeal of its British counterparts.

Business news is provided by the *National Business Review*, also a weekly which covers politics and international news as well. A growing trend is giveaway suburban newspapers.

Specialist news agents in the main city stock overseas newspapers but they are expensive and usually arrive some days late, particularly European editions. Anyone wishing to keep up with the the news from the UK can do so through the *International Express*, a weekly digest of the London Daily and Sunday Expresses widely available in Australasia. In New Zealand it is obtainable from Network Distributors Ltd. (tel 09-443 0245; fax 09 443 0249) and is printed in Auckland. Another alternative for those truly homesick of news from home are the overseas editions of *The Telegraph* or *The Guardian*. These are weekly editions of the major news stories from these and other papers, available either from newsagents or on subscription.

Main Newspapers

The New Zealand Herald: Conservative in tone and appearance. Based in Auckland and news content reflects this, despite its name. Circulation 248,000.

The Dominion: Political focus as might be expected a newspaper based in the capital city. Used to be a liberal, unpartisan scrutineer of government, has become a convert to neo-liberal economic dogma. Circulation 73,000.

The Evening Post: Also Wellington based, more regional news than *The Dominion*, suprisingly good comment and arts content. Circulation 77,000.

The Christchurch Press: Distributed throughout top half of South Island. Good coverage of Canterbury region news, less so of national and international stories. Circulation 99,000.

The Otago Daily Times: Dunedin based. Circulation 52,000.

Magazines

Over 2,300 magazines are available in New Zealand on a regular basis, but only about 60 of these are New Zealand titles. The others include international news magazines such as *Time, The Economist,* and *Newsweek.* Local political comment is provided by the *New Zealand Listener* and the *Political Review.* The *Listener* also carries TV and radio listings, as does the *TV Guide,* which has the biggest circulation of any New Zealand magazine. Next biggest is the *New Zealand Womens Weekly,* a venerable survivor found in every doctor's surgery. Its heyday may be over now that putting the British royals on the cover attracts more indifference than sales. *More* magazine is an upmarket women's magazine which has suprisingly good articles and a no-nonsense practical feminist line. Less mainstream feminist comment can be found in *Broadsheet.* A number of glossy lifestyle magazines have sprung up in the last decade. Of particular note is *Metro,* the Auckland city magazine. Reading *Metro* will help the newcomer understand why the rest of the country can't stand Auckland. Metro's stablemate aimed at readers in the rest of the country is *North and South.* Both are liberal on political issues, conservative on social welfare issues and support the economic liberalisation programme launched by the government in the 1980s. *New Zealand Cuisine* is dedicated to fine food and wine. There are a surprising number of literary magazines, apparently thriving, despite small circulations. The most well established of these is the Christchurch based *Landfall.* Magazines exist for just about every sporting pursuit. Also popular are do-it-yourself and home improvement magazines.

Television

There are three channels available nationally, TV1 and TV2 which are publicly owned and run, funded through TV licence fees, and TV3 which is privately run. Both the public channels have advertising. There are a few regional TV channels, and TAB channel, which broadcasts horse-racing. Cable TV is in its infancy, and is currently available on a trial on the Kapiti Coast north of Wellington, and in two Auckland suburbs. Satellite TV is represented by SKY, another Rupert Murdoch subsidiary, offering three channels; movies, sports and news. The news channel includes the BBC and CNN and may be best option for catching up with the world news as local television news is sadly lacking in its international coverage. New Zealand TV news has unfortunately opted for a poor imitation of American local news programmes. The graphics and visual effects are sophisticated, but the news analysis is not. Unsurprisingly, when the average item does not exceed a minute and half in length, in-depth analysis of stories is rare. TVNZ and TV3 provide a mixed diet of the best of the BBC, popular American sit-coms and home grown soaps.

Radio

Radio New Zealand runs a network of local stations which are funded through advertising revenue and offer a mixed diet of middle of the road popular music, talk back, news and sports. It also runs two non-commercial nationally broadcast stations, the National Programme and Concert FM which are funded through the TV licence fees. The National Programme is broadly equivalent to the UK's Radio 4. Its morning news show, *Morning Report*, is an excellent source of news and comment on political and economic issues. The Concert programme broadcasts classical music and information programmes. It has a commercial rival, Fine Music Radio which takes its programmes, voiceover included, from a classical station in the States. There is a large local private radio sector: 46 AM and 84 FM commercial stations, including student radio, Maori language radio and community access radio. The BBC World Service is broadcast by an Auckland-based private radio station with frequencies in Auckland and Wellington. It plans to extend its coverage into other main centres in the near future.

Post

Postal services are handled by New Zealand Post which has a monopoly on letter delivery. Parcel delivery is also provided by private courier firms. Domestic delivery is once daily, usually mid-morning. There is a network of more than 1200 post offices throughout the country, the majority of which are postal agencies which provide other services as well. There are two classes of mail, Fast Post which promises next day delivery anywhere in the country and ordinary post. The standard cost of a fast post letter is 80c and for an ordinary rate letter, 45c.

Telephones

For information about having a telephone installed in your house, see Chapter Three, *Setting Up Home.* New Zealand Telecom has been overhauling the phone system since 1990, introducing standard seven digit numbers throughout the country. Most of the chaos caused by the change is nowover, although the New

Zealand Number Update Desk is still running and can be contacted on 0155. The international code for New Zealand is 64. There are five area codes for the different regions of the country, 09 for Auckland and northwards, 07 for the Waikato and central North Island area, 06 for the southern half of the North Island, 04 for the Wellington region, and 03 for the South Island. As in the UK, free phone numbers start with 0800. Phone boxes are well distributed but most are now card phones which can be irritating if you donUt have a card handy. They come in $5, $10, $20, or $50 denominations and can be bought from corner stores and Post Offices. Local calls cost 20c per minute. Coin phones still exist as do some of the original model payphones which have a button marked A on the front which you press when the call is connected. In the cities, card and coin phones can usually be found cohabiting, and in some places, credit card phones as well.

Cars and Motoring

Compared with European motorways, New Zealand's highway system is uncongested, although per head of population New Zealanders own as many cars as the Italians or the Swiss and slightly more than the British. Older models are a common sight, a hang-over from the days when new cars were very expensive so people drove their old car for a long time. Most of the older cars are British or American makes. Modern cars tend to be Japanese rather than European. Because of the absence of heavy traffic there is not much of a network of multi-lane motorways. Most state highways are single carriageway and there are no tolls. Multi-lane motorways carry traffic into and out of the four main cities and through parts of Auckland and Wellington. Congestion on these stretches is occasionally a problem, but nothing compared to traffic jams in European or North American cities.

Driving outside the main cities is usually a pleasant experience. The roads are uncluttered and the scenery superb. The weather is often more of an obstacle to getting to your destination than other drivers. Flooding or heavy snow falls sometimes block main routes, particularly the roads through the volcanic plateau in the central North Island and the cross alpine routes in South Island. There are signs at the start of tricky stretches of road indicating which routes are open. In general the signs indicating distances and routes on the highway system are less frequent than in Europe (Although to be fair there is usually only one main route to any destination). Junctions are not as well designed, roundabouts are less common and tend to be poorly signposted.

New Zealand drivers have a reputation for being fast and rather aggressive. It is easy to see why you might be tempted to drive well over the speed limit when there is no other traffic in sight, let alone any sign of the law. City drivers are less considerate than in Europe. It is rare for people to give way to allow cars from side roads to join the main stream of traffic, again perhaps because there are usually fewer congestion problems. Nor do New Zealand drivers willingly move over into the slow lane to let faster traffic past. Unfortunately driving in New Zealand is not very safe. It has one of the worst accident records per head of population in the developed world. The government is trying to improve the statistics by targeting the worst offending group, namely young men who drink and drive, so be aware that the blood alcohol limits are strictly enforced.

Driving Regulations

The maximum speed on highways and motorways is 100 km and in built up areas 50 km. Speed cameras are being introduced at various places in cities and on country roads. New Zealanders drive on the left hand side of the road, and the rules of the road are similar to British driving regulations. One difference is that at cross roads traffic turning left must give way to on-coming vehicles turning right. The sequence of the traffic lights is different from Britain, the lights change straight from red to green, then amber followed by red again. Standard international road signs are being introduced. One sign which may be unfamiliar is LSZ enclosed by a red circle, indicating a limited speed zone in which the motorist should slow down to allow for children or other traffic. This is frequently used when state highways pass through small towns.

As noted above, drink-driving regulations are strictly enforced. The limit is the same as in Britain, 80 mls per 100 mls of blood or less than two pints of beer for the average adult male. Drivers under twenty years old have a lower limit: 30 mls per 100 mls of blood. Police officers are able to stop motorists at random and breath test them. The maximum penalty is a $1500 fine and six months in prison. Repeated offenders can lose their licence. Seat belts must be worn in the front of cars and in the back if they are fitted. Helmets are compulsory for motor cyclists and bicycle riders.

Breakdowns and Accidents

Over 600 people died on New Zealand roads in 1993, nearly twice the number per 100,000 people as in Britain. One of the reasons may be that head on collisions which are more likely to lead to fatalities occur more frequently as New Zealand highways generally do not have a median strip. Another factor, particularly in accidents involving young people, is alcohol. The Government has recently made the driving test much more stringent and introduced restricted licences for the under 20s in an effort to improve road safety.

The New Zealand Automobile Association (POB 1794, Wellington; tel 04-783 739) runs a similar service to its operation in the UK and can be called at any time to assist with mechanical difficulties or breakdowns. Members of the UK AA and RAC have reciprocal rights to use AA services. It costs around $50 per year to join. If you are involved in an accident, you must contact the police. (The emergency number is 111) Unfortunately New Zealand highways are often not well provided with call boxes or emergency telephones.

Driving Licence

A British or International Drivers Licence is valid for 12 months after arrival in New Zealand. At the end of this period visitors must apply for a New Zealand licence which involves sitting a written and oral test, and then an interview with a police officer to obtain exemption from taking the practical test. Drivers under the age of twenty are eligible only for a restricted licence: they are not allowed to drive after dark and are subject to stricter blood alcohol limits.

Car Registration

Cars must be registered with the Post Office and have a current Vehicle Inspection Certificate (VIC). As of 1994 they must also have a Vehicle Identification Number (VIN), a new identification scheme to try and cut down on vehicle theft. At the time of writing, the cost of re-registering an ordinary motorcar was around $195. First time registrations cost about $150 more including the cost of licence plates. They can be registered at any Post Office shop. Re-registration forms are sent out automatically. Most garages offer VIC testing (Warrants of Fitness). It costs about $20. New cars need a warrant every year for the first six years and then six monthly after that.

Transport

Air

As the major population centres are many miles apart, getting between cities by road or rail is time consuming. Air travel is a popular alternative. There are two main internal airlines. Until recently the state owned airline, Air New Zealand had a monopoly on internal air travel. The deregulation of domestic aviation brought one major competitor, the Australian airline Ansett. The two airlines operate out of separate terminals on the same sites in the main cities. The chief benefit from competition was to persuade Air New Zealand to spruce up its terminals which were basic to say the least: Wellington airport was originally a World War Two air hanger, with an appropriately utilitarian atmosphere.

Fare structures between the two airlines are similar. Ansett offers more discounts, while Air New Zealand offers a larger network, incorporating a number of smaller airlines, Eagle Air in the North Islands, Nelson Air, which covers the top of the South Island, and Mount Cook airlines (mostly tourist routes). A variety of discounted fares are available if you book ahead. Air New Zealand offers no frills flights, called City Savers on the main routes. There are also special deals on late night flights or flights during off peak hours. It is worth ringing Air New Zealand or Ansett to find out about what is available. Holders of the International Student Identity Card, can get a 50% discount on standby travel. On the major routes this may entail waiting around in the airport until a flight has spare capacity, but it rarely involves more than a couple of hours delay unless it is a particularly busy period like the start of the school holidays.

If you are visiting New Zealand before deciding whether to migrate permanently, you could look at purchasing a discount air pass. Air New Zealand offers a three sector pass for $435 or an eight sector pass for $1200 which must be purchased before you depart for New Zealand. (The full economy fare per sector is around $250 so the passes offer substantial discounts) Ansett New Zealand offers a similar air pass as does Mt Cook airlines, both of which can be purchased once you arrive.

Trains

The 'rain network is not exactly comprehensive. There are eight train routes around the country and only a few trains to most major destinations each day. Trains cost about the same as the equivalent journey by bus, although there are some faster services which are more expensive. Many of the routes are chiefly designed with tourists in mind, for example the transalpine express from Christchurch to Greymouth, across the Southern Alps. Reservations are advisable during the summer on popular tourist routes. The national reservations number is NZ Rail 0800 802 802.

Coaches

Bus services (usually called coaches) between major cities provide a much more frequent service than the trains. There are three main companies, Newmans, Mt Cook, and InterCity. Mt Cook operates only in the South Island, and Newmans only in the North. InterCity is a subsidiary of NZ Rail. The national reservations numbers are Mt Cook 0800-800737, Newmans 0800-733500, and InterCity 03-3799020.

City Transport

Public transport in most of the major cities does not provide a sufficiently comprehensive network to replace the private car as the major method of getting to work. Because urban population densities are lower than in Europe this does not yet produce enormous pollution and congestion problems. However inner city parking is expensive. Commuter rail networks in Auckland and Wellington replace the car for a small percentage of the working population.

Taxis. Taxis in New Zealand can be found at taxi stands or ordered by phone. They do not drive around waiting to be hired, so there is no point trying to flag one down even if it looks empty. The fares are all metered so you do not need to agree a price with the driver before setting off. In many cities minivans run a taxi service from the airport into any destination in the central city. This is almost always a cheaper option than a taxi, although slightly less convenient as you may not be the first person to be dropped off. They are also often referred to as airport shuttles.

The Inter-island Ferry

Crossing the Cook Strait which separates the North and South Islands takes about three hours. At present there is only one ferry line, the Interisland line, owned by New Zealand Railways. The Interisland line may be about to face some competition from a proposed catamaran service, and NZ Rail is apparently also investigating a high speed ferry service. In the meantime there are four to five ferry crossings a day, with a roll on, roll off service for cars. The standard cost for a small family car is $114 and off peak (non-holiday periods) $92. The fare for foot passengers is $38 standard, and $30 off peak. The North Island departure point is Aotea Quay in Wellington, and in the South Island, Picton. The ferries have recently been refurbished and include such amenities as movie theatres, bars and quite adequate cafeterias. If it is a bad crossing though, probably the last thing on your mind will be food. The Cook Strait is a particularly rough stretch of water.

Useful Addresses

Air New Zealand: Private Bag, Auckland; tel (09) 3797515; fax (09) 388 0575.
Ansett New Zealand: PO Box 4168, Auckland; tel (09) 3096235; fax (09) 309 6434.
InterCity Coachlines: CPO Box 3625, Auckland; tel (09) 3584085; fax (09) 366 4406.
Mount Cook Line: Airline/Landline, PO Box 4644, Christchurch; tel (reservations) 0800-800287
Newmans Route Services: PO Box 90-821, Auckland.
New Zealand Rail Ltd: Private Bag, Wellington, tel (reservations) 0800-802 802.
New Zealand Tourism Board: New Zealand House, Haymarket, London 2W1Y 4TQ; tel 0171-973 0360.
The Interislander: NZ Rail Ltd, Private Bag, Wellington; tel (reservations) 0800-658999; fax (04) 498 3721.

Banks and Finance

New Zealand's banking system is amongst the most advanced in the world and is very convenient to use. Many banks either have or are moving towards computer systems which will allow the overnight clearance of cheques. A visit to the bank no longer need involve any paperwork as most transactions are done electronically using money cards with PINs to access accounts. Outside banking hours which are Monday to Friday, 8.30 am to 4.30 pm, you can use automatic tellers (cash machines) to transfer money between accounts, and order statements or cheque books. Your money card (known as an ATM card (automatic teller machine card) also functions as a direct debit card for EFT-POS transactions. EFT-POS stands for Electronic Fund Transfer at the Point Of Sale. It is the equivalent of Switch in the UK. Most major retailers offer the EFT-POS service. Cheques are still a common method of payment despite the advances in electronic banking. One major difference between New Zealand and the UK is that New Zealand banks do not issue cheque guarantee cards. The onus is on the receiver of the cheque to make sure it is not fraudulent. Retailers usually require ID for chques in the form of a credit card and often take your name and address when you pay by cheque. Credit cards are popular in New Zealand, Mastercard and Visa being the most widely used. Most bills are paid through standing orders (called direct credit) and your wages will probably likewise be paid into your account directly.

Bank Accounts

Most people open an account with one of the four large banks which dominate retail banking: the Bank of New Zealand, Westpac Banking Corporation, the Australia New Zealand Banking Group (ANZ) and the National Bank of New Zealand. Two other banking groups are Countrywide, an amalgamation of former building societies and Trustbank, which formerly operated as local district trusts which have now amalgamated. Branches of foreign banks also operate but if you stick to one of the big four you have access to an extensive network of banking outlets which has developed as result of New Zealand's scattered population.

Some of these banks have branches in the UK and one option to consider is opening an account with them before you leave for New Zealand. There is a generally a fee for this service and a minimum deposit requirement. Contact the National Australia bank for further details. (6 Tokenhouse Yard EC2R 7AJ; tel 0171-606 8070). One advantage of opening an account before you arrive in New Zealand is that it solves the problem of transferring money: you simply arrange for a telexed transfer to your new account. The alternatives to telexing money directly to a New Zealand bank account are outlined in the section on *International Money Transfers* below. Opening an account once you arrive in New Zealand does not take long, but there are a few hitches for the new arrival. Some banks require proof of a regular income before allowing you to open a cheque account, even if you have deposited money with them. You should be issued immediately with an ATM card, which will allow you to withdraw money from a bank or an automatic teller machine. To facilitate opening an account in New Zealand, it is a good idea to bring a letter of introduction from your UK bank.

Investment Advice: Expatriates who are not making a permanent move like to have advice on employee benefits, retirement income funding and personal investments and savings provided on an international basis. Companies specialising in these money related matters include Godwins International Services. (Godwins Ltd., Briarcliff House, Kingsmead, Farnborough, Hampshire GU14 7TE; tel 01252-521701; 01252-375721).

International Money Transfers

There are no foreign exchange controls over shifting money out of New Zealand. Getting money to New Zealand is most quickly achieved through a money wire or a telegraphic transfer. You can either do this through a specialist money-wiring company such as American Express or Western Union, or through the banks. The specialist companies cost more but the process is much faster, less than 15 minutes. Through the banks it usually takes a couple of days but the cost is about half the amount charged by wiring companies.

Money

New Zealand has a decimal money system using dollars as the monetary unit, each dollar consisting of 100 cents. The abbreviation for the dollar is $ and c for cents which stand after the numbers. At the time of going to press the exchange rate was £1$2.56.

Taxation

The taxation system was extensively reformed as part of the economic liberalisation in the 1980s. At one stage under the previous Labour government it was proposed that a single rate of tax apply to everyone regardless of income. This suggestion was vetoed, however the tax system was made less progressive by the lowering of top rates of taxation and the reduction in the number of income brackets. A goods and services tax was introduced, called GST (equivalent to a sales tax). The overall level of taxation in New Zealand is about the same level as in the United Kingdom.

Income Tax

The personal income tax scale has two steps, 24% and 33%, the higher rate threshold currently cuts in at the equivalent of full-time average earnings. Most income is taxed, but a rebate system means that low earners pay only 15% of their earnings in tax. There is a tax credit system for low income families with children and tax surcharge of 25% for those on National Superannuation who receive additional income above a certain level.

For most wage and salary earners income tax is deducted by the employer on a PAYE system. (Pay As You Earn). The tax year runs from 1st April to 31st March. By June wage and salary earners file a tax return (called an IR5) for the previous year. If you are entitled to any rebates or the tax deducted from your earnings was greater than it should have been, you will receive a tax rebate. Self employed individuals pay instalments throughout the financial year. They receive an IR3 form at the end of the tax year to reconcile their assessed with their actual taxes.

Alternatively you may be assessed as having more tax to pay.

There is no equivalent to National Insurance contributions: all social security and health spending is financed through general taxation. Benefits are available to all residents and citizens without any requirement for a contribution record. There is a residency requirement and some benefits are subject to income tests. See below for details.

Table of Income Tax

Rates of tax for the 1993-94 year:

Income up to $30, 875: 24c for every dollar.

Income over $30, 875: 33c for every dollar.

A rebate of 9c in the dollar applies to most income up to $9500. The rebate is clawed back at the rate of 4c in the dollar on income from $9501 to $30, 875. As a result there are effectively three tax brackets:

Income Tax Rate	Tax Rate
$1-9500	15c in the dollar
$9501 — $30 875	28c in the dollar
$30, 876 and over	33c in the dollar

Local Tax
Local authorities finance their activities by levying rates on land and property. The system is similar to that which operated in the UK until the introduction of the Poll Tax. Some local authorities charge for services such as rubbish collection and water supply as well as levying rates. Rates vary around the country and depending on the value of the land and improvements. An annual bill of between $1000-2000 would be typical for a standard family house.

Goods and Services Tax (GST)
GST is an indirect tax, similar to VAT, currently 12.5%. It is borne by the ultimate consumer but is payable at every stage of producing goods or services. It applies to most commodities, exemptions include rental accommodation and financial services. Exports are zero rated. Businesses with a net turnover of greater than $30 000 per annum must be GST registered. They can claim back the GST content of the goods and services they purchase.

Other Taxes
There is no capital gains tax as such or death duties in New Zealand. However certain provisions in the Income Tax Act operate so as to tax as income profits which might otherwise be regarded as capital gains.

Gift Duty: Dutiable gifts consist of property in New Zealand and all property gifted by someone domiciled in New Zealand. Subject to certain exemptions, duty is payable on gifts above $27,000 in any one year. A graduated scale applies rising to 25c in the dollar on gifts exceeding $72,000.

Health Care, Insurance & Hospitals

Health Care
Prevailing public health care standards are generally high. Preventable diseases had been almost eradicated although one of the signs of the social distress caused by the economic restructuring of the 80s is that the diseases of poverty such as rickets, scurvy and tuberculosis are on the rise again. Life expectancy is the same as in the UK but there are significant differences between ethnic groups. New Zealanders smoke less than Europeans.

The general pattern of the public health system in New Zealand is that primary health care system (GPs, prescriptions, out-patients visits to hospitals) has fees while secondary health care is provided free. About a third of New Zealanders have supplementary private medical insurance to cover the additional costs of medical care in the public system and to enable them to afford the costs of private hospitals. The costs of health care not covered by the state are between $30-$40 for a visit to a doctor, prescription charges at $15 per item maximum, optometrists (opticians) and dentists charges at around $60 per visit. People on low incomes can get a Community Services Card which entitles them to cheaper primary care. As in Britain, the GPs provide most basic health care. It is not necessary to register with just one doctor, although for obvious reasons people tend to stay with the same doctor.

Hospitals. Hospital funding and management is currently in a state of upheaval due to the introduction of an internal market system similar to the NHS internal market. Hospitals have been renamed Crown Health Enterprises (which have the unfortunate acronym CHEs, leading to a whole series of cheesy jokes). The quality of care in the public hospital sector does not seem to have declined from its previous high standards but more services are being provided on user-charge basis, and waiting lists are growing. The Government has so far failed to define what core health services it expects CHEs to provide free of charge. Private hospitals exist (there are no private beds in public hospitals) but cater mainly for elective surgery and for those who prefer a private room and more choice of when they have their operation. Waiting lists for standard surgical routines in public hospitals are shorter than in the UK. You are also less likely to be a victim of medical misadventure at the hands of some young doctor at the end of 100 hour shift; young doctors went on strike in the late 80s and successfully negotiated much better pay and conditions than their counterparts in the UK.

Dental Care. Dental care for adults is not subsidised by the government but is provided free for all primary school children through the school dental system. Most New Zealand primary schools will have a dental clinic on the premises. As a result of receiving free basic care nearly half of New Zealand school children have no fillings by the time they get to high school.

Abortion. Abortion is legal under certain strictly defined conditions. If it is judged that the continuation of the pregnancy would result in serious danger to the life or mental or physical health of the woman, oir that there is substantial risk that the child would be born handicapped then an abortion may be approved by two specially appointed consultants. The rate is about the same per 1000 population as the UK and half that of the USA.

Reciprocal Agreements

New Zealand has reciprocal health care agreements with most Commonwealth countries, including the UK. Visitors from these countries are entitled to access to the New Zealand health care system on the same basis as New Zealand citizens and residents. If you are a UK citizen visiting New Zealand to decide whether or not to emigrate, you are entitled to free treatment in the hospital system. You will pay the same as New Zealanders do for doctorUs visits, about £15 for a consultation.

Private Medical Insurance

About 1.3 million New Zealanders have private medical insurance. The main reasons for buying private insurance seem to be to cover the additional costs of using the public system, such as doctors fees and prescription charges, and to cover the costs of private hospital care. Getting insurance just to cover the costs of primary care is unlikely to be cost effective. The average annual costs for doctors' visits and prescriptions charges may be less than the premiums even for a budget insurance deal which only covers primary care. Premiums for this type of package are around $180 per year for an individual and $520 for a family. A comprehensive insurance deal which covers everything from primary care to major surgery in a private hospital will cost anything from $500 upwards annually or an individual or $1500 for a family. However policies vary widely depending on the amount of cover and the exclusions. The main advantages of private hospital care are greater choice over the timing of an operation, and private rooms. You can get hospital only cover which is usually cheaper than a comprehensive policy. Remember though, the public hospital system provides the full range of care. The advantages of having private insurance are mostly the convenience factor of private facilities and the flexibility of choosing the timing of your operation. It is not yet neccessary to have private medical insurance in New Zealand.

The Accident Compensation Corporation (ACC)

New Zealand has a unique system of state protection in the case of personal injury or accident. The government pays out compensation for loss of earnings due to accidents in the workplace, at home or on the sports field. There is no right to sue for personal injury as a consequence. (This includes medical misadventure, although criminal proceedings may still be brought). The cost of ACC is met through payroll levies on employers and employees. It is another area of welfare provision which has suffered from retrenchment in recent years: lump-sum compensation according to a fixed scale depending on the injury, has been abolished, and all assistance is made on a case by case basis. However assistance is available for a wide variety of costs including medical treatment, private hospital treatment, loss of earnings, loss of potential earnings, home help and child care, house modification in the case of permanent disability and training for independent living. The cost of non-work related accidents is met through the earner's premium which is collected through the tax system and for work related accidents, through the employer's premium or levy.

Social Welfare & Unemployment Benefits

Access to the social welfare system in New Zealand does not depend upon establishing a contribution record: benefits are available to all who meet the residency and income criteria. Although entitlement criteria are generous, benefit rates are not: most benefits are worth less than 50% of the average weekly wage ($583.62 in 1993). Increasingly prospective claimants face income and asset tests, for example high income earners who become unemployed may face a stand down period before they are entitled to unemployment benefit and may have to demonstrate that they have used up their own savings before qualifying for state aid. There is a reciprocal social security agreement with the UK which entitles UK residents who move to New Zealand to qualify for New Zealand benefits under the same criteria as New Zealanders. Some UK benefits are payable in New Zealand and in some circumstances it may be advisible to keep paying British National Insurance contributions. Immigrants from other countries will have to satisfy residence criteria before they become eligible.

Invalid benefit: For a married couple the 1993 rate was just under 50% of average weekly wages. It is available to people aged 16 years or more who are severely restricted in their capacity for work due to accident, illness or congenital disability.

Sickness benefit: The married couple rate in 1993 was just over 40% of average weekly wage. It is available those over 16 who are incapacitated for work through sickness or accident.

UK Sickness and Invalidity Benefit: This benefit is payable in New Zealand only if you are absent from the UK temporarily and your absence is for the specific purpose of obtaining treatment for your disability.

Domestic purposes benefit (DPB): The DPB is available to a parent caring for a child without the support of a partner. For a parent with one child the rate is $190.27 weekly or just over 30% of average weekly wage.

Unemployment benefit: Payments are not related to previous earnings and the weekly rate is very low. The married couple rate in 1993 was $221 weekly, or just under 40% of the average weekly wage. Anyone under twenty-five years old is paid a lower rate. The unemployment benefit is payable to citizens and residents only. The UK unemployment benefit is not payable in New Zealand.

Family Allowance: There is a tax credit system for low-income families to top up their weekly wages. Called Guaranteed Minimum Family Income (GMFI) it ensures that their weekly earnings are around 50% of the average weekly wage.

Crime and the Police

Unfortunately New Zealand's reputation for being a peaceful country with few social problems is not entirely deserved. The crime rate has been rising in recent years and the days when people would regularly go out without locking their front doors are over. It has a slightly higher rate of murders than the UK, but many times lower than the US rate. However although you should not have an unrealistically rosy picture of New Zealand society, it is important to keep it in perspective. Violent crime is sufficiently uncommon as to be newsworthy. In general New Zealand cities are safe places to walk around and the police force are not yet routinely armed.

Local Government

Local government in New Zealand is very much subordinate to central government. Its powers and functions are set by parliament. There are two levels, regional councils which have responsibilties broadly for the environmental and land use, including control of pests and noxious plants. They also have some responsibilities over civil defence in the case of flood or earthquake. The next level are territorial or local councils. These are directly elected, and have the power to set rates. Their responsibilities are not as wide ranging as local councils in the UK. They mostly provide services such as rubbish collection and disposal, parks and reserves and libraries. They are responsible for a variety of regulatory measures for example, building consent, health inspection and control of noise, pollution and parking.

Social Life

Meeting people & Making Friends

New Zealanders are very easy to get to know. They are relaxed about opening up a conversation with complete strangers. In fact if you walk into a country pub and fail to say hello to the locals, it would be considered quite rude. People are welcoming in inviting you back to their homes. New Zealanders do not make such invitations out of politeness, they mean it, so never feel you are taking advantage. It is a less formal country than the UK. It is considered quite normal for example to call round without a specific invitation. Neighbours will often drop in and introduce themselves to new people moving in. For all the immediate friendliness, New Zealanders can be quite reserved in some respects. They are not likely to tell you much about their feelings or values until you get to know them well.

Social Attitudes

Perhaps as a result of their pioneering forebears, New Zealanders are an independent people. There is a great tradition of do-it-yourself, whether it comes to building an extension on the back of the house, or cutting off ties with the rest of the Western alliance during the Cold War period by refusing American nuclear armed ships access to New Zealand ports. Innovation is respected. Finding an ingenious, low-cost solution to a problem was obviously an asset in pioneering days. There is even a phrase for it: 'Kiwi Ingenuity' which describes a pragmatic, imaginative approach to problem solving.

Despite approving of innovative and non-traditional approaches to problem solving, rural New Zealand remains quite conservative in outlook. Innovative lifestyles are not generally approved of. However tolerance is also a New Zealand characteristic, perhaps because the independent streak in the average New Zealander leads them to respect the right of others to live their lives as they choose. Urban New Zealand is liberal in outlook. Green issues receive quite a lot of support, perhaps because New Zealanders are aware they live in one of the last largely unspoilt wilderness areas in the world and they have some responsibility to hand it on to their children without ruining it. There is strong support for bicultural and multiculturalism in theory. However Pakeha New Zealanders can increasingly be heard complaining that the Maori are treated more favourably by government. In fact actual positive discrimination programmes of the type common in the USA are comparatively rare. Special grants exist for Maori business and for educational purposes. Few institutions run a formal quota system although all are required to have an equal employment policy. Maori leaders acknowledge that one of the big problems facing Maori society is the increasing dependence on welfare benefits. Maori workers are more likely to be unemployed than Pakeha. They were more severely affected by the economic restructuring of the last decade because job losses were predominantly in the unskilled area and Maori workers have tended to have lower skills levels than Pakeha.

Like the Welsh and the Scots, New Zealanders feel the need to assert their own identity to prove that they are different from the English, the colonial power which shaped the early period of settlement and hence the model for New Zealand culture for a long time. The need to assert themselves usually manifests itself as a fairly critical attitude towards English life, culture and climate, on the part of those who have visited that country. This criticism is usually not intended to be rude, rather it functions as a form of commiseration for the English for having had the misfortune to have been born there rather than in New Zealand. Reciprocal ruthless honesty about the drawbacks of living in New Zealand is unlikely to be welcomed however. In fact they tend to be defensive about New Zealand, even though they think its merits ought to be self-evident.

Smoking. Smoking is a lot less socially acceptable in New Zealand than it is in Europe. Public buildings are smoke free zones by law. Most restaurants provide a smoke free area with some even banning smoking completely.

Entertainment and Culture

New Zealand is not as well-known overseas for its musicians and artists (Dame Kiri Te Kanawa excepted) as it is for its sports men and women, but in fact there is a lively local cultural scene, and increasingly, performers from New Zealand are succeeding internationally. Dame Kiri Te Kanawa, the opera singer is respected throughout New Zealand, not so much because every household is into opera, but because like the All Blacks she is seen as a New Zealander succeeding internationally. She therefore attracts huge audiences, when she

282 Living in New Zealand

returns home to perform. There are two professional orchestra companies, one based in Auckland and the other in Wellington, and most regions have amateur orchestras. International soloists and chamber groups visit frequently, and every two years the Wellington festival of the Performing Arts attracts some top rate orchestras and ensembles from all over the world. Other types of performing arts thrive, particularly in Wellington which has a number of professional theatres, the Royal New Zealand Ballet, a several modern dance companies and the New Zealand Symphony Orchestra. The New Zealand film scene is currently enjoying a lot of success both at home and overseas. *The Piano:* made by New Zealander Jane Campion is one of a long line of quality films.

Sport

What can you say about a country where the Prime Minister gets involved with the choice over the coach of the rugby team? New Zealanders are intensely nationalistic when it comes to identifying with the successes of their national teams, particularly the rugby team, the All Blacks. Losing a rugby match can cast a gloom over the entire nation. It is about more than just losing a game. New Zealand is such a small player in the international political and economic order, that the fact that the country's elite sports teams are capable of taking on the big guys and winning becomes a matter of national pride.

Some of this nationalistic fervour focused on the All Blacks has diminished in recent years. Liberal New Zealand was disenchanted with the attitude of the rugby establishment towards links with South Africa in the days when that country was an international pariah as a result of its apartheid system. Other sporting heroes emerged. For a brief and glorious period the soccer team were in the limelight when they qualified for the World Cup. More consistently successful are the Silver Ferns, the netball team.

New Zealanders are not just enthusiastic about watching sport. A large number of people participate in their spare time. Nearly 50% of the population belong to some kind of sport, fitness or leisure club. The most popular activities are aquatic sports such as swimming, diving, rowing, or water polo. As well as team sports such as hockey, netball, rugby and football (usually called soccer), an increasing number of New Zealanders are involved in individual sports like mountain biking, climbing, skate boarding, triathalon competitions, or trail bike riding.

Maori Culture

The indigenous culture of New Zealand is Maori culture. The Maori have been in Aotearoa (New Zealand) for approximately 1000 years, a long time compared to the 150 years of Pakeha (European) settlement. Maori culture remains distinct from the rest of New Zealand culture, although each influences the other.

Maori Social Customs
The Marae
One of the most distinctive and central parts of Maori culture is the *Marae* or meeting place. A *marae* consists of a *wharenui* (meeting house), a *wharekai* (eating house) and *wharepaku* (ablution block). To the Maori however, it is not the presence of the buildings that is significant, but the spiritual importance of the location, the discussions and exchanges between people and events ranging from marriages to funerals that take place on the *marae*. It is customary to welcome visitors onto the *marae* in a ceremony called a *pohiri* (welcome).

The Pohiri
Visitors (called the *manuhiri*) will gather outside the gate of the *marae*. It is considered improper to walk on to the *marae* uninvited. The visitors will be 'called on' by the host people (the *tangata whenua*). This is called the *karanga* and is usually performed by a woman from the host side. The *manuhiri* will proceed slowly onto the marae as one group. Usually the women are to the front of the group. One of these women will answer the the welcoming call with a *karanga* of her own. The group will pause in silence to *tangi* (remember the dead) and then will move slowly to the seating provided. The front row of seating is reserved for those men who wish to *whaikorero* (speak).

Whaikorero (speeches) are to welcome manuhiri and to thank *tangata whenua* and are always related to the event taking place. Each speech is followed by a *waiata* (song), sung by the speaker's group to show their support of him. The final speaker for the *manuhiri* wll lay down the *koha* (gift). Today *koha* are mostly monetary to contribute to the cost of the *hui* (gathering). The final speech is usually made on the host side.

At the conclusion of the *whaikorero* it is customary for the visitors and the hosts to *hongi* (press noses). Today some people will shake hands instead. It is best to follow the lead of the *tangata whenua*. After the formalities, hosts and guests share a meal together. It is at this point that the *manuhiri* become *tangata whenua* and the *pohiri* is concluded.

Points to Remember
The *wharenui* is for gatherings and for sleeping. You should always remove your shoes before entering the *wharenui*. Never walk on mattresses or sit on pillows. Certain places are reserved for the elders (*kaumatua*) to sit and sleep in. You should never eat in the *wharenui*.

In the *wharekai* (eating house) be careful not to put hair clips, scarves, combs, glasses or anything to do with the head, on the table. Before meals there will usually be grace. It is good manners to allow the *kaumatua* to eat first, and after the first meal once you have become part of the tangata whenua, to offer to help with the dishes or preparation of the next meal.

Do not smoke in any of the buildings on the *marae* and do not use cameras or tape recorders unless given permission. Never be afraid to ask what protocol you should be following. Part of Maori culture emphasises the importance of welcoming guests and making them feel at home, so if you are prepared to be respectful of the culture and traditions, then nobody will mind explaining points of protocol to you. A useful book on Maori culture is *Te Marae- A Guide to Customs and Protocols* (Hiwi and Pat Tauroa, Heinemann Reed, 1986). If you want to find out more about Maori culture during a visit to New Zealand, the New Zealand Tourism Board publishes a leaflet called *New Zealand Maori Cultural Heritage Guide* which lists a number of tourism operators who provide visits to marae and other cultural experiences. (*New Zealand Tourism Board:* New Zealand House, 80 Haymarket SW1Y 4TQ, London; tel 0171-973 0360.) The New Zealand Immigration Service publishes a leaflet called *The Treaty of Waitangi* which explains the relevance of the treaty to new immigrants.

Shops and Shopping

The types of shops in New Zealand will be familiar to the UK immigrant and in some cases even the names are the same. (Although chains with the same names as UK shops often sell different goods in New Zealand which can be disorientating. For example *Woolworths* is one of New Zealand's largest supermarket chains and *Boots* is just a chemists, not a general department store as well). Shops are open 8.30 am until 5pm, five days a week, and 8.30 am until 12pm on Saturday. Sunday shopping is well established. Most shops also have one late night when they are open until 9pm, usually Thursday or Friday. In some larger towns suburban malls and superstores are taking business out of the city centre. Auckland is a case in point, Queen Street, once the focal point of the city centre is almost deserted on a Friday night. In other cities, councils have made determined efforts to revive the town centres. Christchurch's Cathedral Square and Wanganui's Victoria Avenue are good examples.

Food Shopping: Most people buy their weekly groceries from supermarkets. The large supermarkets with the biggest range tend to be located outside the main city area which makes access difficult for non-car owners. You will find the same types of food, as you would find in British supermarkets, but most of the stock will be made in New Zealand as imported goods are expensive. There are probably more distinctions between different types of supermarket chains than in Britain. Some offer a cheap no-frills service with minimal overheads. These tend to be warehouse style places where you pack your own bags and there is not a great range of goods, just all the basics sold very cheaply. Other chains are aiming at the high-income end of the market. They will offer a greater level of customer service, with a range of speciality departments in-store, bakery, butchers, delicatessen, for example, but are comparatively expensive. Most supermarkets are open seven days a week and will usually have at least one late night when they are open until 9pm.

Local shops have not yet disappeared but are threatened by the convenience of supermarket shopping and the cheaper prices. Most city neighbourhoods have a convenience store (called a dairy). Dairies stock practically everything and are usually open late (until 9pm or 10pm), but are rather more expensive than a supermarket. Some neighbourhoods still have their local butcher, fruit and vegetable shop and bakery but these are becoming less common. Serious foodies will probably miss the range of European and speciality foods available in the UK. Delicatessens stock a range of imported foods but at a price. On the other hand, most staple foods are cheaper than in the Europe. The good news is that European style specialities are now starting to be made locally. For example Italian breads such as *foccacia* and *ciabatta* are baked locally in the big cities, and fresh pasta can be found in most towns. A New Plymouth company is producing French style cheeses, although they seem to cost nearly as much as the real thing. New Zealand's varied climate provides suitable conditions to grow a wide range of fruit and vegetables, but you will find that what is available in the shops depends on the season, as it is mostly locally grown. Produce with a short shelf life cannot be imported to cover the off-season because the distances involved are too great. Pacific Island specialities such as taro, coconut and plantains are one type of imported produce that is commonly available in the bigger towns. Fresh fish and shellfish are another New Zealand speciality. Green lipped mussels, pacific oysters, local salmon, smoked eel, trout, are all popular. Because export demand drives up the prices, seafood is not cheap.

Local wines are also generally of good quality. New Zealand white wines were 'discovered' by UK wine writers in the late 80s which had an enormous galvanising effect on the New Zealand industry. The number of vineyards multiplied, and everybody started producing Sauvignon Blanc as that was in demand. New Zealand wines are not any cheaper at home than they are in Europe, but the range is greater. You can buy not just the ubiquitous Sauvignon Blanc but also some seriously good Chardonnay, and even some respectable red wines. Australian wines are readily available and are generally cheaper than

New Zealand wines because their industry does not face the same crippling taxes which hit New Zealand producers.

Non-Food Shopping: Most consumer goods are readily available in New Zealand. Imported goods are cheaper than they used to be as a result of tariffs being lowered in the 1980s. However it is probably not the shopping that attracts most visitors or immigrants. There is no equivalent to Regent Street or Fifth Avenue even in the big cities. Department store chains such as Deka and DIC sell most of the essentials from clothing through to household goods and white goods in rather unimaginative surroundings. Clothing is comparatively cheap although design standards are not particularly high in the chain stores. Independent designers flourish in the larger cities selling well-made and reasonably-priced clothing.

Food and Drink

The New Zealand diet is mostly derived from the eating patterns of the British immigrants, influenced by the relative abundance of dairy products and cheap mutton and beef. New Zealanders tend to consume far too much cholesterol and saturated fat and as a result have one of the highest rates of heart disease in the western world. This is changing slowly as a result of government campaigns promoting healthier eating styles and a new interest in the diet and food of Asian countries. But despite the best attempts of the healthy lifestyle lobby, the standard Sunday lunch in many a New Zealand home remains roast lamb with all the trimmings. during the week the main meal is usually the evening meal, which confusingly, New Zealanders call 'teaU.

Eating out isnUt quite the soul destroying experience it was once, although the countryUs reputation for poor cuisine lingers. In fact now that it is escaping the influence of traditional English cooking, the quality of restaurants in the main cities is very high. The improvement in the domestic wine industry has helped. There is a lot of interest in European food trends. Many New Zealand restaurants have what is called a BYO (BYO stands for Bring Your Own) licence. They are not allowed to sell alcoholic beverages, instead the customer brings their own wine which the restaurant opens. They usually make a small charge called corkage for this. The advantage of BYO establishments is that you avoid the huge mark up restaurants usually put on wine and you have a much wider choice of what to drink. BYO restaurants tend to be cheaper than fully licenced places, at around $25-35 a head for a three course meal, not including what you paid for the wine. A three course meal at a licenced restaurant is more likely to be in the $45-55 range, not including the cost of wine. The cheapest and sometimes the most interesting food can be found at the fashionable espresso bars which are springing up all the time in the big cities. You can eat in these sorts of places for less than $20 (about £8).

The situation in small towns is still pretty grim. Chinese takeaways are probably your best bet anywhere from north of Wellington to the Bombay Hills, and in the hinterlands of Canterbury and Otago. Good local restaurants exist in small town New Zealand but unless a friend you trust (and wants to keep your friendship) has recommended a restaurant, you might be better off with takeaways. Indian restaurants arenUt as common as they are in the UK, but other Asian food establishments are becoming more common. New Zealand fish and chip shops are surprisingly good as instead of frying chips and other goodies in advance and letting them dry out under hot lamps, they fry your order up individually. They still come wrapped in newspaper in most places too, with no European health regulations to interfere. No one has yet died in New Zealand of newsprint poisoning.

Public Holidays

1 January	New Year's Day
2 January	Day after New Year's Day
6 February	Waitangi Day (formerly New Zealand Day)
April	Good Friday
April	Easter Monday
25 April	Anzac Day
June	Queen's Birthday
October	Labour Day
25 December	Christmas Day
26 December	Boxing Day

Time

New Zealand is twelve hours ahead of Greenwich Mean Time. During Daylight Saving the clocks are put forward by one hour, from the last Sunday in October to the last Sunday in March.

Metrication

New Zealand uses the metric measuring system for distances, weights and measures, with a few imperial hangovers. For example beer usually is sold by the pint or half pint. Road signs are all in kilometres as are speed limits. To convert kilometres into miles, multiply by five and divide by eight. Temperatures are in degrees Celsius. As a rough guide, convert to Fahrenheit, double the degrees and add 30.

Retirement

Background Information

There are more than 30,000 British people of retirement age living in New Zealand and a large number from other European countries. Undoubtedly for many older people, the chance to be reunited with children who have already migrated to New Zealand is a major attraction. Having adult children in New Zealand will also make it easier to get permanent residency. Otherwise migration may be difficult for people of retirement age, as New Zealand's immigration policy is aimed at attracting people into the workforce.

New Zealand offers many advantages for those considering a change of scenery upon retirement. The standard of living is high and the exchange rate is favourable so your savings should go a long way. British and American retirees will not have to learn a new language and the culture is sufficiently similar to British culture to be familiar. The climate in most parts of New Zealand is warmer than Northern Europe. There are the attractions of living in a less crowded country, with in general, fewer social problems and a lower crime rate. New Zealand's population is ageing so there are a lot of clubs and services set up with older people in mind. Although doctors' visits cost about £12-14 per consultation, hospital care is still free for New Zealanders and immigrants from countries with reciprocal social security agreements. In general the New Zealand health system is less under-resourced than the NHS. On the other hand, certain types of specialist medical care may be better provided in the UK and other European countries simply because New Zealand is too small to have much expertise in these areas.

The drawbacks of emigrating have to be considered as well. You will be far away from friends and family in the Northern hemisphere and you may find life a little lonely at first. Many retirees mention that one of the hardest aspects of their new life is not being able to afford to return home for family events such as weddings. New Zealand is thirty hours away from London by plane and the trip is not cheap. Most British migrants report that they find it easy to get to know New Zealanders, and although new friends are not a substitute for old, you need not fear being isolated for long in your new country.

The Decision to Leave

Making a permanent move to another country is a very different matter from just visiting it, particularly when you will be adjusting to all the lifestyle changes retirement brings as well. It may be a good idea therefore to spend a longer period in New Zealand before deciding whether to make a permanent move there. Many people make the decision to move after a visit to New Zealand to see family or friends. If you have a British passport you are entitled to visit New Zealand for up to six months without requiring a visa. A visit may be a good opportunity to explore different parts of the country before deciding where you would most like to settle. A number of companies arrange coach and train tours with itineraries that cover most of New Zealand in a short period. Some companies will also arrange farm and home stay tours which will enable you to experience the lifestyle of New Zealand families. One such company is Leisurerail (PO Box 113, Peterborough, PE3 8HY; tel 01733-335599).

As has been noted elsewhere, rental accommodation is generally easy to find, so you may like to try living in your prospective retirement locality for a while. It will also give you a chance to assess the real costs of living in New Zealand. Financial considerations are an important factor when you are living on a fixed income. You can use a visit to assess the property market in order to find out what kind of housing you will be able to afford. In general if you have sold property in the UK, you should be able to afford a New Zealand house of at least an equivalent if not better standard, particularly if you choose to live outside the main cities.

Residence and Entry regulations

Because the general migration category is not open to people aged 55 or above, the most likely route to New Zealand residency for an older person is the family reunification or business development categories. Under the family reunification category, you are entitled to apply for residency if you have an adult child or children living in New Zealand and no adult children living in your own country, or alternatively if you have children living in your home country and you have more children living in New Zealand than any other country including your own. Alternatively if you have sufficient capital you can apply under the business investment category. The minimum amount required is NZ$500, 000. (See Chapter Two, *Residence and Entry*).

Applying for Residence

To qualify for residency under the family reunification category, you will need to provide evidence of the family relationships, and the citizenship or residency status of your New Zealand children, and of children living in other countries. You will need to submit birth and marriage certificates and copies of residency permits. Additionally you will have to satisfy the health and character requirements as outlined in Chapter Two for general residency applications.

Possible retirement areas

Popular retirement areas for New Zealanders are in the warmer regions on the east coast of the North Island and the north of the South Island. Many New Zealanders move to the coast when they retire, often to their beach house or bach. Some communities have a higher proportion of older people than others which you may consider an advantage. One consideration to bear in mind, is that in remoter areas you will certainly need to own a car or to live close to local services as public transport is not convenient enough to rely on. A population retirement option for New Zealanders is the 'ten acre block', a house in the country with a large plot of land. Ten acres may be the size of farm in Europe, but by the standards of New Zealand farms, these are hobby plots, for city folk who want to try the rural lifestyle. Some people cultivate their land, others just enjoy the extra space.

Tauranga and the Bay of Plenty: On the east coast of the North Island, the Bay of Plenty has a pleasant climate and is one of the main horticultural regions as a result. In the summer time, the white sandy beaches and gentle waves of Mt Manganui beach attract many families.

Kapiti Coast: Just north of Wellington, on the west coast of the North Island, the coast is a popular retirement destination for locals. It is dotted with small towns, from Paraparaumu, up to Otaki, many made up largely of holiday homes for Wellingtonians to escape to for the weekends. There are a large number of permanent residents as well, many of retirement age. Transport networks are good, there is a commuter train service into Wellington city, as well as a local bus network. The coast itself can be quite rough, but just down the coast, Porirua harbour provides more sheltered waters for boating or fishing.

Banks Peninsula: Over the Port Hills to the south of Christchurch, the peninsula was called Bank's Island on the first map of New Zealand after Captain Cook's navigator, Joseph Banks who thought its deep inlets cut it off from the main land. In contrast with the flat sweeping plains of Canterbury, the peninsula is all hills and valleys divided by deep harbours. Over the hills is Akaroa, with its echoes of the first French settlers. Streets are called 'Rues' and the building code specifies that new houses are built in the style of the homes of the original French settlers with steeply raked roofs. You would certainly need to be a car owner to live on the peninsula as the bus service to Christchurch is infrequent and the remoter valleys lack local services.

Hobbies and interests

New Zealand offers many opportunities for using your new leisure time. The country is full of keen gardeners and the climate is well suited for those who like to spend time outdoors. If you are planning an active retirement, there is a lot of beautiful countryside to be explored. There are sporting opportunities to suit just about everybody. Golfing is a popular activity. There are public golf courses in most towns and cities. Bowls and croquet are also popular with older people. If you are interested in cultural pursuits, you will probably consider settling near one of the main cities. Fortunately one of the advantages of living in New Zealand is that you can combine proximity to major cities with the semi-rural lifestyle if that is what appeals to you. For example, Banks Peninsula is only 40 minutes away from the centre of Christchurch. Every town has a senior citizens club, equally open to the recent immigrant as to the native New Zealander. These provide a chance to meet other older people as well as social facilities. Many older people use their new leisure time to go back to study, either through night classes or by enrolling at a university part-time. Most New Zealand universities exempt mature students from formal entrance qualifications and instead will assess your ability to study and enrol you at the appropriate level. You can often get used to being a student again by taking a pre-degree certificate in liberal arts which have less rigorous assessment procedures. Night classes are offered in a wide variety of subjects from foreign languages through to car maintenance at local high schools or polytechnics. The following are just some of the clubs available for European and American ex-pats.

Useful Addresses

British Isles Club of Wellington: 38 Webb Street, Wellington; tel (04) 384 8286.
English Speaking Union of the Commonwealth in New Zealand: PO Box 2023, Dunedin; tel (03) 477 2140.
New Zealand American Association Inc.: PO Box 2957, Wellington; tel (04) 367 2202.

Pensions

New Zealand Pensions

New Zealand has reciprocal social security arrangements with a number of countries including the UK, Ireland and the Netherlands. The general principal of these reciprocal arrangements is that people migrating from one country to the other are treated like citizens of their new country with regard to social security arrangements and are entitled to the same range of benefits. However the particular arrangements differ between countries. In the case of UK citizens, if you are entitled to receive a British retirement pension, you can continue to receive it in New Zealand. The level of the British pension is frozen from the point you leave the UK, and is not inflation adjusted. If you become eligible for the pension while in New Zealand, it will be paid at the rate which applies in the UK when you are first entitled to a pension. Under the reciprocal agreement you are entitled to qualify for the New Zealand state retirement pension, National Superannuation if you have been resident in the UK and New Zealand for at least ten years in total. If you qualify, the New Zealand Government supplements the your British pension so that it is at the same level as National Superannuation. National Superannuation pays $230 per week for a single person and $343 for a couple.

If you come from a country which does not have a reciprocal agreement with New Zealand you are not entitled to receive the New Zealand pension until you have been a resident for ten years. National Superannuation is subject to an income test. If you receive additional income other than National Super (your British state pension does not count as additional income), your superannuation payments will be cut back. The basic single person's rate is abated by 25c in the dollar for every dollar of extra income you receive above a certain level, $80 per week for a single person, and $120 per week for a couple. The first half of income from New Zealand based private pension schemes is exempt from the surcharge. Overseas private pension schmemes are not subject to the exemption and are fully taxed.

Receiving Your Pension Abroad

Pension arrangements for ex-patriates vary. In some countries if you have established entitlement in your own country then you can continue to receive your pension in New Zealand. As was noted above, some countries have reciprocal agreements with New Zealand which entitle you to the same range of benefits as a local. You should contact your local Department of Social Security for further information.

Taxation

Once you are a New Zealand resident, you pay New Zealand income tax on your world wide income, including income from any overseas based pension schemes. Residency for taxation purposes has nothing to do with your immigration status. You are deemed to be New Zealand resident for tax purposes if you have a permanent place of abode in New Zealand, regardless of whether you also have one in another country. Having a permanent abode in New Zealand is not limited to owning a dwelling, the courts will also take into account social, personal, and financial ties as evidence of where your permanent abode is. If you are in New Zealand for more than 183 days in any 12 month period you are also regarded as a New Zealand resident for taxation purposes whether or not you have a permanent abode in New Zealand. New Zealand has double tax treaties with twenty-four countries including the USA, Canada, the UK, France, Germany, and the Netherlands. These treaties limit the tax liability for citizens of one country resident in the other, so that an individual does not in theory pay tax twice on the same income.

New Zealand Health Care

One of the drawbacks of the New Zealand health care system for a retired person is that although hospital care is free, doctor's visits are not, nor are prescriptions.

For those pensioners on low incomes from countries with reciprocal social security arrangements, there is the Community Services Card which reduces the costs of health care. There is also a cap on the total amount you will be charged annually for prescriptions so if you need a lot of medication, you do not pay anything for it after a certain point. Private medical insurance is one option to consider to cover the additional costs of health care in New Zealand. See Chapter Four, *The Health Care System* for further details. Private insurance will cover the cost of treatment in private hospitals which may give you more choice about the timing of operations. But as is indicated in Chapter Four, the annual cost of premiums is likely to make private insurance uneconomic, unless you frequently use primary health care services.

Wills and Legal Considerations

You should draw up a will in New Zealand if you are considering buying property and settling there. Dying intestate complicates matters sufficiently for one's heirs without doing so in a foreign country. In the event that a non-New Zealander dies intestate the laws of their own country will apply. As it is more likely that you will be a New Zealand citizen or at least domiciled there in the eyes of the law, New Zealand intestate laws would apply. Under New Zealand intestate laws, your estate would be divided between a surviving spouse and your children, with your spouse getting the major share. This would be the case even if you had separated from but not divorced your spouse.

In New Zealand, a will does not have to be drawn up by a lawyer. There are advantages to having your will drawn up by a lawyer or trust company in that you can nominate them to administer your estate. This may be a good idea, particularly if you have no close relatives in the country to administer your estate for you.

Death

In the event of a friend or relative dying in New Zealand, there are certain formalities which have to be attended to, as is the case in the UK. A death must be certified by a doctor. You should consider as well what you would like your friends or relatives to do in the event of your death, and perhaps leave written instructions with your will. The cost of shipping a body back to Europe to be buried is extremely high.

SECTION II

Working in New Zealand

Employment
Business and Industry Report
Regional Employment Guide
Starting a Business

Employment

The Employment Scene

With a labour market similar to the United Kingdom's, the same language and a similar level of economic development, New Zealand has long been a good place for those wanting to emigrate from the UK to look for jobs. In the past the country enjoyed very low unemployment with the average level throughout the 1970s being less than 2%. However the situation in the last decade has been less favourable. Throughout the 1980s unemployment in New Zealand increased rapidly. A large number of jobs were lost throughout manufacturing industries during the radical economic reforms of the 1980s. Some of the job losses can be attributed to long term trends in the labour market and reflect the same kinds of changes that have occurred in other western countries where manufacturing industries have been unable to compete with cheaper labour costs in the newly industrialised countries of Asia. There has been a similar shift in New Zealand's industrial structure from manufacturing to service industries as has been evident in the United Kingdom. Other job losses can be traced to the lowering of tariff barriers as a result of New Zealand's conversion to neo-liberal economic policies. Tight monetary policy aimed at squeezing inflationary pressures out of the economy also contributed to the economic downturn. Employment in the manufacturing sector dropped by a quarter during the 1980s from 316,000 jobs to 235,000. This sector now employs just over 17% of the workforce, compared to 23% ten years ago. The primary sector (agricultural, horticulture, fishing) has seen a similar drop in employment from 153,000 jobs in 1980 to 131,000 in 1990. Although agriculture has always been the basis of New Zealand's economic prosperity, the primary sector is a comparatively small source of jobs, employing about 10% of the workforce. New Zealand's farms are extremely labour effective and have become more so in recent years and as a result, employment in the agricultural sector has dropped.

The only sector to have experienced growth over this period is the service sector which now accounts for 70% of employment. Within the service sector, the fastest growing source of jobs has been in business and financial services which employs around 12% of the workforce. The biggest employment area in the service sector is wholesale, retail, restaurants and hotels, which employs just over 20% of workforce. The increase in service sector jobs in the last decade has not been sufficient to make up for the loss of jobs in the manufacturing and primary sectors. Overall the total number of people in employment declined by nearly 88,000 between 1981 and 1991.

The current employment situation is more encouraging with an 8% unemployment rate at the time of printing. Although New Zealand like most western countries, was in severe recession at the start of the 1990s, it has been one of the first countries to emerge from the recession. Growth in the last two years was nearly double the OECD average. The number of people in employment has been growing at a faster rate every year since 1991, although because more people are looking for work, the rate of unemployment has not dropped substantially since the recession ended. A recent survey of companies by a Wellington economic research agency showed that 20% of companies were considering increasing their workforce in the short term. Most of this demand is likely to be for skilled labour with some firms shedding unskilled workers to take on workers with skills. Most commentators are predicting a drop in unemployment of 1-2% over the next few years. Improvements in the economies of New Zealand's major trading partners and the signing of the GATT deal should also benefit the New Zealand economic outlook.

Residence and Work Regulations

New Zealand requires that foreign nationals working in New Zealand whether for local or foreign companies obtain work permits for the period of employment which in most cases may not exceed three years. Permission from the New Zealand Immigration Service must be sought prior to arrival and it must be shown that the worker has skills not readily available in New Zealand.

If you are visiting New Zealand and have found a job, you may apply for a work permit within the country, but the maximum period for which it will be granted is nine months. The same restrictions on skills applies. For further details on work permits see Chapter Two, *Residence and Entry.*

Skills and Qualifications

In general British qualifications are recognised and well regarded in New Zealand. New Zealand's university education system derives its structure from British, particularly Scottish universities, so the types of qualifications available from universities are similar in title and content to UK ones. Trade and vocational qualifications have different titles. You can apply to the New Zealand Qualifications Authority, the government agency that oversees the qualifications system, to have the equivalence of your UK qualifications assessed. In some cases you may have to do this as part of the application for residency under the General Category. The necessary forms can be obtained from the New Zealand Immigration Service at New Zealand House in London, or you can write to the Qualifications Authority directly. (New Zealand Qualifications Authority, PO Box 160, Wellington; tel 04-3850459; fax 04-3854929). The Qualifications Authority charges a fee for this service. British school qualifications are accepted as entry requirements for New Zealand universities. Details of entry requirements are available from the Trade Development Board.

Professional Qualifications

Professional employment in New Zealand is regulated by the relevant professional bodies. In order to work in these areas you must register with these organisations. In most cases this will involve an assessment of qualifications and experience and you may be required to take further examinations. In some professions you can arrange for these exams to be taken in your own country. It is important to contact the relevant professional body in good time because applications usually take several months to be considered and qualifying exams are held only once or twice a year in foreign countries. As an example of the type of procedure you have to go through, the following are the requirements for foreign lawyers intending to practice in New Zealand:

Legal Practitioners seeking assessment should write to:

The Executive Director, New Zealand Law Society, PO Box 5041, Wellington, tel (04)4727837; fax (04)4737909.

You will be required to include the following information:

Documentary evidence of tertiary educational standing and attainment, including academic record, showing courses completed and grades.
Documentary evidence of admission as a lawyer in your own country.
A curriculum vitae giving names, dates, and places of practice.
A copy of your law school's handbook showing the structure of the degree and the content and length of each course.
A statutory declaration verifying identity and certifying the accuracy of the above information.
Two bank drafts in payment of application fees:

— One for NZ $100 payable to the New Zealand Law Society
— One for NZ $600 payable to the Council for Legal Education.

Not all professional bodies have such complex registration procedures. Membership of the New Zealand Society of Accountants is automatically granted to any member of the three British Associations of Chartered Accountants. Teachers do not have to join a professional body, but overseas qualified teachers do have to have their qualifications assessed by the Teacher Registration Board. (PO Box 5326, Wellington; (04) 4710852; fax (04) 4710870).

Addresses of Professional Bodies

New Zealand Society of Accountants: PO Box 11-342, Wellington; tel (04)4738 544.
New Zealand Institute of Architects: PO box 438 Wellington; tel 64-4 4735 346.
The Dental Council of New Zealand: PO Box 9318, Wellington; tel (04)3847635; fax (04)3858902.
New Zealand Institute of Draughtsmen Inc: Box 1638 Wellington; tel (04)3846601.
Institute of Professional Engineers NZ (inc): PO Box 12-241, Wellington; tel (04)4739444; fax (04)4732324.
The Medical Council of New Zealand: PO Box 11-649, Wellington; tel (04)3847635; fax (04)3858902.
The Nursing Council: PO Box 9644, Wellington; tel (04)3859589; fax (04)8018502.
Veterinary Association of New Zealand: PO Box 524 Wellington; tel (04)3843632.

Sources of Jobs

Newspapers

Most New Zealand jobs are advertised in newspapers most of which have a daily situations vacant section which tends to be larger on one particular day of the week; usually Saturdays. Some professional jobs will be advertised in specialist publications and at executive level jobs are usually filled through recruitment agencies sometimes without being advertised. The starting place for your job-hunt therefore, is the major New Zealand newspapers. A small number of jobs are advertised directly in the UK in the newspapers listed below. The types of jobs that tend to be advertised directly are in areas where there is a shortage of skills locally, for example in computers and information technology or accountancy.

Newspapers

The major daily newspapers can be read at New Zealand House in London (80 Haymarket SW1Y 4TE) 9am — 5pm weekdays. Subscriptions to New Zealand newspapers can be obtained by contacting their media agent in the UK: Mr Harris Constantinou, (Newspak, Unit 6, Spitfire Way, Spitfire Estate, Hounslow, Middlesex TW5 9NW; tel 0181-8481111). In some cases it may be cheaper to contact the newspapers directly.

Useful Addresses

The Main New Zealand Newspapers:

The New Zealand Herald: PO Box 32, Auckland; tel (09) 379 5050; fax (09) 366 1568 (Distributed throughout the North Island; Circulation 248,000).

The Dominion: PO Box 1297, Wellington; tel (04) 474 0000; fax (04) 474 0350 (Distributed in lower North Island; Circulation 73,000).

The Evening Post: PO Box 3740, Wellington; tel (04) 474 0444; fax (04) 474 0237 (Distributed in lower North Island; Circulation 77,000).

The Press: Private Bag 4722, Christchurch; tel (03) 379 0940; fax (03) 364 8492 (Distributed in Canterbury and Nelson/Tasman region; Circulation 99,000).

The Otago Daily Times: PO Box 181, Dunedin; tel (03) 477 4760; fax (03) 477 1313 (Distributed in lower South Island; Circulation 52,000).

Specialist Publications

Some types of jobs tend to be advertised in specialist magazines. These publications are also useful sources of information about the current job scene in their particular field. Another option would be to place a employment wanted advert with them.

Useful Addresses

GP Weekly: Adis Press Ltd, Private Bag 65-901, Mairangi Bay, Auckland, tel 9-4798100; fax 9-4798066.

Hospitality magazine, PO Box 9596 Newmarket, Auckland, tel 9-5293000; fax 5293001.

Management: PO Box 5544, Auckland; tel (09) 3585455; fax (09) 3585462.

Marketing Magazine: Minty's Media, Private Bag 93-218, Parnell, Auckland; tel (09) 379 4233; fax (9) 3093575.

Mercantile Gazette: PO Box 37-424, Parnell, Auckland; tel/fax (09) 302 5292.

New Zealand Business: Private Bag 93-216 Parnell, Auckland; tel (09) 379 4233; fax (09) 309 3575.

New Zealand Farmer: PO Box 4233, Auckland; tel (09) 5791124; fax (09) 579 9589.

New Zealand Horticulture: PO Box 27-340, Mt Roskill, Auckland; tel (09) 624 1143; fax (09) 624 1145.

New Zealand Manufacturer: PO Box 11543, Wellington; tel (04) 473 3000; fax (04) 473 3004.

Professional Associations

Many professional vacancies are carried in specialist magazines, which are usually published by the relevant professional associations. In some cases all vacancies appear in these publications, for example all permanent teaching jobs are advertised in the *Education Gazette.* They will also usually carry employment wanted adverts. Sometimes it is possible to subscribe just to the employment wanted pages. You can contact the professional bodies listed above for further information.

Useful Addresses
Accountants Journal: PO Box 11-342, Wellington; tel (04) 473 8544; fax (04) 472 6282.

Education Gazette: Legislation Services, GP Print, PO Box 12-418, Thorndon, Wellington.

Law Talk: New Zealand Law Society, PO Box 5041, Wellington; tel (04) 472 7837; fax (04) 473 7909.

New Zealand Engineering: PO Box 12-241, Wellington; tel (04) 473 9444; fax (04) 473 2324.

The New Zealand Medical Journal: The New Zealand Medical Association, PO Box 11-649, Wellington; tel (04) 384 7635; fax (04) 385 8902.

The New Zealand Dental Journal: PO Box 3016, Wellington; tel (04) 801 6187; fax (04) 801 6261.

Trades and Skilled Craftspeople
As is the case with the professional associations, in order to work in New Zealand as a trades or craftsperson, you must join the relevant association or society. If you have qualifications and experience in your own country you will not normally be required to fulfil any additional requirements. You should contact the organisations listed below for further details. Most of these organisations publish a trade magazine which may be a useful source of information about job prospects.

Useful Addresses
The New Zealand Society of Master Plumbers & Gasfitters Inc: PO Box 6606 Wellington; tel (04) 384 4184; fax (04) 384 2456. Also publishes *The New Zealand Plumbers Journal:* address as above.

The New Zealand Master Builders Federation, PO Box 1769, Wellington; tel (04) 473 5094. Also publishes: *Building Today:* PO Box 37-390, Parnell Road, Auckland; tel (09) 309 1112; fax (09) 308 9690.

New Zealand Institute of Surveyors: PO Box 831, Wellington; tel (04) 471 1774; fax (04) 471 1907. Also publishes New Zealand Surveyor: address as above.

The New Zealand Painting Contractors Association: PO Box 15-137, Wellington, tel/fax (04) 388 1516. Also publishes: *New Zealand Painter and Decorator:* address as above.

New Zealand Institute of Valuers: PO Box 27-146, Wellington; tel (04) 385 8436; fax (04) 382 9214. Also publishes: *New Zealand Valuers Journal:* address as above.

UK Newspapers and Directories
As noted above, the trend for the international advertising of jobs has not generally caught on with New Zealand employers because of the obvious difficulties with labour mobility to such a remote country. Only a small percentage of jobs are advertised directly in the UK. For example university lectureships are advertised in the *Times Higher Education Supplement.* The fortnightly publication *Overseas Jobs Express* advertises full time jobs in a variety of areas for many countries including New Zealand. As well there are two newspapers available in the UK for intending migrants to New Zealand, *Destination New Zealand* and *New Zealand Outlook.* These occasionally carry advertisements for jobs and usually carry advertisements for job-search agencies based in the UK which will help you look in New Zealand. The weekly paper for New Zealanders in London, *New Zealand News UK,* is a good source of job advertisements for positions in New Zealand. *New Zealand News UK* is distributed free in London outside central city tube stations and all three papers are available beside the

Immigration Service visa inquiry desk on the third floor of New Zealand House or can be obtained on subscription from the addresses below.

Useful Addresses

Destination New Zealand: Outbound Newspapers, 1 Commercial Road, Eastbourne, East Sussex, BN21 3XQ.
New Zealand News UK: PO Box 10, Berwick Upon Tweed, Northumberland, TD15 1BW.
New Zealand Outlook: Consyl Publishing Ltd, 3 Buckhurst Road, Bexhill-on-Sea, Sussex TN40 1QF; tel 01424-223111.
Overseas Jobs Express: PO Box 22, Brighton BN1 6HX; tel 01273-440220.

Approaching Employers Direct

As in the UK, a large number of jobs are filled without ever being advertised. Advertising and screening applicants is lengthy and expensive. A well written CV which lands on the personnel manager's desk at the right time could save them time and money, and find you the type of job you want. It is also a way of exploiting personal contacts. You can begin your research by finding out the New Zealand companies working in your area of expertise. One place to start is the Yellow Pages which you can consult at the front desk of New Zealand House between 9am and 5pm weekdays. The Information Office on the Second Floor of New Zealand House has business directories and is open 2pm to 4pm weekdays. It is not a job search service however. You can obtain a copy of the *New Zealand Export Yearbook* from the Trade Development Board on the second floor of New Zealand House, which lists New Zealand companies involved in the export market and what range of products they sell. There is a list of major New Zealand employers at the end of this chapter.

Chambers of Commerce & Professional Institutes

Chambers of Commerce exist to serve the interests of their members, local businesses, not as job search agencies but they are usually prepared to help with information. Local chambers of commerce should provide you with a list of their members for a small fee. A list of Chambers of Commerce in the main cities can be found in the *Regional Employment Guide* below. Another type of organisation which will have details of member companies are the professional institutes. Also listed below are the NZ-UK Chamber of Commerce and the Amercian Chamber of Commerce which publish directories of British and American companies respectively with branches, affiliates or subsidiaries in New Zealand.

Useful Addresses

Chambers of Commerce:
American Chamber of Commerce: PO Box 3408, Wellington.
New Zealand Chambers of Commerce: PO Box 11-043, Manners St, Wellington; fax/ tel (04) 4723376.
NZ-UK Chamber of Commerce: Suite 10/16, 3rd Floor, Morley House, 314-322 Regent Street, London W1R 5AJ; tel 0171-636 4525.

Professional Institutes:
New Zealand Merchant Bankers Association: PO Box 540, Wellington; tel (04)4735 787.
New Zealand Bankers Institute: PO Box 3043, Wellington; tel (04)4735 069.
Insurance Institute Of New Zealand: PO Box 1368,Wellington; tel (04)3856 019.
New Zealand Institute of Management: PO Box 67, Wellington; tel (04)4737063.

Placing Employment Wanted Adverts
Another approach is placing an employment wanted advert with the newspapers and specialist publications listed above. You can contact the newspapers directly for details of advertising rates, or place adverts through the *New Zealand Press Association* (85 Fleet St London EC4Y 1DY).

Employment Agencies

UK-based Organisations
There are a number of organisations in the UK which can help you find a job in New Zealand. Some companies specialise in finding jobs for intending migrants, others recruit on behalf of employers and sometimes have New Zealand assignments.The latter type operate on behalf of employers do not search on behalf of prospective workers, however they will fill some vacancies from people they have on their books so it may be worthwhile sending them a cv and a speculative application. As has been mentioned elsewhere, help with job seeking is one of the services which immigration consultancies provide.

Job Search Agencies for Intending Emigrants:
Commonwealth Jobsearch: Oxford House, College Court, Commercial Road, Swindon, Wiltshire SN1 1PZ; tel 01793-535300, 0171-828 1994.
Emigration Consultancy Services, De Salis Court, Hampton Lovett, Droitwich, Worcestershire WR9 ONX; tel 01905 795949; fax 01905 795557.
Leesons Emigration and Demographic Service: 4 Cranley Road, Ilford, Essex IG26AG; tel 0181-5182603.

Recruitment Agencies:
Prime Recruitment Contracts: 105a East Street, Southhampton;
Specialist Consultancy Resources: 14 The Square, 111 Broad Street Birmingham, B15 1AS; tel 0121-631 4030; fax 0121-643 7159.
The Workhouse: 75 New Bond Street, London W1Y 9DD; tel 0171-629 1406; fax 0171-629 1428. (Advertising industry placements)

New Zealand Employment Service
The Department of Labour in New Zealand provides job-search assistance through the New Zealand Employment Service, a network of offices advertising local vacancies. They carry a wide range of vacancies for casual, skilled and unskilled work. There is no fee to use the Employment Service, but you have to be a New Zealand resident or citizen.

Employment Agencies in New Zealand
There are a large number of private employment agencies in New Zealand. As in the UK, these agencies charge the employer when they make a successful placement and are free for the job seeker, although they will offer other services such as career assessment and advice on preparation of CVs for which there may be a charge.

Useful Addresses
Computing/Information Technology
Aacorn International Ltd: PO Box 105-355, Auckland Central; tel (09) 309 7862; fax (09) 309 9034.
Enterprise Staff Consultants Ltd: 3rd Floor, Ferry Building, 99 Quay Street, Auckland, PO Box 1799, Auckland; tel (09) 309 4349; fax (09) 307 1285.

Hawkins McLay Associates: PO Box 10-081, Wellington; tel (04) 473 4385; fax (04) 473 4380.

Information Technology Recruitment (ITEC): PO Box 6798, Wellesley Street, Auckland; tel (09) 302 5304; fax (09) 373 2968.

Mercury Management Consulting Ltd: PO Box 10-605, Wellington; tel (04) 499 2624; fax (04) 499 1655.

Panda Computer Services: PO Box 11-011, Auckland; tel (09) 525 7420; fax (09) 525 7430.

Qube Associates Ltd: EDP Personnel Consultants, PO Box 1849, Auckland; tel (09) 307 3852; fax (09) 366 7171.

Farming
Marvin Farm Services: PO Box 248, Matamata, Waikato; tel (07) 8886025; fax (07) 888 5014.

Finance/Accountancy
Clayton Ford: Level 7, ICL House, 126 The Terrace, PO Box 10083, Wellington; tel (04) 473 6223; fax (04) 471 2100.

Opal Consulting Group: POB 7067, Auckland; fax (09) 377 4127.

Professional/Managerial/General
Advanced Personnel Services Ltd: 399 Montreal St, Christchurch; tel (03)3654322; fax (03)3657356.

Drake International: 10th floor Scollway House 5-7 Willeston Street, PO Box 10063, Wellington; tel (04) 462 6972; fax (04) 473 4930.

IDPE Consulting Group: PO Box 4191, Wellington; tel (04) 472 1151; fax (04) 471 1119.

Lampen: PO Box 2155, Wellington; tel (04) 472 4157; fax (04) 471 0958.

Macfarlane Consulting: PO Box 2292, Auckland; tel (09) 377 4151; fax (09) 337 3221.

Wheeler Campbell Consulting: PO Box 205, Wellington; tel (04) 499 1500; fax (04) 499 3910.

Hotel/Catering
Kelly Recruitment: PO Box 10151, Wellington; tel (04) 499 2825; fax (04) 499 2821.

Medical/Nursing
Acorn Medical Staffing Ltd: PO Box 74-385, Auckland; tel (09) 630 8300.

Auckland Medical Bureau: 469 Parnell Road, Auckland; tel (09) 377 5903.

Medical Personnel: PO Box 67-003, Mt Eden, Auckland; tel (09) 630 1963; fax (09) 630 1965.

Nightingale Nurse Ltd: PO Box 54-137, Plimmerton, Wellington; tel (04) 239 9230.

Secretarial
Opal Consulting Group: PO Box 2209 Wellington; tel (04) 385 4011; fax 1'(04) 385 6704.

Company or Organisation Transfers

One alternative to finding work yourself in New Zealand is to find work with a company with prospects of being transferred to New Zealand. Unfortunately few companies recruit staff with the promise of being posted to a particular country, however if you choose a New Zealand company to work for, your chances are obviously greater. Still this process is likely to be a long term route into New Zealand. The NZ-UK Chambers of Commerce publishes the *New Zealand British Business Directory* which is available for £15.00 and covers New

Zealand companies operating in the UK and vice versa. The Amercian Chamber of Commerce in New Zealand publishes a similar directory of American companies operating in New Zealand. (See the addresses above). The big multinationals also have subsidiaries in New Zealand, sometimes under different names. For example Levers trades in New Zealand as Unilever.

Job Application

The job application process in New Zealand is similar to that in the UK. A typical application will comprise of a letter of application or covering letter and a curriculum vitae (cv). Companies short-list on the basis of CVs and interview the selected candidates before making a decision.

Application Letters and CVs.
If you are sending off speculative letters it is worth taking the time to ring up the company and find out who the personnel or general manager is. A personally addressed letter is much more effective than one which is clearly a copy of one sent to a dozen other companies. Letters, whether applying for a specific vacancy or inquiring about possible future vacancies, should be formal in tone, brief (one side of an A4 sheet), and should outline why you are particularly qualified to work for the company. Curriculum Vitaes are expected to cover much the same sort of ground as CVs in the UK, education, qualifications, work experience, skills and personal details. In New Zealand CVs list jobs and qualifications in reverse chronological order, ie the most recent job first and the earliest last. Try to keep it to two pages and make sure it is clearly laid out. This is particularly important if you are faxing applications to New Zealand as fax machines blur copy slightly and if the typeface on your cv is too small, some important details may be lost. It is worthwhile getting some professional advice on the preparation of your cv; services which assist with CVs can be found under Employment Agencies in the Yellow Pages. Do not send original documents with applications.

Interview Procedure
If you are applying for a job in New Zealand from the UK, and the company wishes to interview you, in most cases they will not be prepared to pay your travel costs. Some companies will arrange interviews by video link or telephone. Another option to consider is to arrange a number of job interviews to coincide with a visit to New Zealand, or your arrival in New Zealand if your residency has been approved. There are job search companies in the UK who specialise in lining up job interviews before you set off for New Zealand. See the section *UK Employment Agencies*, above.
   Job interviews in New Zealand are practically no different to those you might expect in the UK. They tend to be quite formal and you should dress appropriately for a work situation, although the dress code in the New Zealand work place is slightly more casual than in Britain. If you are concerned about brushing up your job search skills, the Centre for Professional Employment Counselling publishes a guide called *The Job Search* (price £10.95) which is available from their offices (67 Jermyn Street, London SW1Y 6N; tel 0171-930 0322).

Aspects of Employment

Salaries

You should not expect a New Zealand salary to be the same as a salary in your home country once the exchange rate is taken into account. Salaries in New Zealand are lower than those forequivalent positions in Europe. On the other hand, living costs are considerably lower. Primary produce, fruit and vegetables, and clothing are all quite cheap. It is difficult to make a direct comparison of living standards between Europe and New Zealand because so many factors are hard to compare. For example, going overseas for an annual holiday becomes very expensive when the nearest country is three hours away, and that is only Australia. On the other hand, you have easy access to great beaches and can enjoy much better climate than northern Europeans, year round. As a generalisation it would be fair to say that living standards are equivalent for most middle income earners. The following salaries for different occupations will give you an idea of relative earnings.

Accountant:	$35,000-$40,000
Accounts Clerk:	$20,000-$25,000
Engineer:	$40,000+
General middle management:	$80,000+
Secretary:	$20,000-$25,000
Stockbroker:	$35,000-$40,000

The minimum wage is currently $6.125 per hour or $245 for a forty hour week. It does not apply to people under 20 or in training schemes.

Working Conditions

Standard conditions of employment used to be a forty-hour week, 8.30am-5pm, five days a week. However with the introduction of more flexible working arrangements under the new industrial relations legislation, variations on this theme are becoming increasingly common. For example Fisher & Paykel, New ZealandUs largest manufacturer of kitchen and laundry appliances has shifted to ten hour shifts, four days a week, in some of their divisions. Rates for overtime are another area changing due to the impact of new legislation. Whereas under the old award system (the equivalent of British collective agreements) overtime in most industries was one and half times the standard rates, in many sectors now particularly for casual workers and in the service sector, overtime rates are being cut back or disappearing entirely. Longer working hours are also becoming a feature of many industries. Holiday provision is still protected by law under the Holidays Act. After twelve months continuous employment, the employee is entitled to three weeks paid leave. In addition there are 11 paid public holidays. Employees do not have to work on public holidays unless they agree or their contract provides for this. The compulsory retirement age is 65, although this is to be progressively phased out by the end of the decade.

Parental Leave

Parental leave is available to employees who have worked for 12 months or more with the same employer, either part-time (for more than ten hours per week) or full time. Employees adopting a child under five years old are also entitled to parental leave. The types of leave are all unpaid and the conditions are as follows:

Special Leave: Up to ten days during pregnancy for women to have ante-natal checks.

Maternity Leave: Up to 14 continuous weeks for the mother which can start up to six weeks before the expected date of birth.

Paternity Leave: Up to two continous weeks for the father around the expected date of birth.

Extended Leave: Up to 52 continuous weeks, excluding any maternity leave taken available in the 12 months after the birth. Extended leave may be shared by both parents but may not exceed 52 weeks in total.

Job Protection
If you take less than four weeks parental leave, your job must be kept open. If you take more than four weeks, the employer may decide that the job cannot be kept open, but you have a right to challenge that decision. If you accept this decision then you are entitled to a preference period of six months when the employer must offer you a job substantially similar to the one you have left. You may not be dismissed for becoming pregnant or for applying for parental leave.

Trades Unions
Prior to the Employment Contracts Act of 1991, New Zealand unions enjoyed a monopoly over workplace representation and union membership in many industries was compulsory. The resulting system of wage determination was highly centralised and inflexible. If unions and employers negotiating in each industry at a national level could not agree, the dispute would be settled through compulsory arbitration by a tribunal made up of members from both sides. As a result of this system, employment conditions were guaranteed at some minimum level in just about all industries, and the disparity between the high paid and the low paid was not very great.

The Employment Contracts Act of 1991 removed union monopolies over bargaining in the workplace, abolished compulsory membership, and the Arbitration Tribunals. Wage fixing is now in theory completely decentralised, although some of the bigger unions still negotiate at national level. Employers and employees negotiate employment contracts which may be either collective or individual. Employees may nominate someone to act as their bargaining agent. Employers are obliged to recognise whoever an employee nominates as their bargaining agent although this does not mean they must negotiate or settle with that agent. Now that trade unions no longer have a protected legal status, total membership has fallen from 683, 000 to 409, 100 in 1993. The number of employees on collective agreements has fallen sharply: 75% of the workforce are now employed on individual contracts. Flexibility has brought benefits to some employees and industries but has weakened the position of others. Part time workers, those in workplaces with only a few employees and the service sector generally all have less job security, fewer employment protections and in some cases have seen a real reduction in pay.

Most New Zealand unions belong to the national body: The New Zealand Council of Trade Unions (PO Box 6645, Wellington tel (04) 3851 334).

Employment Contracts
At the beginning of your employment you will negotiate an employment contract with your employer. You can be covered under an existing collective contract if it provides for new workers to join and if your employer agrees. Otherwise you will negotiate an individual contract. Individual contracts can be either written or oral but it is desirable to have a written contract. If you wish to have a bargaining agent represent you, you have a choice between joining a union or employing a private bargaining agent. Remember though that though your

employer must recognise your bargaining agent they are not obliged to settle with them. An employment contract must by law have certain provisions. There must be an effective personal grievance procedure and disputes procedure. The minimum conditions outlined above, wages and holiday provision and the parental leave provisions, cannot be overridden.

Employment Tribunal & Employment Court

Two institutions for resolving disputes were set up under the Act, the Tribunal, which mostly mediates in disputes, either personal disputes or grievances arising from breach of employment contracts, and the Employment Court which deals with matters referred on by the tribunal, and more serious issues such as disputes involving strikes and lockouts. There is no right to strike while an employment contract is still current.

Women in Work

Around 50% of New Zealand women over the age of 15 work. This figure has been steadily increasing since the 1960s, although it seems to have plateaued in recent years and even dropped off slightly in the late 80s, which may reflect the effects of the economic downturn. The participation rates for women are considerably lower than the corresponding figures for men across all age groups and particularly in the 25-34 age group, reflecting the fact that women are still the primary care givers for children. About a third of the female workforce work part time, a much higher figure than for men.

Despite still bearing more family responsibilities than men, New Zealand women are moving into previously male dominated areas, particularly the professions. Female students outnumber men in areas such as medicine and law, although this is a recent development and men still dominate at senior levels in these professions. Equal pay for the same work was established under the Equal Pay Act of 1972, and other forms of discrimination in the workplace based on gender, race or any other non relevant factor is illegal under the Human Rights Commission Act of 1972. If you believe you have been discriminated against unlawfully, you can either use the personal grievance procedures in your employment contract or you can make a complaint to the Human Rights Commission. Despite the effects of the Equal Pay Act, women's ordinary time earnings remain about 20% lower than men's. Women are still concentrated in a narrower range of occupations which in general, pay less well. Equal pay claims are also harder to establish in the new environment of individual contracts. Discrimination in individual cases is much harder to prove than in a situation where everyone receives the same rate of pay for a job. Despite these negative influences, the attitude towards women in employment in New Zealand is generally positive. Childcare is becoming more affordable now that the government subsidises pre-school care centres. Some of these advances have been achieved through the efforts of women politicians. Women have a high profile in New Zealand public life. Nearly a quarter of the members of parliament are women and the governor general is woman, as is the leader of the opposition.

Permanent Work

Executive Employment Prospects

Prospects are good for executive employment as the recession seems to be finally over. Executive recruitment companies report that the demand for professional staff is high and that the local labour market is unable to provide enough suitably skilled applicants. They note however that the openings are for people with a high level of technical and interpersonal skills. OECD surveys predict strong growth for the New Zealand economy and business confidence is particularly strong.

Information Technology
There is always a demand for skilled programmers particularly with university level qualifications. New Zealanders qualified in these areas tend to be attracted overseas by the comparatively higher salaries. Currently the types of positions being advertised are for software developers with skills in programming in C, C++, Unix, Dos and OS2.

Medical
The numbers of foreign doctors registering with the Medical Council has increased in recent years and the Council is now worried that there may be soon be an oversupply of medical personnel. The increase in numbers seems to be the result of an increase in numbers of skilled immigrants, particularly from South Africa which has resulted in a reverse 'brain-drain'. The situation in New Zealand has usually been the opposite with trained New Zealanders going abroad leaving opportunities for qualified migrants. You should contact the Medical Council for an accurate assessment of employment opportunities. As has been noted already, you must register with the Medical Council in order to practice as a doctor in New Zealand. Doctors from Australia, Britain, Ireland and South Africa who have been registered in their own country are usually accepted for registration without requiring further qualifications. Doctors from other countries will usually have to sit registration exams.

Nurses must apply to be registered with the Nursing Council of New Zealand. The current employment situation is not particularly good for general nurses although the Council notes that there are opportunities for experienced nurses and midwives with specialist skills. Psychiatric, renal, orthopaedics, general surgical are other areas where vacancies are currently being advertised.

Teaching
As noted above, immigrants intending to teach require to have their qualifications approved by the Teacher Registration Board. There is a particular demand for qualified science and mathematics teachers. The *Education Gazette* is published fortnightly and advertises all permanent teaching positions in state and independent schools. You can read copies of the Gazette at the Information Office, second floor New Zealand House, or by subscribing directly to the address above. (See *Professional Associations*).

Short-term Employment

Short-term employment prospects are improving as the economy picks upafter some rather lean years. However, as already noted in Chapter Two, *Residence and Entry* unless you are a New Zealander or have residency you will have to get a work visa to work while in New Zealand, even for a short period. One of the conditions of these visas is that you are doing jobs for which there are no appropriately qualified New Zealanders. Given that the types of jobs most people obtain while travelling are unskilled labouring jobs, your chances of working legitimately are not great. There is a lot of paperwork for your employer to get through, (see Chapter Two) just to hire a fruit picker. Alternatively, if you are a British citizen aged between 18 and 30 you can apply for one of the 500 working holiday visas issued each year, before you leave for New Zealand. (See *Residence and Entry* chapter for details) If you do not have a work permit, many farmers may not be too concerned as they have many short term jobs, particularly seasonal jobs in rural areas and often cannot find locals interested in doing them. Under these circumstances you may find that employers are more interested in whether you are keen on working than whether you are legal. But be careful because in recent years the Immigration Service has been doing sweeps of picking gangs in remote areas to check whether they have work permits. You may endanger your chances of staying in New Zealand if you try to bend the rules on working.

Horticulture and Agriculture

There are a lot of opportunities for keen workers in orchards, even if you have little or no experience. However, since the work is unskilled you will find that pay rates are far from high. Fruit picking tends to be paid at what is called piece rates (rates per kilo or bin filled). Obviously as you get better at the work, your pay rates improve but you may find it discouraging going, as well as back-breaking depending on the crop; asparagus picking is reputed to be the worst. It is possible to follow the different harvests around the country as each type of produce comes into season and to find work virtually year round. In the main horticultural areas during the harvest, work will not be hard to find. Farmers advertise locally, sometimes contacting local youth hostels or backpackers' accommodation, or simply putting a sign up at the gate. They will often provide accommodation, albeit of a rather basic kind, and sometimes even fresh fruit and vegetables or dairy products. Generally the remoter the area, the more difficulty the farmers have in attracting local labour, so the better your chances. However this is no guarantee that they will be able to pay more, they are just more likely to provide non-wage perks such as accommodation or food in order to get the workers. For details of the timing and locations of various harvests see *Work Your Way Around the World* available from Vacation Work Publications (9 Park End Street, Oxford).

Unlike fruit picking, working on farms usually requires some experience. For example you will see almost daily advertisements in the Waikato papers for milkers, but they require people with the skills already. Some unskilled work is available in shearing sheds, for example the job of rousie (the person who picks up the shorn fleeces) does not require much beyond a strong pair of arms. If you have at least two years practical farming under your belt and want to get experience of working on a New Zealand farm, you can contact the International Farm Experience Programme, (YFC Centre, National Agricultural Centre, Stoneleigh Park, Kenilworth, Warwickshire, CV8 2LG; tel 01203-696584; fax 01203-696559).

Au Pair/Nannying

There is some demand for nannies and au pairs in New Zealand. The term au pair is uncommon, and the generic term child-carer is more usual. Posts are advertised in the daily papers or on community notice boards. There are specialist agencies who can be found in the Yellow Pages. Wages are quite low, around NZ$7 per hour, or between $290- 310 per week.

Useful Addresses

Lady-Hamilton Smith Agency: PO Box 445, Papakura, South Auckland; tel (09) 302 3289.
Swift Timbrel: 18 Kings Crescent, Lower Hutt, PO Box 30799.

Teaching English

New Zealand is a popular destination for Asian students wanting to learn English, because of its reputation as a safe and friendly country. As an employment prospect you will almost certainly need the appropriate TEFL qualifications or experience in order to get a work permit, because as has already been noted above, the Immigration Service has to be satisfied that you have skills not possessed by New Zealand job seekers. Speaking English as your first language is not enough to qualify you, however much you may dispute whether Nu Zilindish as spoken by the natives is actually English at all. There are more than 40 public and private English-language schools. Some of the bigger ones are listed below.

Useful Addresses

Aspiring Language Institute: 242 Papanui Road, Christchurch; tel (03) 355 3231.
Capital Language Academy: PO Box 1100, Wellington; tel (04) 472 7557; fax (04) 472 5285.
Dominion English School: 47 Customs St, Auckland, PO Box 4217, Auckland; tel (09) 377 3280; fax (09) 377 3473.
Dominion English School: 28 Salisbury Street, Christchurch; (03) 365 3370.
Garden City English School: 344 Gloucester Street, Christchurch; tel (03) 377 0091.
International Language Academies: PO Box 25-170 Christchurch; tel (03) 3795452; fax (03) 3795357.
Languages International: 27 Princes St, PO Box 5293, Auckland 1; tel (09) 309 0615; fax (09) 3772806.
Seafield School of English: 1/99 Seaview Road, Christchurch; tel (03) 388 3850.
Southern English Schools: 69 Worcester Bvd, Christchurch; tel (03) 365 6022.

Tourism

Over a million tourists visit New Zealand each year and as a result there are a lot of opportunities for casual workers in the tourist regions. Hotel and catering staff positions in tourist destinations are a good place to start looking. Working hours are long and the pay low, but on the other hand, the location may make up for the working conditions. Tourists tip better than locals as New Zealanders traditionally do not tip serving staff. If you can ski, there are a lot of opportunities on New Zealand ski fields for ski instructors or ski patrol personnel. Other types of skills which may help you find employment are aquatic sports skills such as scuba diving, water skiing, or life saving skills. New Zealand beaches are patrolled by mostly by volunteer surf life savers who have specialist skills in rescuing people from the often turbulent waters so you are more likely to finding employment looking after hotel or private pools. Qualified aerobics instructors should find opportunities at the many private gyms around the country.

Voluntary work

If you want to avoid work permit hassles and still be legal, there are voluntary schemes whereby you can work in exchange for food and lodgings. The most well known scheme goes under the name of WWOOF, which stands for Willing Workers on Organic Farms. There are many organic farms in New Zealand so potentially you could see quite a lot of the country without paying for your accommodation. Usually you do about half a day's work in exchange for your board and lodgings. The work can be quite varied and you should be prepared for strictly vegetarian rations Send a s.a.e. to the UK branch of WWOOF (19 Bradford Road, Lewes, Sussex BN7 1RB), who will send you a membership application form; membership costs £8 per year and after you have volunteered for two weekends in Britain you can request the list of WWOOF headquarters around the world. Alternatively you can write directly to New Zealand and request the list of WWOOFer farms from Andrew and Jane Strange, (PO Box 10-037, Palmerston North, New Zealand) for a fee of NZ$15.

Business and Industry Report

After a long period of economic uncertainty, the New Zealand economy seems to have turned the corner and recent indicators are all promising. A recent survey of world competitiveness placed New Zealand ninth overall and well ahead of many of its trading partners which is encouraging news for New Zealand's ability to attract foreign investment. Factor costs are already 20-25% lower than in Australia. Inflation remains steady at just under 1%. Business confidence is at a historically high level. Increased levels of economic activity world-wide should raise the demand for New Zealand exports, still the driving force of the New Zealand economy. A key factor in export performance is the terms of trade, the ratio of import to export prices. These have shown some improvement early in 1995 as a result of better wool prices and low inflation in New Zealand's trading partners.

Agriculture

Agriculture contributes over $3.5 billion annually to the New Zealand economy and accounts for 60% of its export earnings. It is one of the major agricultural exporting countries in the world and is the largest exporter of lamb and mutton, providing over half the world's exports of these products. The New Zealand agricultural industry is highly mechanised and is a low employer of labour as a result. The average family farm employs the farmer, spouse and perhaps one farmhand. It is also one of the most efficient agricultural sectors in the world and has the lowest level of subsidies of any OECD country. The removal of supplementary minimum payments in 1984 was predicted by many in the farming sector to be a disaster. Instead although some farmers were forced to sell up, the sector responded by becoming more efficient and although farm land prices have not yet recovered to their pre-SMP prices, farm profitability is once again favourable. Farmers are now vulnerable to world prices in agricultural commodities and as a result many have diversified in order to spread their risk. Reliance upon traditional production areas has declined: sheep numbers are at their lowest since the 1950s as a result of low wool prices. New production areas such as venison are being developed. Farmers are experimenting with diversification of land use, planting land for forestry while still grazing it, for example. Despite the uncertainty of trading at world prices, the removal of subsidies seem to have done the industry good. The diversity of output has helped the country expand its export markets.

The main products are still sheep meat, dairy products, wool and beef. New Zealand has a natural advantage in agriculture due to its climate which is ideal for grassland farming. The land itself was not originally suited for this purpose being heavily forested and quite hilly. It has been brought under cultivation by lot of effort and the application of grassland management techniques developed in New Zealand's specialist agricultural research stations. Some of this agricultural expertise is being exported overseas in the form of sales of farm machinery, developed in New Zealand, agricultural consulting services, and New Zealand breeding animals. New Zealand is a world leader in animal and plant breeding technology. There were hopes some years ago that 'agri-tech' might double its contribution to export earnings, but this seems to have been an optimistic assessment. On the other hand this sector is primarily responsive to local demand and as farm profitibility improves, it is likely investment in agricultural production techniques will increase.

The outlook for the agricultural industry is optimistic. Agricultural commodity prices are rising steadily in major markets like the USA. In the past year, the US dollar index of agricultural prices has risen by over 30%. The impact of the 1994 GATT agreement is expected to improve market access for New ZealandUs agricultural exports. Under the Uruguay Agreement the European Union will have to lift the current restrictive quotas which prevent access for New Zealand butter and lamb into European markets. Implementation hiccups may delay any immediate windfalls from GATT but it is expected to significantly boost meat and dairy prices by 1995/6 which will have a positive effect upon farm profitability in New Zealand.

Banking and Finance

Banking and financial services was one of the fastest growing employment sectors between 1986 and 1991. In part this was a one-off boom as a result of the deregulation of the financial sector as part of the programme of economic reform instituted by the Labour government in the 1980s. As a result of deregulation there was a rapid growth in money market activity, particularly in the areas of foreign exchange, where all restrictions over transfers were lifted. New Zealand's relatively undeveloped financial industry enjoyed a boom. A range of new financial instruments was introduced such as forward contracts, options and exchange rate futures and secondary markets such as in government securities grew. The share market soared due to the increase in money supply resulting from deregulation. The boom was short-lived however and the inevitable collapse came in October 1987 when the main share price index, the Barclays share index dropped to below its 1984 level. It has not recovered to pre-crash levels and there have been two smaller falls in 1989 and 1990.

The second stage of deregulation in the financial sector occurred in the late 1980s. The regulations governing the supervision and registration of banks was relaxed under the Reserve Bank of New Zealand Act of 1989, and as result most building societies registered as banks and a number of foreign banks established New Zealand subsidiaries. The increase in the number of financial institutions and the range of activities they were involved in resulted in a rapid growth of employment in this area. Activity has levelled off in recently and it seems likely that employment growth will as well.

Construction

Construction is another industry currently enjoying a boom. The construction industry employs more than 6% of the workforce. There is a general shortage of skilled tradespeople and there is likely to be more demand in the future for carpenters, fitters, welders and joiners. New Zealand construction companies have particular expertise in building to earthquake proof standards.

Energy, Coal and Petrochemicals

Coal is New Zealand's largest energy resource, with nearly nine billion tons potentially recoverable according to the Coal Resource Survey programme. New Zealand produces just under three million tons of coal annually, mainly sub-bitumous coal from North Island fields. The West Coast of the South Island is the biggest source of bitumous coal most of which is exported. Industrial usage consumes nearly three-quarters of the remaining production. Coal is no longer a feed stock for thermal power stations as gas is becoming more competitive. In the future dual process stations such as the power station at Huntly, north of Hamilton which can use either gas or coal may go back to using coal as domestic gas supplies decline. The petrochemical industry is concentrated around the natural gas and oil fields off the coast of Taranaki. Six fields produce crude oil, condensate and natural gas which provide about 50% of New Zealand's energy needs. Natural gas is the major product. Around a third of the natural gas produced is used to make synthetic petrol at a processing plant near Motonui.

Seventy to 80% of New Zealand's electricity supply is produced by hydro-electric generators on major rivers. The generating authority currently is the Electricity Corporation of New Zealand (ECNZ), a state owned enterprise. It runs 30 operational hydro-electric stations and eight thermal power stations. The most recent investment in electricity generation was the Clyde Dam project opened in 1992, providing 432 megawatts. The government has plans to break up ECNZ to allow for competitive generation. Distribution of final consumers is currently handled by energy companies owned by a mixture of consumer, local authority and private interests. A Maori trust plans to build another geothermal power station near Taupo.

Major Companies: BP New Zealand, Fletcher Challenge, Dominion Oil Refining, Mobil Oil New Zealand, Caltex NZ.

Forestry

Forests cover about 28% of New Zealand's land area. The bulk of this is native rainforest which is no longer a major source of timber for export. Pressure from conservation groups and the increasing profitability of other plantation species has restricted the harvesting of native forests. Just under 3% of native forests are still being logged under strict conditions. Production forests cover 1.3 million hectares and are a renewable resource. The bulk of these forests are planted in introduced species, mainly radiata pine with a small percentage of Douglas fir and a few other species. The forestry industry is concentrated in the centre of the North Island where the main production forests are located. There are smaller plantation forests in the South Island, mainly in the Tasman area and on the West Coast. The forestry industry is New Zealand's third largest export earning sector after the meat and dairy industries, earning over $1.7 billion annually. Future prospects for growth are encouraging as restrictions on the importing of tropical hardwoods spread. Although export volumes are predicted to keep growing, prices have proved volatile. In the future competition from radiata suppliers in other southern hemisphere countries may depress prices.

The state used to own half the total area of commercial forests but as part of the privatisation move in the last decade, management and cutting rights were sold to the private sector. The private sector now manages 80% of plantations. Major companies involved in the buying of state forestry assets were the New Zealand companies, Carter Holt Harvey and Fletcher Challenge who are now the biggest operators. The state owned Forestry Corporation. Several overseas companies made significant investments.

Major Companies: ITT Rayonier, Juken Nissho, Earnslaw One, Forestry Corporation of New Zealand, Wenita Forestry, Carter Holt Harvey, Fletcher Challenge, New Zealand Forest Products.

Horticulture and Fishing

Horticulture was another booming area in the New Zealand economy during the 1980s-90s. Kiwi fruit is one well known product of the industry. For a brief period, land prices in the chief kiwi fruit growing areas soared. However the entrance of new growers caused a glut on the market and competition from other countries reduced profits to lower levels. Other areas of the horticultural industry are still booming. Fruit and vegetables now account for 11% of agricultural exports and earned over NZ $1.2 billion in foreign exchange. Earnings are predicted to grow to over $2 billion in the next decade.

Another growth export commodity is fresh fish and shell fish. New Zealand's clean waters provide fish of exceptional quality. Fisheries exports were worth NZ $1.4 billion in 1991-2. New Zealand's exclusive economic zone, wherein all fishing is controlled by the Ministry of Agriculture and Fisheries extends for 200 nautical miles from the coast line, and is one of the largest in the world. MAF runs a system of transferable quotas which has been in place since 1986. Assessments are made about the size of the fishstock and the sustainable commercial catch for each species is estimated. The total catch is allocated between fishing companies through individual quotas which companies can buy or sell. Twenty per cent of quotas for new species are allocated to the Maori under a deal between the tribes and the government settled in 1992.

There is a sizable fish and shellfish farming industry. The main export products are pacific oysters, green lipped mussels, and salmon. Increased diversity is expected in the next decade. This industry like much of New Zealand's agricultural and horticultural output is vulnerable to disease which can wipe out an entire season's crop, as happened in the summer of 1992-3 when toxic algae bloom resulted in shellfish harvesting being suspended. The other major threat to the seafood industry comes from trade barriers. About 85% of the revenues of the industry come from exports but most of the markets New Zealand trades with have volume restrictions (quotas) on imports. New Zealand currently has just over 1.2% of world seafood trade and could expand this if the quotas were increased. One target is increasing sales to Europe which currently takes about 9% of New Zealand exports. However the EU usually negotiates market liberalisation in return for access to fishing grounds. This would be difficult to grant directly in the case of the New Zealand industry because of the system of transferable fishing quotas described above. Given the current fierce competition over EU fishing grounds, and the charges being levelled at various countries of over-fishing, leasing the rights to fish in New Zealand waters could be a possible opening to European markets.

Manufacturing

Despite the long term trend away from manufacturing employment, it is one of areas predicted for strong growth at the time of writing. Manufacturing jobs grew by over 11% in 1993. However another round of tariff cuts are in the offing which will threaten existing jobs of those employees in protected industries, mainly apparel, textiles, footware and car assembly. The Ministry of Commerce is currently undertaking a review of New Zealand's tariff regime. According to the Treasury, New Zealand's tariff regime is still high compared to other OECD countries. Manufacturing industry representatives disagree, naturally, and are pushing for continuing protection in some key industries. Examples of local success stories in manufacturing exports are Mercer Stainless Ltd, whose Auckland food service division has a contract with MacDonalds world wide to produce kitchens for their food outlets in 17 countries. It also handles rivals KFC, and expects to expand into Asia.

Automotive: There is no New Zealand owned car manufacturing industry. The majority of vehicles are imported unassembled, mainly from Japan, and assembled locally. The industry suffered a major decline with the lowering of tariffs between 1988-90 and the downturn in the domestic economy which reduced the demand for new cars. Sales fell in 1991 and 1992 but the outlook is currently positive with new vehicle sales stabilising in 1993 as business and consumer confidence improved. There is a small but significant export market for components manufactured in New Zealand.

Major Companies: Ford NZ, General Motors NZ, Toyota NZ.

Textiles: Australia is the major market for the New Zealand textile and apparel industry. It was one of the last industries to retain quotas on the importation of competing foreign goods and still has a higher tariff regime than many other manufacturing sectors. More tariff reductions are proposed which may result in further job losses. Exports are increasing however, particularly to the major market, Australia. The industry is largely made up of specialised small firms.

Steel and non-ferrous metals: Steel and aluminium are the only metals produced in any quantity in New Zealand. Unwrought aluminium from the Comalco smelter near Bluff is a major export earner using raw bauxite imported from Australia. The New Zealand steel works at Glenbrook produces steel by a unique direct reduction process using local ironsands. Gold is a small but fast growing export industry.

Major Companies: BHP New Zealand Steel, Pacific Steel, Comalco-CHH Aluminium.

Electronics: Electronics is one of the surprising success stories of the restructured New Zealand economy. Under the old regime of protected domestic industries the sector was predominantly involved in the manufacture of consumer electronics. Now most of these goods, TVs, videos, etc are imported from Asia where costs are cheaper. The major exception is the domestic whiteware industry (the local term for fridges, dishwashers, ovens etc.) where New Zealanders show a strong preference for long established local brands such as Fisher and Paykel. The electronics industry, instead of declining with the reduction in tariffs, has diversified and found niche markets in high tech commercial and industrial products. For example one Christchurch based company, Dynamic Controls is the world's main manufacturer of controllers for power wheel chairs and scooters. Software is another area where New Zealand firms have developed specialist markets. New Zealand exports $100 million worth of software annually, only half of a percent of world trade in this area, but a good performance for a country better known for exporting dead animals. Job prospects for skilled workers in the industry are good. There is currently a skills shortage from assembly workers through to engineers and software designers. The size of the New Zealand industry has limited the numbers being trained so that it has been unable to keep up with the current leap in demand for its products.

Major Companies: AWA New Zealand, Fisher and Paykel Electronics, IBM New Zealand.

Food and Beverages: The major destination for food manufacturing exports is the Australian market. Food and beverages enterprises employ just over a quarter of the total manufacturing workforce. Large enterprises dominate the industry and employ the majority of the workforce but there are a number of small businesses producing high quality luxury goods such as smoked seafood, speciality cheeses and wines.

Major Companies: Bluebird Foods, DB Group, Cerebos Gregg, Goodman Fielder Wattie, Kraft General Foods, Nestle New Zealand, Lion Nathan, Abels, Montana Wines, Villa Maria Wines.

Tourism
Tourism is now the single biggest earner of foreign exchange, and employs around 171,000 people, making it one of the largest industries in New Zealand.

There are over a million foreign visitors each year or roughly one visitor for every three New Zealanders. Numbers are predicted to continue growing and should continue to generate demand for retail and hospitality services. Hotel occupancy rates in 1994 were just under 60%, the highest level since 1987, resulting in improved profitability for the industry. Overseas visitors make up nearly two thirds of hotel guests. New Zealand is promoted to overseas visitors by the New Zealand Tourism Board which coordinates the visitor information centre network. The Tourism Board also coordinates a number of quality assurance schemes for hospitality services, KiwiHost and the Qualmark scheme. The main attractions for most overseas visitors are the clean environment and beautiful scenery, but a growing number of tourists are after a more active holiday, skiing trips, jet-boat rides, white water rafting, even bungeejumping. This has lead to the growth of a new type of tourism, called 'adventure tourism'. One area which should take off in the future is 'green tourism'. Often thought to be a contradiction in terms because the impact of visitors upon the environment is usually harmful, green tourism aims to combine sharing the environment with tourists and protecting it. Activities such as whale watching off the Kaikoura coast above Christchurch, and visiting bird sanctuary islands already attract the eco-sensitive.

Transport

As a small exporting economy on the edge of the world, the New Zealand economy is highly dependent on maintaining its external transportation links. Internal transportation networks are also important as its small population is spread over two islands, nearly 2,000 kilometres in combined length. Early transport developments were largely the result of government investment. The rail network, harbours, and road building were all extensively developed under a programme of major public works during the 1870s. State ownership and investment was the pattern for transportation development over the next century. The government owned and ran the railways, a shipping line, and eventually the national airline. State ownership of transportation links diminished under the programme of state asset sales begun by the Labour Government in the 1980s. Now private sector investment is behind most new transport projects, with the exception of road building which remains the responsibility of Transit New Zealand, a government authority. Road transportation was deregulated during the 1980s as was public transport in most cities. New Zealand Rail was sold to a consortium made up of a Canadian, an American and a New Zealand company in 1993. Port authorities were set up as companies, largely owned by local authorities, with two partly privately owned. Further private ownership is encouraged by the government.

Regional Employment Guide

THE UPPER NORTH ISLAND
Northland and Auckland
Major Cities: Auckland (pop. 885,000), Whangarei (pop. 44,000).
Newspapers: *The New Zealand Herald* (PO Box 32, Auckland), *Northern Advocate* (PO Box 210, Whangarei).
Chambers of Commerce: Auckland Chamber of Commerce and Industry: 100 Mayoral Drive, Auckland; tel (09) 309 6100; fax (09) 309 0081. Chamber of Commerce of Northland 28 Rathbone street, Whangarei; tel (09) 438 4771.
Industry/Other Comments: The Auckland region is the main business and

industrial centre and employs nearly one third of the total workforce. 50% are employed in the services sector, comprising wholesale, retail, community, social and personal services. The Auckland region provides most of the jobs in manufacturing, construction, business and financial services. Auckland has a container port and an international airport. Employment prospects in the area are good and getting better. The region is predicted to be the leader in economic growth over the next few years and this is reflected in the number of businesses looking to expand their workforce. Numbers of job advertisements increased by 43% during 1994. Growth industries in the future are likely to be construction and manufacturing. North of the greater Auckland area, job prospects are likely to be associated with the growth of tourism and the expected improvement in agricultural export volumes. New Zealand's only crude oil refinery is located at Marsden Point near Whangarei in the east coast. South of Auckland, at Glenbrook is the BHP New Zealand Steel factory which uses a unique production process based on the reduction of local ironsand. West coasts beaches in New Zealand are characterised by the high proportion of iron ore in the sand which results in black coloration.

THE CENTRAL NORTH ISLAND
Waikato, Bay of Plenty, Gisborne and Hawkes Bay
Major Cities: Hamilton (pop. 148,000), Tauranga (pop. 71,000), Rotorua (pop. 54,000) New Plymouth (pop. 49,000).
Newspapers: *The Waikato Times* (Private Bag 3086, Hamilton), *Bay of Plenty Times* (Private Bag 12002, Tauranga).
Chambers of Commerce: Waikato Chamber of Commerce, Arcadia Building, Worley Place, Hamilton; tel (07) 839 5895. Bay of Plenty Chamber of Commerce, Legal House, 29 Brown Street, Tauranga, (07) 577 9823. Hawkes Bay Chamber of Commerce: Clifton Buildings 119 Queen Street East, Hastings; tel (06) 876 5938.
Industry/Other Comments: The Waikato is one of the main dairy farming regions in the country. Horticulture, particularly citrus fruit and kiwi fruit, is the predominant industry in the Bay of Plenty on the east coast. Hamilton, the fourth largest city in the country is home to a number of manufacturing enterprises, a university, and a large wholesale and retail sector. Most light industry in the region is based on the processing of agricultural and forestry raw products. The central region of the North Island is the main centre for the pulp and paper making industry. Large plantation forests of radiata pine provide the raw materials for the production of newsprint, wood pulp, paper and paperboard. The Waikato is the largest coal producing region in the country, with 17 mainly open cast mines producing 1.5 million tons of sub-bitumous coal, over half the total annual output of the country. Gas is main product of the petro-chemical industry based on the Tarankai coast near New Plymouth. The region is also a tourist destination. Major attrations include the thermal region around Rotorua and the network of limestone caves near Waitomo. Economic prospects in the region are favourable particularly for horticulture and forestry, and associated industries, although growth is not predicted to be as high as in Auckland.

THE LOWER NORTH ISLAND
Taranaki, Manawatu-Wanganui and Wellington
Major Cities: Wellington (pop. 325,000), Palmerston North (pop. 71,000), Hastings (pop. 58,000), Napier (pop. 53,000) Wanganui (pop. 41,000).
Newspapers: *The Dominion* (PO Box 1297, Wellington), *Manawatu Evening Standard* (PO Box 3, Palmerston North) *Hawkes Bay Herald Tribune* (PO Box

180, Hastings) *Daily Telegraph* (PO Box 343, Napier), *Wanganui Chronicle* (PO Box 433, Wanganui).
Chambers of Commerce: *Wellington Chamber of Commerce:* 109 Featherston St, Wellington; tel (04) 472 2725; fax (04) 4711767. Wangnaui Chamber of Commerce, Commerce House, 39 Victoria Ave, Wanganui tel (06) 345 0080.
Industry/Other Comments: The capital city Wellington is the headquarters of central government. Most major law firms, accountants and management firms have their base in Wellington as well, although some firms prefer to have their head office in Auckland reflecting that city's commercial dominance. Wellington is the centre of the performing arts, as the national orchestra and dance companies are located there. It has more professional theatres than any other city. Business, government and retail enterprises dominate the main urban area. Manufacturing industry is concentrated in the outerlying suburbs and on the Petone seafront at the northern end of the Wellington harbour. Outside the urban area, to the north, the Wairarapa district is dairy and sheep farming country. The region also contains two major wine making districts. Hawkes Bay is the oldest established wine making region in the country, the Mission vineyard run by Catholic monks first started producing wine last century, while Martinborough, north of Wellington, is one of the newest.

THE UPPER SOUTH ISLAND
Nelson-Marlborough, West Coast and Canterbury
Major Cities: Christchurch (pop. 307,000), Nelson (pop. 47,000).
Newspapers: *The Christchurch Press* (Private Bag, Christchurch), *The Nelson Evening Mail* (PO Box 244, Nelson).
Chambers of Commerce: Canterbury Employers Chamber of Commerce: 57 Kilmore St, Christchurch; tel (03) 366 5096. Nelson Chamber of Commerce, 54 Montgomery Square, Nelson; tel (03) 548 1363.
Industry/Other Comments: Christchurch and the Canterbury region are predicted to be one of the fastest growing local economies. Job advertisements rose by 22% during 1994. Improvements to market access for New Zealand lamb resulting from GATT should boost the Canterbury region which is the largest sheep farming region in the country. It has a container port nearby at Lyttleton and the second busiest international airport in the country. As well as agricultural industry, Christchurch is the largest region for manufacturing employment after Auckland. It has a number of high-tech electronic and software firms. Canterbury is to be the site of a new 'Hard Business Network' supported by the Ministry of Commerce through the Canterbury Business Development Board. Networks are intended to be partnerships between small businesses which individually would have difficulty in promoting themselves overseas. Tourism is the other major source of economic activity in the region. Tourist attractions are the scenery and the skiing. Christchurch is only an hour away from the ski fields of Mt Hutt. The first legal casino is due to be opened in the former railway station in Christchurch at the end of 1994. Further north, the Nelson/Marlborough region is a major wine growing district, and a centre for forestry and fishing. Exports of timber through Port Nelson are predicted to quadruple over the next five years. The West Coast is the main source for export grade coal. At the time of writing a new deep-water port in the South Island is under consideration. Two locations are being backed, one in Nelson by timber companies, the other on the West Coast, by the state owned mining company CoalCorp.

THE LOWER SOUTH ISLAND
Southland and Otago
Major Cities: Dunedin (pop. 149,000), Invercargill (pop. 52,000).
Newspapers: *The Otago Daily Times* (PO Box 181, Dunedin) *The Southland Times* (PO Box 805, Invercargill).

Chambers of Commerce: Otago Chamber of Commerce: PO Box 5713, Dunedin; tel (03) 479 0181. Southland Chamber of Commerce and International Trade, PO Box 100, Invercargill; tel (03) 218 9059.

Industry/Other Comments: The agricultural base of the rural economy in Otago and Southland is mainly concentrated on sheep farming with smaller numbers of dairy and beef farms. Horticultural activity in the region is based on stonefruit orchards. Vineyards are relatively new to the region. Until recently the climate was thought to be too cold for grape growing. Manufacturing in the region is concentrated around the cities of Dunedin and Invercargill with the exception of the Comalco Aluminium smelter located at Tiwai point near Bluff. Bluff is also known for its production of oysters. American forestry company Rayonier is currently looking at siting a fibre board plant somewhere in Southland which should boost employment prospects in that area.

Directory of Major Employers

Accountancy

Arthur Anderson: Arthur Anderson Tower, National Bank Centre, 209 Queen St, PO Box 199, Auckland; tel (09) 302 0280.

BDO Hogg Young Cathie: Quay Tower, 29 Customs St West , Auckland; tel (09) 379 5285.

Coopers & Lybrand: Coopers & Lybrand Tower 23-29 Albert St, Auckland, PO Box 48, Auckland; tel (09) 358 4888; fax (09) 358 1210.

Ernst & Young: National Mutual Centre, Shortland Street PO Box 2146, Auckland; tel (09) 377 4790.

KPMG Peat Marwick: KPMG Centre 9 Princes St Auckland; tel (09) 367 5800.

Price Waterhouse: Price Waterhouse Centre 66 Wyndham St PO Box 748, Auckland; tel (09) 309 3421.

Banking

ANZ Banking Group (New Zealand) Ltd: 215-229 Lambton Quay, PO Box 1492, Wellington; tel (04) 496 7000; fax (04) 473 6919.

Bank of New Zealand: BNZ Centre, 1 Willis Street, Wellington, PO Box 2392, Wellington; tel (04) 474 6999; fax (04) 474 6687.

Citibank: PO Box 3429, Auckland.

Countrywide Banking Corp. Ltd: PO Box 5445, Wellesley Street, Auckland.

CS First Boston: PO Box 5333, Auckland.

National Australia Bank: Private Bag, Auckland.

National Bank of New Zealand: National Bank House, 170-186 Featherston St, Wellington, PO Box 1791, Wellington; tel (04) 494 4000; fax (04) 473 3642.

Reserve Bank of New Zealand: PO Box 2498, Wellington.

Westpac Banking Corporation: Westpac House, 318-324 Lambton Quay, Wellington, PO Box 691, Wellington; tel (04) 498 1000; fax (04) 498 1889.

Business and Management Services

Databank Systems Ltd: PO Box 3647, Wellington.

Deloitte Touche Tohmatsu (Management Consultants): 32 Oxford Tce, Christchurch; tel (03) 379 7010.

Fuji Xerox New Zealand Ltd: 17 Hargreaves Street, Ponsonby, PO Box 5948, Auckland; tel (09) 377 3834; fax (09) 356 4444.

Opal Consulting Group: PO Box 7067, Auckland; fax (09) 377 4127.

Morgan and Banks: Level 6, Ports of Auckland Building, CPO Box 579, Auckland; tel (09) 367 9000; fax (09) 367 9001.

PA Consulting Group: 53-59 Cook Street, Auckland; tel (09) 303 2743; fax (09) 303 1276.

Unisys New Zealand Ltd: 3 Owens Road, Epsom, PO Box 5144, Auckland; tel (09) 630 1333; fax (09) 638 7650.

Wang New Zealand: Wang Terraces, 9 City Road, Auckland; tel (09) 307 8600; fax (09) 309 3960.

Forestry, Pulp and Paper
Carter Holt Harvey Ltd: 640 Great South Road Manakau City, Private Bag 92-106 Auckland; tel (09) 262 6000; fax (09) 262 6099.

Forestry Corporation of New Zealand Ltd: 32 Pukaki Street, PO Box 1748, Rotorua; tel (07) 347 9012; fax (07) 347 9103.

Juken Nissho Ltd: 101 Customs Street East, PO Box 1450, Auckland; tel (09) 309 1750; fax (09) 309 0326.

Hotel Chains
Quality Hotels: PO Box 5640, Wellesley St, Auckland; tel (09) 309 4411; fax (09) 377 0764

Southern Pacific Hotel Corporation: PO Box 3921, Auckland; tel (09) 3732269; fax (09) 309 3577.

Insurance Companies
AMI Insurance: 63 Albert St, Auckland; tel (09) 377 4640

AMP Insurance: Cnr Queen & Victoria Streets Auckland tel (09) 377 4630.

Commercial Union General Insurance Company Ltd: Commercial Union House, 12-14 OUConnell Street, PO Box 4039, Auckland; tel (09) 377 0650.

NZI Insurance: 3-13 Shortland Street, Private Bag 92-130 Auckland; tel (09) 309 7000

State Insurance: Cnr Wakefield & Rutland Streets, Auckland; tel (09) 308 9989.

Law Firms
Russell McVeagh McKenzie Bartleet & Co: The Shortland Centre 51-53 Shortland St, Auckland; tel (09) 309 8839.

Rudd Watts & Stone: 125 Queen St, Auckland, PO Box 3798, Auckland; tel (09) 309 4863.

Simpson Grierson Butler White: Simpson Grierson Butler White Building, 92 Albert St, Auckland; tel (09) 358 2222.

Bell Gully Buddle Weir: The Auckland Club Tower, 34 Shortland St, Auckland, PO Box 4199, Auckland; tel (09) 309 0859.

Manufacturing and Marketing
Abels Ltd: 101 Carlton Gorge Road, Newmarket, Auckland, Private Bag 99919, Newmarket, Auckland; tel (09) 520 5858; (09) 524 1161.

AWA New Zealand Ltd: Wineera Drive, Porirua, Wellington, Private Bag, Porirua, Wellington; tel (04) 237 0159; fax (04) 237 1267.

Bayer New Zealand Ltd: 3 Argus Place, Glenfield, Auckland, PO Box 215, Auckland; tel (09) 443 5500; fax (09) 443 5487.

BHP New Zealand Steel: Private Bag 92121, Auckland; tel (09) 375 8999; fax (09) 375 8959.

Bluebird Foods Ltd: 124 Wiri Station Road, Manukau City, Auckland, Private Bag 76903, Manukau City, Auckland; tel (09) 262 3383; fax (09) 262 8898.

Cadbury Confectionery Ltd: 280 Cumberland Street, Dunedin, PO Box 890, Dunedin; tel (03) 474 1126; fax (03) 474 1889.

Cerebos Gregg Ltd: 291 East Tamaki, Auckland, PO Box 58095, Auckland; tel (09) 274 9099; fax (09) 274 6293.

Colgate Palmolive Ltd: 415 Church Street, Penrose, Auckland; tel (09) 525 2300, Fax (09) 525 2353.

318 Working in New Zealand

Comalco: 30-32 Bowden Rd, Mt Wellington, Auckland, PO Box 14107, Panmure, Auckland; tel (09) 573 0531; fax (09) 573 0539.

DB Group Led: Citibank Centre, 23 Customs Street East, Auckland; tel (09) 377 8990; fax (09) 309 9422.

Fisher and Paykel: 78 Springs Road East Tamaki, Auckland, Private Bag 14917, Panmure, Auckland; tel (09) 2730660; fax (09) 273 0560.

Ford Motor Co. Ltd: Private Bag 96912, Manakau City.

General Motors NZ Ltd: PO Box 40413, Upper Hutt.

Goodman Fielder Wattie Ltd: 66 Wyndham Street, Private Bag 92096, Auckland; tel (09) 309 1719; fax (09) 309 1069.

IBM New Zealand Ltd: IBM Esplanade, Petone, Wellington, PO Box 38993, Petone, Wellington; tel (04) 576 5711; fax (04) 576 5902.

Kraft General Foods Ltd: 11 Dalgety Drive, Manurewa, Auckland, PO Box 97348, Mail Centre South Auckland; tel (09) 268 0888; fax (09) 268 0866.

Levene & Co.: Head Office Harris Road, East Tamaki, Auckland; tel (09) 274 4211.

Lion Nathan Ltd: PO Box 190, Auckland; tel (09) 303 3388; fax (09) 303 3307.

Montana Wines: 171 Pilkington Rad, Glen Innes, Auckland, PO Box 18293; tel (09) 570 5549; fax (09) 527 1113.

Nestle New Zealand Ltd: 1 Broadway, Newmarket, Auckland, PO Box 1784; tel (09) 309 6509; fax (09) 309 3303.

Proctor and Gamble: PO Box 5861, Auckland.

Toyota NZ Ltd: Private Bag 13909, Johnsonville, Wellington.

Villa Maria Estate Ltd: 5 Kirkbridge Road, Mangere, Auckland, PO Box 43043, Auckland; tel (09) 275 6119; fax (09) 275 6618.

Oil and Petrochemicals

BP Oil NZ Ltd: PO Box 892, Wellington; tel (04) 495 5000, fax (04) 495 5400.

Fletcher Challenge Petroleum Marketing Ltd: Natural Gas Corporation House, 22 The Terrace, Wellington, PO Box 1818, Wellington; tel (04) 499 022; fax (04) 499 0033.

Mobil Oil NZ Ltd: PO Box 1709, Auckland; tel (09) 302 4700, fax (09) 377.

Shell NZ Ltd: PO Box 2091, Wellington.

Telecommunications and Utilities

AT&T: PO Box 5945, Auckland.

Coalcorp: PO Box 439, Wellington.

Electricity Corporation NZ: PO Box 930, Wellington.

NZ Post Ltd: Private Bag 39990, Wellington 1.

Transport, and Shipping

Air New Zealand: Private Bag 92007, Auckland; tel (09) 366 2400; fax (09) 366 2764.

Apex International Forwarding Ltd: 9A Mahunga Drive, Mangere Bridge, PO Box 2427, Auckland; tel (09) 6343616; fax (09) 622 2264.

Beacon Chartering and Shipping Ltd: Level 8 Anzac Avenue, Auckland, PO Box 418, Auckland; tel (09) 309 7994; fax (09) 309 3427.

Columbus Maritime Services Ltd: 52 Symonds Street Auckland, PO Box 3551, Auckland; tel (09) 377 3460; fax (09) 309 3003.

DHL Worldwide Express: 49 Mahunga Drive, Mangere, Auckland, PO Box 13509, Onehunga, Auckland; tel (09) 636 7124; fax (09) 636 7634.

NZ Rail Ltd: Private Bag, Wellington

Pacific Forum Line (NZ) Ltd: 49-55 Anzac Avenue, Auckland, PO Box 796, Auckland; tel (09) 307 9100; fax (09) 309 2683.

Shipping Enterprises: Barneys Building, 78 Maunganui Road, Mt Maunganui, PO Box 5144, Mount Maunganui; tel (07) 575 9684.

Starting a Business

In principle, it is quite feasible for foreigners to set up a business or to buy part or all of an existing business in New Zealand. The prevailing attitude towards business ventures, whether started by New Zealanders or immigrants is positive and helpful. To make a success of the venture requires, of course, the same blend of careful planning, energy and luck that you need in any country. More than anything, you need to research your chosen potential market or markets to ensure that the products or services that you offer are geared to meet a real demand at an appropriate price. Much of your groundwork can be done in advance, but there is no substitute for visiting and seeing for yourself the environment in which you wish to try the venture. It may well be worth considering spending substantial time living and working in New Zealand before making a final commitment to a particular enterprise.

In most cases therefore, it is likely that you will have obtained New Zealand residency before setting up a business on your own. If you are not a New Zealand citizen or resident and you are investing substantial sums of money (more than NZ $10 million) in New Zealand shares or assets, or you are investing in certain areas of the economy such as broadcasting, you will require the permission of the Overseas Investment Commission (*OIC:* 2 The Terrace, PO Box 2498, Wellington; tel 04 472 2029 Fax. 04 473 8554). Permission is dependent on the extent to which the projected business will contribute to the economy. Similarly permission is required if you are not a New Zealander and you are the principal of a business with a turnover of greater than NZ $10 million or it is particular restricted areas of the economy. However these restrictions will not affect most immigrants considering setting up a small business in New Zealand.

If you are organising your application for New Zealand residency with the intention of setting up a business there you should note that a special scheme exists to attract business investors. (See Chapter Two, *Residence and Entry*). The sums required to qualify for the Business Investment category are fairly substantial. If you do not have the necessary capital to qualify under this category, then you will need to apply under the General or Family categories.

In recent years, regulations governing setting up business in New Zealand have been relaxed. The Companies Act was substantially ammended in 1994 to make the process of incorporating a company simpler. There are a number of government agencies set up to help small businesses and the attitude towards entrepreneurs is positive. The operating environment for businesses is quite similar to the UK. Telephone, computer systems, and financial services are advanced. The workforce has a similar level of qualifications to UK workers. As part of encouraging individual initiative and competititive economic environment, the government is trying to cut down on the amount of red-tape involved in doing business, and to encourage small businesses to set up. The result is that it is a good time to be starting up a new business in New Zealand. This chapter will look at what is involved in buying a business in New Zealand or in starting your own.

Preparation

Choosing a Business

Since in broad terms, New Zealanders engage in similar business, cultural and social activities to Europeans, there are similar potential markets for anyone contemplating setting up a new enterprise. The differences need to be borne in mind, however, not the least of which is that the comparatively small total population and its distribution will have a significant effect on the structure of potential markets. For example if you are considering setting up in the restaurant industry you will find that in the larger cities restaurants and wine bars abound: the market is pretty well saturated and thus very competitive. Such businesses are stretched to find some new competitive advantage and that is often manifested as gimmickry which of course has a short-lived novelty appeal. In the rural areas, there are fewer restaurants and wine-bars, however, there is less population to support them as New Zealand is not particularly densely populated. An opportunity, yes, but maybe one that requires a lot of 'up-front' investment in marketing and publicity. Given that moving to a new country is going to be pretty challenging in itself, it may be wise to opt for a safer bet such as selecting an enterprise for which there is a known or an established market, or one in which you have particular skills and experience. Obviously there is an advantage in buying an already established business in this respect, however before you buy you should research the track record of your chosen enterprise. Remember that the majority of businesses succeed not on the uniqueness of the concept but on the application of sound and careful management techniques.

Researching Your Business

Whether it is your intention to buy a business or to set up from scratch, researching the potential market for that business is essential. The specific information that you need to determine whether there is a viable market will depend greatly upon the type of business, the services or the products you have in mind. There are companies specialising in market research in the major cities in New Zealand, which would be able to provide data on most aspects of the market or would offer to conduct specific enquires, for a fee, in areas of the market which were less well researched. This type of service is usually beyond the budget of those setting up a small business. There are some companies offering research services specifically tailored for small businesses and you can do some of the research work yourself. One of the first places to start looking for information is the local public library. Most public libraries run an information service for local businesses and for those intending to set up a business. They will have information on market trends, local suppliers, possible competitors, planning and development strategies. Some libraries offer a contract research service and will do a lot of the legwork by investigating the feasibility of a project for you. This may be a cost-effective option simply because they will be familiar with the sources of information and will be able to find out quickly what you need to know. Information on businesses and commerce in specific regions can be obtained from the local Chamber of Commerce. Chambers of Commerce in the main cities are listed below. The Department of Statistics, now called Statistic New Zealand, runs a professional consultancy service for data on imports, prices, population etc. They publish the *Quarterly Economic*

Survey of various sectors of the economy. Predominantly this is income and expenditure data, although they also collect investment data. Each year this is gathered into the more detailed *Annual Enterprise Survey*. More general data on the New Zealand economy is published in the monthly *Key Statistics*. They also publish the *New Zealand Year Book* (see below). If your business is involved in the export market, the Ministry of Foreign Affairs and Trade can help with economic and political information about your target markets.

Researching market opportunities in New Zealand from Europe is naturally more difficult than doing the ground work once you arrive. There are companies which offer an information gathering service specifically for intending immigrants, in areas ranging from business opportunities to education prospects. (One such company is *Infoseek*, listed below). Other sources of information are the *New Zealand Year Book*, which provides a highly detailed picture of social, demographic, and economic trends in New Zealand. It is a useful introduction to the structure of the economy and the main business sectors. The disadvantage of the yearbook is that the information is based on five yearly census data, so while it is very detailed, it is not always up to date. Copies of the yearbook can be bought at the Kiwifruits shop (25 Bedfordbury, Covent Garden, London WC2N 4BL; 0171-2401423), which specialises in New Zealand products, or can be found in some libraries. The Information Office at the New Zealand High Commission has a copy of the yearbook as well as individual chapters on specific topics.

Useful Addresses
Chambers of Commerce
New Zealand Chambers of Commerce: PO Box 11-043, Manners Street, Wellington; fax/tel (04) 472 3376.
Auckland Chamber of Commerce and Industry: 100 Mayoral Drive, Auckland; tel (09) 309 6100; fax (09) 309 0081.
Canterbury Employers Chamber of Commerce: 57 Kilmore St, Christchurch; tel (03) 366 5096.
Otago Chamber of Commerce: PO Box 5713, Dunedin; tel (03) 479 0181.
Wellington Chamber of Commerce: 109 Featherston St, Wellington; tel (04) 472 2725; fax (04) 471 1767.

Business and Market Research Organisations
Business Research Centre, Marac House 105-9 The Terrace, PO Box 10617, Wellington; tel (04) 4993088.
Business Information Service, Wellington Public Library, PO Box 1992, tel (04) 8014059; fax (04) 8014088.
Business and Economic Research Ltd, Weddel House, 158 The Terrace, tel (04) 4725564; fax (04) 473 3276.
Infoseek: PO Box 10-194, The Terrace, Wellington; tel/fax (04) 476 5948.

Government Departments
Ministry of Foreign Affairs and Trade: Private Bag 18901, Wellington; tel (04) 472 8877; fax (04) 472 9596.
Statistics New Zealand: Information Consultancy Groups:
Auckland: 70 Symonds Street, Private Bag, 92003, Auckland; tel (09) 358 4588; fax (09) 379 0859.
Christchurch: Winchester House, 64 Kilmore Street, Private Bag 4741, Christchurch; tel (03) 374 8700; fax (03) 374 8864.
Dunedin: Civic Centre (4th Floor) The Octagon, Private Bag 1935, Dunedin; tel (03) 477 7511; fax (03) 477 5243.

Wellington: Aorangi House, 85 Molesworth Street, PO Box 2922, Wellington; tel (04) 495 4600; fax (04) 472 9135.

Choosing an Area
Having decided on your line of business, the next logical step is to decide where to locate it. Obviously the type of business will determine this in many cases, for example choosing where to site a horticultural enterprise will largely be determined by climate. The tourism industry has until recently been concentrated in the geothermal area around Rotorua, and the South Island more generally, with most visitors staying in Christchurch or Queenstown. Auckland is attempting to attract visitors for longer stays and is likely to be a growth area for tourism in the future. Another growing sector is adventure tourism, with the south of the Waikato region around Waitomo caves, Nelson and the West Coast likely to benefit. Export manufacturing is strongest in Auckland and Christchurch. Forestry, another export sector predicted to grow is likely to benefit the region around Rotorua, Taupo and Turangi. Overall according to *Metro* magazine, Auckland is likely to enjoy the highest economic growth over the next few years with the Bay of Plenty, Canterbury and Otago following behind.

Useful Publications
Books
The Small Business Book, a New Zealand Guide: Robert Hamlin and John English, Bridget Williams, 1993.
Your Successful Small Business: A New Zealand Guide to Starting Out and Staying In Business: Judith Ashton, Viking Pacific, 1992.

Periodicals
ABC Directory of Business and Commercial Opportunity: PO Box 9087, Newmarket, Auckland; tel (09) 307 0598; fax (09) 309 3076.
Business Development News: Ministry of Commerce, PO Box 1473, Wellington; tel (04) 472 0030-xt 8057; fax (04) 471 2658.
The National Business Review: PO Box 1734, Auckland; tel (09) 307 1629; fax (09) 309 7878.

Small and Medium Enterprises
Specific assistance for people wanting to set up their own business is available from the Small Business Agency. (PO Box 11-012, Wellington; tel 04-472 3141; fax 04-499 5545.) The agency provides advice to individuals as well as running more general courses on how to set up a small business. The Inland Revenue Department also runs a small business advisory service which provides help with working out your tax obligations. They can be contacted at local IRD offices.

Buying a Business v Setting up from Scratch
The decision between buying a business or setting up your own is basically about the degree of risk you are prepared to take and what kind of capital you can raise. Buying a business requires more more money, but on the other hand, you will be buying a going concern which will provide an immediate source of income. Setting up from scratch can be done on a shoestring, but if you underestimate your financial needs at the beginning, your enterprise may not last long. Your first years in business may be difficult for cash flow and unanticipated expenses so it is important not to miscalculate the size of the budget you can realistically manage on. You may also find that the stress of changing your country of abode is enough to cope with during your first years in New Zealand and the move to set up your own operation may be easier after

you have acclimatised to New Zealand in other ways. If you do decide to go ahead and buy an existing business, the place to start looking is the daily newspapers classified sections. Specialist business estate agencies can be found by looking in the Yellow Pages. To give you some idea of the types of opportunities and the prices, the following businesses were recently advertised for sale: Auckland: Restaurant/bar for sale, top North Shore location, $98,000; North Otago, Motel and Restaurant on State Highway 1, $370,000; Dunedin: Convenience store with a three bedroomed house, weekly turnover $7000; $71,000.

Raising Finance

Banks & Business Plans
There are various sources of loans for small businesses available, the most common being the banks. However, any lender or giver of grants will expect some reassurance of serious commitment from the person or persons asking for help. This means in most cases, evidence that they are committing a significant amount of their own capital to the venture. As was noted above, the major reason for small business failure is bad financial planning so in order to convince a bank that you are a worthwhile investment you need to produce a business plan. Without going into too much detail here, your business plan should include:

A summary containing a broad outline of your vision of the business.
A brief CV of each person involved in the business, highlighting skills and expertise relevant to the scheme.
A description of the main services or products that you intend to offer.
Evidence that a viable market exists for your services or products.
An outline of your marketing communication strategy (how you intend to contact your potential customers)

Financial information:

Expenditure: Start-up costs, cash flow projections, salaries, running (operating) costs including materials, production, heating, lighting, premises (rent) etc., other expenses
(Remember to make a generous allowance for contingencies)
Projected income: (Sales).

Remember that you are trying to present a positive case to your audience — the more professional and credible the plan, the more chance you have of success: clarity and a realistic rather than optimistic view will enhance your proposal and if realism tells you that the idea is not sound, then you must review it or even come up with another idea.

A final comment on business plans: there are people who can offer advice on how to write your plan; listen to that advice; there are also people who will write it for you, but if you prepare it yourself, then you will be that much closer to an understanding of your projected business.

Investment Incentives

There are very few investment incentive schemes available directly from central government. The main sources of funding are local Business Development Boards funded by the government which offer grants and incentive funds to attract businesses into their regions. (see below) The one exception is tourism where government loans are available through the Tourist Accommodation Development scheme.

Regional Investment Offices
The Ministry of Commerce's a network of local Business Development Boards
provide information and assistance both for existing businesses and for intending
business people. They also distribute Business Development Grants. Three types
of grant are available:

1. *Business Development Investigation Grants:* Up to $20,000 available to firms
or individuals investigating the commercial and technical viability of a potential
commercial activity.
2. *Expert Assistance Grants:* Up to $8,000 for firms to engage consultants in key
management areas where better performance will lead to efficiency improvements.
3. *Enterprise Growth Development Grants:* Up to $20,000 to help firms improve
their level of competitiveness.

The recipient firm or individual will be required to meet half the cost of any
proposal for which they receive a grant, themselves. The Ministry also publishes
Business Development News, a monthly publication providing information about
business initiatives. If you want further information about how regional development boards decide to allocate grants, you can contact the *Business Development
Board Network:* (Ministry of Commerce 33 Bowen St, PO Box 1473, Wellington;
tel 04-472 0030; fax 04-473 4638).

Addresses of Business Development Boards
Aorangi Business Development Board: Stafford and Sefton Streets PO Box 779,
Timaru; tel (03) 688 8106; fax (03) 688 1712.
Auckland Business Development Board: 47 Wakefield St PO Box 7040, Auckland;
tel (09) 308 9141; fax (09) 308 9138.
Bay Of Plenty Business Development Board: Cameron Rd& First Ave, PO Box
568, Tauranga; tel (07) 577 6000; fax (07) 577 6010.
Canterbury Business Development Board: 109 Cambridge Tce, Christchurch; tel
(03) 365 1918; fax (03) 379 0697.
East Coast Business Development Board: Treble Court, Peel St, PO Box 517,
Gisbourne; tel (06) 867 9744; fax (06) 867 9183.
*Hawkes Bay Business Development Board:*174 Hastings Street, PO Box 1041,
Napier; tel (06) 835 2044; fax (06) 835 4038.
Kapiti/ Horowhenua Business Development Board: 29 Queen St, PO Box 673
Levin, tel (06) 367 9669/(04) 298 8207; fax (06) 368 1925.
King Country/Taupo Business Development Board: King and Taupiri Streets,
PO Box 44, Te Kuiti; tel (07) 878 8685; fax (07) 878 6740.
Manawatu Business Development Board: Corner Church and Princess St, PO
Box 1846, Palmerston North; tel (06) 355 0195; fax (06) 355 0196.
Marlborough Business Development Board: 3 Main St, PO Box 652, Blenheim;
tel (03) 578 2313; fax (03) 578 7343.
Nelson Bays Business Development Board: 37 Bridge St, PO Box 840, Nelson;
(03) 548 8622; fax (03) 546 6455.
Otago Business Development Board: 282 Moray Place PO Box 5558, Dunedin;
(03) 477 6528; fax (03) 479 0649.
Southland Business Development Board: 27 Kelvin Street, PO Box 979, Invercar-
gill; tel (03) 218 9860; fax (03) 214 4654.
Tai Tokerau Business Development Board: Walton Plaza, Albert Street, PO Box
221, Whangarei; tel (09) 438 1339; fax (09) 430 0552.
Taranaki Business Development Board: 5 Queen Street, PO Box 349, New
Plymouth; tel (06) 757 9993; fax (06) 758 8173.
Thames Valley/Coromandel Business Development Board: Normanby Road PO
Box 86, Paeroa; tel (07) 862 7423; fax (07) 862 7421.

Waikato Business Development Board: Victoria & London Streets, PO Box 960, Hamilton; tel (07) 862 7423; fax (07) 834 0105.

Wairarapa Business Development Board: 32 Perry St, PO Box 251, Masterton; tel (06) 378 2705; fax (06) 378 9548.

Wanganui Business Development Board: 259 Victoria Avenue, PO Box 7045, Wanganui; tel (06) 345 0949; fax (06) 345 0666.

Wellington Business Development Board: 249 High St, Lower Hutt; tel (04) 566 9192; fax (04) 566 9191.

*West Coast Business Development Board:*100 Mackay St, PO Box 361, Greymouth; tel (03) 768 6334; fax (03) 768 5408.

Business Structures and Registration

Businesses in New Zealand can take similar forms to those in the UK, namely: Public Limited Company, Partnership, Joint Venture, Trust, or Sole Trader. The three most common forms for small businesses are sole trader, partnership or public limited company. The form of your business determines who benefits from it but also who is liable should something go wrong. It is not uncommon for businesses to start up in one form then change into another as they expand so you don't have to make a once and for all decision before you start.

Sole Trader: In this structure, you are the sole owner and controller of your business. This is the simplest form of business structure to start up: you simply tell the IRD you are becoming self-employed. If your business has a turnover greater than $30,000 you will also need to register for Goods and Services Tax, but these are the only legal formalities required. The disadvantage of the simple structure is that as a sole trader you are personally responsible for any debts incurred by your business and your personal assets can be taken as payment.

Partnership: Partnerships are formed by private agreement between the partners and their form is quite flexible, dependent upon the terms of that agreement. It is a good idea, although not legally necessary, to have the agreement drawn up or checked by a lawyer. Juliet Ashton in her book *Your Successful Small Business* suggests that the agreement should cover the name of the partnership and the business, the date of the agreement and an indication of how long the partnership is intended to last, as well as how much capital has been invested by each partner in the firm and the interest on it, the way the profits will be split and who is responsible for management and control of the business, arrangements about holidays, illness, division of responsibilities and what will happen if one of the partners dies. There is a tendency to assume you will work things out as you go along, particularly if you are going into business with a friend, However there are many pitfalls in this approach, and although it may seem legalistic it is a better idea to have written clearly who is responsible for what aspect of the business rather than put your partnership under strain by not having a clear understanding from the beginning. You should in any case think twice before going into business with a friend. You need to assess objectively their strengths and weaknesses as a potential business person, as well as how you will get along with them under pressure. As with a sole trader structure you are personally responsible for any debts incurred by your business, even if your partner made the decisions that led the business into difficulties.

Limited Companies: As distinct from partnerships and sole-trading operations, if you own a company you are not personally responsible for its debts. The company has a separate legal existence and your liability is limited to the extent of your share ownership. However it is worth noting that if you have to borrow money to set up your company, banks will commonly require personal guarantees from the directors, so you will not be protected by the company's legal status. You can either buy a company off the shelf from one of the businesses that specialise in selling shelf companies (advertised in the *Yellow Pages*) or you can set one up yourself. Company incorporation in New Zealand has recently been simplified under the *Companies Act* of 1993. There is now only one type of company and there is no longer any minimum or maximum number of directors or shareholders required. To set up a company you require the following:

1. A name
2. At least one shareholder
3. At least one director
4. At at least one share
5. A registered office and an address.

The director and shareholder can be one and the same so in fact it only needs one person to set up a company. You begin by registering the name you have chosen with the Registrar of Companies. Obviously you have to pick a name which no-one else has used already. Once the name has been approved you can apply to have your company registered. Along with your application (which must be signed and must state the company's name, registered office and address) you must include signed consents from all directors to act as such and certificates stating that they are not disqualified from acting, consents by shareholders to take the stated number of shares, notice from the Registrar reserving the company's name, and the constitution of the company if there is one. Companies need no longer state their objects in a constitution. Once he receives a properly completed application the Registrar will issue a certificate of incorporation. The current cost of incorporation is $300.

Ideas for New Businesses

Most new immigrants will need a chance to look around once they arrive in New Zealand before deciding what line of business to take up. There are a lot of established avenues for the first time business person as you will see when looking at the businesses for sale section in the papers. Should you want to consider trying something different, the following suggestions may give you some ideas.

Accommodation: As long as the tourist boom continues, providing accommodation is likely to be a reasonably safe bet. B&Bs are not as common in New Zealand as they are in the UK although the idea is beginning to catch on, as an inexpensive accommodation option. However you will need to research the potential market carefully. Many tourists arrive on package deals with accommodation organised through the large hotel chains. On the other hand, many Asian tourists travel to New Zealand, particularly Christchurch because of its English associations. You could market your B&B as a real English experience. Another relatively undeveloped type of accommodation in New Zealand is the country house hotel. While there are a number of luxury country lodges at top prices, the market is by no means oversupplied at the high end.

Publishing: There is no newspaper aimed at European expats, although the size of community could support one. The main cities lack a weekly arts and events magazine. There are a number of give-away newspapers providing a listings service but production standards are not high. There is an opportunity for a well produced magazine covering the music scene, arts, leisure and general listings.

Tourism: The most recent development in tourism is so-called adventure tourism, not just taking pictures of the scenery but actively getting into the environment, through for example jet boat rides, white water rafting, bungee jumping, big game fishing, and helicopter or balloon rides. Some of these areas are already well catered for and in some cases, where the rides take place in Department of Conservation lands for example, only a few operators may be licensed. Other areas could be developed, for example horse trekking.

Running a Business

Employing Staff

As an employer you negotiate individual contracts of employment with your staff, who can either nominate a bargaining agent in the negotiations or represent themselves directly. While there is a lot of flexibility over negotiating terms and conditions relevant to your workplace, Certain statutory protections remain for workers. There is a legal minimum wage of NZ $245 for a 40 hour week. This does not apply to people under the age of 20, apprentices and other trainees. There are eleven paid public holidays, and after 12 months employment, employees are entitled to three weeks paid annual leave. There are also provisions for special leave in the case of bereavement, and parental leave (both maternity and paternity, although new dads get less time off than new mums). See under *Working Conditions* in Chapter Six for further details.

Contracts. Employment contracts must contain a section on dispute settlement, and there are standard procedures for dealing with personal grievance cases against employers for unjustified dismissal.

Wages & Time Record. You are required to keep a wages and time record for each employee.

Taxes. Your other legal obligations as an employer concern taxation. You are required to deduct payroll taxes (known as PAYE) from your employeeUs wages and make returns of the same to the Inland Revenue Department. You must get all your employees to fill out a tax deduction certificate called an IR12, and you must pay an accident compensation levy for each employee, yearly. If you provide any perks for staff as part of their employment package, then you have to pay fringe benefit taxes on them. (See *Taxation* below for more details.)

Accountants

As has been noted, the major reason for small business failure is poor management, usually poor financial control. You would be well advised to consult an accountant who specialises in dealing with small businesses to help you look after this important area. Your local small business advisory service should have a list of local accountants. In the case of companies there are certain statutory requirements you must fulfill with regard to financial reporting. Every company is required to keep full, true and complete record of its affairs and transactions including providing a Profit and Loss Account and a Balance Sheet. Accounting practice is regulated by the New Zealand Society of Accountants (PO Box 11-342, Wellington; tel 04-473 8544; fax 04-472 6282) which provides mandatory standards for company financial reporting called Statements of Standard

Accounting Practice (SSAPs). Any material departure from these has to be disclosed in financial statements. The standards are intended for use by other types of business though not compulsory.

Taxation

The Inland Revenue Department publishes a guide for small businesses on their tax obligations. You can obtain copies from any IRD office. They also run the Small Business Advisory Service which advises beginning business people about what taxes they need to know about, what records to keep, how to complete tax returns and when to file returns and make payments. To get in touch with the service, you simply indicate when you register for GST or as a new employer that you would like an advisory consultation. You can either come into an IRD office for an appointment or an advisor will come and visit your office. They also run regular seminars.

Applying for an IRD number
One of the first requirements of any type of business operation is an Inland Revenue Department number. (IRD number) If you already have a personal IRD number and you are a sole trader, then you can continue to use this number. If your business location is different from your home address and you are registering for GST or as an employer then you may obtain another number for your business. Companies and partnerships must have their own numbers. You apply by contacting the nearest IRD office and filling in a form. You will need a passport or birth certificate as identification for a personal IRD number. In the case of a partnership, you must provide the IRD numbers of the partners, and for a company IRD, a copy of the certificate of incorporation.

Types of Taxes
There are four major types of taxes which you will have to deal with when doing business in New Zealand; income tax and company tax, Goods and Services Tax (GST), Accident Compensation Levies and Fringe Benefit Tax.

Income Tax and Company Tax: Income tax is payable by all persons or business entities. Individuals are taxed on a progressive rate system whereby 24% is payable on earnings up to NZ$30,875, and 33% over that figure. Resident companies are taxed at a flat rate of 33% on income earned, whereas non-resident companies are taxed at 38%.

Goods and Services Tax (GST): All businesses with an anticipated turnover of greater than $30,000 per annum are required to register for GST. GST is not a tax on your own business, it is a tax on sales to your customers which you collect on behalf of the IRD. It is similar to VAT, but the threshold is comparatively lower for GST so more small businesses are covered by it. Under the $30, 000 threshold you can choose whether or not to register. If you deal with other registered businesses it may be worthwhile because they will be charging you GST which you will not be able to claim back. You pay GST on all your business inputs, supplies etc. You then add GST to all the sales you make. You make GST returns either monthly, two monthly, or if your business has a turnover of less than $250, 000 you can opt for six monthly returns which will simplify the amount of paperwork.

Fringe Benefit Tax and Accident Compensation: If you provide any extra benefits to your employees such as a company car then you must pay fringe benefit tax. Even if you do not provide any perks, you must send in a yearly return. ACC is a fixed levy on each member of your workforce.

Annual Tax Returns
Different returns will be required depending on whether you are a sole trader, a company or a partnership. The tax year runs from 1st April to 31 March, and although businesses can use different year end dates for reporting purposes, the balance date will be related to the nearest 31st March for tax purposes. Sole traders must complete an IR3, the return for self employed people. In a partnership, each partner must fill in an IR3, plus an IR7 must be filled in for the partnership as a whole. A company must fill in an IR4, and each shareholder must also file an individual return. Included with each return must be a copy of the accounts.

Useful Publications
Doing Business In New Zealand: Ernst & Young, Publications Department, Beckett House, 1 Lambeth Road, London SE1 7EU; tel 0171-9282000.
Running a Small Business?- A guide to your tax obligations: Inland Revenue Department, available from local IRD offices.

Personal Case Histories

Australia

JONATHAN CROSSEN & GARY LOVE

Glaswegians Jonathan Crossen and Gary Love, both aged 24, travelled together to Australia after graduating in English and Risk Management repectively. Their idea was to use the trip as a way of exploring Australia and checking out the possibilities for future long-term employment. During nine months from September until the following May they worked and toured in Australia and their experiences and advice may be useful to anyone wishing to follow in their footsteps.

What preparations did you make for the trip?
We arranged to stay in Perth with Jonathan's relatives so we didn't have to decide where to start our Australian trip. We began by getting round-the-world tickets; our itinerary was London-Bangkok-Hong Kong-Perth-Sydney-Auckland-Los Angeles-New York-London. To our surprise the RTW ticket only cost slightly more than a return flight to Perth/Sydney, and it included the airfare from Perth to Sydney, thus saving us A$800 each.

What about visas?
We applied for one year working visas about eight weeks in advance. Having evidence of a confirmed return flight and saying that you are staying with relations in Australia definitely makes the process easier. However it is not essential to have relations there in order to get the one year working visa.

What about the work part of your trip?
We were lucky to have a contact before we left the UK and when we arrived we had no difficulty picking up demolition work on a vineyard in the Swan Valley (Perth) at $8 per hour (cash in hand). This gave us the time to ask around in pubs and clubs, scan job ads in the press and to see if there was any thing going through the CES (Commonwealth Employment Service).

Were you successful?
After persevering, we both got jobs in the Berlin Nightclub (in Perth) run by Showbusiness Australia. SBA have an office in Perth (tel +00 61 9 481 1156). To our surprise it was not our carefully prepared references which interested the manager of the club, but our previous experience. We did bar work and PR for the club. Later, we both found pub work in Sydney through contacts.

Would you say it was easy or difficult to get work?
Actually, it was rather difficult.

Have you any tips for making it easier?
Well, for a start there's this myth that Australians are very casual so most people turn up in scruffy jeans or shorts. This is a big mistake and I advise anyone looking for work, to take care to look neat; you don't have to wear a suit, just make an effort to look respectable. It can make a big difference to your initial reception and favourably affect your chances.

How easy was it to find accommodation?
This is a catch-22; on the working holiday visa you can only work three months in one place. Unfortunately most leases are for longer. Again, after dogged insistence we got a place in suburban Perth for ten weeks. Sydney is much easier to find accommodation in as there are so many travellers there and there is a supply of short-term places. But of course you are one of thousands looking for it. We ended up in the lively and infamous (but cheap) Sydney suburb of King's Cross. In retrospect, Perth was better because there were a few thousand less working travellers there.

Can you sum up some of the highlights of your trip?
Perth was definitely the highlight and we wished we could have stayed there longer than the four months we did.

What, if any, were your misconceptions about Australia?
Well, for a start it was much more difficult to find work than we had anticipated. It took a lot of hard looking and asking and we learned the hard way about avoiding jobs which paid 'commission only' and said 'travellers welcome'. Such jobs usually involve selling door to door are are hard work for uncertain rewards.

Have you any other advice for other working travellers?
You must be persistent. If an employer turns you down once but does not appear to have an instant antipathy towards you; ask them again a couple of weeks later. This may not result in a job with that employer, but they may be in a position to refer you on to someone else because your obvious keeness has impressed them. Also be prepared to be flexible. If there are only manual jobs available, take one in the hope it will lead to something better. In any case manual work is not looked down on in Australia like here and it is considerably better paid.

On returning to the UK, Gary took up a job with Standard Life and Jonathan started work on his D.Phil in Metallurgy at the University of Oxford. Both would consider living and working in Australia at some future date and would recommend spending a year in Australia on a working holiday visa as a way of getting to know the country.

THE AYRE FAMILY

Dr and Mrs Ayre, originally from Scotland, decided to emigrate to Australia in 1976 from Malaysia where both of them had worked for seventeen years. Their children Alexander and Frances were however, born in Scotland, although they were brought up mainly in Malaysia. The children were ten and seven respectively when their parents decided to move permanently to Australia.

The parents, Peter and Jean, had to decide between moving to Australia, which they had never seen, or moving back to the UK which had changed a lot.

What made you decide to emigrate to Australia?
The decision to go to Australia was a very difficult one to make. We both had very good jobs in the Malaysian education system, but we felt we had to leave because the Malay goverment wanted all secondary education to be in Malay which we felt would be inappropriate for our own children, who had minimal Malay. We had already decided to move back to the UK where a post was waiting, when a lucrative job offer came from the Western Australia College of Advanced Education for Peter so we thought we'd take the big step.

What type of accommodation did you live in when you first arrived?
We rented a small flat for three months while we looked for a house to buy.

What were your first impressions of Australia?
That even though we had arrived in winter, the climate was beautiful. We were also impressed by the incredible sense of spaciousness of the country and the fact that all the houses were different from one another.

What did you miss from the UK?
At first we found the vegation and wildlife very strange compared with Britain and we missed the lush green-ness and richness of the vegetation. Since then we have come to love the sparse landscapes of the bush.

What things do you like most about your lifestyle in Australia?
Apart from our first favourable impressions, which have remained true, we like the very sport-oriented outdoor lifestyle, the wide variety of foods from the many different communities represented in Australia, the large number of parks which separate the suburbs and of course our work

Are the employment conditions more attractive than in the UK?
We have been lucky in that our employment situation has always been good. When Peter retired from Edith Cowan University where his specialist area was Teaching English as a Second Language, he formed his own educational consultancy, ICARE, in 1991 and has been employed on a contract basis ever since. I (Jean) got a job teaching English to migrants soon after arriving in Australia and specialised in working with Vietnamese refugee children who were in need of special care as many of them had been traumatised. It was very rewarding seeing them respond positively to various aspects of their new lives.

Is there a downside?
We certainly found some things very hard; in particular being so far from the family, especially as our parents became frailer and in need of attention which we were not able to give because of the distance and expense. Regretably, visits back to Britain to see them were very rare. [When they finally died, the airfares were at a peak and in any case the return flights from Australia to UK are more expensive than vice versa].

Also Perth is remote from other cities in Australia and the vast distances involved in travelling within Australia can be a great expense as well as not being very easy to make.

The other downside for us is the lack of a strongly educational or academic tradition in Australia. We have both found this very difficult to cope with, although generally the children's education has been of a very good standard and blue-collar workers are well paid.

Oh, and probably the worst thing to plague us, ever since we arrived in Australia, are the flies.

Do you feel you made the right choice in deciding to move permanently in Australia?

On the whole we do. We feel our children have benefitted by being very well accommodated in terms of their different abilities and needs. Travel to Britain is now a lot easier and cheaper so we can consider making homesickness trips to see family and friends. We have not ruled out the possibilty of eventually returning to Britain as we both still miss it to a certain extent, even after so many years as expatriates.

What about Alexander?

After arriving in Australia from Malaysia, he attended the local primary school and then a private boys's secondary school which he left to complete a pre-apprenticeship training in automotive paint-spraying. Since completing the course he has had a variety of jobs and is currently employed by an office furniture company as a truck driver which he really enjoys. He did try working in the mines for a while as a driller's off-sider, and the money was great, but it was in the middle of nowhere and there was nothing to spend the money on except drink. He had to work with a driller who spent $1000 dollars a week on alcohol. He (the driller) was very abusive as you would expect from someone permanently under the influence.

I don't think he would ever consider leaving Australia. His love of sports finds its outlet in Australia. He captains an indoor cricket team at Super League level. He hasn't been back to Britain since he was fifteen. Perhaps he'd go there for a holiday but his priority is to travel around Australia first.

And Frances?

Her memories of a childhood in Australia are a mixture of sun, surf and endless opportunities. She went to the local primary and then to a state high shool that specialised in music. Although it was difficult at first to attend a school out of the local area where she didn't know anyone, she settled in to enjoy five excellent years there. She had the opportunity of performing in concerts and her school band, orchestra and choir even travelled to Geneva in 1985 to compete in an international festival. After high school she went to Scotland for a year to work and then returned to do an arts degree at the University of Western Australia. She then did a graduate diploma of education at Edith Cowan University followed by a nine-months teaching stint at a private high school in Perth. Then she went to Oxford to do an MA in English Literature which she completed in 1994.

'I am currently teaching at a private boys' school in London which makes sense while I pay off my student debts, but I may return to Australia at some stage particularly if I ever get married and have children as Australia is a wonderful place to grow up'.

New Zealand

NIGEL ATKINSON

Thirty-year-old Nigel Atkinson has just moved to New Zealand. His partner whom he met in Britain is a New Zealander. She wanted to return home so he decided to move to New Zealand out of desire for adventure and to try a different way of life. He worked as an accountant in the UK but is going to change careers and is planning to study viticulture at a New Zealand university next year. His partner is a trained horticulturist currently working as a teacher and they hope eventually to set up a vineyard. He is working on a Marlborough vineyard over the summer to gain experience in the industry before starting his course in February.

What made you decide to make the move?
My girlfriend wanted to return home for a while and given that I wasn't particularly enjoying my job at the time, the move to New Zealand gave me the ideal opportunity to try something new career wise.

Did you know anything about New Zealand?
Just what my partner and other New Zealanders had told me, what I read in the papers, and from a visit there in March.

What, if any, are the problems you have faced so far?
I wouldn't describe any problems as major. It is annoying to have to continually ask people to explain what they are talking about, because they use New Zealand terms for things or abbreviations. If you accept that you are a foreigner, even though you speak the same language and ask questions, it's easier.

What research did you do before arriving in New Zealand?
I spoke to potential employers on my visit here in March. I had contacts through my partner's family and from friends of mine back in the UK. I demanded to see a recruitment consultant in Wellington — they tend to be reluctant to talk to you for some reason.

How do you find the New Zealanders?
I knew roughly what to expect because my partner introduced me to other New Zealanders when I was in the UK.

What are your first impressions of New Zealand like?
The main surprise has been the hostile attitude shown by some people towards Asians now coming to live in New Zealand. I thought New Zealanders were generally a tolerant lot. I don't know if it's racism or envy of the perceived wealth of the new Asian immigrants.

What advice would you have for others thinking applying for residency?
You should find out as much as possible about New Zealand before taking the plunge. Visit the country first and investigate fully the red tape you will encounter on arrival. I didn't find obtaining residency difficult because I fit the criteria and had sufficient points but I had to be very careful in presenting all the appropriate evidence in support of my application.

ANN OAKTHORPE

Ann Oakthorpe is 33 and moved to New Zealand in 1992 with her husband and two children. They were attracted by the clean, green image of the country and the outdoor lifestyle. Her husband is a computer programmer who has found work in Christchurch. They have settled in Sumner, a suburb beside the beach about fifteen minutes from the centre of Christchurch.

How easy was the New Zealand red tape to get through?
It seemed like we had to send them a copy of just about every document we possessed — marriage certificates, medical certificates, even character references. The information the High Commission sends out so you can assess whether you qualify for permanent residency is quite straightforward, it's the next step, actually applying which is rather a headache.

How did you go about finding work?
My husband contacted a New Zealand recruitment company who were advertising in London for staff. The job wasn't confirmed until we arrived in New Zealand but the company told us that he wouldn't have any trouble finding work because people with his kind of skills are in demand. I've found it more difficult — I was working in real estate in the UK but we arrived in New Zealand just at the end of the recession and it took a while for the property market to start moving again. It's much better now but I was unemployed for a short period.

What, in your opinion, are the main differences between living and working in New Zealand compared to the UK?
People are a bit more relaxed here compared to London. We don't spend so much time travelling to work which is a relief, it gives us more time to spend with the children.

How have the children reacted to the move?
They like it here a lot, in some ways I think they've made the adjustment much faster than I have. It's a great place for children. The schools have much better playing facilities than the schools at home and they both enjoy sport.

How do you like the lifestyle?
We all really like the outdoor lifestyle. Christchurch is close to the mountains and the sea is just ten minutes walk away.

What is accommodation like? Is it expensive?
We rented a house to start off with. It wasn't an ideal home but it was adequate for a couple of months and it wasn't expensive. While looking for houses I saw a lot of very ordinary places and it was my impression that New Zealand houses lack variety to a British eye. I think this is partly to do with the fact that very old houses do not exist. We finally found one we really like on a hillside overlooking the sea. We certainly couldn't have afforded to buy anything like this in the UK.

What are your impressions of New Zealanders?
The sense of humour here is different, quite dry and laconic. People are also keen to point out how things are better and they like to knock the 'Brits' in a not unfriendly sort of way. However, if you retaliate they get very touchy. I think it is advisable to avoid the kind of conversations that can lead to mutual put downs, if at all possible.

How, if at all, has moving to New Zealand affected your preconceived views or misconceptions of it?
On one hand you have older New Zealanders referring to Britain as 'home' which sounds odd to us. Having been here for a while, I think I've moved away from noticing the similarities with the UK to being aware of the real differences. Some basic attitudes are quite different — a friend described New Zealand as like England 20 years ago, but I reckon that it's the old fashioned values that have survived. In some ways I think New Zealand is way ahead in its outlook and by the way, we also get the new films before they open in London!

What is your advice for those thinking of taking the plunge?
It's definitely a good idea to visit New Zealand first before deciding if you want to move. The image of New Zealand you get from newspaper reports in the UK has not always been accurate until recently when a new note of realism has crept in. New Zealand is far from being a backwater paradise and it has its share of social problems. Some parts of the bigger cities are pretty dismal and even though the economy is improving, unemployment is still very high. On the other hand nearly everywhere in New Zealand is still safer than London. I don't worry about letting the children walk to school. I think if you enjoy your visit and like the feel of the place then you should make the move. There are lots of opportunities here, its just a matter of settling in and finding your feet.

Vacation Work also publish:

	Paperback	Hardback
The Directory of Summer Jobs in Britain	£7.95	£12.95
The Directory of Summer Jobs Abroad	£7.95	£12.95
Adventure Holidays	£5.95	£10.95
The Teenager's Vacation Guide to Work, Study & Adventure ...	£6.95	£9.95
Work Your Way Around the World	£9.95	£15.95
Teaching English Abroad	£9.95	£15.95
The Au Pair & Nanny's Guide to Working Abroad	£8.95	£14.95
Working in Ski Resorts — Europe & North America	£8.95	£14.95
Kibbutz Volunteer	£5.95	£8.95
The Directory of Jobs & Careers Abroad	£9.95	£15.95
The International Directory of Voluntary Work	£8.95	£14.95
The Directory of Work & Study in Developing Countries	£7.95	£10.95
Live & Work in the USA & Canada	£8.95	£14.95
Live & Work in Scandinavia	£8.95	£14.95
Live & Work in Germany	£8.95	£11.95
Live & Work in Belgium, The Netherlands & Luxembourg	£8.95	£11.95
Live & Work in Spain & Portugal	£8.95	£11.95
Live & Work in Italy	£7.95	£10.95
Travellers Survival Kit: Russia & the Republics	£9.95	–
Travellers Survival Kit: Western Europe	£8.95	–
Travellers Survival Kit: Eastern Europe	£9.95	–
Travellers Survival Kit: South America	£12.95	–
Travellers Survival Kit: Central America	£8.95	–
Travellers Survival Kit: Cuba	£9.95	–
Travellers Survival Kit: USA & Canada	£9.95	–
Travellers Survival Kit to the East	£6.95	–
Travellers Survival Kit: Australia & New Zealand	£9.95	–
Hitch-hikers' Manual Britain	£3.95	–
Europe — a Manual for Hitch-hikers	£4.95	–
The Traveller's Picture Phrase-Book	£1.95	–

Distributors of:

Summer Jobs USA	£10.95	–
Internships (On-the-Job Training Opportunities — in the USA)	£19.95	–
Sports Scholarships in the USA	£17.95	–
The Directory of College Accommodations USA	£5.95	–
Emplois d'Ete en France	£7.95	–
Making It in Japan	£8.95	–
Jobs in Japan	£9.95	–
Teaching English in Asia	£8.95	–

**Vacation Work Publications, 9 Park End Street, Oxford OX1 1HJ
(Tel 01865-241978. Fax 01865-790885)**